Before the Raj

BEFORE THE RAJ

Writing Early Anglophone India

James Mulholland

Johns Hopkins University Press
Baltimore

Published 2021
Printed in the United States of America on acid-free paper
2 4 6 8 9 7 5 3 1

Johns Hopkins University Press
2715 North Charles Street
Baltimore, Maryland 21218-4363
www.press.jhu.edu

Library of Congress Cataloging-in-Publication Data

Names: Mulholland, James, 1975– author.
Title: Before the raj : writing early Anglophone India / James Mulholland.
Description: Baltimore : Johns Hopkins University Press, 2020. |
Includes bibliographical references and index.
Identifiers: LCCN 2020011648 | ISBN 9781421439600 (hardcover) |
ISBN 9781421439617 (paperback) | ISBN 9781421439624 (ebook)
Subjects: LCSH: Anglo-Indian literature—18th century—History and criticism. | Journalism, Regional—India—History—18th century. | Newspaper publishing—India—History—18th century. | British—India—History—18th century. | India—In literature.
Classification: LCC PR9485.2 .M85 2020 | DDC 820.9/95409033—dc23
LC record available at https://lccn.loc.gov/2020011648

A catalog record for this book is available from the British Library.

Special discounts are available for bulk purchases of this book. For more information, please contact Special Sales at specialsales@jh.edu.

Johns Hopkins University Press uses environmentally friendly book materials, including recycled text paper that is composed of at least 30 percent post-consumer waste, whenever possible.

CONTENTS

ACKNOWLEDGMENTS

It is customary in acknowledgments to indicate when a book began, and I will not break that pattern. This book originated as I was completing the final revisions for a different book at Emory University's Fox Center for Humanistic Inquiry. That book had a final chapter on Anglo-Indian poets, some of whom reappear here, and their profusion at a time when I was just trying to finish felt overwhelming. During the late eighteenth century, British people seemed to be everywhere, colonizing the globe while scribbling away in notebooks and letters. How did they imagine themselves as writers?

From that initial curiosity, it has been ten years, and *Before the Raj* has developed through many phone calls, meals, meetings, and events. It is a testament to the collective endeavor of bookmaking that I cannot do justice to all the people and places that have contributed to this work. I feel fortunate and grateful for all of the opportunities to share what could have been just as easily ignored. I have probably indelicately omitted an important piece that you contributed to its making, and for that I apologize.

One of the principal institutions that assisted with the completion of this book has been North Carolina State University. It became my intellectual home in 2012 and has produced for me many friends, particularly within its lively English department. Thanks go especially to two outstanding department heads, Tony Harrison and Laura Severin, for guiding a large department through turbulent changes in academe and modeling what it means to be a scholar. Laura has been an important counselor and guide for my career; it is rare to find someone as attentive and thoughtful about mentoring younger academics, and I thank her for it.

Numerous colleagues at NC State have shared in the creation of this project. Thanks to the writing group—Rebecca Walsh, Raja Abillama, Shea McManus, and Suzanne Katzenstein—who read early versions of this work. Leila

May, Don Palmer, Sharon Setzer, Jay Setzer, Paul Fyfe, and Maggie Simon have been avid colleagues, intellectual companions, and good friends. (Vive the Danish Drinking Club!) Huiling Ding and Belle Boggs were fellow travelers as I dipped my toes into program development. The administrative staff of the NC State English department have been a constant help: Jenny Tiet, Stephanie McBroom, Melissa Jackson, Molly Scott. The College of Humanities and Social Sciences, and the university, have been supportive with time and money, and thanks go to the leadership of Deanna Dannels, Tom Birkland, Victoria Gallagher, and Jeff Braden, as well as our provost, Warwick Arden, and chancellor, Randy Woodson. In addition to scholarly leaves, this work was supported by a Junior Faculty Development Award and a Lightning Rod grant (coauthored with Rebecca Walsh). My appreciation to the taxpayers and legislators of North Carolina for their continued support of higher education and its goal of expanding knowledge.

Before I came to NC State, I was a faculty member at Wheaton College, Massachusetts, and still number many friends there. Thanks to Rolf Nelson, Francisco Fernandez de Alba, Alberto Bianchi, Touba Ghadessi, Shawn Christian, and Josh Stenger for conversation and wit during my time there. Paula Krebs and Claire Buck were both official and unofficial mentors at Wheaton and, happily for me, remained so even after I left.

During the 2016–17 academic year I was in residence at the National Humanities Center with support from the Frederick Burkhardt Residential Fellowship for Recently Tenured Scholars from the American Council of Learned Societies. Special thanks to Pauline Yu, Matthew Goldfeder, and the rest of the ACLS staff for believing in my research. The National Humanities Center is tucked away in a lovely grove of tall pines in central North Carolina, but it is the staff there that make it a national treasure. Thanks to the Center's director, Robert Newman; the director of academic programs (much missed), Tony Kaye; the head of publicity, Don Solomon; and to Joel Elliott, Lois Whittington, Marie Brubaker, Felisha Wilson, Stephanie Tucker, and everyone else who helped me make my way while I was there. The library staff of the National Humanities Center—Brooke Andrade, Sarah Harris, and Joe Milillo—are recognized as among the best, and they worked with me to find archives and papers from across the world, all of which expanded the scope of this project immensely. Thanks to all of the fellows of the National Humanities Center's 2016–17 class, especially Matthew Booker, Douglas Campbell, Marlene Daut, Florence Dore, Laurent Dubois, Mary Floyd-Wilson, Kim Hall, Nicole

Marafioti, Kate Marshall, Ian Newman, Tamara Sears, Tatiana Seijas, Miguel La Serna, and Luise White.

The ideas in this book were presented to many audiences, but a few deserve special mention. Some of the earliest versions appeared in a 2013 Folger Seminar, "Law as Politics in England and the Empire, ca. 1600–1830." The seminar modeled how to handle the difficulties of interdisciplinary research, and the organizer, Paul Halliday, was electric, knitting together legal jurisdiction, race and slavery, empire, and subjecthood. While not always directly named, the insights of that seminar shimmer on the edges of this book, and I thank the Folger and NC State for material support that allowed me to attend.

A 2016 American Comparative Literature Association seminar, "Imperial Publics," convened together with Tanya Agathocleous, clarified much about the idea of publics and publicity. It is always a joy to think about the institutional forms of research in the academy with Tanya, and I thank all of the seminar participants, particularly Dan White and Tillman Nechtman, who alerted me to new dimensions about eighteenth-century India.

The participants in the Material Texts seminar at Caltech in 2016—Jonathan Eacott, Keith Pluymers, Ben Wurgaft, Chandra Mukerji, and Julia Barr—heard early work about Eyles Irwin; many thanks to Alex Dubé for organizing that visit (and for a lovely time in sunny California). Alex Beecroft invited me to attend the University of South Carolina's "Worlding the Disciplines" conference in 2016, where I presented on translocalism and authenticity and was able to meet with Anne-Marie McManus and Vilashini Cooppan. Thanks always to Alex, and to David Greven, for high-spirited friendship.

A lovely invitation from Jonathan Beecher Field took me to Clemson University, where I had the pleasure of meeting Erin Goss and hearing her thrilling ideas (bad poetry forever!). The faculty at Louisiana State University also commented astutely on this project in 2016, especially Michael Bibler and Chris Barret. "Romanticism's Futures" at The Stonybrook Humanities Institute provided an occasion for thinking about the complex captivity material in chapter 6. Thanks go especially to Kathleen Wilson for the invitation, to Kathleen and Peter Manning for organizing, and to its other participants: Paul Hamilton, Margaret Russet, and Brent Sirota. Porscha Fermanis invited me to join the revelatory "Cultural Geographies of the Colonial Southern Hemisphere," part of her SouthHem project, where portions of chapter 7 were worked out. It was so helpful to speak with conference-goers, especially Elleke Boehmer, Alex Bubb, Manu Samriti Chander, Alan Lester, Nikki Hessell, Jason Rudy, and Kathleen Wilson.

The Triangle Global British History Seminar has been an important place for me to learn a lot more about what it means to think like historians. Special thanks to the organizers—Phil Stern, Brent Sirota, and Susan Pennybacker—and to all of the participants there for welcoming me, especially my fellow NC State colleague Julia Rudolph. The C18 Historical Poetics working group has heard me stammer my way through versions of this project for years now. Anna Foy, Jeff Strabone, Lisa Lynne Moore, Brad Pasanek, and Dustin Stewart deserve much for their forbearance and for what they have contributed to this project. Thanks to Meredith Martin for being intermediator and interpreter between the centuries and thanks to other members of the nineteenth-century Historical Poetics group who have commented on this project (sometimes without knowing it): Jenny Jackson, Yopi Prins, Jason Rudy, Tricia Lootens, Carolyn Williams.

Special mention must be made of the annual conventions of the American Society for Eighteenth-Century Studies and the Modern Language Association, both of which have been regular way stations for these ideas. The ASECS Race and Empire caucus has been a key place for my research, in part because it finally brought together others who were thinking about the same problems. The founders of that caucus, Suvir Kaul and Ashley Cohen, invited me to join early on and have created a new institution for eighteenth-century studies. Suvir has always been a model academic and an intellectual aspiration: striving to match his example and falling short still means one does well. Ashley's capacious knowledge of these subjects has always been inspiring. It was through the Race and Empire caucus that I met Kathleen Wilson, whose own work has been a strong guide and who has always been game for a chat about what the British had been doing around the world; her storehouse of knowledge has been a wonder. Kathy Lubey, in addition to being an interlocutor about professional matters (at times, yes, over martinis), has been a friend since grad school and invited me to the Columbia University eighteenth-century seminar in a fateful November 2016 that clarified a lot about the stakes of this project. Evan Gottlieb and Juliet Shields offered an early opportunity for me to think about issues of localism and regionalism in postcolonial literary studies with the edited collection *Representing Place in British Literature and Culture, 1660–1830*. The published part of this project all started there.

Many friends sustained me during those muddy middle moments of despair that everyone feels in the making of a book. Phil Stern and Kim Stern have been weekly dinner companions for years and witty relief from the concerns of academic life (5:36?). Roxann Wheeler has been a confidante, sounding board, and supporter. Dan White and Mary Ellis Gibson have both been pathbreakers in this field. Dan has always directed me to new places and championed my work. Mary Ellis read the manuscript with care, attention, and the kind of confident overview that only her years of expertise in this subject could provide. She is an exemplar of what academic community is supposed to be. The enthusiasm of Courtney Weiss Smith for the ideas in this project is infectious, and she commented with a passionate insight that only a real intellectual could muster. Special thanks go to Courtney, Jeff Strabone, and Anna Foy for working through my many agonized versions of the book title. Crystal Lake has made me smile about the eighteenth century whenever we are together. Dave Alff brought insights to these chapters that show the careful discernment of an astute thinker. Hillary Chute is a decades-long friend who has been a constant source of advice and of long-running jokes. Benjy Kahan read just about every word of this project (and many of the words that did not make it into the final version, thanks to his timely intervention). He has always seen clearly what matters at moments when things have seemed cloudy to me. This book began in the final days of an extraordinary year at Emory's Fox Center for Humanistic Inquiry where we were both fellows, and it continued when we had the great luck to be cofellows again at the National Humanities Center (revelry!). I am grateful to have such a good friend as a writing partner extraordinaire.

Many colleagues contributed ideas that clarified my own thinking but, more importantly, refreshed my faith in this long-running project: George Boulukos, Michelle Burnham, Tita Chico, Daniel DeWispelare, Doug Fordham, Mitch Fraas, Yvonne Fuentes, Humberto Garcia, Kristin Girten, Tony Jarrells, Collin Jennings, Betty Joseph, Ramesh Mallipeddi, Bob Markley, Dave Mazella, Anupama Mohan, Sal Nicolazzo, Danny O'Quinn, Joe Ponce, Aaron Santesso, Norbert Schürer, Vanessa Smith, Rajani Sudan, Charlotte Sussman, Nicole Wright, Chi-ming Yang, and Gena Zuroski. Thanks to all of them.

There were many libraries, archives, and collections that assisted with the completion of this project. Special thanks go to the staff of the British Library, particularly its Manuscript and Asia, Pacific, and Africa reading rooms. I spent summers sifting through what they have archived there, and I am appreciative that such an institution exists. The National Library of Scotland, the library of the School of Oriental and Asian Studies, the Beinecke Library at Yale University, the Public Records Office Northern Ireland, the Fitzwilliam Museum at Cambridge University—all of these contributed material to the project. The Australian Defence Force Academy Library, especially Rose Holley, crucially assisted with the parts of James Romney's papers. The Senate House Library of the University of London was essential in helping with the archives of Eyles Irwin. Thanks to the staff of NC State's library system, especially D. H. Hill Library, who were indefatigable with all of my questions, requests, and, yes, overdue interlibrary loans. Other collections at the Victoria and Albert Museum, the British Museum, the Anne S. K. Brown Military Collection at Brown University (thank you, Peter Harrington), the Yale Center for British Art, the David M. Rubenstein Rare Book and Manuscript Library at Duke University, the National Army Museum in London, and the National Library of the Netherlands assisted with materials and images.

Touba Ghadessi and Aazam Daroneh helped at crucial moments with Persian. Miles Ogborn and Fiona Ross assisted with the spelling of South Asian names. Paul Losensky helped me with understanding *ghazal* and the transregional migrations of Persian more generally. Imre Bangha offered important insights into the context of Brajbhasha and Persian versus Urdu scripts. Annette Dowd was essential to this project for her incisive help with Dutch translations. Darby Orcutt and Will Cross gave great advice about my contract. Thanks to Emily Chilton for bibliographic assistance. Special thanks to Katy Garcia for vital fact-checking and to Joe Abbott for expert copyediting. Catherine Goldstead guided this book with acumen and helped me to finalize a title and subtitle that had bedeviled me for years: that was more of a relief than you can know. Johns Hopkins University Press has been fabulous to work with, and I appreciate its commitment to mission-driven academic publishing. Thanks to the trustees of Johns Hopkins University for continuing to support their press.

My family has been a constant presence throughout this book. Thanks to Hugh and Cyndie, Mike and Michelle, Tyler and Dylan. There is not enough appreciation that can be given to Rachel Brewster. Her love and support have made so much possible since we first met, and I cannot express how lucky I am. This book is dedicated to our daughter, Evie, who wanders into my office as I write this to give me a hug and remind me it is morning. She makes it easy for me to finish, to put it away, to do something else.

A NOTE ON SPELLING AND USAGE

In this book I generally follow usage patterns established by the historians and literary critics that have informed this study. For quoted text, I have retained the original spelling of places, personal names, and documents (with modernizations added in parentheses if necessary). For nonquoted text I have retained the eighteenth- and nineteenth-century spelling of people and places, with modern place names included in parentheses where appropriate. When the name of a geographical location has diverged from the accepted period usage, I have placed it in quotation marks.

Throughout I italicize words from non-English languages, except for those that are proper nouns, common words and phrases that appear often in English, or words and phrases from Dutch (the last for ease of reading in chapter 7). I have not used diacritics except in cases where it was necessary to identify an author's name. For the spelling of Persian names I have followed the *Encyclopædia Iranica*. After an initial occurrence in each chapter, references to the British East India Company are typically shortened to EIC or Company.

Before the Raj

Translocal Anglo-India

Recalled to England by his longtime employer, the British East India Company, and soon to be tried before the House of Commons for corruption, India's first governor-general, Warren Hastings, sat aboard the Company ship *Berrington* in 1785 and composed in a small leather-bound memorandum book an imitation of Horace's ode "Otium divos rogat in patenti."[1] Hastings was a controversial colonial administrator and unpopular among Britain's politicians, who consistently fought for control over the Company.[2] He in turn felt anger toward his opponents and assertive about his record. The journey from India to England, which lasted five months, allowed him ample time for contemplation.

His rewriting of Horace's poem was an early part of his defense, which continued for nearly a decade until he was saved from punishment by the House of Lords in 1795. Hastings transforms Horace's classical meditation on contentment and peace into an account of the existential character of the colonizer. He repositions the literature of the Roman Empire to India, replacing Horace's references to warlike Thracians and Parthians with "Mahrattas" (Marathas) and "Seiks" (Sikhs). He resists the "printed lies" of his parliamentary detractors, who seek to "destroy" the "fame" that his "labour'd years have won," by arguing that knowledge and arts had flourished in India under his control. He accrued no wealth or titles, "nor Robes, nor gems," he pouts, but instead he let minds "unfetter'd tread / Far as the paths of knowledge lead."[3] The poem's telescoping time frame looks back to classical antiquity while still anticipating a future in which art-making and orientalist knowledge absolve him of criminality.

The combination of art and governance is a central axis that runs throughout eighteenth-century anglophone Asia, as it does in Hastings's poem.

Multilocal, transhistorical, culturally allusive, and geopolitically savvy, anglophone literature in pre-1800 Asia sought to manage the contradictions of aggressive nationalism and desire for empire, much as British literature did.[4] Without understanding these contexts, literary works like Hastings's ode have been passed over too quickly by critics who struggle to reconcile their exploitation and cruelty with the creative imaginations that animated colonizers' art and the institutions that made that art viable. Understanding how modernity, globalization, and British cultural superiority triumphed in Asia requires that we comprehend how the art and culture created there was driven by local and regional institutions.

With that goal in mind I propose three primary arguments in this book. First, anglophone literary culture took shape in India during the late eighteenth century and was institutionalized during this period. Second, this literary culture developed a distinct translocal imagination and regional awareness that reconciled its attachment to British cultural traditions with its composition in the new environments of India. Third, regional links and exchanges, within India and throughout the Bay of Bengal to places like Penang, Sumatra, and Java, were as significant as those longer global connections to Britain and Europe that have been the interest of scholars in the aftermath of Edward Said's *Orientalism*.

Together, these three arguments explain Anglo-Indian literature's incremental cohesion and emergence between 1770 and 1820. My institutional literary history of anglophone Asia focuses not just on cultural concepts and imaginations but also on the physical realities of writing and print that informed those imaginations.[5] I recover the mostly forgotten figures and associations of Anglo-Indian writing to describe how it was organized and how it began to understand itself as unique during this period. Authors constructed a literary culture that operated within a web of colonial cities and trading outposts that borrowed from each other and produced important interlinked aesthetics.

Their translocal imaginations and regional institutions undermine the idea that they were beholden to London; British India did not mean simply acting British while in India. Anglo-Indian literature could not exist without Britain, of course, but neither was it the home nation's arts annex or British culture's indigent dependent. At the same time, these authors were often dismissive of indigenous traditions even as they engaged them for their own writing. I do not mean their study to constitute a "white recovery project" by which their history of marginalizing ramifies in such a way as to narrow the canon of eighteenth-century literature.[6] Scholars in postcolonial studies and imperial history have documented extensively how European culture contributed to colonialism, and the goal of *Before the Raj* is to expand our understanding of how the forces that created an elite orientalist discourse also created an anglophone colonial public sphere in Asia. Anglo-Indian literature, in addition to being an imperial instrument, an imposition of Orientalists, and an expression of national identity, was a regional literature composed of mobile participants and moving publics related to, but detached from, the nation-state that secured its existence.

Although at least two centuries of European writing about India preceded Hastings's 1785 poetic justification of his governance, the country he left behind had only recently developed vibrant local literary institutions of English. Writing was always an essential skill among EIC employees, appearing most often as the dispatches and consultations that dominate Company records. Beginning in the 1770s, however, printers and printing presses multiplied, the space for amateur theater and public performance expanded, interest in circulating libraries increased, and newspapers proliferated, carrying with them opportunities for rapid publication and belletristic literature, especially in poetry columns, instructive essays, and readers' letters. Madras possessed a printing press—the first to print English consistently in South Asia—by 1761. Bombay formed its first amateur theater in the 1770s, and Calcutta established the first English-language newspaper in 1780. Developments like these roused the printer William Duane to exclaim in 1791 that "the civilized world affords no similar instance of the rise and culture of the arts" as what he saw occurring in Calcutta, whose practitioners, he argued, were examples of an "anglo-asiatic taste."[7] It remained true decades later, when the French botanist Victor Jacquemont visited in 1829 and enthusiastically described the city as possessing "journals without number, both political and literary," as well as "learned societies . . . of every denomination."[8] Before the advent of steamship travel between Britain and India in the 1820s, which shortened travel times from months to weeks and more easily connected Europe and Asia, and before the nineteenth-century Bengal Renaissance and its eruption of native language printing, there was a robust self-generated anglophone literary culture, the contours of which I document in this book.[9]

While Asia's anglophone literature often shared generic forms similar to those of Britain, its subject matter could differ considerably. Some topics were conventional and might have felt as familiar to 1770s English provincial towns or New England farming hamlets as it would be in India—polite poetry about virtues like perseverance and fortitude; light satirical verse of courtship and marriage; epitaphs for lost loved ones; accounts of exotic locales and essays about distant destinations in Scandinavia, China, or Islamic central Asia. But there was also writing more *local*, in the multiple senses of that term. This writing was geographically proximate to its authors and its audience. It appeared in several languages or promised access to less-familiar linguistic and cultural knowledge. It commented on military, economic, and geopolitical concerns of South Asia. It reported on and responded to India's long-enduring societies and to its recently established sociabilities.

Nineteenth-century historians excluded this energetic cultural creation from the English canon. Twentieth-century scholars, in turn, assumed that Anglo-Indian culture merely imitated metropolitan Britain, absorbing and reiterating its fashions. They disregarded its self-created artistic worlds because the limited populations of Europeans in eighteenth-century South Asia were thought to exist in small pockets too divided from Eurasian and indigenous populations to produce a distinct sociability.[10] Such accounts of culture typically consider it within a metropolitan framework that perceives Anglo-Indians as desirous of their British home and slavishly mimicking its fashions while secluding themselves from local peoples and traditions.[11] The few nineteenth- and early twentieth-century attempts to assemble a canon of Anglo-Indian poets consciously and consistently subordinated them to a British national standard, naming them "Our Indian Poets" who composed "British-Indian poetry."[12] They describe this canon as a trivial subset, a curious offshoot, a "tiny niche," a "minor tributary," or a "regional variety" of a larger body of English literature originating in Britain.[13]

Twenty-first-century scholars have begun to revise these positions, discarding the notion that anglophone authors were sad exiles nostalgic for a homeland many of them rarely saw.[14] Daniel White describes a "powerful current of imperial culture" that tethered London and Calcutta in the early nineteenth century and created the "rise" of anglophone Indian literature.[15] Mary Ellis Gibson suggests the "transperipheral" spaces of Britain's empire were "as important" to its constitution as "metropole/colony exchange."[16] Both have attuned readers to the vibrancy of Anglo-India, an "alternative modernity" formed by the "complex linguistic contact zone" that messily mixed English with the classical languages of Mediterranean antiquity and the regional vernaculars of South Asia.[17] Historians of science have dismantled diffusion models of modernity by focusing on the many interacting scales of place-based cultural creation and on the production and circulation of knowledge in colonial spaces.[18] Archivists and geographers have reported on the history of printing in India before 1800 and demonstrated the importance of writing for the advancement of empire there.[19] Book historians have looked beyond metropolitan-peripheral relations, "decentring print culture history" to demonstrate how colonial outposts also functioned as sites of "creative ferment."[20]

Yet we still know little about eighteenth-century Anglo-Indian literature outside of Bengal and even less about imaginative writing that appeared in newspapers, manuscripts, or other vital but nonelite forms. India's anglophone poetry in particular remains an "unclaimed tradition," according to Rosinka Chaudhuri, still in need of a "proper history" for most of its "beleaguered and secret existence."[21] There has been slight interest in the aesthetic features of the sizable archive produced by soldiers, junior officers, and middling merchants who made up the majority of India's white population and who attended plays, wrote poetry and travel accounts, and participated in Indian life. These figures tell a different story about the relationship between literature and empire. Much like those captives documented by Linda Colley who reveal imperialism's "underbelly," their writing reveals the violence of empire's creation but also how it could be dispersed, chaotic, and boring.[22]

Attending to this archive of literature would extend the postnational and transnational turns in cultural studies and work against the idea that English literary history should be considered "an exclusive national property."[23] The peculiar mixtures of nonnational sovereignties at work on the Indian subcontinent reveal the way that national literary traditions organized under the headings of British literature or English literature are insufficient for our understanding of the authors and texts from this period. Instead, a new literary history of early British Asia would subject Anglo-Indian writing to the same scrutiny that has been so usefully devoted to the essential yet disregarded scribes of the "document raj," whose policies were supported by natives' personal labor that systematically transformed British India into a vast administrative state ruled through paper.[24] The assumption that literary discourse contributed to the power of colonialism, much as the documentary mechanisms of Company governance did, necessitates that we possess a clearer picture of those readers and writers who formed the nascent art world of these pivotal decades. The goal is not to assert the dominance of one mode of identification or another—that is, to resolve whether these authors, artists, and cultures are British or Indian, "Anglo" or "Asiatic"—but rather to discover and assess the significance of local and regional attachments for the emergence of publics in the eighteenth century.

Let me state from the outset that I do not think of Anglo-Indian literature as unified and contiguous, like a tectonic plate colliding with other plates on the earth's surface or a National Geographic globe that represents its different continents in bright distinguishable colors. I see the regional organization of this literature as often discontinuous and frayed, riven with the cultural relations and the physical realities of travel into and out of these spaces. Its more local and regional addresses do not mean that anglophone texts could not be transported to Britain, or even produced there, as examples drawn from India's orientalist scholarly societies (see chap. 1) or EIC army captivity narratives (chap. 6) demonstrate. In these cases, especially, India acted as the origin of an oceanic dissemination that turned into a small craze for vivid examples of exoticism and imperial violence in distant lands.

Yet these submetropolitan practices are still too often perceived as parochial and provincial, when in fact they operated according to a "logic of self-differentiation" from metropolitan norms.[25] Literary scholars might apply to histories of English literature the same attention to change that has appeared in social scientific ideas about "multiple modernities," which teach us to abandon ideas about the diffusion of knowledge from metropoles to peripheries in favor of a dispersed, interactive picture of scientific creation.[26] Adopting this model would mean recognizing that anglophone literature replaces metropolitan norms with new practices for the accordingly new, complexly mixed social spaces of India. Such an approach requires us to reconceive imperial publics as composed of individuals who neither identify wholly with a national homeland, defining themselves by its fashions and forms, nor think of themselves as wild exotics precariously rooted in alien terrain and always seeking to go native. Anglo-Indian literary culture is the imaginative product of a community that possesses disparate social and political constituencies rather than the aspiration to accede to the homogenizing "vast anonymous address" of British literature whose writers appear to be "variations on the same pattern" of European colonialism.[27]

What follows is not a complete historical account of literary creation in Asia by English users at the end of the eighteenth century and the beginning of the nineteenth. Nor does it expand on the lengthy indigenous artistic cultures of India and South Asia. These artistic cultures were essential to anglophone India's literary publics, and native Indians were instrumental to the creation of the anglophone public sphere, working as language instructors and translators, transmitting knowledge essential for the operation of orientalism in Asia, which in turn was necessary for the creation of foundational humanistic concepts like literature and historical truth.[28] These early ventures led to more energetic nineteenth-century native anglophone literary production by Henry Derozio, for instance, the mixed-race Bengali poet who is an early expression of the heterogeneous people of India and their opposition to colonialism.[29] Indigenous Indians were avid contributors to the infrastructure of the anglophone public sphere at a moment when Britain was not yet ascendant in South Asia, meaning that their experience differs from the marginalization that Manu Samriti Chander describes as constitutive of the nineteenth-century's "Brown Romantics."[30] Native Indians manufactured type for printing presses, co-owned newspapers, were targeted as readers, and served as agents of Anglo-India's censorship and control. Their writing in the dialects of South Asia and transregional tongues of prestige, like Persian, contributed directly to Asia's multilingual anglophony, even as their authorship of imaginative writing in English was still sparse. My emphasis on infrastructure, art worlds, and literary publics is an attempt to capture their complementary contributions, which cannot be easily identified by authorial attributions and title pages.

They were part of the several overlapping areas and interwoven adaptive lineages that brought the anglophone public sphere into being in Asia. Each chapter of *Before the Raj* delineates a different set of elements that, when put together, answer how anglophone literature in Asia operated and who made up its audiences. For this reason the chapters proceed in broadly chronological fashion and are organized largely by geography, focusing on the three primary locations of EIC administration (Madras, Calcutta, and Bombay) but also on trading stations throughout the Bay of Bengal and the Strait of Malacca (Melaka). Some of the chapters are author-based, while others are ordered more by genres, media, and the routes that distributed them. Literature, Nancy Glazener notes, is a "collective invention" that necessitates institutional support from the state, not just from authors and readers, who might offer only "discretionary participation."[31] My first chapter expands on this notion by describing the institutionalization of anglophone literature in late eighteenth-century Asia that led authors to develop translocal techniques of inspiration and reading audiences that saw themselves in regional registers. The EIC, which I term a "cultural company-state," acted not just as a trading corporation or a governmental organization but as a cultural patron and censor. The focus of chapter 2 is on newspapers and their printed poetry, a vehicle that was essential to the formation of a multilingual reading public and the colonial public sphere that emerged with it. Chapter 3 examines a Company employee, Eyles Irwin, who was born in Calcutta and stationed in Madras from 1766 until 1785. He cultivated a portable literary reputation by coupling his writing to authors and markets anchored in London, India, and China, a condition that he describes as his "vagrant muse." Chapter 4 expands on the notion of Anglo-India's suitability for translocal poetics by analyzing two late eighteenth-century authors essential to the Calcutta literary scene: the jurist and orientalist Sir William Jones and the anonymous "Anna Maria," whose collection of poems provoked celebrations about the vitality of Bengal's literary culture. Jones imagines India to rejuvenate British literature, which Anna Maria takes up in her verse, so successfully mixing literary fads from London like the anonymous love poetry of 1780s Della Cruscanism with Indian themes that some reviewers worried poets might abandon England for the East.

James Romney (1745–1807), the central figure of chapter 5, was a Bombay army officer who, like Irwin, Jones, and Anna Maria, perceived India as an opportunity to revisit English literary fashions. He was a prolific letter writer, poet, and playwright (penning a stage adaptation of Laurence Sterne's *The Life and Opinions of Tristram Shandy, Gentleman* [1761–67]), whose example of eighteenth-century Bombay sociability and artistic culture has been completely overlooked by postcolonial scholars and empire historians. More familiar are the martial verse, prison memoirs, and captivity narratives written by lower-class military men in response to the four Anglo-Mysore wars (1767–99) that I examine in chapter 6, which indicate how warfare was a stimulus for Anglo-India's literary institutions and publics. When positioned within a translocal and regional framework, however, these verses and narratives demonstrate the importance of proximate and immediate audiences as opposed to transnational or imperial British readership. Translocal literature was a tool with which to examine imperialism, as when Dutch-speaking natives debated with English occupiers in the *Java Government Gazette* after the British captured Java from the Netherlands in 1811, which I detail in chapter 7. This final chapter moves in three steps across settlements in the Bay of Bengal from Penang to Sumatra and ultimately to Java, offering along the way insights about the outpost literature of Britain's Asian colonies and its relation to India. Throughout, I expand on the notions, suggested later in this introduction, that scholars compose literary histories in a "minor key" from the archives, authors, and occasions that I describe in this book.[32]

Translocal Regionalism in Anglo-India

A more comprehensive account of Anglo-Indian literature requires the adoption of new methods that together I call translocal regionalism. These methods combine postcolonial theory's notion of culture as a contest over power together with the circulation of people, goods, and ideas found in histories of science and the geopolitics and trade apparent among commonwealth and empire histories. But rather than treat empire as a single analytic field, as historians such as Catherine Hall and Ann Laura Stoler do, I break it into regional frames to isolate their influence on anglophone literature as an organized institution during the late eighteenth century.[33] Translocal regionalism moves beyond hub-and-spoke and dyadic models that see imperialism as diffusing from centrally controlled nodes in Europe. It supplements the sense that European empires were a "complex agglomeration of overlapping webs" by adding new attention to how local interactions constituted and changed anglophone Asia.[34] This approach differs from those of important predecessors, such as Sara Suleri, who argues for a unifying "rhetoric" about English India, or Kate Teltscher, who examines the "European tradition of writing about India" that appeared after the British accession to greater geopolitical power that occurred during the late eighteenth century.[35] Instead, like Miles Ogborn, I seek out the "small-scale geographies" of Britain's imperial literature among sites that coexisted with one another.[36]

Ideas about the translocal originated when social scientists returned to insights from the 1970s and 1980s about "local knowledge" to correct the overemphasis on the nation-state and deterritorialization in theories of transnationalism and globalization.[37] In response, anthropologists, geographers, and communication scholars developed the concept of translocality, which defined place as pervious and extensive rather than insular and restricted. This shift turned attention away from the idea that immediate physical copresence was the most genuine form of human relationship and toward an account of how movement through space structured social interactions and cultural change. Studies of migration, missionary and aid workers, and transnational political resistance offered new accounts of humans in motion, media-generated identities, and "agency-oriented" approaches in "cross-border social space."[38] These accounts began a decade-long discussion of translocality as an intermediary between the local and the global, a strategy for "local-to-local relations," a "grounded transnationalism," an assemblage of social movements, and the geopolitics that ensued from that assemblage.[39] All of these positions shared an interest in concepts that transcended locality through actors or objects that organized themselves across scales (local, regional, national, international).[40]

Literary criticism has focused on the authorial strategies that have developed in response to translocal migration. Jahan Ramazani's "translocal poetics," for example, captures the potential for locality to be "relational" that he inherited from social scientists when he rejects the idea that poetry must be either "rooted or rootless, local or universal."[41] Translocalism was a companion to the transnational turn, overcoming the bounded regions of area studies while also suppressing the importance of the national literary traditions by focusing on overlapping networks that "facilitate the circulation of people, resources, practices, and ideas" that extend beyond direct physical proximity.[42] But Ramazani's translocalism is drawn from twentieth- and twenty-first-century examples of cultural hybridity and exile, such as those enunciated in African American and black British poetry. Eighteenth-century Anglo-Indian literature, however, is driven by the peculiar state-dependent yet nonnational sovereignty of the EIC. This significant historical difference requires that we join translocalism with critical regionalism to understand literature as an intercessor between porous localities and clotted global structures like those created by imperial ventures.[43]

One drawback of regional thinking is the still-prevalent sense that regions are contiguous, internally coherent, and resistant to the homogenization of culture that occurs in the modern world. Critical regionalism, which is one answer to that drawback, began as a form of architectural theory that resisted homogenization—an "architecture of resistance"—but was later taken up by cultural scholars seeking to understand how the region might mitigate the overuse of local, global, and transnational structures by focusing on the interstitial and the incidental.[44] Ideas developed from critical regionalism capture the shifting, fluctuating nature of regions that achieve stability temporarily as "relational yet interdependent spaces" rather than as enclosed territorial sites that are natural and opposed to the manufactured modern world.[45]

When all of these traditions, investments, and scholarly motives are united, translocalism and critical regionalism teach scholars to see the region as porous, not as rigid, autonomous, or self-contained. In this model the local and the regional interact with social and cultural formations that manifest at other scales (such as the national or the interimperial) rather than simply resisting them in some way that should be seen as sincere and authentic.[46] Translocal relations were crucial components of the infrastructure and imaginative conception of Anglo-India's regional reading publics that interacted with but did not mindlessly copy the characteristics of a growing modern world. The notion of a translocalized region explains how Anglo-Indian authors could be situated in the specific environments of South Asia that they were changing with their presence while retaining ongoing associations with European culture without resorting to theories of unitary national identity or a common colonial discourse. This new sense of translocal regionalism understands that the transcendence of local boundaries is not always an expression of liberatory tactics of resistance among the oppressed but is also an essential feature of the long-distance cultural relations produced by colonizing modernity. Joining translocalism with critical regionalism allows scholars to move away from the connotation of the region as a geographic fact toward understanding it as a "social convention" and a "human accomplishment" that recognizes the association between culture and a series of places, not all of which are physically adjacent in space and not all of which perceive "society" and "state" to be one and the same.[47]

For the Anglo-Indian authors I describe in this book, the translocal and the regional are not the antithesis of European Enlightenment's universal ideals, but neither are they an endorsement of more narrow "local color." These authors vacillate between appeals to common humanity and the depiction of resident customs in ways that Joseph Rezek shows define provincial aesthetics, but they do not subordinate themselves to metropolitan culture, petitioning it "for approval."[48] They do not seek for translocal identities of "universalizing localism" that Trish Loughran defines as the aspiration of early America's champions, like Thomas Paine, who sought to overcome the atomized fragmentation of the Atlantic colonies by creating an American nationalism that was simultaneously local and cosmopolitan.[49] Nor are they the literary equivalent of what Natasha Eaton describes as visual art's attempt to "provincialize metropolitan taste" by bringing images of India to Britain and drawing attention to the "contingency of Britishness."[50] Anglophone authors sought acclaim and praise within their own self-devised domains, existing in between the "world literary space" of literature and the "zigzagging movements" of nonnational literary networks.[51] Reconceptualizing anglophone Asia as a region shot through by the translocal travels of authors who are defined by their semiautonomy from Britain focuses scholars on the interacting scales of place-based cultural creation rather than the connections between metropole and colony.

Oceanic to Regional

Anglo-Indian authors, in particular, exemplify the need for these interventions because national designations—"British," for example—have frequently acted as frictionless ways for scholars to assume shared habits of consumption and aesthetic mentalities among peoples in enormously different locations, geographies, and life circumstances.[52] The disciplinary category "British literature" has typically included regional constituencies that scholars have presumed are strongly related to one another owing to their shared linguistic origin in Britain and the expectation that because many of their authors were white, they must have an affinity for Europe. By combining the techniques of translocalism with new understandings of the region and colonial modernity, in this book I guide readers toward other archives that alter the history of British literature.

The Indian Ocean and the Bay of Bengal play crucial roles in this institutional account of Anglo-Indian literary history because they were essential vectors for the subjugation of Asia. Examinations of the Indian Ocean world have placed the subcontinent in a wider Asian context with "connected histories" that supplement understandings of its colonial relationships to Europe and account for its central role within an "inter-imperial" system that had endured for centuries.[53] Already established regional commercial networks and transregional cultural links aided European entry into the Asia trade.[54] British imperialism should be seen as a local, regional, and global system (rather than a "core-periphery" or "cross-colonial" one), with many of the artistic and cultural exchanges between Asia and Europe occurring within a "market framework."[55] At the same time, there were regional networks within a larger global system that transformed nineteenth-century India into a "subimperial center" of the British Empire and the "fulcrum" of the Indian Ocean arena.[56] Overall, this period is defined by an integration between European empires and regional polities that demonstrates the collaborative nature of economic and cultural ties rather than the superiority of European ingenuity or the preeminence of its trading corporations.

Within this system the structure of the EIC was elemental. Because it was conceived as a series of interlinked plantations, islands, and trading stations, the EIC was always a "fluid, networked entity" that was "influenced by and interacting with the regional dynamics of areas such as the Bay of Bengal."[57]

This networked model of corporate action, which I describe in greater detail in chapter 1, meant that the anglophone Indian Ocean world was a "cultural milieu" as much as a "trading zone."[58] My project responds to worries from Sugata Bose and Lauren Benton that imperial historiography and world-systems theory have obscured flows of culture and ideas.[59]

In the English tradition, to imagine the oceans as elements of an interconnected network dates back at least as far as George Savile, the Marquis of Halifax, who in 1694 offered a stereoscopic vision of English empire as having its "Root" in the sea "from whence it sendeth its Branches into both the *Indies*."[60] This image, as much octopus as arbor, has persisted even as thinking about empire evolved throughout the twentieth century from one that perceived metropoles and colonies to be linked by economic domination and cultural imposition to more recent views that see it as a dispersed network activated by hybridity and creolization. Scholars of anglophone Asia have focused primarily on the relationship between Calcutta and London, and Graham Shaw rightly stresses the importance of Britain's capital during this era.[61] As the home of Parliament and the location of the Company's headquarters, London remained indispensable for knowledge about India, whether in the voluminous written dispatches and consultations that make the India Office Records or the petitions addressed to Parliament, public prosecutions and defenses of prominent EIC figures like Hastings, and accounts of military actions or economies of India's territories.[62]

But alongside this reciprocal relationship of entangled roots existed regional English-language literary culture in Asia. Poems, essays, narratives, and letters to the editor were being contributed from and distributed throughout Anglo-India and were not confined within tightly bounded urban locales. The Literary Society of Bombay not only sought to purchase a "pretty extensive library" as a "public utility" for the inhabitants of the city but also offered reduced rates for members outside of Bombay proper and free access to members of Calcutta's Asiatick Society or the Literary Society of Madras.[63] The *Bombay Gazette* advertised itself to Calcutta readers as a way for them to collect information from "circumjacent English, Dutch, and Portuguese settlements" and to encounter "Poetical Articles" and "polite amusements, such as Theatricals, and Accounts of Festive Assemblies."[64] Sharing was not always reliable, and the *Madras Courier* was forced to apologize to its readers in Bengal who had not received recent issues, insisting that "they may in the future depend on the most exact punctuality."[65] The placement of this announcement from the editors of the *Madras Courier* in the *Calcutta Gazette* suggests that Anglo-Indian readers consumed many newspapers from different cities and that Calcutta was not always dominant. An author seeking subscriptions for two volumes of "original poetry" to be printed in Madras "in an elegant small Type and on fine Letter paper" boasted of agents accepting money in Madras, Calcutta, Bombay, and Masulipatam, four cities along the central postal routes of British India.[66] Another poetry collection from Madras presented the mobility of people and literature in Anglo-India quite literally when it advertised itself as written in an "easy and humorous stile" that would "prove an *agreeable companion in the Palanquin*," referring to the sedan chairs carried on the shoulders of native Indians that ferried Europeans around the city, like the officer depicted reading a small handbook in a watercolor from the 1830s (fig. 1).[67]

Figure 1. An officer reading in a palanquin, ca. 1830s, while natives literally support the consumption of books in India. Unsigned original native watercolor. Courtesy of the Anne S. K. Brown Military Collection, Brown University Library.

From these items emerges some sense of the continent-wide scope and movement of cultural information and written compositions. They demonstrate that local connections and exchanges among British India resulted in a strong sense of regional literary identity, bolstered by the structure of its new institutions, and of regional fashions made through translocal pathways of travel. Far from being imitators of British cultural norms, Anglo-Indian authors began a concerted effort to see India as a fertile place for regionally based artistic creativity. Sir William Jones depicts India as a "fountain head" whose Sanskrit traditions were more antique than those of classical Greece and Rome. It was precisely the distance from Britain that allowed India to be an incubator of poetic taste. Eyles Irwin claimed the South Asian climate itself was fecund inspiration for his earliest pastoral poetry of the 1770s, and William Marsden argued that although Britain had an extensive network of playwrights and critics, the amateur theater of Sumatra, his home from 1771 to 1779, was more pleasing to his imagination. Nonelite authors and newspapermen were just as enthusiastic about the artistic possibilities of residing in India. They saw Anglo-Indian literature and its institutions as competing with and even exceeding those of metropolitan Britain. William Duane, as I noted earlier, was an advocate for "anglo-asiatic taste" and thought "Calcutta rivals the head of empire," London, nowhere more so than "in her publications."[68] Madras author and newspaper proprietor Hugh Boyd credits the productivity of empire with the achievements of Anglo-Indian art. He asserts that no other "establishment, remote from the mother country," has "command[ed]" so much "regard and astonishment" as British India.[69]

Claims to cultural success—even superiority—like those of Duane or Boyd are really claims to difference that was experienced as a semiautonomy from British literature: dependent on its norms but seeking to adapt them to their particular circumstances, institutions, and ambitions. Such semiautonomy was theorized by eighteenth-century Anglo-Indians, who were explicit about their debts to the literature of the British nation-state but also keen to establish a sense of cultural independence from it. Whether it was elegies for shared intellectual societies, mobile newspaper subscriptions, or palanquin poetry, Anglo-Indian authors took pride and pleasure in imagining themselves as part of an interconnected regional public. While Britain, especially London, remained an arbiter of literary success, it was also an important contrast with Asia, which itself acted as a site of imaginative creation and public-making.

Middle Reading

One of the dramas of place-based analysis is that as comparative scales grow in complexity, detail and nuance are lost. Scale and value are intertwined, and decisions scholars make about one necessarily affects evaluations about the other.[70] That is why I advocate for translocal regionalism as the best way to isolate and contextualize late eighteenth-century Anglo-Indian regional literature. Isolating a set of undervalued yet representative authors, genres, and media is necessary for an institutional analysis of early anglophone Asia because such a process is based in historical realities (to the extent that they can be ascertained) and differentiates Anglo-Indian literature from other contemporaneous literary currents.

Translocal regionalism, therefore, functions best through analysis that is middling in scale and with reading that is "poised between the close and the distant" (like Susan Lanser's "large reading").[71] The close and the distant are markers of both geography and methodology. In this sense translocal regionalism offers historically specific causal examples that stand in for general patterns about the growth and organization of a body of literature. Such reading is informed by the abundance of theories about the middle, including "middle ground" evaluations of world-systems theory, which seek to counter grandiosity by "pushing simultaneously out toward global and in toward local phenomena"; "meso-level" analysis in organizational theory and "theories of the middle-range" in analytical sociology that operate "in between" micro and macro descriptions and identify a few crucial factors to explain large social and historical events; the accommodations that can occur when alien peoples meet in the middle ground; and the "middling" scale that James English describes as a mode of textual criticism that "falls somewhere between ordinary human reading methods" and the broad data patterns constructed by computational analysis.[72] The advantage of "midrange theorizing," in Aihwa Ong's estimation, is that it operates in the spirit of Clifford Geertz's injunction for scholars to remain "rather close to the ground" with their observations.[73] It shares Cannon Schmitt's desire to combine close reading with "gathering more, and different, data" about the objects that are taken literally in literature so that critics can describe how they work physically and institutionally, not just what they might mean symbolically or ideologically to different audiences.[74] Middle reading therefore seeks innovations in the types of objects that are meant to be analyzed and the methods that are used to do so. By combining different kinds of goals for literary criticism (reporting vs. interpretative meaning; thin and thick description), middle reading identifies unique cultural groups, such as Anglo-Indian reading publics, while at the same time theorizing their entanglement with larger phenomena, such as British literature or European colonialism.

Middle reading involves incremental and aggregative approaches, examining an assortment of unexceptional texts to assess the systematic values of a colonial literary culture at its origins. It is meant to mitigate what might be called the keyhole problem of literary criticism, which is the reality that critics not only read a limited amount of textual material but that what critics read is distorted by the apertures and analytics through which we have historically encountered that material. Every room looks like the keyhole we peek through to see it; likewise, every text looks like the dominant theories that we use to read them. Rather than emphasizing the microlevels of close reading or the macrolevel of distant reading, I strive for a midlevel reading that produces granular analysis of representative literary works with systematic discussion of their historical and geopolitical context. It necessitates the isolation and elevation of particular variables. Of course, I also want middle reading to resonate with the idea that most of the authors and topics I take up in this book are thought to be of middling talent by literary critics who are rewarded for searching out unusual and innovative artists and patterns to anchor their own stand-out arguments. My amalgamation of institutional history, author biography, archival recovery, and formal interpretation hopes to salvage some value for the ordinary, traditional, and unremarkable aspects of writing.

Middle reading is suited to the problems of evaluating Europe's colonial literatures because it insists that scholars negotiate among geographical scales, especially the local and the global that have so preoccupied postcolonial theory and imperial history from their beginnings. Kathleen Wilson, Tillman Nechtman, and many others have demonstrated that it is impossible to disentangle these scales in late eighteenth-century India.[75] The salient task for any scholar of European imperialism is not to determine whether or when the world finally acquired a worldly or global orientation but to describe how its differing scales were interconnected by specific actors at precise moments. The translocal and regional orientation of this book therefore advocates not for eradicating the distinctions among these places in time but rather for demonstrating how authors' and administrators' literary imaginations and geopolitical strategies made those distinctions traversable in contextually definite ways. Describing these locally disparate but globally joined cultural formations is a means of overcoming the instinctive recourse to concepts of indigeneity and autochthony, with their rubrics of authentic belonging and their perception of culture as a possession, that confounded colonial discourse's attempts to produce historically and geographically differentiated accounts of colonialism.[76]

Middle reading is a type of reading that recognizes "repetitions with change" across interconnected geographies within a sharply defined time period that make Anglo-Indian literature "locally disparate" but "globally integral."[77] It reintroduces values for imaginative literary creation that are not easily acknowledged by literary criticism, which prizes formal innovation and demonstrations of scholarly ingenuity. Sociologists Craig Calhoun and Richard Sennett have complained that theoretical (that is to say, nonempirical) studies of culture have perpetuated the notion that culture is a "distinct domain, separate in particular from economy and society." They propose, instead, to merge these domains and to identify how "social processes are turned by practical activity into cultural forms" that in turn "inform the improvisation of social practices."[78] Middle reading offers such an approach, understanding that Anglo-Indian literature requires a mode of reading and of storytelling that comprehends its alignment with "social transmission"—dissemination to readers based on intelligibility and relevance rather than permanence and canonicity, which can be closely linked with the expert's hunt for hidden meaning.[79]

Middle reading dispenses with the rewards granted to maximally adept critics who seek to startle their colleagues with increasingly unforeseen and clever interpretations. Instead, I follow the instinct to seek overlooked actors, forgotten circumstances, and patiently reconstructed frameworks. The texts I analyze here are often social histories in another form. My goal is not to surprise readers with the astonishing fluency of these authors but to contextualize their unsurprising existence. Such focus returns to these practitioners' reality rather than the scholars' present of reading and the "charisma" of the critic acting as a "privileged messenger."[80] I do not assume the documents I have included here plainly tell what needs to be known or that the distortions of European colonialism and the opaque rhetoric of their historical archives can be overcome.[81] But decisions about what to read and how to read it matter because they indicate resolutions about cultural value: scholars cannot read everything, and even if we could, digesting the results of reading everything is a Borgesian dilemma.

Middle reading therefore has much to add to new imperial and new global histories that have literature as their primary object.[82] Its methods apply to literature the values derived from decades-long debates about microhistory, "big history," shorter histories, and the longue durée.[83] It relies on context-specific analysis in a way consonant with what Avner Greif describes as historical and comparative institutional analysis and on understanding that literature is a "means of historical agency" rather than an "intransitive" inert object in the world, in Jonathan Arac's words: an always changing vehicle for inaugurating authors and audiences rather than a set of static infrastructures.[84] Middle reading is needed for literary histories that "put books back in contact with [the] hard surfaces of life including trade, industry, craft traditions, marketplaces, publics, geography, and discourse networks," as Heather Love advocates, but also for retrieving and valuing properly all of the normal boring writing produced by authors who were motivated to maintain social connections, enact geopolitical strategies, or simply live with a sense of purpose.[85]

Bad Writing, Normal Literature, Boring Things

Any institutional literary history of eighteenth-century colonialism in India and Asia that wants to get in touch with the "hard surfaces of life" needs to admit that much of Anglo-Indian literature (like most writing) is ordinary, conventional, sometimes even bad. I see Anglo-Indians as creating a "minor literature" tilted more toward "collective enunciation" than toward the "abundant" talent of an identifiable canon.[86] Anglo-Indian writers composed within a language (English) that was not yet dominant in its geographical location (India) but was instead minor and mingled among others that were spoken by more people (Bengali, Tamil, etc.) or that possessed greater cultural prestige and political power in the region (Sanskrit, Persian). Yet from the beginning English was used by native Indian merchants and clerks, as well as by the language teachers and agents (*munshis*, *banyans*, and *dubashes*) of white Europeans, all of whom led to what Vinay Dharwadker calls the "partial Anglicization" of Indian society.[87] The collectivity of Anglo-Indian literature operates through an attachment to European metropolitan literary culture that is altered by its adaptation to new terrains and multilingual and multiethnic social circumstances.

Within this environment a literary history in a minor key must seek out the everyday and repetitive with the same vigor as the extraordinary, distinguished, or pioneering (those elements that have traditionally driven literary criticism).[88] Historians of colonial literature in particular should be more engaged with examining not its elite practitioners but its unexceptional, run-of-the-mill authors. In this type of literary history the place and circumstances of texts' composition and publication make a material difference in how we interpret them, altering the attentions of literary criticism, which have revolved primarily around form, content, or authorial biography.

With this principle in mind I reconstruct the physical infrastructure and social relationships that make up the constellations of Anglo-India's art world, which is populated not just by aristocratic administrators and Enlightenment scholars like Hastings and Jones but also by those clerks, soldiers, and surveyors who as yet have no literary history because their written productions have been largely ignored.[89] Often these works exist in between popular and elite literature, skewed toward disposal and deletion rather than preservation and posterity. The ordinary is valuable because of its proliferation—by definition the majority of material composed—but also because it is rapidly changeable. The transitory and ephemeral nature of everyday writing is an argument for its value, not for its inferiority.

One representative example of this incremental adaptation that can be identified by middle reading is the continued prevalence of neoclassicism in early nineteenth-century Calcutta. For centuries knowledge of the classics served as an important imaginative benchmark and training tool for colonial elites in India.[90] Many of the civil buildings in Anglo-India were neoclassical, and visitors from Europe compared them to those of Mediterranean antiquity: the Government House in Madras, for example, was modeled on the Parthenon.[91] Commemoration of returning soldiers and their commanders, like Lord Cornwallis, was vaguely Roman, with the Accountant General's Office in Calcutta displaying a "medallion" of Cornwallis's face with "laurels and cornucopia" after his successes in the third Anglo-Mysore War of 1791–92.[92] And the heroic couplet, that most neoclassical verse form, remained pervasive among Anglo-Indian poets well into the nineteenth century. The satire of India, *Calcutta: A Poem* (1811), was written entirely in heroic couplets and laughs that what was old in Britain becomes new again in India as

> London's fluttering fashions, six months old,
> Their antiquated charms display to view,
> In distant realms how elegant and new![93]

Though the author of *Calcutta* thinks otherwise, the use of neoclassicism and the heroic couplet in "distant realms" are not indicators of bad design or of belated authors incapable of artistic innovation. Instead, Asian colonialism reglobalized neoclassical aesthetics, turning the early eighteenth-century British reinvention of classical antiquity into an imperial art form. This is not necessarily the "superficial adoption of European elements" that Holger Hoock intuits with the adoption by "indigenous elites" of neoclassical values.[94] It is no more superficial than the British adopting the Roman cultural poses that produced neoclassicism in the first place. Rather, the embrace of Greek and Roman elements, routed through neoclassical Britain, is a manifestation of Anglo-India's translocal aesthetic that aspires to compete with those metropolitan values on which it depends. Old techniques ("London's fluttering fashions, six months old") are reinvigorated in new contexts, which lead to new social affiliations, literary publics, and reputation-making apparatuses.

It is helpful to think of this collective conventionality and repetitive reinvigoration of "fluttering fashions" as the infrastructure of Anglo-Indian literary culture that enables the majority of artistic production, though it is often unnoticed. As the sociologist Susan Leigh Star observed, unremarkable aspects of social institutions allow them to function.[95] "Study the unstudied," she suggests, and literary scholars could productively turn such a mandate not only toward overlooked authors and (non)canons—the familiar routes of archival recovery—but also toward the discarded, unfashionable techniques of a period, especially those literary forms, like the heroic couplet, that predominate despite having given way elsewhere to what are seen as more inventive practices.[96]

Rewriting literary history in a minor key thus requires that scholars situate neglected works, authors, and forms in the social contexts that "produced, distributed, and consumed" them "to the extent that available records and materials allow."[97] But it would also raise questions about the standards that have made certain topics intellectually interesting and professionally rewarding. Late twentieth-century debates about the composition of the canon and art's intrinsic value still retain an ability to shape literary criticism because those debates have been reformulated into twenty-first-century archival decisions about what gets preserved, transmitted, and studied.[98] For this reason, scholars of empire should follow Margaret Cohen's call to excavate the coherent aesthetics of forgotten works that have been dismissed as uninteresting or mediocre.[99] The works I examine in this book are a colonial variation of Franco Moretti's insight that "most literature is normal literature" and correspondingly demands a literary history able to assess its normalcy.[100] Literary criticism rates novelty and generic change higher than stasis and traditionalism, reinforcing the "persistence of liberal humanist notions" of value in the academy because it allows for an easily outlined and rationally continuous evolution of ideas.[101] In this view the best writers are leaders, and the rest catch up too late. Early innovations eventually turn into widely adopted conventions, and the cycle starts all over again. The consequence has been that the works I discuss here, which are primarily ordinary literature (even if about extraordinary circumstances), rarely rise to visibility unless they appear as those "bad objects" of empire that W. J. T. Mitchell suggests provoke crises among critics because of their politics.[102]

In its historical moment the conventionality and studied triviality of much Anglo-Indian writing demonstrates both adoration and contempt for the perceived power of English literature. The moral components associated with bad writing have a long history of being challenged during the eighteenth century (as scholars of women's writing and laboring-class poets have consistently pointed out), and the perception that artistic invention might repair or compensate for immorality has its own lengthy story.[103] It also cannot be forgotten that the authors I examine here were directly responsible for the pain and trauma of colonial dispossession and subjugation; they were the officers and administrators who made empire possible, and they often relished their sense of superiority. They played a part in the longer, larger exploitation of India that led to countless lost lives and the stagnation of economic growth, which in many industries shifted from "prosperity to poverty" over two centuries of colonial rule.[104] That exploitation was not reserved for India only but intensified throughout Asia over the course of the nineteenth century.

But theories of orientalism and colonial discourse, for all their creative power and illuminating politics, have become a roadblock to understanding Asia's earliest anglophone culture, leading either to what Kuan-Hsing Chen calls an "obsessive critique of the West" that only reinforces its singular dominance or to pursuit of an elusive and original Asia that somehow evaded the effects of European intrusion.[105] All of those boring ordinary poems and plays and narratives that were the standard fare of late eighteenth-century anglophone Asia were ignored because they did not conform to the kind of postcolonial print culture scholars expected after Said's *Orientalism*.

This does not mean scholars should practice postcolonialism without politics, if such a thing was even possible. But the reasons why these Anglo-Indian authors have been forgotten are evidence as much of the institutional politics of twenty-first-century literary criticism as of eighteenth-century colonialism. If they published in London, as the Calcutta-born Eyles Irwin did, they are perceived as being an extension of its values rather than local ones. But if their audience primarily included Anglo-India, as the Bombay Army officer and playwright James Romney's did, they are excluded from the English canon that has been fashioned since the early twentieth century. Because they are typically white Anglo-Indian colonizers, they are outside of postcolonialism's worthy goal of recovering the nonwhite perspectives of those subjected to the British Empire. They are not considered to be a diaspora and are thus resistant to its tactics of community retrieval. Programming literary history through vectors of nation and authenticity has had an especially strong exclusionary effect on Anglo-Indian authors: their work lacks the telos of nation-formation, which was available to American literature, so they are seldom integrated into the national traditions that for decades have organized the discipline of literary studies. The obsession with influence has caused us to disregard authors like Irwin and Romney, whose innovations occur in subject matter or political stance, in favor of more obvious formal experimenters like Sir William Jones.[106] These authors' neglect has been exacerbated by their limited numbers of readers, as well as by the practical difficulties of researching archives that have been poorly preserved, lost among a glut of other documents, or only recently digitized.

These difficulties make Anglo-Indian writing a worthy beneficiary of postcolonialism's impulse to recover significant yet obscured portions of the imperial archive. Anglo-India's authors remind us that recovery can reinforce unspoken, preexisting aesthetic judgments that were the reason those authors were omitted from the canon in the first place. They reveal that literary criticism integrates previously neglected authors either by conferring on them the status of genius they are presumed to have warranted all along (Aphra Behn) or by reading them as representative of popular topics and genres created retroactively (working-class poets). Rather than accept this restrictive binary, we should compose literary histories that valorize ordinary authors whose writing, while formally conventional, nonetheless offers insights about understudied places and historical moments. Such a project would require us to track the coherent aesthetics of unheeded works that scholars have determined only afterward were the dead ends of literary history. It would bring back into visibility authors obscured in the "great unread" and would weigh the status of culture's dark matter, which resonates with and lends mass to human production but endures now only faintly in our fuzzy memories.[107]

CHAPTER ONE

A Cultural Company-State and the Colonial Public Sphere

In a well-known argument for the geographically wider and historically deeper origins of American literature, Wai Chee Dimock describes the ecstasies Henry David Thoreau felt while reading the Bhagavad Gita at Walden Pond and sensing a connection between its waters and the Ganges. This moment of mixed continents and temporalities leads Dimock to the notion of American literature's "deep time."[1] In her exposition of this foundational scene she notes a critical detail: at Walden Pond Thoreau was reading the first English-language translation of the Bhagavad Gita, produced in 1785 by Charles Wilkins, an employee of the East India Company, whose project was completed in India and authorized and funded by Wilkins's close friend and literary interlocutor Warren Hastings, the governor-general of Bengal.[2] Hastings claimed, presciently, that Wilkins's linguistic work would "survive when the British dominion in India shall have long ceased to exist."[3] In the *longue durée* of American literature Hastings and Thoreau share sightlines into a future in which the Bhagavad Gita outlasts the British Empire, which seemed to be growing relentlessly as Thoreau was reading and writing during the 1840s.

There is another consequence of Dimock's insights about Thoreau. She perceives Thoreau to be a "conduit" and "a carrier" of earlier literary cultures, as if conveying unopened letters from an earlier age, but Thoreau, Wilkins, and Hastings were also actors within that culture.[4] The Bhagavad Gita may have outlasted the British Empire, as Hastings predicted, yet it was inexorably altered by it too.[5] Thoreau's ecstasies and American literature's "deep time" are only imaginable because of a concerted effort by colonial administrators, military men, radical printers, and native craftsmen, many of them supported and directed by the monopolistic EIC, to create a regional anglophone literary culture that engaged with the enormous cultural and linguistic diversity of South Asia. Specific choices made by individual actors and quasi-governmental bodies created and defined eighteenth-century anglophone literary culture in India. I draw attention to Dimock's routing of American literature through British India because it so effectively reignites questions about the material and textual intermediation that makes reading publics, civil societies, and literary canons (and noncanons) possible. Returning to their examples is necessary to complete a new history of governing apparatuses, artistic worlds, and political public spheres that arose as a result of late eighteenth-century European colonialism.

Why Now? 1765–1819

Anglo-India's regional literature was a practical and imaginative response to a pivotal period in South Asia: the decades between 1765, when the Treaty of Allahabad made the EIC *diwan* (agent) of Bengal, Bihar, and Orissa in northern India for the Mughal Empire, and the founding of Singapore by Thomas Stamford Raffles in 1819 and the arrival of the steamboat (to Bombay in 1820 and Calcutta in 1823), after which connections to Europe and conditions for regional literary publics changed rapidly.[6] The decades in between, especially the 1780s and 1790s that form the centerpiece of this book, were decisive for the administration of India. Geopolitically, this was a period when the EIC consolidated its territorial gains in northeastern India—especially after the Permanent Settlement of 1793, which regularized the collection of tax revenue in Bengal—and defeated the Kingdom of Mysore in the south, killing one of their most fearsome enemies, Tipu Sultan, at the 1799 siege of Seringapatam (Srirangapatna). This was also the period when the Company was placed under greater parliamentary scrutiny, especially after the impeachment of Hastings, the governor-general (1772–85) who was tried in Parliament for corruption in spectacular fashion (1788–95) by, among others, Edmund Burke and Richard Brinsley Sheridan.

The historian C. A. Bayly defines this unusual epoch as the "first global crisis," when the world transitioned from the "archaic globalization" of the Qing Chinese, Ottoman, Mughal, and Javanese empires, which were primarily agrarian with "patchy and contingent" sovereignties, toward an international system of national ideology.[7] This crisis involved mobile sentiments of revolution (Polasky), "vectors" of the Atlantic resistance exploding as rampant piracy and American rebellion (Linebaugh and Rediker), slave revolts in Jamaica motivated by the enormous cruelty of the plantation system

(Walvin), and liberal upheavals in Haiti driven by enslaved Africans and Enlightenment ideals (DuBois).[8] Its aftermath was the system of European nation-states and overseas imperialism that Bayly calls the "modern world," and it was during this period that British India stabilized as a territorial dominion. In the 1750s the subcontinent was not yet seen by the British as a potential settlement colony or an important sector, dwarfed as it was by trade with the West Indies and American seaboard. By the 1810s it was a dominant issue of British domestic and overseas politics, eclipsed only by the abolition debate and Napoleon Bonaparte.[9]

The transformation in prominence occurred because of the military, political, and economic success of the British in Asia. This success was punctuated by notorious setbacks that have led scholars to presume that the art and literature of this period attempted to salvage national pride from the psychic toll of defeats against American revolutionaries and native Indian leaders.[10] Nonetheless, during these decades the British shifted into a dominant position, confirmed with the removal of their last considerable opponent in South Asia, the Maratha Confederacy, in 1818.

Added to these geopolitical events were infrastructural and demographic changes. Though population totals are difficult to ascertain with confidence, more English-speaking Europeans arrived in India starting in the 1780s, expanding interest in the creation and distribution of anglophone literature. Their interest, together with EIC direction, produced the impetus for a vigorous cultural infrastructure—presses, newspapers, poetry collections, letters, papermaking and selling, circulating libraries, and amateur theaters. Examining these elements inverts the relationship between cultural infrastructure and its identifying products, embedding them in their ambient background while bringing to the fore the social relations, artistic imaginations, and physical instruments that created and motivated Anglo-Indian publics.[11]

But this cannot be the only explanation; British people had been resident in India since the mid-seventeenth century. Determining why Anglo-Indian literary publics cohered during this period requires reexamination of the relationship between English writing and imperial power in a way that moves beyond the easy correspondence of literature as an instrument of empire and the "rhetoric of English India."[12] While Edward Said and Sara Suleri have sensitized generations of scholars to associate cultural creation with imperial administration, they do not answer why anglophone literature in Asia took the institutional forms that it did and pursued its semiautonomous agenda of self-differentiation. In succeeding sections I consider how Anglo-Indian literature operated in concert with a cultural company-state to establish unique institutions. Understanding when and why this art was created requires attention to the concerted, often contentious, interactions of the British crown, the EIC, and Anglo-India's authors, artists, and audiences.

The primary exponent of these changes was the East India Company, the crucial yet institutionally byzantine vector of colonialism in Asia. Britain, and England before it, had extensive commercial contacts with India, dating to before 1600, when Queen Elizabeth offered the EIC a monopoly on trade between the Horn of Africa and the Straits of Magellan in South America. Competing with Dutch, French, and Danish outfits, the EIC established trading outposts called factories along the eastern and western coasts of India—at Surat in 1613, Madras in 1639, Bombay in 1668, and Calcutta in 1690. Between 1600 and 1833 the EIC was estimated to have financed forty-six hundred voyages—averaging one ship per week after 1800—which placed it among the largest commercial ventures emerging from Britain.[13]

But the EIC was more than a joint-stock trading company or a precursor to multinational corporations. As Philip Stern has noted, it behaved more like a "form of early modern government" and a "political community and polity" that pursued many of the same functions as nation-states or global empires—administering law, collecting taxes, inflicting punishment, engaging in warfare, supporting armies, and conducting diplomacy.[14] Its monopoly over trade to Asia was guaranteed by monarchical charter, renewed and reinforced by parliamentary debate. These debates opposed observers worried about the power of the EIC with MPs who often explicitly acted as Company factors. The result was a series of concessions and compromises, most notably with the 1773 Regulating Act, which established the Supreme Court system in Bengal and the position of governor-general, and the 1784 India Act, which instituted a Parliament-appointed Board of Control to oversee the operation of the Company. The EIC was further constrained after its monopoly on trade was revoked in 1813, though it was not finally disbanded, and India reorganized as a British Crown colony, until 1858, after the widespread Indian Rebellion.

In practice, however, the vast distances required for communication, the complicated political ambitions of Company officials, and their convoluted interactions with other European trading companies and South Asian political powers meant that control was contested and dispersed. This situation was exacerbated by the close connections between the EIC's trade and

Britain's domestic governance and economy. EIC stock was a central holding for Britain's creditors and essential income for prominent politicians, so that potential bankruptcies in the early 1770s and the 1780s threatened the entire system (even as individuals amassed large fortunes).[15] Lord Chatham unashamedly voiced his hope that Indian wealth, transferred to individuals like himself, would "fix the ease and preeminence of England for ages"; they would live off Asia's industry, he cheered.[16] Early on, EIC trade required bullion because Asian economies did not want European manufactures, which led to greater global integration as swelling mineral wealth from South America financed western European commerce with India and China.[17]

After 1765, when the EIC assumed control of Bengal's finances, taxation rather than its own supply of money paid for oceanic trade.[18] Textiles and opium provide examples of how revenue collection, territorial administration, and trade worked together. By 1750 Indian textiles accounted for 60 percent of EIC sales in London.[19] Textile weavers had to fill EIC demands at a compulsory low price, and eventually those cloth purchases were financed with the land revenue the EIC took from Bengal peasants.[20] Similarly, the Company collected monopoly rights in Asia for opium beginning in 1773 and outlawed private cultivation in 1797, meaning that peasants had to cultivate a fixed amount and deliver it to the EIC at a set price. Through these mechanisms of coerced commerce Britain's trade deficits with the Americas and Europe were balanced by the extraction of Indian surpluses.[21]

Nonetheless, the fiscal militarism of the EIC was diffuse, especially before the reforms of the 1770s and 1780s, when each presidency had a unique administration, institutional culture, financial system, and even different currencies (with Bengal using the sicca rupee, Madras the gold pagoda, and Bombay the Bombay rupee).[22] The Company was often in debt and between 1794 and 1810 lost tens of millions of pounds sterling that it sustained by borrowing heavily on money markets, loans supported by the promise of Indian tax revenue. Its lavish expenses included not only civil servants and standing armies but also the expenditures for costs of Indian goods and the support of colonial services, like those of the printing presses and newspapers that I discuss later in this chapter.[23] As a profit-making enterprise the EIC was a disaster, but as a wealth-extracting administrator it was superb, spending nearly all (and sometimes more) of its revenues to expand and maintain its dominion in Asia and its political influence in Britain.

Although there was a tendency toward closer ties between the EIC and the British government until dissolution in 1858, Company strategy in Asia never fully accorded with British foreign policy, particularly around issues like piracy or religious missions, which were officially banned from proselytizing in India until 1813.[24] Our notion of empire as a projection of a nation-state's wishes overlooks the evolving ways in which other organizations like the EIC participated in governance by advancing it, resisting it, debating it. Indeed, the creation of a British Empire in Asia required the British government to conquer not just the territory of India but also the EIC, which became "British," Stern cannily suggests, only when Parliament asserted rights to it, a process that occurred gradually (and with concentrated defiance) between the 1770s and 1820s.[25] The multiple competing interests of monarchy, Parliament, and traders meant the British imperium was a multiregional, tessellated endeavor throughout the period I describe in this book.

Complicating matters was that the EIC existed within a larger world of connected sovereignties that existed before the arrival of Europeans, which meant its employees were exposed to different cultures, most of which were uncommon in Britain. The Ottoman axis extended from Venice to India, while the Qing Empire in China had an economic output likely equivalent to all of Europe.[26] Even with the volume of European oceanic shipping, most of the maritime trade in Asia was local and regional, which produced rapid cultural contact there. Parsis, who had fled Islam in the eighth century and settled in Gujarat, acted as intermediaries between the British and Hindus and functioned as shipyard owners whose Indian craftsmen built vessels for the British fleet, often crewed by *lascars* (native Indian sailors) and East Africans.[27] Jews, who traveled to India after the destruction of the Abbasid Caliphate by Mongols in 1258, were an important merchant diaspora that facilitated trade in South Asia.[28] Armenians, who had relocated to southern Asia, were exponents of this integrated trade because although they were Christians, they used Persian, could operate in Muslim areas, and had a network that reached to the Mediterranean.[29] Despite the withdrawal of the Ming China navies from the Indian Ocean world in the fifteenth century and the chaotic succession of the Qing dynasty, diasporic Chinese trading communities were ubiquitous, especially in Southeast Asia.[30] These groups formed what Gagan Sood calls the "connective tissue" of the Asian region.[31]

At the center of this region was the Mughal Empire. Founded by Muslims invading from central Asia in 1526, over the next two centuries it expanded across the subcontinent, absorbing, though never completely subordinating, many of the smaller kingdoms of central and southern India into what John Richards calls a "war-state" whose dynamism was driven by military conflict.[32] The "patchwork quilt" of imperial control these conflicts created made it possible to affiliate with nonindigenous sovereignties like the EIC.[33] Military successes at Plassey (Palashi) in 1757, after which the EIC secured control of Calcutta, and at Buxar (Baksar) in 1764, where it smashed the residual powers of Bengal, captured Bihar, and weakened the Nawab of Awadh, were "later seen as milestones" by historians, but they provoked little comment in Delhi, the capital of the Mughal Empire, because its vastness had made it vulnerable to a range of contemporaneous threats to its centralizing power.[34]

By the late eighteenth century, Mughal India was fractured and dispersed, with polities in Punjab toward the north and Maratha states in the west all asserting different degrees of independence, though the vitality of Mughal culture survived and even insinuated itself into its successors' forms of governance.[35] Southern Indian polities, especially the Kingdom of Mysore under Haidar Ali and Tipu Sultan, contended with these North Indian states and each other to establish their own dominions on the Deccan plateau.[36] The EIC was simply one among many competitors within the region that had been unified uneasily a century earlier by the indispensable Mughal statesman Aurangzeb (1618–1707).[37] As Jon Wilson notes, it is hard to separate political practices from social life in eighteenth-century India, since much of the British power in Bengal arrived with the approval of the Mughal state.[38] When the EIC assumed the *diwani* for Bengal in 1765, for example, the Company became an agent of the Mughal Empire: in effect, a semisovereign trading company sanctioned by the British monarch and certified by Parliament operated on behalf of a South Asian emperor. The arrangement was as confusing as it was lucrative.[39]

Anglo-Indian literature reflected this knotty geopolitical situation and cultural intermixture at a moment when the Indian subcontinent's colonial future was not yet assured. Recognizing this fact is an important component of Partha Chatterjee's polemical retelling of colonial modernity, which imagines other outcomes than the "teleologically predetermined" British rule over India.[40] Different endings were still vivid in late eighteenth-century India; one evening in 1792, Tipu Sultan dreamed he had expelled the British from India. He recorded his dream in a diary not as a comforting fantasy but as a political aspiration.[41] The anglophone literature of this period likewise is a feature of an as-yet-unassimilated colonial modernity, still in flux and incompletely integrated. Remembering this is the literary critical equivalent of understanding that even in 1800 it was not clear that the British would survive in India, let alone produce a literature that reflected their dominion.

Who Were the Anglo-Indians?

Although the exact number of white people inhabiting India between 1770 and 1820 is unknown, it is evident their population was small compared to that of indigenous inhabitants. Madras had approximately eighty thousand residents in 1800 but only a few thousand white civilians, soldiers, and sailors.[42] Bengal, with thirty million people, was three times more populous than all of Great Britain and dwarfed its few hundred Company administrators. EIC civil personnel in India probably never totaled more than two thousand at any time before the nineteenth century, but the Company, which possessed privately funded armies, employed many more soldiers, which might have raised the population to twenty thousand or more as the EIC governed larger territories and involved itself in conflicts with Mysore and the Marathas, its two primary adversaries on the subcontinent during this period.[43]

Most scholars dismiss the uniqueness of eighteenth-century India because of this small population, which they assume meant isolation for its elites.[44] Percival Spear assumed that by the late eighteenth century the British in India were "beginning to adopt English rather than Indian standards of living and amusement" and seeking to make each settlement an "exact replica . . . of an English town."[45] P. J. Marshall believed their association with the EIC meant few opportunities for Anglo-Indian literary society and authorial careers because it was a "community dominated by official employment, recruited in Britain and set on returning to Britain."[46] "Assimilation to metropolitan values seems to have been what most articulate British people in India also wanted," he contends, and they maintained a "strictly British life style" that emulated "self-consciously British norms" and "gloried in its Britishness."[47] Likewise, Bayly wonders if Britain's expatriates were "too small in numbers, too dependent on the Crown and Company, and too divided from Eurasian and Indian society by racial exclusiveness" to fashion their own "creole nationalism."[48]

The prominence of the EIC within the Anglo-Indian colonial economy meant that most whites came into contact with the Company.[49] Debates—especially between William Dalrymple and Pankaj Mishra—about the significance and the degree to which elite Company men adopted indigenous customs and dress, took Indian wives and mistresses, and created mixed-race families have shifted scholars away from the idea that the British either were going native or were a "people apart" from their surroundings.[50] Yet whatever cultural attitudes toward India existed and however pervasive they were, still overlooked is that the white population of India's presidency cities (Calcutta, Madras, and Bombay) were each equal to that of a British market town that exhibited characteristics of both imitation and originality, assimilation and ghettoization.

The range of professions, too, was wider than is typically imagined. Often thought to be composed of only merchants and military men, by the 1790s the Anglo-Indian population included attorneys, notaries, translators, accountants, record keepers, printers, coroners, police officers, harbormasters and ships' pilots, store owners and shopkeepers, bookbinders, insurance agents, ship inspectors, indigo planters, jewelers, tailors, carpenters, hairdressers, carriage-makers, and dance instructors. To date, scholars have primarily focused on the Enlightenment impact of erudite orientalists like Sir William Jones and William Marsden, but, as we will see, paying attention to this larger population of nonelite soldiers and workers is crucial for a more complete picture of the nascent literary culture of Anglo-India. They depended on the "Crown and Company," but they also came into contact with other cultures in ways that differ from the more segregated nineteenth-century Raj.

The ethnic and national origins of this population varied widely. The EIC drew employees from around the British Isles, including Irish and Scottish gentry families. These differences were evident in the associations of Anglo-India, for example the Highland Society, first convened in Calcutta in 1788, or by the printing of Scots songs and the popularity of Walter Scott.[51] Most traveled from Europe, though some, like Eyles Irwin, the focus of chapter 3, were born in India. Others were not white at all, like Julius Soubise, the mixed-race former slave and companion of the Duchess of Queensbury, who had fled to Calcutta in the 1770s and became an equestrian, a fencing instructor, and a theatrical performer.[52] Whether or not they thought of Britain as home, returning there was uncommon.[53] The nabob who traveled back to the British Isles with a vast fortune was a rare occurrence, and short-term visits to Britain were impossible when journeys required six months and departures were narrowly constrained by the monsoon's seasonal wind patterns.[54] In fact, though scholars have emphasized imperial operators who moved across colonial domains, such as Lord Cornwallis, who served both in the American Revolution and as governor-general of Bengal, most inhabitants of British Asia were men who spent long periods there by decision or necessity.[55] For junior army officers and soldiers enlistment was a "speculative risk" as they assessed the unusual climate against pay that was "modest."[56] The journey between Europe and Asia was treacherous, and South Asian weather was thought to be unhealthy for white people, which provoked anxiety about their clothes, food, and drink.[57] These anxieties have been corralled as evidence of fatalism among Anglo-Indians and nostalgia for Britain's temperate healthfulness. Less frequently considered is the obverse: that long travel times and increased mortality provoked many Europeans to see India as perhaps their last home. A glance at *The East Indian Kalendar* from 1797, one in a series of yearly listings of the EIC's employees, shows that many serving in India first arrived in the 1760s and 1770s; most of these spent their entire lives there. Mrs. Oldstander, a long-lived Anglo-Indian character that I discuss in chapter 5, pointedly insists she would never leave India for Albion's cool breezes. She would rather "turn Braminy" and be burned with her husband as a white *sati*, choosing flames over frigidity and India over England.

White women were a small part of Anglo-India's population. There were perhaps one hundred white women in Bengal and eighty-five women (and children) recorded in Madras during the 1770s, yet they were imaginatively significant.[58] James Romney thought women the arbiters of Anglo-Indian sociability. The printer William Duane believed the pseudonymous poet "Anna Maria" to be the vanguard of a new "anglo-asiatic taste." Their rarity led to social fluidity that Joan Mickelson Gaughan argues differed from stridently gendered spheres of Britain, making eighteenth-century India a "transgressive space" (Franklin) with an "unorthodox femininity" (Nussbaum).[59] Eliza Draper, the Indian-born object of Laurence Sterne's late-life erotic fascination, lived in Bombay, which made her a muse for Anglo-Indian writers decades after she had left the region. Elizabeth Marsh's dramatic adventures in Asia, when she traveled without her husband, courted Company officials, and flirted with soldiers, shows that working-class women's sexuality could result in economic advancement.[60]

Residencies and outposts dotted India and the Bay of Bengal, yet most Anglo-Indian men and women resided in Calcutta, Madras, or Bombay, new colonial port cities that arose via EIC trade and that displaced previously important sites like Surat, Masulipatam (Machilipatnam), and Dacca (Dhaka).[61] Most scholars argue that whites were segregated from indigenous Indians, unlike in the "creole" societies and settler colonies of the Caribbean, North America, and Australasia.[62] Others suggest there was closer contact between white Europeans and native Indians before the nineteenth-century Raj.[63] Sexual intimacy and mixed-race children were common—a third of all children baptized in 1780s Calcutta were multiracial—and works such as William Dalrymple's *White Mughals* have popularized the sexual connections between Europeans and Indians.[64] Recent literary scholars such as Mary Ellis Gibson and Daniel White, however, have suggested more nuanced depictions of these relationships that emphasize the multilingualism of Anglo-Indians dependent on language teachers and scribes (*munshis* and *maulvis*), personal agents (*banyans* or *baniyas*), and servants, whose English training began a "partial Anglicization" of Indian society.[65]

Indigenous Indians worked imaginatively in concert with the anglophone public sphere, as when Muthuswami Dikshitar set Sanskrit lyrics within Irish jigs and European military music like "God Save the King" and Thomas Moore's "Remember the Time (The Castilian Maid)."[66] Ghulam Husain Khan Tabatabai's *Sëir Mutaqharain*, a history of the Mughal Empire in the eighteenth century, was translated from Persian by an Armenian friend of Sir William Jones, who went by the sobriquet Haji Mustafa; he warns in prefatory remarks about the "general turn of the English individuals in India" toward "contempt" for Indians, claiming that his is a "voice that has spoken among a million of others that could speak, but are silent."[67] Resistance to this "contempt" was shared by the few lower-class mixed-race authors who made it into print, such as "Old Nell," an Irish-Indian woman who asserted in *Hicky's Bengal Gazette* that although her "skin may not be so white as your fine ladies," she was as "sleek as the best of them," despite toiling as a gardener in Bengal.[68] Such anglophone voices spread outside of Asia in the works of Dean Mahomet (also known as Din Muhammad), who published an account of his service in the EIC armies and his travels through India in 1794 in Cork, Ireland, where he had traveled with his commanding officer.[69] Mahomet was known to later Indian travelers such as Mirza Abu Taleb Khan, whose description of a visit to England was translated from Persian into English by an EIC scholar and published there in 1810 and 1814. Theirs were among the six narratives from Indians to Britain that exist before 1800.[70]

But the vast majority of the anglophone literary public was dominated by white authors who were typical in that they occupied administrative positions and military roles. They were involved in the infrastructure of commerce and territorial governance, a rule by writing, an administration of paper. The Orient may have been a projection of European ideas about a place that suited their motives and perceptions of superiority, as Said and Suleri argue, but it was also a specific and material place with which many administrators interacted during daily routines. Those routines shaped their writing, even if not always in ways directly represented by their content. These authors were not those "imperial Britons" and returning nabobs who redefined Britishness as "global and performative" rather than "geographically rooted," nor were they the cultural brokers, "go-betweens," or "trans-imperial" subjects who intermediated between Europe and Asia at residencies around the globe.[71] They were not metropolitans abroad or a traveling Little England.

Instead, they were cognizant of their existence as British nationals in an interimperial world but also as cultural agents who fashioned identities in concert with (and distinct from) empires past and present. I attempt to capture this intermixture by referring to them as *Anglo-Indian*, a term whose meaning shifted significantly from the eighteenth century to the present. It was first used in an official capacity during the 1911 census of the British Empire, when it acquired its current connotation of mixed-race individuals. During the eighteenth century, however, it was grouped with a cluster of terms—*half-caste, Indo-Briton, East-Indian, Eurasian,* and *country-born*—that implied genealogy, geographical origin/occupation, or both.[72] This book reconnects the term with its earlier usage, which was driven less by parentage or ethnicity than by location, referring to a class of Europeans who lived and worked in Asia.[73] While many of the writers I examine in this book thought of themselves as British or referred to themselves as "English," they also understood their place in an Anglo-Indian context. We could see them as a diasporic community composed of individuals who redefine themselves in India without "going native," or we could see them as one of the identities being "carved out in diverse colonial settings," often in antagonism to metropolitan codes.[74]

From these vantages a complex picture emerges of a relatively small, mobile, multilingual audience that vigorously adapted British literary forms and cultural fashions to the local and regional concerns of India. They were civil servants and military men, merchants, and traders who produced imaginative writing in response to their surroundings. They engaged with the multi-ethnic world of South Asia while celebrating their national origin and assuming their superiority over indigenous Indians. The two categories of "going native" (ostensibly benign, appreciative colonialism) or rigidly maintained Britishness (cultural superiority and orientalism) are insufficient to describe how they interacted with the environment and the varied populations who also inhabited the place. It is the literature of this experience, in these physical places and under these conditions, that I take up with this book.

Printers, Patrons, Readers, and Libraries

Assessing the translocal and regional scales of writing in eighteenth-century India requires understanding the confluence of two sizable historical forces: how patronage and finance shaped the production and dissemination of Anglo-Indian literature and how orientalist learning and South Asia's many languages constructed a multilingual anglophony from which that literature emerged. The Indian subcontinent may have been the first "fully formed print culture to appear outside of Europe and North America," but the knowledge of this print culture has not led to much description of its pre-1800 Anglo authors and readers.[75] This is especially odd when one realizes that writing was an essential skill for EIC employees and that printed matter and books were an important part of EIC servants' possessions.[76] Beyond primers, dictionaries, and unofficial guides, like Thomas Williamson's *The East India Vade Mecum* (1810), employees carried imaginative literature to India and purchased it while there. A late eighteenth-century list of "necessary expense[s]" for India included "books of amusement and instruction" worth at least £3; the Supreme Court of Bengal Justice John Hyde possessed many more—1,321 titles—when he died in 1796.[77] Thomas Madge, a captain in the Madras Army from 1768 to 1773, owned editions of Shakespeare, Jonathan Swift, and Alexander Pope but also contemporaries like Henry Fielding, David Hume, Tobias Smollet, Laurence Sterne, Robert Dodsley, Moliere, Jacques Rousseau, Montesquieu, and a "number of Persian manuscripts."[78]

Missionary societies were the largest exporter of texts to India in the early eighteenth century, but scholars estimate that anywhere from 10 to 20 percent of Britain's overseas book trade involved India by the 1770s, having started irregularly but grown rapidly after 1763.[79] Those ship captains often reserved space for personal economic speculation, and many chose books, which they sold to local agents who passed them on through storefronts and auctions.[80] From the 1750s onward, book exports to India surged, increasing from twenty-two hundred volumes in the 1750s to twenty-seven thousand in the 1770s, most of it driven by the private trade of passengers.[81] India was so important that John Murray, father of Byron's publisher, lost money if new publications "were not ready in time for the India ships."[82] Because shipping costs were high, only the wealthiest could transport collections back to Europe; most books and manuscripts remained in India, recycled among readers and passed on to new collections, as Mitch Fraas has shown.[83]

Beyond these private collections were also EIC-established libraries, all of which created a density of reading material. These libraries originated in the late seventeenth and early eighteenth centuries, and their holdings suggest that these metropolitan structures were adjusted to the specific desires of Anglo-India's reading publics (rather than the formation of a national literary canon of English literature).[84] Madras's Fort St. George library already possessed 1,235 titles by 1730, including "Hebrew and Arabic books," more in Greek, Latin, and French, as well as "Books Translated into the Tamulic [Tamil] (or Malabars) and into the Gentu [Hindu] Languages."[85] The Asiatick Society of Bengal commandeered the three to four thousand manuscripts and books of Tipu Sultan after his 1799 defeat at Seringapatam.[86] The Literary Society of Bombay, founded in 1804, absorbed an earlier Medical and Literary Library of Bombay (est. 1789), before agreeing to spend £1,000 to expand its collection and then £100 each subsequent year on "newspaper, literary and scientific periodicals."[87] The EIC subsidized these collections, though private circulating libraries became so successful that by the late eighteenth century the Company began to dismantle the libraries it had earlier supported.[88]

Libraries expanded readers' range. Whereas the first circulating library established in Calcutta in 1781 likely had a limited readership owing to the great expense of joining (one gold mohur, about thirty-six shillings), later versions, like Calcutta's Cock, Maxwell, and Co., reduced prices and had agents in Dinapore (Dinapur or Danapur) and Cawnpore (Kanpur) to assure customers "books for circulation at those stations" by 1788.[89] A 1790 plan for a Madras circulating library promised "two thousand volumes of the latest and most choice books" to subscribers "within 50 miles" of Madras, who could keep books for three months (and those in "Out-stations" for six months), demonstrating that the arteries of its customer base ranged well beyond city limits.[90]

This massive print trade was aided by warfare. The first English-language press was captured during skirmishes with the French in Pondicherry and relocated to Madras in 1761 along with its printer, Charles Delon.[91] Warfare was a perpetual topic of newspapers, which printed military announcements, prisoner lists, and captivity narratives (especially of the four Mysore wars, 1767–99). The EIC saw the advantages of a pliant press and, as a later section shows, used military conflict as a pretext to reduce the possibility of criticism, but even EIC critics and "radicals" relished how war provoked increases to their readership.[92] On the anniversary of their second year in publication in 1786, the editors of the *Calcutta Gazette* joked that "peace . . . deprives the news-writer of his best fund" with which to attract readers.[93] John Collegins, in his 1802 poetic celebration of the Asiatick Society of Bengal, makes explicit the link between warfare and artistic ascendancy when he suggests "all the arts shall prosper like our arms"; when "warriors burn," he continues, "each man of letters warms."[94] Newspaper articles, poetic elegies, and captivity narratives supplied tools for Anglo-Indian readers to think about their role in British imperialism and was an example of the culture-facilitating effects of the EIC war machine.

This political environment supported the creation of a local printing industry. There were forty printers and at least seventeen different presses (though only ten at any one time) in Calcutta between 1780 and 1800; more were located in a dozen cities across South and southeastern Asia working in numerous languages, especially English.[95] Presses sold business forms, like bills of lading or powers of attorney, and printed newspapers, which helped support other ventures, such as book publishing or type foundries. The first type foundry was established by Charles Wilkins in 1778 and the type foundry of the Chronicle Press in Calcutta, established in 1786, manufactured Bengali, Nasta'liq, and Devanagari type for the *Calcutta Chronicle* and the press's other publications.[96] Printers in Madras produced Tamil and Telugu, and those in Bombay produced Marathi, Malayalam, and Gujarati, including two Parsi compositors at the *Bombay Courier* who used the newly cast Gujarati type to print the *Khordeh Avesta* (1798), a Zoroastrian religious text that marks the first time non-Europeans used movable type to print a text in India.[97] Paper remained expensive because it was imported from Europe or China, though the Baptist missionary Serampore Press had an extensive operation that included a paper mill by the early nineteenth century.[98]

The EIC was crucial for providing financial and infrastructural support to what we would now consider cultural and creative projects. Hastings supported artists, aided the foundation of the Asiatick Society of Bengal, and personally financed a madrassa in Calcutta to satisfy regional Muslim leaders who worried that knowledge of Islam might deteriorate alongside the Mughal Empire.[99] He benefited from ecological disasters, like northern India's 1770s famine, that disrupted indigenous forms of patronage and pushed *pandits* toward Company service.[100] He established a permanent printing office for the purpose of printing business forms "whether in Persian, Bengal or English" but also to demonstrate his was a "liberal" and "enlightened" government.[101] Printed products were subsidized by the government and resold to Company audiences or supported by the promise of a large body of purchasers, as was the case when members of the Asiatick Society of Bengal each agreed to purchase one copy of its publication, *Asiatick Researches* (1789).[102] When the Company refused direct support, Hastings often intervened, such as with Francis Gladwin's edition *Ayeen Akbery: or, The Institutes of the Emperor Akber*, a translation of the extensive late sixteenth-century survey of Mughal domains (*Ā'in-e Akbari*), published in three volumes between 1783 and 1786.[103] Company support was always complicated by worries over cost and disagreements about effectiveness, but these efforts were not simply Hastings's whim; his successor, Cornwallis, often seen as a stolid response to Hastings's orientalist government, supported the creation of a Sanskrit college in Benares to house a "precious Library of the most ancient and Valuable General Learning and Tradition."[104]

The shifting and contentious politics of the Company support for printing and translation had indirect effects, such as gathering together individuals who by necessity worked in different languages with diverse people and cultures. Hastings personally funded Nathaniel Brassey Halhed's *A Grammar of the Bengal Language* (1778), a tool for teaching Bengali that, following from Sir William Jones's *A Grammar of the Persian Language* (1771), helped establish the "historical grammar" as an authoritative form for language learning and cultural knowledge.[105] Ogborn has called Halhed's *Grammar* a "co-production" by Europeans and natives because while Halhed collected samples of Bengali and Charles Wilkins designed fonts, indigenous religious scholars provided manuscript materials that native craftsmen like Panchanan Karmakar, a blacksmith descended from metallurgists and calligraphers, used to manufacture the intricate cursive type (fig. 2).[106] The "artful combination and alignment of linguists, scribes, engravers, founders, and printers" required physical immediacy and local control in ways that were not possible with earlier attempts at printed Bengali that were distant from the subcontinent, like the London-based William Bolts's project from the 1770s.[107]

Local control was encouraged by Hastings. He justified his support for Halhed's *Grammar* to his superiors in London by arguing for state-funded and company-aided art that advanced both intellectual and business interests. He wondered rhetorically whether "in the present State and Constitution of this

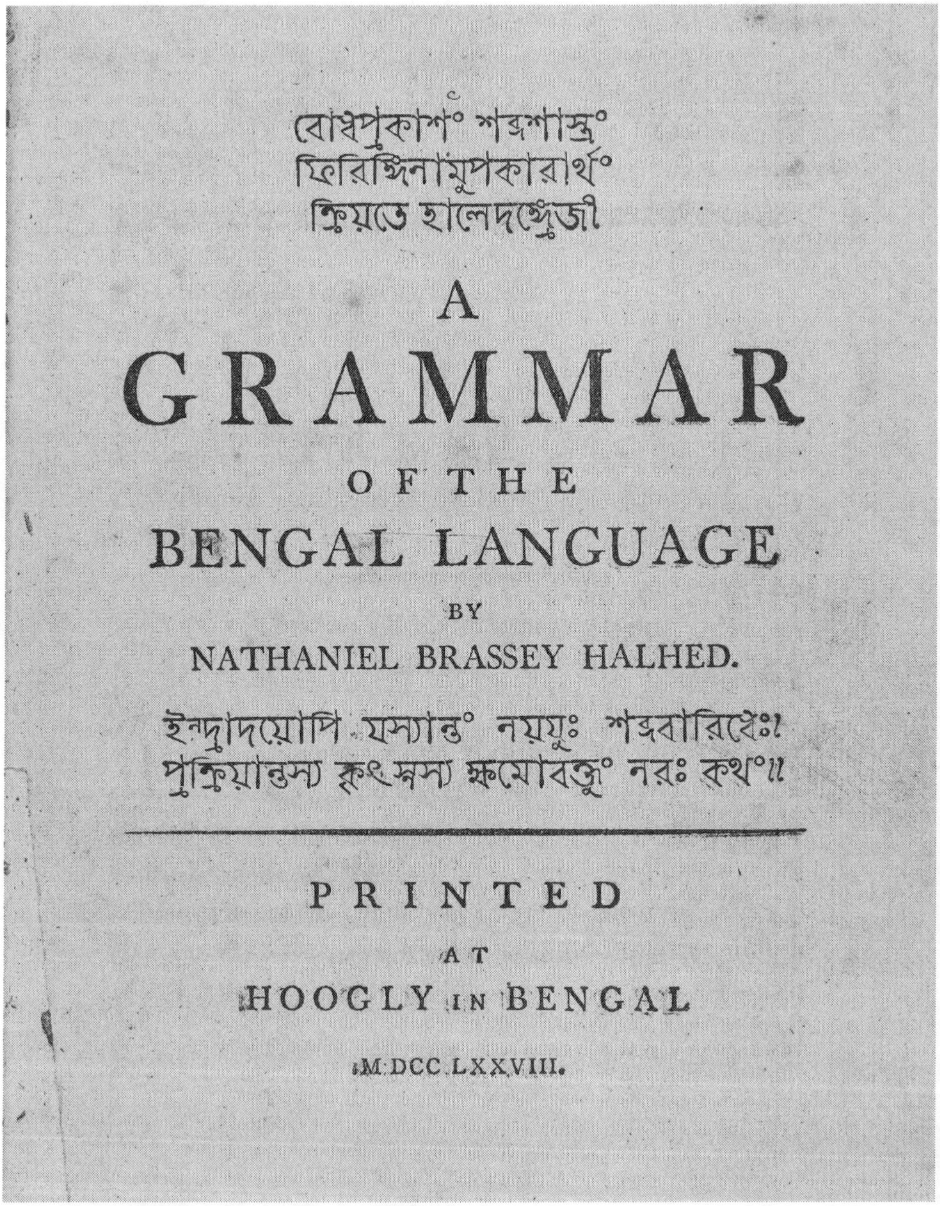

বোধপ্রকাশং শব্দশাস্ত্রং
ফিরিঙ্গিনামুপকারার্থং
ক্রিয়তে হালেদঙ্গ্রেজী

A
GRAMMAR
OF THE
BENGAL LANGUAGE
BY
NATHANIEL BRASSEY HALHED.

ইন্দ্রাদয়োপি যস্যান্তং নয়য়ুঃ শব্দবারিধেঃ।
প্রক্রিয়ান্তস্য কৃৎস্নস্য ক্ষমোবক্তুং নরঃ কথং॥

PRINTED
AT
HOOGLY IN BENGAL

M.DCC.LXXVIII.

Figure 2. Title page of Nathaniel Brassey Halhed's *A Grammar of the Bengal Language* (1778), including its delicate Bengali typefaces, designed by Charles Wilkins and struck by Panchanan Karmakar. The second line of Bengali in the title page translates as "for the benefit of the foreigner" (F. Ross, 33). Courtesy of the Beinecke Rare Books and Manuscript Library, Yale University.

government"—referring to the governorship of Bengal and of EIC possessions in Asia—"it ought to be reckoned a part of its Duties to encourage the Effects of Genius,—or to facilitate the Introduction of new arts, by which the dispatch of business may be quickened."[108] For Hastings, Halhed's *Grammar* was one of those "effects of Genius" and "new arts" that quickened business. Halhed celebrates that his *Grammar* was created by government, comparing it to the "Supreme Court of Justice" in Bengal (*Grammar*, i). He anticipates the better-known sentiments of Thomas Macaulay's "Minute on Indian Education" (1835), with its call for a class of "interpreters" to mediate between colonizers and those they rule, when he claims that his *Grammar* was needed for the "cultivation of the right understanding and of a general medium of intercourse between the Government and its Subjects" (*Grammar*, ii). But his reason differs considerably from those of the mid-nineteenth century's imperialists: Halhed claimed such cultivation was necessary because the British were ignorant, like the ancient Romans ("people of little learning and less taste"), of native customs (*Grammar*, ii). He hoped that, like the Romans who studied Greeks, Anglo-Indians would study Bengalis, whose learning was valuable even if "utterly disregarded in Europe" (*Grammar*, ii).

Printing Bengali before 1800 was not purely "functional" in its motives and effects, as Anindita Ghosh assumes.[109] In fact, the "language of command" that Bernard Cohn believes motivated British orientalist learning to objectify India was paired from the outset with the aesthetic desires of an emergent Anglo-Indian art world.[110] Halhed insisted on the importance of the visual dimensions of his work, noting that "public curiosity must be strongly excited by the beautiful characters which are displayed" in his *Grammar* (xxii). He was proud of the local origins of his type, noting the failures of the "ablest artists in London" (xxiii) and praising Wilkins, who built a set of type "remote from all connexion with European artists" and with "rapidity unknown in Europe" (xxiv). (Halhed pointedly ignores Karmakar's contributions.)[111] Hastings provided samples of the *Grammar* to the Bengal Council, with whom he governed, as evidence that his government should support printers. Yet another explicit goal was to sell the book to EIC employees across India as a company manual.[112]

In the process they meant to distribute culture. Halhed's *Grammar* included translations of the massive Indian epic the Mahabharata, and his earlier work, *A Code of Gentoo Laws* (1776), included passages of Sanskrit verse alongside its legal arguments.[113] Hastings defended Wilkins's translation of the Bhagavad Gita (and the salary he paid Wilkins to complete it) by boasting that it was a work of "very high and ascertained antiquity" whose "wonderful Fancy" would "open a new and most extensive Range for the human mind."[114]

Fiona Ross reminds scholars that the motives for patronage and public works among Company administrations were driven by self-interest; the title page of the *Grammar* confesses in Bengali that it is "for the benefit of the foreigner."[115] Yet the promotion of art in Anglo-India was an aesthetic, as well as utilitarian choice. Hastings offered his own "pleasure" at reading Wilkins's Gita—the same translation Thoreau read at Walden—as a sign of its value.[116] Personal patronage and finance "shaped the patterns of dissemination and distribution" in eighteenth-century Bengal, as Ogborn notes, but patrons and artists alike attested to the importance of aesthetic criteria as well.[117] Even as the EIC was entangled during this period with complex, money-losing global trade and debates within Britain about state oversight, administrators pressed for the value of local control, indigenous participation in publishing, and the importance of translating aesthetic desires into material infrastructure and literary imaginations. These men argued for corporate-sponsored creativity that merged colonial politics with finance and culture.

Sponsorship and Censorship

Its support of printing presses, grammar texts, educational institutions, translations and translators, artists and writers made the EIC a ubiquitous actor in the realm of Anglo-Indian cultural creation. Imperial politics necessitated the comprehension of Asian languages, which, though essential to EIC commerce from the beginning, expanded rapidly through Company-sponsored orientalist scholarship and practical language training that ensured an India-based print culture would be "hybrid," in the description of Kenneth Hall. Hybrid print culture sustained British rule, but it also reinforced regional rather than national identities predicated on "locally initiated creativity."[118] Because all of these advances were closely aligned with the trading ventures and resource extractions of the monopolistic EIC—and were supported by its patronage and regulated by its censorship—the Company carried considerable weight in Anglo-India's art world. Few corporations have so greatly influenced an entire literary culture, making the EIC akin to a cultural company-state.

With the phrase *cultural company-state* I combine two recent interventions in understandings of the state and sovereignty. Attention to private projects and public works has redefined the British state as what Holger Hoock calls a "cultural state" that thrust national institutions into the artistic sphere to complement its fiscal-military power. Hoock argues that the period I describe in this book was a "transitional phase," when the "cultural state was first forged at the metropolitan and imperial level," delineating a framework for its practices that included such varied elements as copyright for literature, imperial commemorative sculpture, and institutions like the British Museum, which funded archaeological exhibitions and sanctioned artifact appropriation, all of which demonstrate the "porous boundaries between state institutions and the cultural sphere."[119] A significant aspect of the cultural state's imperial dimensions occurred through the EIC, which, as I noted earlier, Philip Stern calls a "company-state" that pursued functions typically reserved for nations.[120] Maintaining its state-like sovereignty obsessed its directors and troubled observers. Adam Smith thought the EIC was a "strange absurdity" with its violation of market principles; Edmund Burke called it a "state in disguise of a merchant"; and Thomas Macaulay sought to accentuate its oddness by asking readers to imagine any other corporation, such as the "Merchant Tailors' Company," possessing armies, consolidating territory, and controlling people as the EIC did.[121]

Nick Robins cautions that examining the EIC through the "lens of culture" might cause us to forget why it was trading in India, but, as postcolonial scholars have noted from the outset, culture is inextricable from colonialism.[122] Rather than obscure its intentions, I would suggest that Anglo-Indian literature was one of many complicated legacies of EIC actions in Asia. Aesthetics were a unifying justification for infrastructure. For that reason scholars must examine that literature through its cultural institutions to understand the Company's trading practices and its state-sanctioned colonialism but also the constitution of English literature as a category, scholarly discipline, and methodology fashioned partly overseas from the British Isles.[123]

Some of the effects of this cultural company-state have been documented in different ways without being categorized as such, including the direct support for literary creation that Michael Franklin identifies with the "circle" of authors around Hastings; EIC patronage of scholarly communities, like the Asiatick Society of Bengal; or the lucrative market for portraits of Company officials that drew many European artists, like Johann Zoffany and Robert Home, to India in search of commissions.[124] The effects took shape as governmental favoritism, such as those newspapers that were able to access the Company-administered postal network for free.[125] When Madras's first paper, the *Madras Courier*, was founded in 1785, its editor, Richard Johnston, requested the same support as that of the *Calcutta Gazette*, including governmental purchase of "types of all sizes [as] are absolutely necessary" and the promise to transport them for free on EIC ships.[126] Johnston maintained that Madras would benefit from having a newspaper that allowed for widespread governmental notifications, arguing it was an improvement on the old system of posting handwritten notices on the city's "Sea Gate."[127] The *Bombay Gazette* used the example of the *Madras Courier* to convince its city government to make it the official newspaper.[128] When it fell into financial trouble in 1792, it asked the Bombay government to put it on a "better footing" while also seeking approval for its merger with another paper.[129]

It was not just financial and material inputs but also legal arrangements and political disputes that reveal EIC interventions in the cultural sphere. Surveillance and censorship were potent structuring devices for anglophone Asia because, as Robert Darnton notes, repressive censorship is instrumental to an institution's function, not just an external force acting on it.[130] The modern premise that the free press is virtuous and its curtailment is deleterious was not shared by the EIC, whose views aligned more with early modern judgments that saw censorship as a legitimate response to acute crises and political struggles. Those crises typically involved Company anxieties about maintaining its monopoly on trade with Asia and how to control transplanted Europeans and indigenous inhabitants.[131] The EIC technically determined which Europeans could reside in their domains, and it thus shaped the population of writers and printers by deporting those who resisted back to England. They gathered information about these populations from its intermittent and haphazard system of surveillance and censorship that Bayly has called the "information order."[132]

Surveillance was a general concern among authors. Bombay resident Charles Forbes was quite worried about his correspondence, warning one colleague not to send unsealed letters, especially if they contain "railing at men in Power."[133] But there was no systematic preproduction censorship of books or the theater until the nineteenth century, and postproduction consequences were vigorously resisted. In fact, it was not authors and letter writers but newspaper editors and proprietors who received the most attention from EIC regulation. John Shore, a friend of Hastings and the governor-general from 1793 to 1798, peevishly assumed that newspapers spread "licentiousness, too dangerous to be permitted in this country."[134] His successor, Ricard Wellesley, wondered how he could "tranquillize the editors of . . . mischievous publications."[135] By 1799 the EIC had established a series of regulations aimed at exerting explicit and comprehensive surveillance of British India's newspapers.[136] This date marks an important shift toward more systematically supervised interaction between newspapers and their reading publics.

Before then, however, censorship of newspapers was largely arbitrary and personal. Anglo-India's first newspaper, *Hicky's Bengal Gazette* (est. 1780), was prevented from using its mail system after repeatedly offending EIC administrators. Its owner, James Augustus Hicky, protested by publishing "The *Printer's* Solilqui [*sic*]," which asks "To Print—or not to Print—that is the Question" and complains about the "damn'd *Post Office*" that caused his newspaper's issues to "die away and loose [*sic*] their Circulation."[137] Hicky was prosecuted by the EIC, his press was confiscated, and he served a prison sentence as a result of a libel case against Hastings.[138] His legal claims to the rights of an English subject and to due process were dismissed.

When another Calcutta printer, William Duane, published a rumor about a senior EIC official's death, he was forced to undergo an interrogation, during which he advocated for uncensored newspapers and stated his hope that "all matters of Public Report and General concerns are discussed in them freely."[139] His confidence dissipated quickly when he was imprisoned. He begged for pardon, writing to the Secretary of Bengal: "I am punished, I am humbled, I am sorry."[140] While seeking bail, he offered security from two native Indians, even apologizing at one point when he misidentifies a native's name owing to his "want of a sufficient knowledge of the Native Language."[141] His reprieve did not last long. After being released, he was expelled from Asia and soon settled in the United States, where he became closely identified with the Democratic-Republican Party of Thomas Jefferson, who claimed that Duane's Philadelphia newspaper, *Aurora*, was instrumental in the party's victories in the 1800 US presidential election.[142] In America Duane participated in the type of political discourse that EIC sovereignty had blocked him from joining in India.

In Madras and Bombay the governmental attitude was perhaps even more interventionist than in Bengal, where Hicky and Duane were located. A controversy over the publication of an essay titled "The Chinese Anecdote" (1791) in the *Madras Courier* reveals how censorship was more personal than systematic during this early period of Anglo-Indian printing. The essay was an allegorical travel narrative about rapacious Chinese Mandarins who abuse the gentle inhabitants of the central Asian state.[143] It includes familiar elements of the oriental tale, such as depictions of Chinese despotism, bribery, and luxurious living, which had made the genre an important vehicle for political satire.[144] But it also crosses the oriental tale with the politics of European colonialism, which led one EIC official near Pondicherry to perceive it as a critique of his administration. He demanded that the newspaper be punished, arguing that it was "licensed and authorized by Government" with the "expressed condition" that nothing "disrespectful" nor "injurious" would be printed about the Company or its employees.[145]

When the editor, James Stuart Hall, was asked to name the essay's author—it could have been Hall himself—he protested his ignorance, asserting dubiously that he simply found the lengthy essay "on the table" of his printer's shop after he had returned from an errand.[146] Throughout the eighteenth century in Britain, such appeals to anonymity were a common defense of printers and were forcefully contested by governments. One reason the oriental tale became identified with such powerful mechanisms of satire was that the genre itself was associated with the safety of geographical distance and anonymized critique. Nonetheless, Hall offered to print an apology and insisted his newspaper would be "extremely guarded and delicate" about the reputations of private individuals.[147] The consequences of confrontation were so great that he agreed his printing would protect intimate secrets rather than publish them.

Perhaps the most adventurous conflict over the censorial powers of the cultural company-state involved Samuel Augustus Humphreys's 1790s Madras newspaper the *India Herald* (of which no copies are extant). The EIC accused Humphreys of printing a rumor that an incestuous affair existed between the Prince of Wales and one of his sisters.[148] The Secretary of Madras called this insinuation "the most daring libel," never exceeded in its "scandal, wickedness, and atrocity."[149] Evidence for the libel was secured by a native servant (a "Peon named Eerlapah") who was sent by the Madras government to the printer's office in the guise of a reader.[150] In response Humphreys tried to protect himself and his business partners ("many of whom are Natives, who look to the sale of the Paper for support") by asserting labor and property rights.[151] Duane's bond holders and Humphreys's business partners show that indigenous Indians were directly involved in the production of Anglo-Indian newspapers and in the apparatus of state-based surveillance used to monitor them, and they succeeded and suffered in turns as newspapers expanded.

Humphreys's assertions were unsuccessful; he was imprisoned on a ship and set to be deported from India, like Duane, but somehow escaped. (He reappeared five years later in Bombay. Again, newspapers played a role: the government of Madras only learned that Humphreys remained in India when an official in Madras noticed an announcement in a Bombay newspaper that Humphreys had been appointed as an attorney.[152] In this instance it was Anglo-India's regional reading network that foiled Humphreys's escape.) But before he vanished in the middle of the night from Madras, Humphreys orchestrated a campaign against the EIC from his prison hulk, including a handbill titled "To the Public" and datelined from his own Herald Press. In it Humphreys excoriates the Madras government for imprisoning him "without [his] being charged with any crime" and describes his confinement as "so unmanly an attack."[153]

What makes this handbill resonant is Humphreys's mention of the "public" of readers he imagines can be persuaded by his handbill's arguments. This public is avowedly local and immediate—imagined as allies knowledgeable of the specific cultural landmarks and political terrain and also potentially sympathetic to his plight. He laments to these readers how "even here"—that is, even in India—he should be allowed to claim the protections of English common law, which were dismissed by the EIC.[154] Within Company domains Anglo-Indians were viewed legally as British subjects; in practice, however, these rights were often abridged, and issues of jurisdiction were uncertain.[155] In his case, as with other newspaper proprietors such as Hicky and Duane, the global relations of civil discourse and rights shatter against Company prerogative. When Humphreys failed in his appeals to English law, he shifted toward the realm of sociability and local public opinion, using the printing apparatus that was about to be seized from him to portray the EIC as effeminate, cowardly individuals engaged in an "unmanly . . . attack" on another person.

These examples demonstrate the degree to which the EIC involved itself in the intellectual forms and physical infrastructure of Anglo-India's public sphere. The complicated dependence between newspapers and the Company administration became more pronounced after 1799, when editors accepted a systematic censorial regime that required them, for example, to submit proof sheets for examination before publication.[156] Censorship extended well into the 1820s and merged with concerns about a native Indian free press, exemplified by Thomas Munro's 1822 memorandum on the Indian Press, which argued that an uncensored press was a threat to foreign control of India, warning that a free press would "generate insubordination, insurrection, and anarchy" and lead "inevitably" to the expulsion of Europeans.[157]

Scholars have rightly emphasized the degree to which the EIC entangled itself in the politics of printing on the Indian subcontinent, describing a pervasive orientalist attitude among its officials and Britain-based scholars that regimented and rationalized the administration of India's people and its economy. Some scholars describe newspaper proprietors as "servile"; others saw them as a counterweight to EIC power, and still others perceived a continuous contest over liberalism and the free press.[158] But at their origin the relationship between Anglo-Indian newspapers and the EIC was more equivocal than these arguments credit. Even as newspaper editors sought to evade government censorship, they desired governmental legitimacy and used its machinery (particularly the postal service) as a financial and marketing strategy. They begged the EIC explicitly for financial assistance, as was the case for the *Bombay Gazette*. At other times newspaper proprietors promoted themselves as a check on Company intrusion and dishonesty, as Hicky, Duane, and Humphreys did. None of these men succeeded, but their imprisonment and deportation did little to extinguish critiques of the EIC.

The two prevailing positions about orientalism—that it was an imposition and "conquest of knowledge," as Edward Said and Bernard Cohn suggest, or that it indicated Britain's "desperate ignorance" and dependence on native information, as C. A. Bayly argues—appear quite differently when set alongside a better understanding of the EIC's attempts to control an anglophone printing world it helped to create.[159] In these cases the EIC exercised its sovereignty as a company-state to draw the contours and determine the composition of its colonial public sphere. Of course, the EIC was not always unified, nor was it autonomous from the larger fiscal-military state. Its actions mimic those of the British government that often sought to control the distribution of information, especially in the press, through subsidy and prosecution, but there was more absolute constraint for the press in India.[160] To the extent that the EIC was able to maintain a semblance of sovereignty over Asia, it was also able to contribute material and imaginative resources to the constitution of a public sphere and a literary culture in Anglo-India.

If scholars have undervalued the EIC as a patron of the visual arts, as Natasha Eaton convincingly demonstrates, they have also underappreciated its role as both a benefactor of imaginative literature and a creator of its infrastructure but also as a censor whose surveillance designed literary publics and controlled its population of producers.[161] Support and censorship of newspapers were an early artistic and infrastructural example of the historically lengthier control over trade that motivated Adam Smith to conclude that the EIC was an unnatural organization "which oppresses and domineers in the East Indies."[162] Attention to the EIC's dual role as patron and censor would help fracture the sense that British literature cultivated a universal address and substitute instead a sense of how legal regimes specific to EIC Asia shaped what was written and printed and how it was distributed or how it was suppressed.

Making a Colonial Public Sphere

Can corporations create publics? If so, what is their relation to those conceptual features typically seen to organize modern social life, the public sphere and civil society? Here I reflect on those questions by extending my previous description of the EIC's essential role in the formation of Anglo-India's art world.[163] Owing to the influence of Jürgen Habermas and Benedict Anderson, scholars tend to associate public spheres with nation-states, especially with the example of the early American republic, in which to participate in public was to craft a national identity. Likewise, transnational public spheres, often aligned with the anti-imperial resistance described by Elleke Boehmer and Isabel Hofmeyr, seem nonetheless to result in national self-determination (few twentieth-century Indians hoped to replace British occupation with a return to the Mughal Empire).[164]

It is not clear where a state-charted joint-stock company like the EIC might fit within these models of Enlightenment or anticolonial public spheres; the EIC is not exactly a nation-state, does not belong within the private realm, and cannot be considered a construction of civil society, though it has stems in all those domains. It seems more akin to a modern media conglomerate "intricately intertwined with the state and the economy" than an exponent of rational debate and political critique that Habermas found in the eighteenth-century public sphere.[165] As a cultural company-state, the EIC seems to exist in an uneasy relationship to these categories: directly sustaining elements that produce a public sphere in anglophone India yet constraining its participants and organs through its power to administer courts, censor printing, seize property, and deport individuals from Asia.

Typically, scholars perceive the corporation as co-opting art worlds and the public sphere to create profits and restrain criticism of its practices.[166] Yet, as John O'Brien noted, the corporation is not just a legal entity with a history; it is also an "imaginative construct" whose central premise is to extend the principles of the human body into the sphere of social life.[167] In this sense we might use EIC activities to understand better the consequences of the corporation's intimate role in the formation of the public sphere. Central to this program would be the assessment of how far the Anglo-Indian public sphere diverges from the Habermasian model and in what ways Anglo-Indian publics contributed to the "dynamism" of imperial British identities and cultures that, as James Livesey notes, are usually associated with the Atlantic world of colonial America and the early American republic, not with imperial British Asia.[168]

The concept of a "colonial public sphere" generally evokes two possibilities in South Asia. The first is the isolated social world of expatriate Europeans whose actions reproduced European models of sociability, and subordinated Asian ones, to assure racial separation and white superiority.[169] Seema Alavi calls these organizations "imperial assemblages" productive of what Mrinalini Sinha describes as an "imperial social formation" whose ideas were sustained, for instance, through social clubs that made the colonial public sphere the "quintessentially imperial institution."[170] Such thinking about publics and publicity has led Partha Chatterjee and Sudipta Kaviraj to describe how South Asians had to adapt Western concepts of civil society to their own history and ideals.[171]

The second model evokes resistance to the exclusivity and orientalist racism of imperial social formations through political organizations of indigenous Indians. These publics drew inspiration from early modern Mughal sociabilities, such as the literary salons (*musha'irahs*) of Delhi and Lucknow and poetry competitions in Persian and Urdu, or they "grafted" and "transmuted" Western European notions of the public to India.[172] This colonial public sphere is thought to have emerged in the early nineteenth century in "attenuated" forms before spreading through an "imperial network of steamer routes, telegraph lines, and railways" to form an "ocean-wide colonial public sphere."[173]

Rather than perceive the colonial public sphere as one or the other, I suggest that we examine it as an outgrowth of the trade and politics that motivated EIC contributions to artistic creation in the first place. The anglophone colonial public sphere in Asia is like the public described by Michael Warner as a "practical fiction" of organized strangers, "self-creating and self-organized" and "essentially imaginary," which "exists by virtue of being addressed."[174] It was explicitly political in ways accounted for best by respondents to Habermas, such as scholars of the gendered and minoritized American nineteenth century, who have shown how private matters of the intimate sphere responded to and reverberated within the outward orientations of the public sphere.[175] Distinctions between private civil society and the public sphere of debate have eroded in the decades since *Structural Transformation* was disseminated widely in other languages. My examples from late eighteenth-century Anglo-India and early nineteenth-century British Asia reveal a literary public in the process of its creation whose codes of civility and sociability were interpenetrated with the workings of the public sphere. Newspaper proprietors appealed to notions of a "republic of letters," arguing that the proliferation of printing would preserve those "hidden Treasures of Indian Learning" that otherwise might "continue [to be] buried in the oblivion of past Ages"; without this printing, they reasoned, these "curious and interesting acquisitions to the republic of Letters must be entirely forfeited."[176] But in much the same way that the republic of letters borrows elements of the state to describe the operation of a literary public sphere, the colonial public sphere appealed to the example of the cultural company-state to explain how it interacted with structures typically categorized as civil society.[177]

The history that I have traced here is important for understanding this intermixture. India's anglophone publics existed alongside energetic indigenous ones, and the combination of native sovereignties with state-like entities, such as the EIC, alters the sense that cultural creation and political critique might be easily separated from the authority of the state. Before the nineteenth-century bifurcation of colonial publics into either Eurocentric exclusivity or oppositional indigeneity, opportunities for civil society existed in relationship to the British nation-state and the EIC. In much the same way that categories of colonizer and colonized are not "fixed or self-evident," neither are the social forms and organizations they create;[178] rather, these social forms are always being redefined and rearticulated in response to the cultural company-state. Asia serves as a site of public-making distinct from those models devised from the British public sphere. Anglo-India was an arena for the construction of social identities, not just the dissemination of public opinion already accepted in Europe.[179]

Therefore, the EIC was an ambivalent patron of civil society's ideals, not its "enemy," as Livesey suggests it was.[180] It sought to construct publics and sociabilities that bolstered its sovereignty but did not preclude civic discourse or artistic critique. The EIC understood that founding publics was a means of expressing its power and for that reason actively supported the publicity capacities of its state-assisted art worlds. At the same time, it shaped that publicity to create a civil society less confrontational toward its goals and stratagems, a task it only partially accomplished.

Anglo-India offers an alternative model of the public sphere, in which the assumed separation between the realm of public authority and the ability of the private realm to project publics—either as the literary or the political public sphere or the more intimate civil society of "town"—is more tenuous and transparent than in the idealized, oppositional model that originates with Habermas. The company-state is a condition in which civil society is not composed of communities able to organize themselves independent of the state.[181] Rather than the public sphere as an intermediary between public and private realms, Anglo-Indian colonial publics are a projection of state authority—that is, the authority of the cultural company-state. And because the anglophone public sphere was in an embryonic condition in late eighteenth-century Asia, it did not yet possess the same degree of exclusivity that would surround nineteenth-century Eurocentric clubs that Sinha has described as an adhesive for imperial identity.

The eighteenth-century Anglo-Indian model of a colonial public sphere conflated without collapsing the difference between the public sphere and state authority. Such conflation answers the question about why states might allow civil society and the public sphere of debate to survive even when they were directed at restraining state power (what Livesey terms the "Gellner problem").[182] In this history the "contradictory institutionalization" of the public sphere, in which the public's rational-critical function eventually becomes manipulated into serving state power, is not quite so contradictory as it first appears. Reviewing the origins of the public sphere beyond Europe and America allows us to see the importance of the corporation for the operation of what Howard Becker calls art worlds, Michael Warner calls publics, and Bruno Latour calls the associations that make up the social.[183] These publics were an "improvisation" in much the same way that Livesey characterizes civil society as improvisational rather than regimented and dictated; similarly, empire amplified and altered the function of publics like those described by Habermas.[184] Although civil society is often idealized as a process unencumbered from (and anathema to) market manipulation and governmental control, such a definition excludes important historical experiments that occurred in the domains of colonial empires, such as the eighteenth-century Indian public sphere supported by the cultural company-state. Understanding this history revives, rather than deletes, the possibilities for a global civil society predicated on the connections across space that Dimock observes in the impossible temporalities of Thoreau reading the Gita by the gentle shores of Walden Pond.

CHAPTER TWO

Newspaper Poetry and Reading Publics in Eighteenth-Century India

The pre-1800 Anglo-Indian literary canon, so far as there is one, is split. Its better-known contributors are the gentlemen poets involved in colonial administration whose artistic and scholarly projects coincided with the intellectual apparatus of orientalism that they helped to create. It is anchored by the jurist, language polymath, and poet Sir William Jones. Jones has been anglophone Asia's indispensable figure. In the 1780s, after he arrived in India, he was hailed by his compatriots as the originator of English verse on the subcontinent. Elegies celebrated him as a Brahmin bard, more eastern than India's actual indigenes. Theodore Douglas Dunn's influential 1921 *Poets of the John Company*—another term for the East India Company—begins with Jones. Robert Sencourt's *India in English Literature* (1923) asserts that Jones did for literature what Robert Clive and Warren Hastings did in "life and affairs": consolidate India for the English.[1] Jones's visibility increased again when Edward Said depicted him as the archetypal orientalist who sought to turn India "into a province of European learning."[2]

The scholarly shifts that occurred after Said's *Orientalism* were numerous, but among the most important was a renewed effort to recover native voices and to examine how indigenes responded to and resisted European colonization. Recovery of native voices led to a more complete picture of South Asian literary culture, one that renewed interest in the contours of anglophone Asia. New anthologies still featured gentlemanly poets like Jones but placed them in broader language and cultural traditions that made up what Mary Ellis Gibson calls Calcutta's "complex linguistic contact zone."[3]

This chapter seeks to add to that scholarly momentum by focusing on poetry published in the late eighteenth-century Anglo-Indian newspapers that spanned the entire region beginning in 1780. Newspapers were an essential part of a nascent colonial public sphere and were particularly important for pre-1800 verse. Newspapers became a clearinghouse for artistic ventures and the mechanism by which a distinct Anglo-Indian culture was made and publicized.[4] The newspaper, already a robust European institution by the late eighteenth century, was adapted to the promulgation of Anglo-Indian norms.[5] Anglo-Indian newspapers, poignantly aware of their debts to Britain, perceived verse as establishing unique literary institutions. These institutions often incubated in Calcutta but quickly migrated to other parts of Anglo-India, spawning an intraregional anglophone literary network.

Newspapers were the most immediate way—in time and space—for authors and their local readers to access each other, and each of these groups could look to newspapers for ways to read about their habits and norms. Printed matter directly addressed this audience and used its social codes to bolster its sense of distinctiveness. Calcutta's reading public, as Michael Franklin notes, "was anxious not only to read about itself, but to (re)write itself, and print was revealing colonial society to itself."[6] The multilingualism, visual variety, and pervasive use of pseudonymity in anglophone newspaper poetry suggest a way to merge the image of writing as a social practice with the history of anglophone literature and thereby shift scholars' attention toward the coexistence of these vibrant quotidian forms with better-known gentlemanly orientalist authors such as Jones.

Poetry and the Business of Newspapers

Anglo-Indian newspapers first appeared in 1780 and proliferated rapidly in the ensuing two decades, often supporting other publishing ventures.[7] Unlike in the American context, Anglo-Indian newspapers appeared soon after the establishment of printing presses in South Asia. No city in India could match London's density of newsprint, but Calcutta had numerous weeklies, including *Hicky's Bengal Gazette* (est. 1780), the *India Gazette, or Calcutta Advertiser* (est. 1780), the *Calcutta Gazette* (est. 1784), the *Calcutta Chronicle* (est. 1786), the *Asiatic Mirror* (est. ca. 1788), *The World* (a.k.a. *The Indian World*) (est. ca. 1791), that equaled or exceeded the number in most provincial towns in England.[8] Calcutta has captured the vast majority of scholarly attention, as Dennis Rhodes notes, because cities like Madras were "never as prolific in [their eighteenth-century] printing program[s] as was Calcutta," but Bombay and Madras had weeklies too, including the *Madras Courier* (est. 1785), *Bombay Gazette* (est. 1791), the *Bombay Courier* (est. 1793), *The Hircarrah* (est. Madras, 1793), and the *Madras Government Gazette* (est. 1795).[9] Between 1800 and 1820 there were anglophone newspapers in Penang (the *Prince of Wales Island Gazette* [1806–30]), Ceylon (the *Ceylon Government Gazette*, thought to have begun in 1802 on the island now called Sri Lanka), Java (the *Java Government Gazette* [1812–16]), and Sydney (the *Sydney Gazette and New South Wales Advertiser* [1803–42]).[10]

India's newspapers borrowed their forms from Britain, reported on European news, and mirrored economically what was occurring in provincial England between 1770 and 1800. During that period in England circulation increased and the number of newspapers doubled, which in turn served as a "financial prop" for most provincial printer-booksellers.[11] In Asia, as in Britain, newspapers anchored other commercial ventures, such as the involvement of *India Gazette* proprietor Bernard Messink with the Calcutta theater, or the *Prince of Wales Island Gazette* printer, A. B. Bone, selling local merchandise.

Although British and European newspapers provided obvious models, scholars have overemphasized their importance for Anglo-India's literary culture and reading publics. Jeremy Black argues for a worldwide British "colonial press" that produced useful information and "underlined the urban character" of the British colonial presence (something lacking, he argues, among French colonies).[12] James Belich names these connections "Angloworld," a "politically divided but culturally and economically united intercontinental system."[13] Graham Shaw suggests that newspapers from Britain were "eagerly awaited" in India because information "available locally . . . was extremely limited."[14]

The opposite was the case. Anglo-Indian newspapers depended on local news: births, marriages, deaths, eminent people's departures, ships' arrivals, debtors' auctions, reports of criminality (especially homicides), transcripts of jury trials, theater reviews, accounts of parties and masquerades, notes for dancing instruction, riding classes, items for sale, runaway slaves, military news, and all manner of poetry, essays, and correspondence with readers. One advertisement from 1784 offered prints of Governor-General Warren Hastings, and another from 1789 announced the services of Samuel Gold, a "Horse and Dog Painter."[15] Consistently printed were advertisements for pedestrian commodities, like Madeira wine (ever popular), or more specialized ones, like the sale of Company elephants in Benares.[16] They abutted descriptions of South Asian military victories or defeats with that most local of news items, pleas for lost animals.[17] Newspapers were visually complex, multilingual, and formally variegated vessels for the anglophone public sphere and, like the culture that surrounded it, were not yet as regimented into the fine segmentations and hierarchies that would typify the late nineteenth-century Raj. The sense that there was a "dearth of local news" so that "British newspapers were shamelessly cannibalised for column inches" by proprietors in Calcutta, Madras, and Bombay, is wrong, as is the notion that newspapers were national institutions that primarily built national identities.[18]

Among the most consistent and robust local contributions to newspapers was poetry. Opportunities for versifying were plentiful because every newspaper dedicated regular space to poetry: the *Calcutta Chronicle* carried a "Poet's Corner"; the *Asiatic Mirror* published the "Parnassian Corner"; Madras's *The Hircarrah* called its section "The Parnassian Spring"; the *Calcutta Gazette* named its section simply "Poetry." The *Madras Courier* also ran a regular poetry column, called variously "Poetry" or "Poet's Corner," that averaged one poem per issue before 1800 and often more.[19] These verses filled interior pages and were easier and less expensive to print than pamphlets or books. They could be composed quickly and were immediately responsive to political and social events, whether news reports of military conflicts or local masquerades and balls, and they were shared among other regional audiences through reprinting.

Newspapers in eighteenth-century South and southeastern Asia operated through republication and redistribution of material, particularly from other newspapers. This was a common practice in eighteenth-century England but also in nineteenth-century America, where reprinting was a strategic way to form a post-Revolution literary culture, and recirculation was an instrument for national unity: a way for small, local publishers to access readers outside their more immediate boundaries.[20] Anglo-Indian newspapers likewise drew on regional and global publishing phenomena, reproducing reports from other newspapers on issues, primarily from the Anglocentric world. But they did not make local writing into a national literature in the way Ellen Gruber Garvey contends newspaper republication did in the United States.[21] Instead, republication and the sharing of newspapers created a regional colonial network among towns, cities, and factory outposts more than it hinted at what would become Britain's nineteenth-century "imperial press system."[22]

Republication was a strategy that extended to newspaper verse. But authors of poetry were rarely identified, whether in republications or submissions of original verse; instead, newspaper poetry functioned primarily through anonymity and pseudonymity. Many authors adopted names such as "Nauticus," "Omicron," or "Candidus" and used them consistently.[23] Practices of anonymity and pseudonymity affect what gets preserved in cultural memory, as Mark Vareschi has observed, and in Anglo-India pseudonymity helped authors establish lasting relationships with editors and readers.[24] These newspapers possess all of the fine distinctions among pseudonyms, attributions, and honorifics that Katherine Bode believes require a more expansive sense of what it means to be an author—a "spectrum of authorship," as she calls it, that necessitates a new literary history that groups texts by region or by topic rather than by individual author.[25]

Such a reorganization is essential to understanding Anglo-Indian newspapers because editors were responsive to local and regional audiences and portrayed themselves as proxies for the larger Asian public: a reconciling, critical functionary alert to a new body of readers that was in the process of cohering. Correspondence between readers and editors was not only of practical importance to newspaper publication but was a structuring feature of the newspaper itself, often highlighted in specific sections that made apparent the papers' intake of submissions from readers. Over time, editors took on a curatorial attitude, as when the editors of the *Calcutta Gazette* apologized to one contributor for rejecting his poems because "the circumstances upon which they are founded being now out of date, we think it best not to publish them," demonstrating how newspaper verses were dispatches from the present slanted toward immediate relevance rather than posterity.[26] The *Madras Courier* developed a regular column titled "Correspondents," which announced information to readers, such as what poems had been received and when they would be appearing in future issues. Sometimes this column reads more like criticism, such as when the paper publicly rejected a poem called "The Party of Pleasure" because "it did not promise to be ANY thing, rather than what it calls itself" and would have been better titled "a PARTY WITHOUT PLEASURE," the capitals seeming to emphasize the editors' dismissal of the poem.[27]

These gleeful rejections occasionally offered insight into how the newspaper functioned. In another case the *Madras Courier* announced in print it was rejecting a poem called "Christmas Day," pronouncing the poem a failure that caused "much social pleasantry" among the staff, suggesting that they shared reading duties and aesthetic perspectives (as well as jokes at authors' expense).[28] Sometimes these aesthetic judgments arose from explicitly societal and racial coordinates, as when in a separate instance those same editors implied obscurely that the contributor "Sable" is "of much too dark complexion for our paper," though it's not clear whether this comment is directed at the poet's ethnicity, the "dark" sentiments of the unnamed poem, or both.[29] Newspapers encouraged competition among readers, such as when a pseudonymous "Sahib" complained to the editors of the *Calcutta Gazette* about a Persian translation of the "Bostan of Sadee" (the *Bustan* of Sa'di, a text from thirteenth-century Persia) published in the *Calcutta Chronicle*, which he wanted to counter with his own published translation in the competing newspaper.[30] While the structure of Anglo-Indian newspapers was similar to that of other anglophone domains, its poetry demonstrates how local issues became an important driving force for the economics of its nascent literary culture.

Multilingual Reading Publics

One significant local force was the close interaction between Anglo-Indian poetry and the multilingualism of South Asia. While much of the writing in late eighteenth- and early nineteenth-century South Asian newspapers was generic and conventional, a substantial amount drew from its immediate environment. Anglo-Indian newspaper verse is a rich source of information about the contours and mechanics of Anglo-Indian readers and their interactions with indigenous cultural and artistic practices. Expenditures on physical infrastructure—printing presses, language guides, teaching colleges, and libraries—made an Anglo-Indian cultural sphere possible, and language training contributed directly to its literary productions. Classical Persian poets such as Hafez, Ferdowsi, and Sa'di formed a central part of the orientalist canon from the early eighteenth century, but knowledge of these authors expanded with the publication of Jones's *A Grammar of the Persian Language* (1771), which the EIC recommended to employees.[31] In 1804 the New Calcutta Academy advertised instruction not only in French and Latin but also in Persian and noted that it employed "two Persian moonshees [*munshis*]" in addition to a "fencing and dancing master and a music master."[32] This kind of knowledge allowed an anonymous "learner of Persian," who was identified simply as "A.," to submit his "lesson of yesterday evening," a translation from Sa'di's thirteenth-century *Bustan*, a collection of didactic tales, for publication in the *Calcutta Gazette*, expecting it would meet with approval because it was the "produce of Asia" and acquainted readers with its "diversity of books and authors."[33] Another poet, "Senex," argued that newspaper translations were essential for spreading Persian wisdom lest it be reserved for "the instruction of a few only" who already knew the language.[34] In an editorial to the *India Gazette* Senex praises its poetry and notes that there are many "in the circle of my acquaintance, who employ their leisure hours in Literary pursuits."[35]

These examples imply that the cultural company-state actively fostered Anglo-India's translocal and multicultural affiliations. As Anna Winterbottom has argued, the study of Asian languages, so crucial to the commerce of the Company from its inception, was the origin of European orientalism.[36] Language study was akin to the practical orientalism (Bayly) or Enlightenment orientalism (Aravamudan) that preceded Said's impositional orientalism. These early forms of orientalism practiced by Europeans drew substantially from the indigenous traditions of publicity and civility that C. A. Bayly terms the *ecumene*.[37] Before South Asia became a society of mass literacy and print, handwritten media and oral performances coincided with "intimate social relations," rather than being separated from them.[38] This protoindigenous public sphere was avowedly multilingual and converged with the commercial and cultural motives of the EIC. For many members of the gentry bureaucracy of Mughal India, for example, speaking and writing Persian with a "fine hand" and in an "elegant epistolary style" were important markers of social and political rank.[39] By the 1790s, Persian publications like *The Works of Dewan Hafez* (1791), edited by the Mughal poet Mirza Abu Taleb Khan, coexisted with visually rich newspapers that announced important events, such as the resignation of Warren Hastings and the ascension of John Macpherson with a 1785 proclamation in English, Persian, and Bengali (fig. 3).[40]

Bengali may have been considered lowly and clerical, unlike Persian or Sanskrit, but it appeared frequently alongside those languages in newspapers, presaging its role as what Anindita Ghosh calls the "vital instrument" of nineteenth-century Indian national identity.[41] And though Sanskrit and Persian were the focus of eighteenth-century orientalists, the more local language, Tamil, was India's first printed language.[42] Sixteenth- and seventeenth-century Portuguese experiments in Goa and Lisbon were later taken up by Danish and British missionaries in southern India so that by 1800 there were already 266 Tamil titles in print, among them a Tamil-English edition of John Bunyan's *The Pilgrim's Progress* (1793), the first novel printed in South Asia (fig. 4).[43] Published outside of Madras in Vepery by the Society for Promoting Christian Knowledge, it culminated from earlier editions of the Bible (in 1715, 1766, and 1772) and dozens of interlingual grammars and dictionaries.[44] That Bunyan's novel reflected an "intellectual of the world" might explain its appeal to global audiences and its effectiveness as a method of conversion, but its

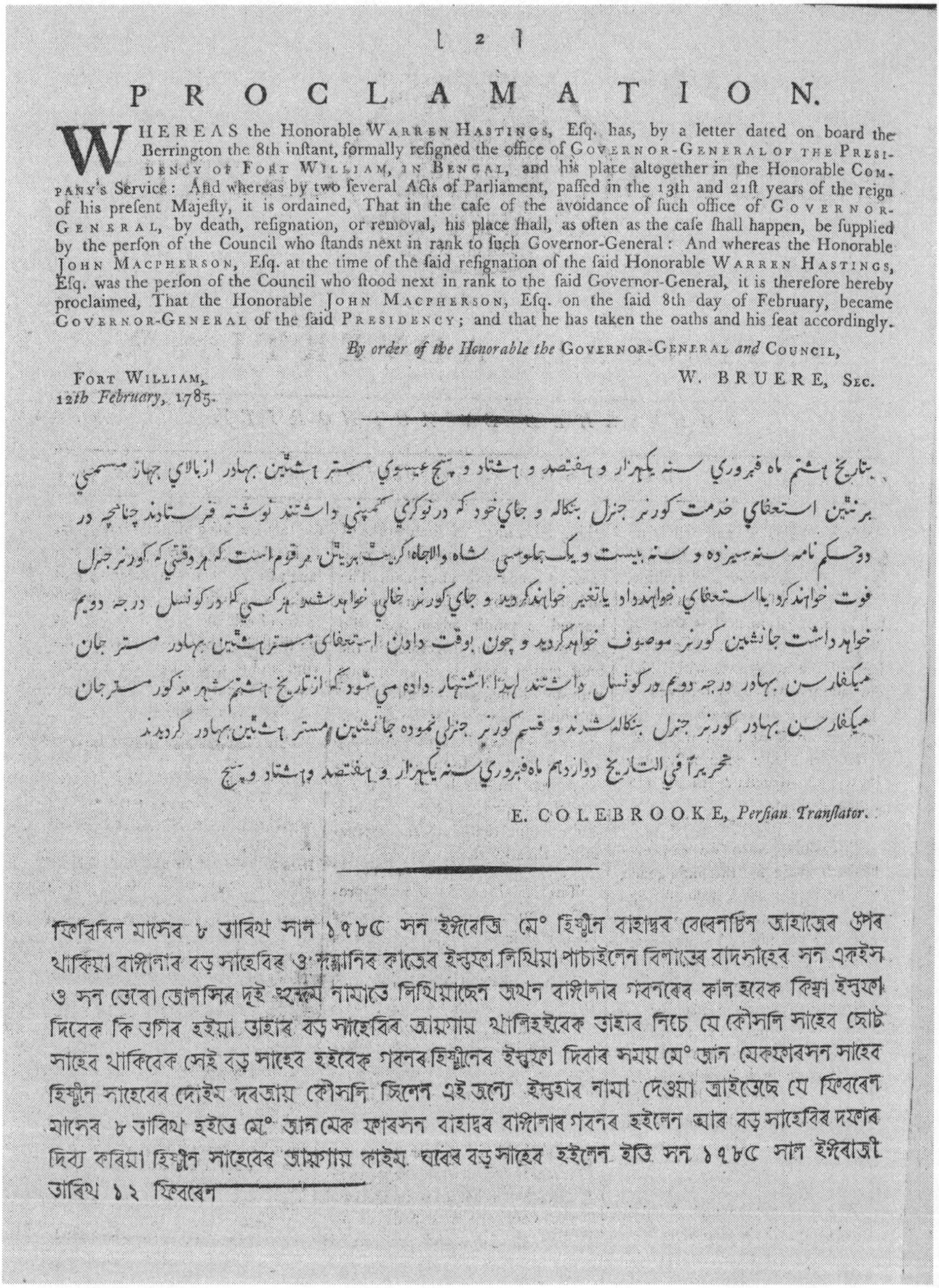
[2]

PROCLAMATION.

WHEREAS the Honorable WARREN HASTINGS, Esq. has, by a letter dated on board the Berrington the 8th instant, formally resigned the office of GOVERNOR-GENERAL OF THE PRESIDENCY OF FORT WILLIAM, IN BENGAL, and his place altogether in the Honorable COMPANY's Service: And whereas by two several Acts of Parliament, passed in the 13th and 21st years of the reign of his present Majesty, it is ordained, That in the case of the avoidance of such office of GOVERNOR-GENERAL, by death, resignation, or removal, his place shall, as often as the case shall happen, be supplied by the person of the Council who stands next in rank to such Governor-General: And whereas the Honorable JOHN MACPHERSON, Esq. at the time of the said resignation of the said Honorable WARREN HASTINGS, Esq. was the person of the Council who stood next in rank to the said Governor-General, it is therefore hereby proclaimed, That the Honorable JOHN MACPHERSON, Esq. on the said 8th day of February, became GOVERNOR-GENERAL of the said PRESIDENCY; and that he has taken the oaths and his seat accordingly.

By order of the Honorable the GOVERNOR-GENERAL *and* COUNCIL,

FORT WILLIAM,
12th February, 1785.

W. BRUERE, SEC.

بتاریخ هشتم ماه فبروري سنه یکهزار و هفتصد و هشتاد و پنج عیسوي مستر هشتین بهادر ازبالاي جهاز مسمي برنتین استعفاي خدمت گورنر جنرل بنگاله و جاي خود که درنوکري کمپني داشتند نوشته فرستادند چنانچه در دوحکم نامه سنه سیزده و سنه بیست و یک جلوسي شاه والاجاه گریت بریتن مرقوم است که هروقتي که گورنر جنرل فوت خواهند کرد یا استعفاي خواهند داد یاتغیر خواهند گردید و جاي گورنر خالي خواهد شد هرکسي که درکونسل درجه دویم خواهد داشت جانشین گورنر موصوف خواهد گردید و چون بوقت دادن استعفای مستر هشتین بهادر مستر جان میکفارسن بهادر درجه دویم درکونسل داشتند لهذا اشتهار داده مي شود که ازتاریخ هشتم شهر مذکور مستر جان میکفارسن بهادر گورنر جنرل بنگاله شدند و قسم گورنر جنرلي نموده جانشین مستر هشتین بهادر گردیدند

تحریرا في التاریخ دوازدهم ماه فبروري سنه یکهزار و هفتصد و هشتاد و پنج

E. COLEBROOKE, *Persian Translator.*

ফিবিরিল মাসের ৮ তারিখ সাল ১৭৮৫ সন ইঙ্গরেজি মে° হিষ্টীন বাহাদুর বেরেনটিন জাহাজের উপর থাকিয়া বাঙ্গালার বড় সাহেবির ও কোম্পানির কাজের ইস্তুফা লিখিয়া পাঠাইলেন বিলাতের বাদসাহের সন একইস ও সন তেরো জোলসির দুই হুকুম নামাতে লিখিয়াছেন যখন বাঙ্গালার গবনরের কাল হবেক কিম্বা ইস্তুফা দিবেক কি তগির হইয়া তাহার বড় সাহেবির জায়গায় খালি হইবেক তাহার নিচে যে কৌনসলি সাহেব মোট সাহেব থাকিবেক সেই বড় সাহেব হইবেক গবনর হিষ্টীনের ইস্তুফা দিবার সময় মে° জান মেকফারসন সাহেব হিষ্টীন সাহেবের দোইম দরজায় কৌনসলি ছিলেন এই জন্যে ইস্তেহার নামা দেওয়া জাইতেছে যে ফিবরেল মাসের ৮ তারিখ হইতে মে° জান মেক ফারসন বাহাদুর বাঙ্গালার গবনর হইলেন আর বড় সাহেবির দফার দিব্য করিয়া হিষ্টীন সাহেবের জায়গায় কাইম ঘাবের বড় সাহেব হইলেন ইতি সন ১৭৮৫ সাল ইঙ্গরাজী তারিখ ১২ ফিবরেল

Figure 3. A "proclamation" published in the *Calcutta Gazette*, announcing the ascension of John Macpherson to the position of governor-general of Bengal after the resignation of Warren Hastings, printed in English, Persian, and Bengali. This page indicates the overlapping, but not entirely shared, language fluencies and reading publics of eighteenth-century India. Courtesy of the Beinecke Rare Books and Manuscript Library, Yale University.

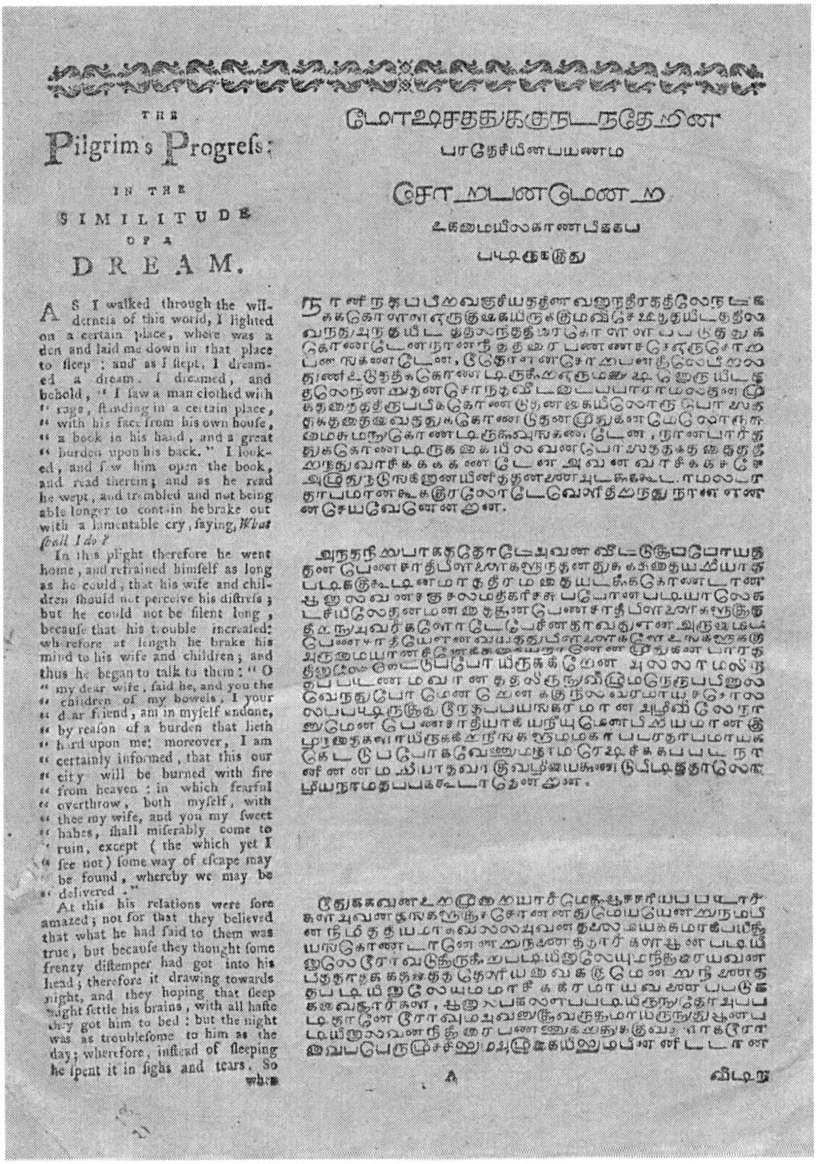

THE

Pilgrim's Progreſs:

IN THE

SIMILITUDE

OF A

DREAM.

AS I walked through the wilderneſs of this world, I lighted on a certain place, where was a den and laid me down in that place to ſleep; and as I ſlept, I dreamed a dream. I dreamed, and behold, "I ſaw a man clothed with "rags, ſtanding in a certain place, "with his face from his own houſe, "a book in his hand, and a great "burden upon his back." I looked, and ſaw him open the book, and read therein; and as he read he wept, and trembled and not being able longer to contain he brake out with a lamentable cry, ſaying, *What ſhall I do?*

In this plight therefore he went home, and refrained himſelf as long as he could, that his wife and children ſhould not perceive his diſtreſs; but he could not be ſilent long, becauſe that his trouble increaſed: wherefore at length he brake his mind to his wife and children; and thus he began to talk to them: "O "my dear wife, ſaid he, and you the "children of my bowels, I your "dear friend, am in myſelf undone, "by reaſon of a burden that lieth "hard upon me: moreover, I am "certainly informed, that this our "city will be burned with fire "from heaven; in which fearful "overthrow, both myſelf, with "thee my wife, and you my ſweet "babes, ſhall miſerably come to "ruin, except (the which yet I "ſee not) ſome way of eſcape may "be found, whereby we may be "delivered."

At this his relations were ſore amazed; not for that they believed that what he had ſaid to them was true, but becauſe they thought ſome frenzy diſtemper had got into his head; therefore it drawing towards night, and they hoping that ſleep might ſettle his brains, with all haſte they got him to bed: but the night was as troubleſome to him as the day; wherefore, inſtead of ſleeping he ſpent it in ſighs and tears. So

when

A

Figure 4. Initial page of the Tamil-English edition of John Bunyan's *Pilgrim's Progress* (1793), the first novel published in South Asia. It separates languages into columns, suggesting the desire for comparison. © British Library Board (Asia, Pacific & Africa 14170.cc.1).

Tamil translation also signals how missionaries sought to establish trust with South Asia's different ethnicities and religions by routing Anglo-India's multilingual reading publics through English literary works.[45]

The strategic multilingualism of Anglo-India spilled into its newspaper verses. The twin columns of Tamil and English in the Vepery *Pilgrim's Progress* were a familiar layout for newspaper poetry, which suggests cultural relationships driven by comparison and appropriation. Consider the untitled Persian ode of Candidus, translated from a *ghazal* by the thirteenth-century Sufi poet Amir Khusrau, an Indian Muslim of Turkish descent and a courtier of the Delhi Sultanate who, according to Aziz Ahmad, sought to harmonize Islam with India.[46] Drawing from this tradition, Candidus's Persian ode sets Persian alongside English in a 1790 issue of the *Madras Courier* (figs. 5, 6).[47] Ghazal is a genre of love lyric that originated in seventh-century Arabic before migrating into Persian as it moved through central Asia to India.[48] Typically, a speaker addresses a loved figure, entreating that person for affection. The genre involved song-making, ambiguous genders, and complex quasi-religious philosophizing and mysticism, and Khusrau was its most important popularizer in India.[49] Persian's elegant cursive was, like Tamil or Bengali, difficult to make into type, and Candidus's Persian ode indicates how quickly technologies for multilingual printing had advanced since Halhed's 1778 *Grammar*. The poem's geometry proposes multiple ways of reading: one might begin, for instance, along its slim central spine of white space and move toward the margins, comparing Persian and English (since the languages read in opposite directions), or scan back and forth between lines to assess the translation's qualities.

Little is known about the pseudonymous Candidus, who was identified in another poem printed by the *Madras Courier* as an officer with the "Grand Army in India" during the third Anglo-Mysore War.[50] An author using the same pseudonym in 1784 published multiple poems in the *Calcutta Gazette*, including an imitation of Horace ("An Ode on the Introduction of the Cold Weather"), an English ode rewritten from Anacreon ("An Ode"), and a translation of a ghazal by Khusrau ("A Song of Amir Khoseru"). The repetition of this pseudonym in Calcutta and Madras cannot confirm it is the same person, but it hints at a mobile author or someone who could publish across British India.[51]

A bit more can be ascertained about who might have read the Persian ode, because the content and visual presentation of Candidus's translation reveals what propelled Anglo-India's reading publics. The poem's layout suggests the

POETRY.

TO THE EDITORS OF THE MADRAS COURIER.

PERMIT me, Gentlemen, to send you a very pretty Persian Ode by *Ameer Khosru*, the favourite Poet of Hindostan, with a literal translation into English Verse of the same number, nearly as the Original.

TRANSLATION.

I told my friend, in artless lay,
I could not sleep from night till day,
And asked his skilful aid:
He felt my pulse, and smiling said,
'Tis love alone has turned your head,
Pray who's the lovely maid?

Go tell her first, how much you love!
How much you grieve! if she approve,
Her lips will life impart.
I went and told my melting tale,
How love for her had made me pale,
And pressed upon my heart!

And who are you? the scornful said,
For me a hundred hearts have bled;
Inform me of your name!
Your hapless lover, I replied,
For whom this heart so oft has sighed;
——She knew I was the same;

And bid my Khusroo, never fear,
This honey'd lip thy heart shall cheer,
And own thy grateful flame.

CANDIDUS.

A SIMILE.

CELIA, arriv'd at forty-nine,
To spread her fame still tries,
And tho' she feels her charms decline,
She feels her passion rise!

Thus Oaks, three hundred winters told,
Just like herself expire,
Turn touchwood, wither'd, grey and old,
And at each spark take fire.

FORT St. GEORGE 20th. July 90.

NOTICE is hereby given that an application was this day made before the Kings Ordinary in the Honorable the Mayor's Court for Letters of Administration to the Estate and Effects of Edward Sutter deceased to be granted to Mr. Thomas Parry as a mortgage Bond creditor to the said deceased.

J. HAMILTON, Proctor.

TO be SOLD.

A LARGE Commodious house with the appurtenances, Situated in St. Thomas Street, and adjoining to that of Geo. Moubray Esquire.

ADVERTISEMENT.

MADRAS PRICE CURRENT.

CHRISTIAN ADMONITION. A TALE.

FORT St. GEORGE, Printed by CHARLES FORD, at the *Register Office*,

THE Editors request the Subscribers to the Courier will give them notice when they are about to change their residence that no mistake be made in the Direction.

Figure 5. A page from the *Madras Courier*, July 28, 1790, showing Candidus's Persian ode, with Persian on the left and English on the right. © British Library Board (Asia, Pacific & Africa SM 126).

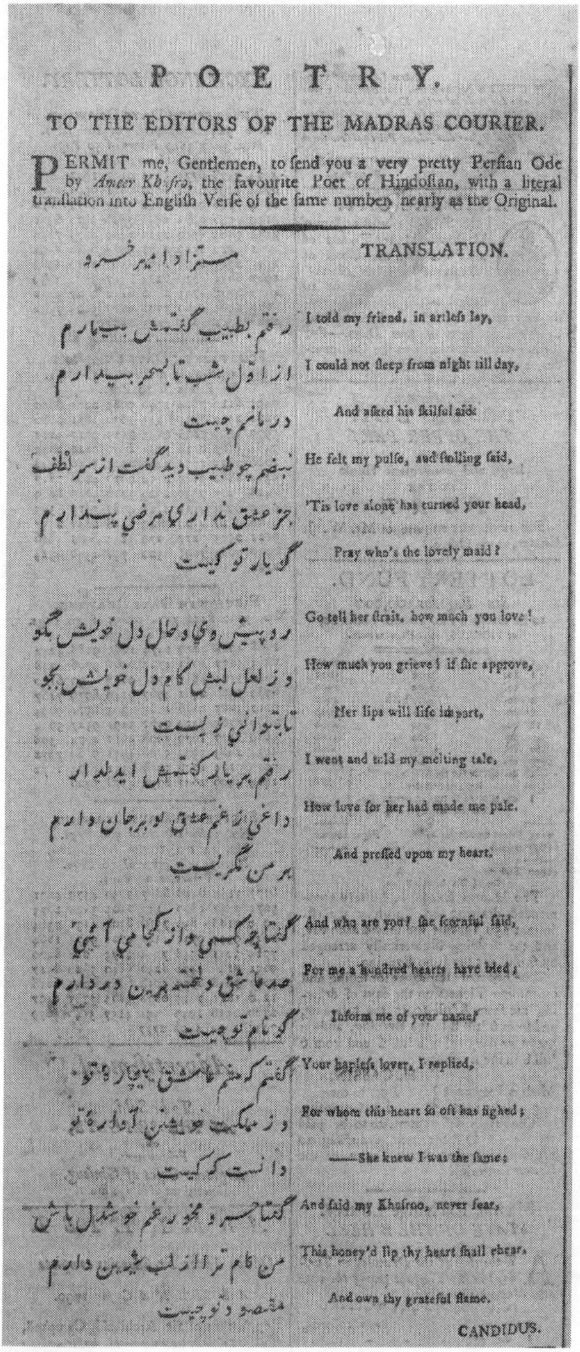

POETRY.

TO THE EDITORS OF THE MADRAS COURIER.

PERMIT me, Gentlemen, to ſend you a very pretty Perſian Ode by *Ameer Khuſro*, the favourite Poet of Hindoſtan, with a literal tranſlation into Engliſh Verſe of the ſame number, nearly as the Original.

مستزاد امیر خسرو

رفتم بطبیب گفتمش بیمارم
از اول شب تا بسحر بیدارم
درمانم چیست
بنضم چو طبیب دید گفت از سر لطف
جز عشق نداری مرضی پندارم
گو یار تو کیست
رو پیش وی و حال دل خویش بگو
وز لعل لبش کام دل خویش بجو
تا بتوانی زیست
رفتم بر یار گفتمش ای دلدار
داغی ز غم عشق تو برجان دارم
بر من نگریست
گفتا چه کسی و از کجا می آیی
صد عاشق و مستمند چون تو دارم
گو نام تو چیست
گفتم که منم عاشق بیچاره تو
وز مملکت خویشتن آوارهٔ تو
دانست که کیست
گفتا خسرو مخور غم خوشدل باش
من کام ترا از لب شیرین دادم
مقصود تو چیست

TRANSLATION.

I told my friend, in artleſs lay,
I could not ſleep from night till day,
And aſked his ſkilful aid:
He felt my pulſe, and ſmiling ſaid,
'Tis love alone has turned your head,
Pray who's the lovely maid?

Go tell her ſtrait, how much you love!
How much you grieve! if ſhe approve,
Her lips will life impart,
I went and told my melting tale,
How love for her had made me pale,
And preſſed upon my heart.

And who are you? ſhe ſcornful ſaid,
For me a hundred hearts have bled;
Inform me of your name?
Your hapleſs lover, I replied,
For whom this heart ſo oft has ſighed;
——She knew I was the ſame;

And ſaid my Khuſroo, never fear,
This honey'd lip thy heart ſhall chear,
And own thy grateful flame.

CANDIDUS.

Figure 6. Detail of Candidus's Persian ode. © British Library Board (Asia, Pacific & Africa SM 126).

sophistication and variety of the audiences it pursued. Although the English translation dispenses with the repeated end-stopped lines (*radif*) and internal rhymes (*qafia*) of ghazal, it maintains its couplets and mentions Khusrau's name in the last stanza, a technique called *takhallus* in which an author includes a "signature verse" that "identifies the poet" and closes the poem.[52] It also marks a startling transition when the speaker of the ghazal presents himself in the third person, which ultimately reveals the poet as the admirer of the beloved but also asserts the poet's rhetorical skill.[53] Paul Losensky believes this type of turn is the speaker's sign of subservience to the beloved mentioned in the poem, but in the case of Candidus's translation it also has the convenient effect of identifying an author from a preceding literary tradition.[54] As the translation ends, Candidus writes:

> said my Khusroo, never fear,
> This honey'd lip, thy heart shall chear,
> And own thy grateful theme.

Retaining this sign-off, while disregarding other techniques, implies that Candidus sought to transmute the traditional subject matter of ghazal—the affection between lover and beloved—into affiliations between Anglo-Indian versifiers and the Persian lyric. Most of the poem is a speaker's "artless lay" addressed to the person he loves, but it also expresses Candidus's relation to Khusrau and Persian poetry. His "honey'd lip" speaks Khusrau's "grateful theme" as a form of intergenerational inheritance and multilingual posterity. The obvious intermediations of the poem, such as its translations from one language to another printed beside it, stand, as well, for emotional connections that transcend differences in culture, place, and time. But the poem is also an intervention into a competitive multilingual literary sphere in which EIC employees broadcast their skill by associating themselves with artistic predecessors and publishing poetic imitations of them. With his Persian ode Candidus makes clear to other writers like Senex and the "learner of Persian" that he, too, knows the classical canon.

This close relationship between English versifiers and Persian poetry reformulates an appropriation of traditions as a literary affiliation across time. Candidus's translation displays visually, even ostentatiously, the generative potential of Anglo-Indian literature to draw on other cultures and adopt the authority of the Persian lyric's long history in South Asia. Because ghazals had spread to Asia from Arabia, Robert Fraser describes them as a "transregional" genre, while Thomas Bauer and Angelika Neuwirth argue that to understand them requires comparing cultures.[55] Before the ghazal became an exponent of highly localized exotic traditions for authors like Ralph Waldo Emerson, authors like Candidus sought to access a courtly cosmopolitan tradition of the ghazal that, as Fatima Burney shows, had disappeared by the nineteenth century.[56] Cultural comparison is built into the form of Candidus's ode, much as it was in the Tamil-English *Pilgrim's Progress,* but it also binds Persian transregionalism and British economic globalism together by locating and aestheticizing India's politics, which prized knowledge of Persian because it was the language of Mughal Empire officials.

Cultural comparisons such as those formalized in Candidus's Persian ode attempted to obviate the distance between Anglo and India, and the newspaper was the vehicle by which Persian culture, reformulated within South Asia, merged with anglophone poetic institutions. The European attraction to Persian culture proved essential for the construction of bourgeois public spheres outside of Europe, with the paradoxical effect, according to Hamid Dabashi, of creating shared anti-imperialism among its native participants.[57] Siraj Ahmed claims that the cross-continental popularity of the ghazal would become an inspiration for the category of world literature.[58] But Persophilia's earliest Indian manifestations were also anchored within the local worlds of newspaper verse and were not always recognized as an extension of Europe.

Although Persian dominated nonanglophone contributions to Anglo-Indian verse, there were other experiments in South Asian languages. A 1788 *Calcutta Gazette* issue included a "little epigram" that originated in "Birj," referring to Brajbhasha (which was occasionally written as "Birj"), a dialect of Hindi based in north central India.[59] Brajbhasha was a "newly ascendant form of Hindi" during the early modern period, a moment when Hindi was more various and not yet stabilized into an official language of the nation-state of India.[60] It was "North India's most important literary vernacular," according to Allison Busch, and offered a "highly versatile poetic idiom" for members of the Mughal courts that were established at Agra and Fatehpur Sikri. Brajbhasha coexisted with Khari Boli, another dialect of Hindi that became more prominent as the Mughal court moved from Agra to Delhi (then named Shahjahanabad, after the ruler Shah Jahan) in 1648.[61]

The author, Sahib, presents Braj poetry as a "species" unique to this Indian dialect and without any comparative form in Europe ("I do not recollect any of the same class in the poetry of Europe").[62] Sahib's poem is described as a "little epigram" that asks readers to guess what the speaker "bore" on his "heaving breast" at night. The unexpected answer revealed at the poem's conclusion is a "flow'ry wreath" rather than the speaker's beloved. Another poem published that same year, also in Brajbhasha and using that same pseudonym of Sahib, identified the genre as "peheilee" (*paheli*), a riddle-poem translated from the "dialect of Birj" that over two rhyming quatrains asks the reader to identify a tree that "in few short breaths . . . blooms and dies."[63] *Paheli* involves playful erotic verse that elides the reader's expectations at the poem's conclusion. The existence of these riddles, and Brajbhasha poetry generally, in the *Calcutta Gazette* confirms that newspapers were receptive to literary idioms from beyond the prestige languages of English and Persian and outside of the immediately local settings of presidency cities like Calcutta.

As telling is that readers of poetry in Bengal were being exposed to a courtly literary tradition that evinced Mughal power and linguistic multiplicity rather than its decadence and decline.[64] The printed form of the "little epigram" repeats the overlapping audiences evident from Hastings's resignation announcement from 1785. Its multilingual presentation is a direct result of the cultural and political circumstances of South Asia: Brajbhasha poetry came to prominence at the height of Mughal dominance over the subcontinent. It was a companion literary idiom to the more dominant use of Persian in the Mughal Empire and demonstrated the linguistic and cultural pluralism of Mughal courts. The headnotes of these two Brajbhasha translations nod toward the language learning and knowledge acquisition from South Asian sources that produced these riddles.[65] At the same time, the poems recognize the pluralism of the subcontinent and acknowledge alternate polities, such as the Mughal Empire, itself composed of competing cultural forms. This Mughal knowledge intrigued Company administrators as they sought earlier models of the relationship between writing and Indian sovereignty.[66] To publish translations of Brajbhasha poetry is to look into the past of the Mughal Empire for some inspiration about the poetic present. Scholars have focused on how language learning produced orientalist knowledge in regimes of European Enlightenment or how it operationalized itself through practical effects of colonial surveillance and surveying. They have largely ignored its contributions to more localized Anglo-Indian and anglophone Asian literature. It was essential to this process that local materials moved into translocal (Brajbhasha), transregional (Persian), and quasi-global (English) languages. These poems suggest the potential for a profoundly multilingual readership in Bengal but also for an aesthetic ideology that prized moving among many languages rather than the dominance of English.

In eighteenth-century South Asia, newspapers were an essential venue for multilingual reading publics conversant in techniques of appropriation and cultural comparison supported by the cultural company-state. Non-English traditions provided opportunities for authors to innovate within appropriated forms and to appeal to the new literary publics of educated readers aware of the linguistic legacies around them. Newspaper authors like Candidus and Sahib "reach into and manipulate" the "indigenous systems of communication" that C. A. Bayly calls the information order with the goal of constructing a translocal poetics that reflects their circumstances.[67] That their aesthetic forms legitimized appropriation only intensifies the need to acknowledge such overlooked contributors to eighteenth-century orientalism.

Punch Houses, Hookahs, and Cheroots

Newspaper poems function as the most succinct expression of the diverse and multilingual public sphere of Anglo-India. If printed artifacts are a "metonym for an abstract public," as Michael Warner suggests, then the form of those artifacts captures not only the imaginative qualities of that public but also the nonabstract forces that organized it.[68] These poems take seriously the physicality of an immediate readership and its abstraction as a public or an audience. In the last section this link between identifiable readers and abstractions like an Anglo-Indian reading public is evident in the multilingual printed forms of the poems. This section describes a separate class of poetry that reflected on the institutions of eighteenth-century Anglo-Indian literature. Those institutions connect the textual publics of newspaper verse with the physical meeting places of Anglo-India, such as the punch house, the tavern, and the marketplace. I have selected poems that exhibit the presentism of the verse, responding to immediate social and cultural issues of Anglo-India. Their descriptions of public spaces present a dual vision of Anglo-India's multilingualism as a chaotic spoken audience and a more distant yet responsive reader of newspapers.

Owing to Habermas, the public sphere has typically been conflated with the coffeehouse, but in Anglo-India it was also associated with the punch house. The term *punch* is thought to have originated with Sanskrit, and its popularity in Britain is attributed to the commodity trade in spices; in India it was often made from arrack (coconut liquor) and citrus.[69] Punch houses were taverns located on the poor fringes of South Asian society and were locations where different nationalities and economic classes mixed. For this reason they were thought by many to be unseemly and dangerous. Editorials printed in the *Calcutta Chronicle* whined that punch houses were the "receptacles for vagrant Europeans" or for "vagabond Europeans," primarily the sailors "who had run from their ships" upon arriving in India rather than face the dangerous return passage.[70] The *Calcutta Chronicle*'s editors called for punch house denizens to be conscripted into the Company's military as soldiers or impressed as sailors. The *India Gazette* worried that the "Punch-house mob" was "maudlin with cramming and swilling," presumably of rich foods and alcohol.[71]

Some Anglo-Indian poets wrote about this frenzied "cramming and swilling" as a particular form of sociability. Perhaps in response to pious editorials, a pseudonymous "Timothy Twicelaid" composed "The Punch House" for a 1790 issue of the *Madras Courier*.[72] Twicelaid is described as a sailor who provides a meticulous account of his night at a Madras punch house. He depicts the specific figures and voices of this especially communicative public that differs considerably from the reasoned debate and philosophical criticism found in Habermas's coffeehouse.[73] The tavern's unruly characters include an "obsequious Landlord," his servant "Sawmy" (the "master's head Dubash [servant]"), and the Landlady who in the poem threatens to call the "Sepoys" (native militias) as the sailors become too rowdy.[74] These locals assemble together with the "Boatswains, Gunners, Mates, and common Sailors" who "Consort with Stewards, Midshipmen, and Taylors" while "self-dub'd Captains, Bailiffs, Barbers join, / and drown reflection in adulterate Wine." "In noise and novelty" these ordinary figures of Anglo-India "pass the days." The scene is mixed with European and Indian, oceanic and terrestrial inhabitants, all of whom are assaulted by news and entertainment. Information disseminates rapidly—"throughout the Black-town quick the news is handed"—by the tavern's waiter, who "speaks of Tippoo," referring to Tipu Sultan, the British antagonist and leader of Mysore. News competes with other attractions, such as the "Snakemen, Conjour[er]s" and the "dancing Dogs and Monkeys" that "beguile" the crowd while they drink. Against this, the speaker worries, poetry cannot compete:

> What verse can tell the motley things that meet,
> In this inhospitable dull retreat,
> Where fraud, chicane, and every art combine . . . ?

Whether the author of this poem is indeed some sailor on shore leave or, more likely, a local writer experimenting with a transient persona, the crucial element of the poem is the attempt to capture the "motley things" of Madras's punch houses, where "every art combine" to eradicate reason and reflection.

What does it mean to conjure a punch-house in an eighteenth-century Anglo-Indian newspaper? One answer would point to the translocal and global features of the tavern and of punch drinking in particular. Bärbel Czennia describes punch consumption and the punch bowl as indicators of British anxieties about becoming a global power, where the punch bowl offers an "alternate world history cast in porcelain."[75] While punch might reflect the British beginning to embrace a global identity, wrapped in a set of objects and consumption habits, a poem like "The Punch House" also demonstrates the regional aesthetic dimensions extrapolated from punch's association with drunken socializing.[76]

Another answer might focus on the critique of these arts of convivial mixing. In this important way the textual form of the poem follows from the physical realities of the people and publics described there. While Anglo-India's city governments and newspaper editorials opposed the punch house, its "arts" and low characters nonetheless enter the arena of newspaper verse. "The Punch House," like the physical space it describes and the textual public sphere that it defines, is a place where "every art combine[s]," much like the newspaper itself. Snake charmers compete with the news of war, and sepoys fight with Europeans. This aesthetic of chaotic combination made the poem, and the newspaper that printed it, so invigorating for art but so worrisome for those who advocated instead for the domestic space as a civilized and welcome retreat.

Even as "The Punch House" offered one vision of Anglo-India's highly mobile, socially volatile public culture, poems about tobacco smoking offer an adjacent meditation on the unique qualities of its art-making. Tobacco cultivation spread rapidly when the Portuguese imported it to Asia from the Americas in the seventeenth century. Hookahs—long elaborate water pipes that use hot coals to produce smoke and pass it through a tube—were introduced from the Near Eastern world at the same time as tobacco.[77] They became an aristocratic luxury item in the early seventeenth century, their ornate designs and intricate metalwork separating them from more modest clay pipes (called "chilims" or "chillums"). This separation of the hookah from other smoking implements established a new craft industry in early modern India.[78]

Europeans adopted the habit for smoking tobacco in hookahs. For EIC officer Philip Dormer Stanhope hookahs symbolized the luxurious indulgence of Anglo-India. He noted that even writers, the lowest-level servants of the EIC with the smallest salaries, still "contrive to be attended" by a "Hookah-burdaar" (from the Persian *huka-bardar*), a servant "whose duty it is to replenish the Hooka."[79] The attorney and Calcutta *bon vivant* William Hickey believed everyone required a *huka-bardar* on staff, which led to Arthur William Devis's depiction of a gentleman, rumored to be Hickey himself, sitting at ease with his hookah while being waited on by a servant (fig. 7). Another author in the *Bombay Courier* describes his hookah as the item that

Figure 7. Arthur William Devis, *Portrait of a Gentleman and an Indian Servant*, ca. 1785. Oil on canvas. Courtesy of the Yale Center for British Art, Paul Mellon Collection.

adds some "zest" to his "snug bungalow" and that he smokes with his "Cup of Tea and a book."[80] The hookah was much more frequently paired with private spaces than public ones, and, like the palanquin, was often combined with reading. Devis's portrait shows a man at ease in his parlor who looks to be examining a letter while smoking his pipe.

The prevalence of tobacco smoking led, of course, to satires of its distractions. One correspondent to the *India Gazette*, identified only as "Hy. Wildmore," jokes that "smok[ing] my Hookah and sleep[ing] 'till twelve" is part of the "perfection" involved in the "happy art of Time Killing in Bengal."[81] The 1789 poem "The Hookah" describes the smoking instrument as the "solace of life" and the "best of pleasures / That this sultry clime allows," a device that assists the consumption of alcohol ("improv'st young Bacchus' treasures") and the admiration of women ("Venus' self thy aid avows").[82] But most pointed were a series of poems that appeared in the *Madras Courier* during 1791 that use tobacco smoking as an index of Anglo-India's unique literary arts. The first poem, titled "The Hooker" (meaning hookah), was composed by a poet who had named himself "Fumigator" and who lauds hookah smoking as the "delight of my soul!" insisting he's "eager" to "seize the dear snake"—the hookah's hose that delivered the smoke—to forget a lost love. Despite its easily mocked enthusiasm for tobacco, the poem philosophizes that smoking has "deaden'd the smart" of his loss with "mildness replete."[83] Within one week two poems responded to "The Hooker" in the *Madras Courier*, inveighing against the idea of escaping life through hookah use. One author, named "Brevity," warns that while hookah smoke might "deaden the smart," it also might encourage the author to mount "castles in air" by means of "a stool and a rope"—a reference to suicide by hanging. Another poem warns anyone who attempts to "puff [Cupid] from his due" will find instead that "Cupid in turn smokes you."[84]

These poems show the responsiveness of newspaper verse by turning the original poem's vocabulary and conceits to playful ends. But a third response, titled "A Song," most explicitly transforms the act of smoking into a conscious reexamination of the role of newspaper verse in Anglo-India's multilingual publics and local literary marketplace.[85] "A Song" is a debate between two speakers, and it compares the complicated indulgence of the hookah to the relative simplicity of the cheroot (cigar). Ultimately, the poem uses two different types of Anglo-Indian speakers to differentiate between two Anglo-Indian aesthetics. It begins in the voice of a "gay *Feringy*" (or "alien," from the Persian word *farangi*), who is overheard by the poem's speaker explaining to a servant the pleasures of the hookah in a mixture of dialect and English.[86] Stretched at ease, this "feringy" exclaims:

> *"Qui hy?"—"Saib"—"Tazzy Chillm lacw,"*
> "My palate well to suit;
> "I feel myself I don't know how,
> "O, curse that vile Cheroot!"
>
> "Dear Hooka! Source of kind relief,
> "From heart-corroding care,
> "With thee I puff away all grief,
> "Give sorrow to the Air."

The poem is placed in the *Burra Choke* (or *Burra Chowk*), meaning a large market or main street.[87] The bazaar, like the punch house, combined social mixing with commerce in late eighteenth-century Calcutta. The italicized passage at the beginning verbalizes in Hindi an exchange between an employer and a servant overheard by the poem's speaker. In this exchange the employer calls to his servant with a "Qui hy?" a phrase (in Hindi, "koi-hai") that means roughly "Is anyone there?"[88] The use of phrases such as "Qui hy?" and the servant's response of "Saib" ("sahib": a term of respect that was closely associated with the whites of India) indicate the multilingualism of the poem and of the Anglo-Indian social life that it depicts: a foreigner conversant with local languages and indulging in Indian customs.

Provoked by the hookah-smoking sahib, the poem's author endorses different artistic values. Instead of the hookah, the remainder of the poem celebrates the cheroot, as the author claims that he

> too will sing,
> What smoker can be mute?
> Egad! I'll make the *Black Town* ring,
> In praise of my Cheroot.

A cheroot was a small cylindrical cigar that was easy to roll; hence, the author claims his cigar, unlike the hookah, does not require "spice, nor fruit / No Sugar sweet, no fragrant Rose." The uncomplicated cigar becomes a model of this English verse. The "plain Cheroot" is smoked "in its unadulterate state," he exclaims, which makes it into a "sovereign treat."[89] To assert the unadorned cheroot is also to assert the author's sovereign aesthetic taste.

The hookah and the cigar are two ways to think about poetry's ability to convey cultural intermixture and apprehend regional details. To select the simple cigar instead of the ornate hookah has strong connotations of embracing European masculinity instead of weak Asian luxury (and femininity). But the poem does not stop there: "A Song" might characterize itself as a simple cigar and its user as a manly man, but the cheroot, like the hookah, is a product of Asian history. In fact, the word *cheroot* begins in Tamil and arrives in English via southern India.[90] The hookah and the cheroot are cultural cousins as much as antagonists—two artistic traditions that in different ways combine the "anglo" and the "asiatic," to repeat the terminology of the eighteenth-century Calcutta newspaperman William Duane. Colonial discourse has taught us the overlapping connotations of masculinity and femininity with colonizer and colonized, but this multilingual newspaper poem reveals another tradition of local and regional writing, whose imagination somewhat comically drew from two popular forms of relaxation, the hookah and the cheroot.

Literature's Infrastructure and the History of Conventional Forms

As these descriptions show, poems that at first seem frivolous become important meditations on artistic creation and the reading publics of Anglo-India. At the outset of this chapter I drew attention to an alternate Anglo-Indian literary canon that existed alongside the more established writing of orientalists like Sir William Jones. These socially elevated individuals wrote within a tradition that aligned with academe's emphasis on literature's formal innovation and genius across periodized literary history.

Anglo-Indian newspaper verse offers a contemporaneous archive of imperial literature to that of elite orientalists, made up of common, ordinary textual productions that are tilted toward disposability rather than posterity. To describe artistic practices as ordinary is not to say they are not unique; rather, it is to note how shared features are adapted to new circumstances. For me, this method has been inspired by Susan Leigh Star, who defines infrastructure not only as physical emplacements, like roads and sewers, but also as a "trace or record of activities" that provide scholars with some access to the information order as it is created.[91] This conceptual reorientation seeks to capture how the patterns of material realities influence the construction of imaginations, not only those that are *about* those infrastructures but also those that show traces of how they were constrained and routed by them, as in the case of poems about punch houses, hookahs, and cheroots. Infrastructure, in this sense, is fundamentally relational, effected through shared boundaries, so that scholars must consider not just what qualifies as infrastructure but when it is recognized as such.[92]

I asked earlier in this chapter why an author would conjure a punch house in a newspaper poem. The answers take scholars closer to a model that is able to see Anglo-Indian infrastructure as more than simply printing presses and paper imports but also the self-devised artistic imaginations that arose from its social complexities and that created its unique textual spaces. James Livesey claims that the onerous EIC "seemed to be the enemy of the coffee house," with its ideals of civil society that were abstracted from the babble, noise, and argument that defined its new forms of sociability.[93] Examining the punch house allows for a different sense of where publics emerged, and newspapers allow us to analyze anew the venues where civil society was debated in Anglo-India. Tellingly, many of these poems about Persian translations, punch houses, or tobacco smoking address concrete audiences, engage with specific author-audience relationships, and identify obvious dedicatees, all of which are part of what Paula Bernat Bennett has called insistently "public speech."[94] It is precisely this aesthetic locality that can make these poems seem boring, especially when they thematize the modes and venues of their distribution. They seek to succeed within their immediate geographical and temporal domains rather than to reach out to us, their future readers.

Writing about nineteenth-century American poetry, Michael Cohen asks, "What happens to poetry if we think of poems as potentially cheap, disposable, timely, and local?"[95] Daniel White trended toward an answer when he noted that the "light reading" and comic verse published in Anglo-India's 1820s newspapers was often self-consciously bad poetry intended to reject European aesthetic rules and embrace mobility.[96] Such an impulse toward light reading and comic verse originated during the late eighteenth century, and although it might be no more distinguished because it was written in Bombay instead of Brighton, it nonetheless offers valuable insights into the convergence of art-making with Anglo-India's increasingly populous and mixed social world. The debates in newspapers about the representation of these languages and spaces show that Anglo-Indian authors were quite self-conscious about the aesthetics of the textual publics they erected in their writing and the physical spaces in which it was read and distributed.

Presenting punch houses and tobacco smoking in newspaper poetry gives scholars new ways to think about Anglo-Indian versus European sociability and art-making. Even as they were avid adopters of European social customs and spaces, Anglo-Indian artistic practices were not simple reproductions of European ways of life, nor were they naive repetitions of European forms. New literary histories of anglophone Asia will need to account for the dynamics by which authors devised their own artistic domain without resorting to the concept of artistic evolution that operates in concert with political, especially national, self-determination. Instead, scholars will need to focus on the translocalism and regionalism of the period to explain how anglophone authors utilized conventional generic forms. The easiest way to become invisible to literary scholars is to be a capable writer of consciously conventional verse absent of social commentary and without attachment to memorable historical events. To be a writer on the periphery of the metropolitan social sphere is to be almost undetectable and for that reason the majority of Anglo-Indian literature in this period has been perceived as unworthy of sustained analysis.

But what if scholars were rewarded for examining merely competent or good writers—those figures who seem undistinguished as formal experimentalists but who have nonetheless mastered the prevailing generic conventions and codes of the period and who make up its collective social witnesses? To focus on them would create a different history, fixated less on literature's elite practitioners and more on its conventional forms, assessing how they arose from the changes in the physical and social infrastructure of modern life. This is scholarship often described as author rehabilitation. My study of Anglo-Indian literature borrows many of the tactics of author rehabilitation but combines them with an analysis of infrastructure to identify a new archive that has been waiting for our attention. To examine it now is to answer lingering questions about why literature composed in Britain's Asian empire took the form it did and what it can tell us about how cultural production contributed to the creation of the modern world.

The Vagrant Muse

Making Reputation across Eurasia

This chapter defines the translocal poetics of Eyles Irwin (1751–1817), a colonial administrator and global traveler who cultivated what I call a portable literary reputation by coupling his writing to authors and markets in London, India, and China. He believed his associations with and travels through these domains secured for him a literary position that distinguished him from his contemporaries. He describes this artistic outlook as inspired by a "vagrant muse" who traveled with him across the globe and throughout Asia.

Born in Calcutta to an Irish family employed by the East India Company, Irwin was educated from a young age in England before training for service in Asia, as his father did.[1] Posted to Madras in 1766, Irwin acted as a clerk, revenue collector, and surveyor within the EIC's Fort St. George presidency in Madras, ultimately leaving the Company in 1794 after traveling to China as an advance party for George McCartney's first-ever British embassy to the Qing Empire. During Irwin's three decades as an EIC employee, he traveled through Venice, Alexandria, Baghdad, Sana'a, Canton, Macau, and across southern India, writing poetry and prose that sought to capture the vastness of what he called the "world of waters" that served as the medium of his administrative career and the facilitator of his literary one.

I begin the closely contextualized case studies of this book with Irwin because he exemplifies the category of late eighteenth-century India-based authors who should be understood in translocal and regional frames and whose literary history may be uncovered only by examining conventional genres of the type I described in the previous chapter. Irwin's writing extended across decades and included numerous topics, continually relating the oceanic world of Company service to the specific movements and dispositions of his body. His life is akin to the peripatetic existences that have come to typify the global eighteenth century.[2] Although largely forgotten now, Irwin is also an important figure for anglophone India's regional writing: he is arguably the first identifiable anglophone author to sustain a writing career from India and was well-known enough in 1805 that a survey of Indian writers named him among the "distinguished votaries of the *Oriental British Muse*."[3]

Irwin composed travel poetry, orientalized pastorals, and poems on political subjects, such as the imperial conflicts in India (*Ode to Robert Brooke, Esquire: Occasioned by the Death of Hyder Ally* [1784]), British naval victories (*Nilus; An Elegy Occasioned by the Victory of Admiral Nelson over the French Fleet* [1798]), the Peninsular Wars (*Ode to Iberia* [1808]), and Napoleon Bonaparte (*Napoleon: or, the Vanity of Human Wishes* [1814]). He published prose narratives of his travels across the Arabian Sea and in Egypt, as well as a comic opera called *The Bedouins: or, Arabs of the Desert* (1802). To all of this he added orthodox love lyrics and unconventional poems of place. Irwin was a prolific writer, and understanding his corpus requires attention to issues of historiography, close contextualization, and the conscious making of literary publics through translocalism at a moment when a regional anglophone literary culture of Asia was beginning to cohere. His career indicates the difficulties of being an author who appealed to audiences in England while promoting more proximate ones in India.

His vagrant muse put him in touch with prominent authors and artists throughout Britain, including the poet and patron William Hayley, the Sumatran expert and author William Marsden, and the painter George Romney. His works were printed in London by an established literary publisher, Dodsley, and mentioned regularly in well-known publications like the *European Review* and the *Gentleman's Magazine*. But his writing also associated him with the social and literary communities of interimperial spaces in Asia, the Indian Ocean, Arabia, and the Mediterranean, while also rooting him in the history of classical Greek, Roman, Egyptian, Ottoman, and Qing cultures. He presented his familiarity with these distant histories and antique lands as evidence of his value as an anglophone author outside of Britain.

Irwin's translocal poetics aimed to carry localities, accreting them into an intertwined set of authorial and political identities that fit uncertainly into national categories. He created connections across the component pieces of various and competing empires that recall what Seema Alavi names "imperial assemblages," which overlaid already existing networks with the changes forced by colonialism.[4] He emphasizes locality but always in relationships that transcend spatial and temporal boundaries. The literal routes of his administrative career, and their imaginative representation in writing and drawing, show Irwin as a version of those travelers that James Clifford describes as foundational to the experience of translocalism because they exchange knowledge among cultures.[5]

Anglo-India's literary publics were structured by the mobility and itineracy of authors like Irwin, though literary scholars have been slow to appreciate these qualities. Irwin was required to be mobile in his career, and, for that reason, his chronicles look quite different from the authentic localism or reciprocal networks of imperial identity that operated according to binaries of home and away, metropole and colony, domestic and imperial. In contrast to these satisfyingly balanced pairings, Irwin's writing assembles geographical, historical, and cultural multiplicities across the fractured eighteenth-century interimperial world. "Literature is the home of nonstandard space and time," Wai Chee Dimock notes, and collecting artifacts, cataloging ruins, and composing travel poetry and narratives were Irwin's way of accessing nonstandard space-time.[6] He appealed to his readers as the inheritors of the delocalized but unabsorbed ruins of other cultures. The vagrancy that made such writing possible required crafting a writer's reputation that might resonate with Anglo-Indian audiences while still attracting British ones. Irwin reveals now-forgotten ambitions among eighteenth-century Anglo-Indian authors. In his personal history we can glimpse the new chronologies and contours that were necessary for Anglo-Indian writing to emerge from a tricky combination of local anchors and transimperial topics and affiliations. Examining the different scales, genres, and media of Irwin's translocalism suggests how scholars might understand anew the literature of the British Empire as a planetary phenomenon with shifting local components.

Reading Charlotte Smith in Canton

Irwin is best known—if he is known at all—as an author who performed Indian identities for audiences in England. His second published poem, *Bedukah, or the Self-Devoted* (1776), represents the dying speech of a *sati*, who, by immolating herself, resists imperial power by crying out to the poem's narrator, who observes her death.[7] "Ramah: or, The Bramin" (1780) similarly represents the protests of an Indian holy man who with "rage possesst" delivers a lengthy rebuke of British colonial policy and Mughal oppression of Hindus before throwing himself to his death from the top of a temple in Conjeveram (Kanchipuram) as "a lesson to the British throne."[8] Irwin, especially in the early part of his career, was a frequent impersonator of native

Indian characters who expostulated on the dangers that the British Empire created with its conduct.[9]

In addition to this poetry of empire, however, Irwin solidified his reputation by placing himself in relationships that were unapologetically local yet elastic. One of his last published poems written in Asia, "To Mrs. Charlotte Smith, on Her Various Works" (1794), provides some semblance of his literary program. In the poem he allies himself with Smith, an innovator of British poetry, to describe his distinctive Eurasian "vagrant muse" (fig. 8).

His sonnet to Charlotte Smith was written in 1793 from Canton, China, where Irwin had traveled to assist Britain's first embassy to the Qing Empire. Irwin was part of a team of EIC employees who sought to facilitate the much larger embassy—the first of its kind—from the British Monarchy to the Qing Empire headed by George McCartney, Irwin's former superior in Madras.[10] The Company was worried that McCartney's embassy might actually harm trade with China, and Irwin arrived in Canton in 1792 as part of a three-person team deputed by the Company to prepare the representatives of the Qianlong emperor for McCartney's arrival.[11]

In retrospect, the Company's fears were legitimate; McCartney's commercial overtures were rejected, and the embassy was a failure. But as James Hevia notes, there were other goals beyond the expansion of trade that seemed more successful, such as the ceremonial establishment of "sovereign equality" between Britain and China and the assertion of British "national character" in the form of displaying artistic and scientific objects, such as globes, chemical apparatus, and Wedgwood pottery.[12] All of these gifts were attempts, Hevia argues, to erase British anxieties about its low standing compared to China. A 1793 article from the *Calcutta Gazette* discussing the McCartney embassy presented these anxieties plainly when it wrote that the "Chinese profess such utter contempt towards all European nations, as well as for their arts and sciences"; it argued that "before we can hope to be admitted into their good opinion," it was necessary to "surprize [*sic*] them with our ingenuity and splendour."[13]

The vigorous self-promotion of British arts is one background on Irwin's sonnet to Smith. In this context, what does it mean to be a reader and admirer of Charlotte Smith in Canton? One answer is found in Irwin's attempt to transfer Smith's poetic fame to himself. Irwin portrays Smith, who renewed interest in the sonnet with her *Elegiac Sonnets* (1784), as a "Creative mind!" whose poems were "treasures to the dazzled day."[14] For Irwin she exemplifies the "ingenuity and splendor" of English-language writing.

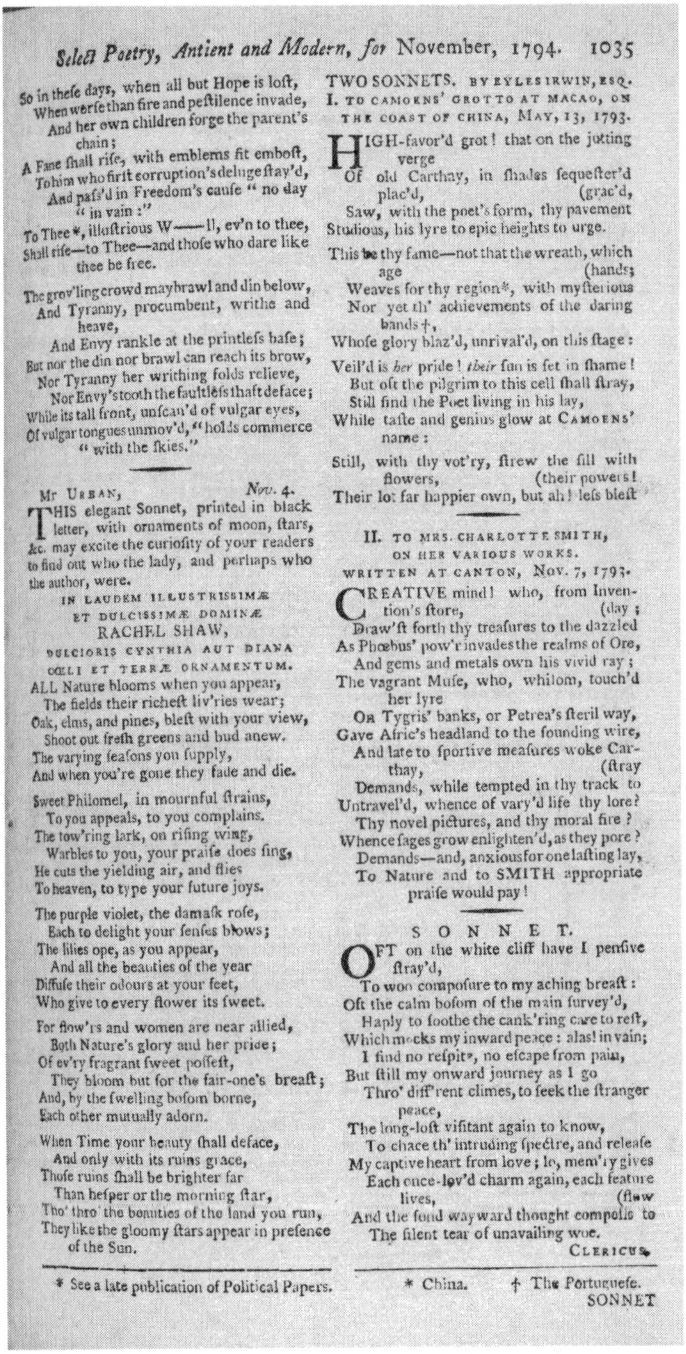

Select Poetry, Antient and Modern, for November, 1794. 1035

So in theſe days, when all but Hope is loſt,
When worſe than fire and peſtilence invade,
And her own children forge the parent's chain;
A Fane ſhall riſe, with emblems fit emboſt,
To him who firſt corruption's deluge ſtay'd,
And paſs'd in Freedom's cauſe "no day in vain:"
To Thee*, illuſtrious W——ll, ev'n to thee,
Shall riſe—to Thee—and thoſe who dare like thee be free.

The grov'ling crowd may brawl and din below,
And Tyranny, procumbent, writhe and heave,
And Envy rankle at the printleſs baſe;
But nor the din nor brawl can reach its brow,
Nor Tyranny her writhing folds relieve,
Nor Envy's tooth the faultleſs ſhaft deface;
While its tall front, unſcan'd of vulgar eyes,
Of vulgar tongues unmov'd, "holds commerce with the ſkies."

Mr URBAN, Nov. 4.

THIS elegant Sonnet, printed in black letter, with ornaments of moon, ſtars, &c. may excite the curioſity of your readers to find out who the lady, and perhaps who the author, were.

IN LAUDEM ILLUSTRISSIMÆ
ET DULCISSIMÆ DOMINÆ
RACHEL SHAW,
DULCIORIS CYNTHIA AUT DIANA
COELI ET TERRÆ ORNAMENTUM.

ALL Nature blooms when you appear,
The fields their richeſt liv'ries wear;
Oak, elms, and pines, bleſt with your view,
Shoot out freſh greens and bud anew.
The varying ſeaſons you ſupply,
And when you're gone they fade and die.

Sweet Philomel, in mournful ſtrains,
To you appeals, to you complains.
The tow'ring lark, on riſing wing,
Warbles to you, your praiſe does ſing,
He cuts the yielding air, and flies
To heaven, to type your future joys.

The purple violet, the damaſk roſe,
Each to delight your ſenſes blows;
The lilies ope, as you appear,
And all the beauties of the year
Diffuſe their odours at your feet,
Who give to every flower its ſweet.

For flow'rs and women are near allied,
Both Nature's glory and her pride;
Of ev'ry fragrant ſweet poſſeſt,
They bloom but for the fair-one's breaſt;
And, by the ſwelling boſom borne,
Each other mutually adorn.

When Time your beauty ſhall deface,
And only with its ruins grace,
Thoſe ruins ſhall be brighter far
Than heſper or the morning ſtar,
Tho' thro' the bounties of the land you run,
They like the gloomy ſtars appear in preſence of the Sun.

TWO SONNETS. BY EYLES IRWIN, ESQ.

I. TO CAMOENS' GROTTO AT MACAO, ON THE COAST OF CHINA, MAY, 13, 1793.

HIGH-favor'd grot! that on the jutting verge
Of old Carthay, in ſhades ſequeſter'd plac'd, (grac'd,
Saw, with the poet's form, thy pavement
Studious, his lyre to epic heights to urge.
This be thy fame—not that the wreath, which age (hands;
Weaves for thy region*, with myſterious
Nor yet th' achievements of the daring bands†,
Whoſe glory blaz'd, unrival'd, on this ſtage:
Veil'd is *her* pride! *their* ſun is ſet in ſhame!
But oft the pilgrim to this cell ſhall ſtray,
Still find the Poet living in his lay,
While taſte and genius glow at CAMOENS' name:
Still, with thy vot'ry, ſtrew the ſill with flowers, (their powers!
Their lot far happier own, but ah! leſs bleſt

II. TO MRS. CHARLOTTE SMITH, ON HER VARIOUS WORKS.
WRITTEN AT CANTON, NOV. 7, 1793.

CREATIVE mind! who, from Invention's ſtore, (day;
Draw'ſt forth thy treaſures to the dazzled
As Phœbus' pow'r invades the realms of Ore,
And gems and metals own his vivid ray;
The vagrant Muſe, who, whilom, touch'd her lyre
On Tygris' banks, or Petrea's ſteril way,
Gave Afric's headland to the founding wire,
And late to ſportive meaſures woke Carthay, (ſtray
Demands, while tempted in thy track to
Untravel'd, whence of vary'd life thy lore?
Thy novel pictures, and thy moral fire?
Whence ſages grow enlighten'd, as they pore?
Demands—and, anxious for one laſting lay,
To Nature and to SMITH appropriate praiſe would pay!

SONNET.

OFT on the white cliff have I penſive ſtray'd,
To woo compoſure to my aching breaſt:
Oft the calm boſom of the main ſurvey'd,
Haply to ſoothe the cank'ring care to reſt,
Which mocks my inward peace: alas! in vain;
I find no reſpite, no eſcape from pain,
But ſtill my onward journey as I go
Thro' diff'rent climes, to ſeek the ſtranger peace,
The long-loſt viſitant again to know,
To chace th' intruding ſpectre, and releaſe
My captive heart from love; lo, mem'ry gives
Each once-lov'd charm again, each feature lives, (flow
And the fond wayward thought compells to
The ſilent tear of unavailing woe.
CLERICUS.

* See a late publication of Political Papers.

* China. † The Portugueſe.

SONNET

Figure 8. Eyles Irwin's sonnet to Charlotte Smith, composed in Canton and published in the *Gentleman's Magazine.* Note the way that the date and location of its composition figures prominently in the poem. Courtesy of the Lewis Walpole Library, Yale University.

Yet Irwin's appreciation of Smith's creativity is really an account of his translocal poetics, which he argues emerge from "Tygris' banks" (Mesopotamia), in "Afric's headlands" (the Nile), and in "Petrea's steril way" (the Arabian desert), each of which had "woke Cathay" (China). Irwin had traveled through all of these locations as an EIC emissary. He portrays himself as having brought poetry to each place or having rejuvenated it when it had gone silent, making "To Mrs. Charlotte Smith" an account of his culture-giving poetic gifts. In combining topographical features, geographical locations, continents, and imperial formations, the poem is an act of aesthetic affiliation. The poem simultaneously demonstrates Irwin's familiarity with Britain's literary scene and his participation in it from afar. His poem seeks to reinforce the perception of his literary skill by recording a vision of itinerant cultural production that does not perfectly overlap with British norms. Irwin acts as a kind of array that refracts Smith's literary standing, turning it into a model for the anglophone Asian literary world. His association with her coerces an affiliative network of distanced intimacy. With his personal geography, enumerated in the poem, Irwin provides a map of anglophone poetry's power to knit together seemingly disparate locales. He distinguishes himself from Smith's "track" by arguing for an alternative mode of inspiration evolving from Eurasia rather than the roots, rocks, and rivers of Smith's England.

Irwin's sonnet to Smith may declare the ingenuity of anglophone Asian verse, the consequences of which he can identify more clearly from China, but another of his poems also written in China, "To Camoens' Grotto at Macao" (1794), assesses the imperial prehistory of his vagrant muse. This poem is an appreciation of the sixteenth-century Portuguese poet Luis Vaz de Camões, the author of *The Lusiads* (1572), a ten-canto *ottava rima* epic in the style of Virgil that renders Vasco da Gama's fifteenth-century voyage to India in heroic fashion. Camões composed his poem while resident in Macau, where he superintended the property of deceased and absent soldiers. He had traveled to Asia, perhaps unwillingly, during the 1550s, to serve as an exponent of Portuguese commerce. While there, he was frequently in conflict with authorities, often in prison for debt, and all the while carrying with him a manuscript of his epic. That epic was so successful that, in Richard Helgerson's estimation, Camões is unrivaled as a national poet and still integral to modern Portugal's identity.[15]

Camões's reputation drew Irwin's admiration and imitation. While in China, Irwin claimed to have rediscovered the small rocky outcropping above the city of Macau where Camões was supposed to have written his

Figure 9. The bust of Luis Vaz de Camões at the "Poets Grotto" in Macau (ca. 1917–19), supposed to be the location where Camões composed *The Lusiads* that Irwin celebrates with his own poem. Courtesy of Sidney D. Gamble Photographs Collection, David M. Rubenstein Rare Book and Manuscript Library, Duke University.

poem (fig. 9). He describes that spot as Camões's "high-favor'd grot [grotto]" in which he could still hear the old poet's "lyre" soar "to epic heights," praising the "daring bands" of Portuguese sailors who first arrived to trade with China. Camões infused Macau with a "glory blaz'd, unrival'd, on this stage" and any "pilgrim to this cell"—the tight space tucked underneath its two overhanging stones—would "still find the Poet living in his lay." The conflation of poet, poem, and locale aligns Irwin's vagrant muse with earlier settings, as did his Smith sonnet, and with earlier authors who might spur recognition of his own artistic achievements.

Irwin was familiar with *The Lusiads*; he had purchased the most recent English edition, which had been translated almost two decades earlier by fellow Company employee William Julius Mickle, who had styled the epic poem a "manifesto for building the right and most moral kind of empire."[16] Mickle saw poetry as a tool of governance and argued that the "establishment of improved governments in the East" was not just the "dream of theory" but something evident in Company administration.[17] Mickle's ultimate goal was to translate Portuguese failures in China into British successes. Understanding the mistake of the Portuguese—which, according to Mickle, was "ignorance of the true principles of commerce"—would ensure that it would not be repeated by the Company in India.[18] The Portuguese presence in southern China had always been the target of European competition, especially among EIC traders, who believed their opportunities must come at the expense of the Portuguese, despite their nations' frequent alliances against the Dutch.[19] But it also required the replacement of those commercial desires with heroic ones, a "collusion between commerce and empire" that Balachandra Rajan notes was the obscured undertone of *The Lusiads*.[20]

Poetry and governance have a lengthy entwined history in the anglophone tradition, particularly from the sixteenth-century examples of Sir Philip Sidney and Edmund Spenser. The collusion between empire and reputation serves for Irwin as the model for merging poetry and governance, making the translations involved in his appreciation of Camões not literal and linguistic as much as historical and cultural: he seeks to affiliate himself with the triumphs of imperial epic while detaching his verse from the history of Portugal's decreasing influence in Asia. As with Charlotte Smith, Irwin's appreciative poem revives the memory of *The Lusiads* to bolster his status. The power of a place like Macau, and a poem composed there, was to reach across time and teach anglophone authors what to emulate and what to avoid. China, like India, appears as a route to literary fame, and Irwin's admiration of Camões is paradoxically Irwin's strategy for supplanting him.

The invocation (and projection) of Camões and Smith from China elucidates some of the complex poetics necessary for Irwin to stylize himself as a vagrant muse who refracts the literary reputation of predecessors and contemporaries to imagine his own literary power. Chi-ming Yang has noted that China acted as a "cultural intermediary" and "placeholder" for Britain's "historical concerns and cultural anxieties." This imperial competition between established empires, like the Qing and British, Yang argues, made the figure of the foreign commentator resonate within eighteenth-century English fiction.[21] Irwin represents a variation of this yearning for intermediation when he lauds Smith or identifies with Camões, becoming, in essence, a foreign correspondent of anglophone poetry, announcing the conditions of English verse elsewhere around the world while arguing that his vagrancy represents another prototype to be emulated by authors, whether in London or Madras. The "imagined distance between East and West" that was so enabling for the foreign characters of English fiction is literalized by Irwin's sojourn in China.[22]

Parnassus in Madras

Irwin imagined all of these Asian locales as audiences for, not just influences on, his poetry—as publics that might grow along what he called in his sonnet to Smith the "steril way" of his travel. Though Madras goes unmentioned in the poem, it was the most significant location of his career, and its artistic culture is the subject of his "Prologue Written for the Opening of the Lyceum at Madras 1782." Though never published, it was read aloud at the Lyceum's inauguration and provides an aperture into Madras as it was institutionalized as a literary public in the early 1780s. Little historical information exists about the Madras Lyceum beyond Irwin's poem, in which it is represented as surrounded by enemies, particularly Haidar Ali, father of Tipu Sultan, and the ruler of the Kingdom of Mysore, who was a perpetual antagonist of the EIC.

As with his poem to Smith, Irwin's "Prologue" portrays his public as sustained by art's ability to amalgamate translocal and transhistorical affiliations. Rather than accentuate the interlingual exchanges that spurred translations like the Vepery Press's Tamil-English *Pilgrim's Progress* (1793) or those geographically proximate multilingual readers targeted by newspaper poets like Candidus, Irwin looks toward the Hellenic past for models of Madras's anglophone world. He describes the Lyceum's audience as akin to "Thermopylae's devoted band," reconceiving Anglo-Indians as those Greeks who sacrificed themselves in 480 BCE to oppose the invading Persian armies of Xerxes.[23] But unlike the ancient Greeks, Madras's Anglo-Indians can be saved by listening to poems. In response to the question "Amid this strife on what shall wit rely, / Where taste resort, or Sentiment apply?" (246). Irwin offers the Lyceum and his poem that sanctifies it:

> some bolder minds their views proclaim,
> To blow the dying ember into flame;
> With wit's remains to make our glorious stand,
> And from unleashed darkness, shield the land.

Irwin's depiction of Anglo-Indian audiences as soldiers who stand against "unleashed darkness" is culturally dismissive and reflects the violent militarism essential to their economic survival.[24] Yet in overlaying the geography of Thermopylae with that of Madras, Irwin associates his immediate audience with those "bolder minds" that seek with their "views" to "blow the dying ember into flame" and thus "shield the land." In the process he makes hearing his poem a matter of life and death. The poem is the mechanism by which, and the Lyceum the place where, multiple forces converge into the nascent public sphere of Madras that saves Asia's anglophone poetry in its infancy by encouraging others to "proclaim."

To be seen as advancing beauty in Asia was the impulse that initiated Irwin's authorial career. His first composition, *St. Thomas's Mount* (1774), argued that southern India was more nurturing for writers than England and used pastoral, georgic, and topographical modes to explain how Asia might revitalize English-language poetry. The poem, which was started in India when Irwin was just seventeen years old and employed as a writer (a kind of junior accountant), refers to the English name of a hill (in Tamil, *Parangi Malai*) that overlooks Madras. Irwin turns it, and the city's immediate surroundings, into a pastoral poem. The pastoral genre has continually adapted itself through relocation and recontextualization, and it is the promise of geographical mobility and generic innovation that pushed Irwin to compose in that form.[25] His epigraph to *St. Thomas's Mount* cites the concluding lines of Alexander Pope's *Windsor-Forest* (1713)—themselves adopted from Pope's *Pastorals*—about being the "first in these fields," as Irwin seeks to establish himself as first in the "fields" of Anglo-India.[26] The poem is his preliminary statement of India as a coherent field for English verse with himself as its initial explorer.

Irwin understood that his identity as an Anglo-Indian writer was valuable; the title page of *St. Thomas's Mount* advertises that it was "Written by a GENTLEMAN in INDIA." India appears as a route to literary fame, a means of apprenticeship, and an archaeological past to draw on. It had figured prominently in English writing since at least the late seventeenth century, with John Dryden's political drama of Mughal India, *Aureng-Zebe* (1675), or the now well-known references to the "glitt'ring Spoil" of "*India's* glowing gems" that exist within the private rooms of Belinda in Pope's *The Rape of the Lock* (1714).[27] But before the publication of *St. Thomas's Mount*, Madras appeared primarily in geography manuals, sailors' handbooks, dictionaries, and travel accounts that exhibited an instrumental attitude toward southern India. When Madras did surface in imaginative literature, it was as a distant locale for a dramatic plot device, as in the epistolary novel *The Artless Lovers* (1768), whose protagonist, Lucy Wheatly, gets to receive an inheritance and marry for love when she learns that her male cousin, Richard, has died in Madras, eliminating him as an heir.[28] Unlike these other authors, Irwin is among the earliest we know of who wrote imaginative literature about Madras while in India.[29]

Yet, much as he did with his sonnet to Charlotte Smith, Irwin associates himself in *St. Thomas's Mount* with John Denham and Pope primarily as a means of bolstering his own art. By making *St. Thomas's Mount* commensurate with "Cooper's Hill" or *Windsor-Forest*, he announces a new literary tradition that relocates pastoral England to India. "In DENHAM'S lays the hill of Cooper shines," and "Windsor blooms in POPE'S immortal lines," Irwin writes, but after his poem, *St. Thomas's Mount* will "without a rival reign" (canto 1, 7–11). Just as *St. Thomas's Mount* exceeds "Cooper's Hill" and *Windsor-Forest*, so India exceeds Britain, and Irwin surpasses his rivals Denham and Pope.

Therefore, when Irwin affirms that the climatological newness and geographical exoticism of India are advantages other poets like Denham and Pope cannot match, he seeks to establish an alternative tradition away from and outside of Britain and Europe. He orientalizes the pastoral by replacing its central conceit of singing beneath the oak tree with singing underneath a "Mango shade"; "to sing" the "lively hues" of the mango and its "ambrosial fruit," he writes, "would transcend the Muse" (canto 1, 39–40). Likewise, his pastoral is energized by southern India's nurturing coastal climate, with its "genial spring" and its "happy fields" (canto 1, 15) so different from Britain's "havock of . . . boist'rous skies" and long winters of "universal gloom" (canto 1, 18, 22). Claims of verdancy were not new to eighteenth-century pastoral, and climatological difference had frequently acted as an explanation for the need to alter its generic features, but Irwin seeks to establish his literary reputation by asserting to English readers that southern India's nurturing coastal climate is also an anchor for new anglophone poetics. Denham writes near the beginning of "Cooper's Hill" that "where the Muses & their train resort / *Parnassus* stands."[30] With *St. Thomas's Mount* Irwin asserts that there are poets in Anglo-India, so there is a Parnassus, too.

It was an Indian Parnassus, moreover, that might compete with England's adoption of the classical one. While England may "the court of Beauty boast," Irwin imagines an exodus to India of "Heroes and Bards" who "seek this distant land" to "gain the honor" of the Muse's "lovely hand" (canto 3, 131–34). As with the myth of St. Thomas, the apostle who supposedly traveled to Asia to convert Indians to Christianity and whose name was attached to the hill by seventeenth-century English colonialists, Irwin's poem publicizes India as a locale of beauty and Christian conversion alike that seeks adherents (and readers) for its new publics.

The eastward migration across the globe to India becomes a mode of literary promise that persists as an organizing conceit throughout his career, functioning as a vanguard for the "court of Beauty" that transforms defunct literary locales with his abundant poetic gifts and his appreciation of their past and present cultures. In this model Madras, and its prospect from St. Thomas Mount, establishes new traditions by drawing from Britain's neoclassical conception of the classical Greek and Roman past. The East serves as prologue and epilogue to reading publics that are seeking to "blow" the "ember into flame." Anglophone India thus acts as a counterweight to denunciations of empire arising in England among skeptical writers and thinkers, most famously Edmund Burke. But it was also, as Irwin notes, a mechanism by which England may boast of its beauty through the possibility of national regeneration and cultural renewal in Asia.

As celebrations of the Madras Lyceum and St. Thomas Mount indicate, Irwin's translocal poetics is more like what historians of science have termed "moving localities," in which specific places are not "coincident or constrained by location" but rove beyond it as a "complex set of connections, allegiances, and commitments" that stretch the boundaries of what is proximate in space and time.[31] While rooted in physical locations, it also binds those locations to others across the globe (Cooper's Hill, Windsor Forest) that serve as models and precursors yet also competitors. Irwin's translocalism is a cluster of formal innovations and cultural positions organized around locations, written about and remembered, motivated by the movements of his career but portable, not entrenched in those places as residue. It is constituted in contradiction: Irwin is inspired by these locales but also revives them from sterility; anglophone poetry is life-giving and yet rejuvenated by those places that Irwin has visited. What James Clifford identifies as culture's dual attention to routes and roots appears within Irwin's writing as a way to define literary success in Asia as a set of authorial connections (Charlotte Smith), historical commitments (ancient Greece), and evocative localities (St. Thomas Mount) whose relationship is guaranteed by, and generative of, their author's reputation.[32]

Ruins, Relics, and the Near Eastern Past

"What a World of Waters!" Irwin exclaimed in a 1784 letter to his friend and quasi-literary agent William Hayley, who throughout Irwin's career oversaw the correction and publication of many of his poems to British audiences.[33] With this exclamation Irwin expresses his enthusiasm for a life that was insistently global in its imagination and imperial obligations. The locales of his travels provided the content for his poetry and prose, while his vagrancy was the strategy he used to piece together the constituent elements of his poetics. As Irwin journeyed through the commercial cities of the Mediterranean and the Near East, he materialized their ancient relics and contemporary cultures as drawings, maps, and writings. Through these collections Irwin associated himself with the vibrancy of empires that had disappeared or gone silent as a means of gathering a literary reputation while in Anglo-India. He aimed to produce a composite art of place located along longitudinal axes of imperial movement and within sediments of history. He contrived a method by which to affiliate with the deep past available in its landscapes and ruins.

Irwin's ambitions were hardly unique. Eighteenth-century literature—its poetry especially—ransacked classical Greece and Rome to articulate imperial aspirations and reputational desires.[34] A few Anglo-Indian authors, like Sir William Jones, turned to ancient India as a means of identifying an origin even more temporally distant than those of classical antiquity.[35] Irwin shared this attention to alternate origins, but instead of Sanskrit culture, Irwin focused on examples from Roman Egypt and the pre-Islamic Near East. He reveals what can happen when an anglophone author looks back on the Panhellenic past from India, not England.

Imagining authors as revivifying literature as they travel through the world's imperial spaces was a constant conceit of Irwin's career. It functioned as a crucial gear in the spatially and temporally distended poetics of his four *Eastern Eclogues* (1780), which are set across northern Africa, Arabia, and southern India.[36] As with *St. Thomas's Mount*, Irwin presents his eclogues as valuable because of their novelty, arguing that they emerge from "other Climes, where new Subjects occur" (3). They arrived to him as visions collected during his "novel and perilous Journey" from Madras to London and back again, a journey necessitated by the bureaucratic politics of his colonial career (4). While he admits to being influenced by earlier pastorals—a genre, he notes with obligatory self-deprecation, that has been "pursued by so many able Pens, that an Author could have little Success to Hope for" (3)—he suggests their influence is mitigated by the relative newness for English-language readers of the places he describes. Rather than attempt to "rival celebrated Writers" (3) with his formal innovations, Irwin proposes to outdo them with his content and political relevancy, even though perceiving the Near East as a novel subject forces Irwin to forget European predecessors, such as Richard Pococke, Frederick Norden, James Bruce, and Constantin, Comte de Volney, all of whom had visited and published about these places.[37]

What distinguishes Irwin's writing, therefore, is biographical and geographical rather than formal. Irwin is careful not only to account for what he sees but also to react emotionally to his experiences. He capitalizes on what Nigel Leask has termed the "aesthetics of distance" and its ability to facilitate the comparison of cultures.[38] His first eclogue in *Eastern Eclogues*, "Alexis: or, The Traveller," for example, is set within the ruins of Alexandria and follows a speaker who, like Irwin, has traveled from "northern climes" to "the spicy isles" (lines 11–12). Alexis sees the ruins of Alexandria as "Relics of antient taste! by Time betray'd" and "Disjoin'd by wars, by ignorance defac'd" (lines 3, 6). As Alexis wanders, he "hold[s] sweet converse with the mighty dead" (line 8) among a landscape littered with their artifacts: "useless aqueducts obstruct the way" along "gaping catacombs" with "long canals"; buildings with "tow'rs unroof'd" present the "Wonders of art decay'd" (lines 27–31). The poem moves from the famed Alexandrian lighthouse to the Catacombs of Kom el Shoqafa, the city's subterranean cemetery that dates back to Roman Egypt.

The most significant object embedded in the poem, however, is Pompey's Pillar, which Irwin sketched for the title page of *Eastern Eclogues* (fig. 10). Pompey's Pillar is a Roman triumphal column, erected not by Pompey, as was commonly thought, but by Diocletian in 297 CE. In Irwin's inaccurate history the pillar plays an important role, telling the tale of "Egyptian honor" and "Roman shame" when Pompey was defeated by Julius Caesar and fled to Egypt to mark the end of the Roman Republic (line 36). In a version of the trope later popularized by Percy Bysshe Shelley in "Ozymandias" (1818), Irwin imagines the pillar to perpetuate Pompey's name even after he was defeated and killed.

Irwin projects onto this pillar his concerns about the effects of worldly expansion on Britain. The political situations overlap inexactly: Alexis never renounces imperial ambitions, nor does he make explicit how violent Roman factionalism might correspond to Britain's imperial politics. But the impetus for the journey that brought Irwin to Alexandria offers a clue. Irwin temporarily left India in 1777 after his superior, the governor of Madras, Lord Pigot, was overthrown and imprisoned by rival colonial administrators in a dispute about money loaned to the nawab of Arcot, a native Indian prince. After al-

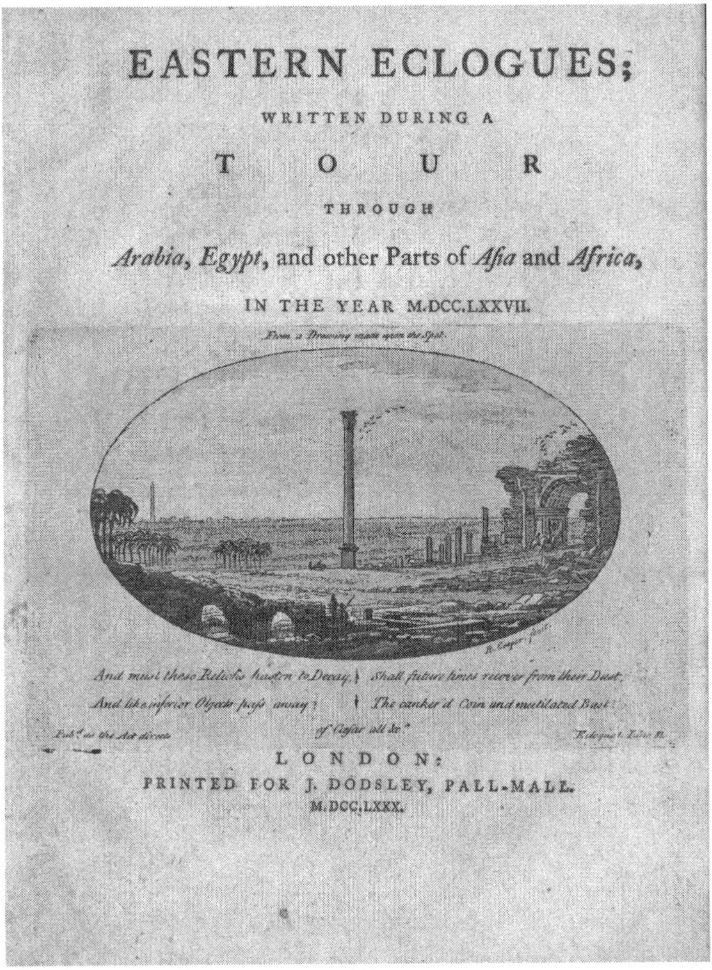

EASTERN ECLOGUES;

WRITTEN DURING A

T O U R

THROUGH

Arabia, Egypt, and other Parts of *Asia* and *Africa*,

IN THE YEAR M.DCC.LXXVII.

And must these Relicks hasten to Decay,
And like inferior Objects pass away?
Shall future times recover from their Dust,
The canker'd Coin and mutilated Bust!
of Cæsar all &c.

LONDON:

PRINTED FOR J. DODSLEY, PALL-MALL.

M.DCC.LXXX.

Figure 10. Title page of the *Eastern Eclogues* (1780) that shows Eyles Irwin's sketch of Alexandria's ruins. The closer monument is a column Irwin incorrectly identifies as a pillar erected by Pompey. In the left background is one of two obelisks, each of which was referred to as Cleopatra's Needle. Both of these obelisks were removed from Egypt in the nineteenth century, one to New York City's Central Park and the other to London's Thames Embankment. Courtesy of the Library Special Collections, Charles E. Young Research Library, UCLA.

lying himself with Pigot, Irwin was expelled from Madras; he trekked to London carrying petitions on his superior's behalf via an unusual route that took him through Egypt and the Mediterranean. While traveling, he composed a poem attacking Pigot's captors as traitors who were "leagued with

Mahomet's perfidious race," referring to the allies of the Muslim nawab, and portraying Pigot as a "Noble Sufferer" tormented by greedy EIC employees.[39] The dissenting factions of Madras hang over Irwin's interests in Pompey's Pillar, which commemorates the consequences of an earlier empire's internecine conflicts. Irwin's drawing of Pompey's Pillar confronts readers with an image that unsettles the typically boisterous analogy between Rome's ancient imperial might and Britain's eighteenth-century Asian expansion. It looms in the center of the drawing like an uncomfortable splinter of memory, reminding readers that empires' end gestates in their triumphs.

Irwin's composite art offsets the potential dangers of such factionalism. Seeing the ruins of Alexandria inspired "concern" and "regret" in him for the "beauty and pride" of these ruins. Irwin's drawing of Pompey's Pillar testifies to its desolate surroundings, which are populated only by the silhouettes of resting herdsmen and soaring birds. He anthropomorphizes Alexandria's artifacts, describing that he felt for them as he would if he saw "a venerable character in distress."[40] Gazing on the same ruins that Irwin sketched, Alexis wonders "must these relics hasten to decay, / And like inferior objects pass away?"[41] Of course not, the poem answers confidently; as long as Irwin documents these relics in his writing and his drawing, they remain animate and alive.

Scholars have linked landscape's representational modes to the changes brought about by European colonialists like Irwin. Every culture has a landscape tradition, W. J. T. Mitchell notes, but landscape helped build the "'dreamwork' of imperialism" by appealing to the "utopian fantasies" and "perfected imperial prospect" of overseas adventures (while also hinting at the "unresolved ambivalence" about Europe's conquests and some of the "unsuppressed resistance" to it).[42] For Sara Suleri the picturesque landscape has always depicted the treacherous dynamics of cultural encounters in an arrested form, whereas Leask sees landscapes as an analogy for expropriation of territory and the "ruinous agency of time."[43]

Irwin indicates that time's ruinous agency had human collaborators whose pointless conflicts accelerated the devastation of past architectural achievements. Ruins become warnings rather than triumphs of empire. His was not a system for packaging relics to soothe Europe's metropolitan audiences with sentimentalized visions of empires past. In a prose account of his 1777 journey from India to England, titled *A Series of Adventures in the Course of a Voyage Up the Red-Sea* (1780), which functions as a companion to his *Eastern Eclogues,* Irwin recalls the story of an English ship crew who affixed ropes to the side of Pompey's Pillar so they could "initial . . . the[ir] names" in "very legible black paint" on its side. Afterward, while getting drunk on punch at the pillar's crown, the crew broke off a piece, which their ship captain carried back with him to England. Irwin confesses that he also acquired little relics from the ruins of Alexandria, adding these pieces to the "small collection" he had been amassing during his journey from India to England. He even suggests that Pompey's Pillar would make "a beautiful termination . . . to one of the vistos [vistas] at Chatsworth! What a noble addition would it prove to the collection at Stowe!" referring to two great English country estates.[44]

With these examples Irwin argues that Alexandrian ruins should become mobile and be absorbed within even larger imperial collections, energized by their proximity to other artifacts (and by the collectors who value them). By suggesting that they can only be secured in England and their aesthetic worth can only be appreciated in concert with other looted artifacts, Irwin indulges in the appropriation and deterritorialization that was central to cultural imperialism. But Irwin's imaginative reconstitution of Near Eastern relics functions quite differently from the artifacts and riches extracted by nabobs, such as those who imprisoned Pigot or the ostentatious Sir Matthew Mite of Samuel Foote's 1772 play *The Nabob*, who boasts that when "richly dispensed," wealth has the "magical power" to "closely conceal the source from whence [it] proceed[s]."[45] For Irwin these artifacts operate in the reverse of Mite's dictum: rather than conceal their origins, relics persistently reveal them. The appeal of the deterritorialized object is that it can be inserted into a larger translocal and transhistorical collection without eradicating the story it tells. What is so compelling about Irwin's ruins is that they do not exhibit the types of "ruination" that allows empire to rule by simply eroding indigenous sovereignties and infrastructure, as Ann Laura Stoler notes is common in European colonialism.[46] Instead, he seeks ways to reanimate already eroded ruins as a means of legitimizing new imperial forms and connecting to an alternative past.

Irwin's 1783 collection of travel poetry, *Occasional Epistles: Written during a Journey from London to Busrah, in the Gulf of Persia*, continues his preoccupation with using antique ruins to review the current status of Britain's empire. Irwin's roving is like a manifesto for his vagrant aesthetics, as he reports from across the Mediterranean, the Indian Ocean, and the Arabian Sea. Irwin's journey embeds him in history and mythology, so that traveling across the Peloponnesian peninsula is the same as digging into Greece's past, which places him "where wise Ulysses" received "a warrior's due" and where

"Helen still inflames in Homer's lay."[47] His poetry is complemented by lengthy footnotes and, much like the *Eastern Eclogues*, by reproductions of Irwin's original sketches, leading a reviewer for the *Scots Magazine* to laud the collection as at once "a poem, a history-piece, and a landscape."[48] The poems can be tedious to read because they are formally quite conventional (written in heroic couplets) but enormously allusive and replete with obscure references.

With his epistles Irwin seeks to create cultural mnemonics that revivify the past in the present; not to do so is to risk deterioration or obliteration, a danger akin to leaving Pompey's Pillar in Egypt. Irwin's third epistle, which begins with an epigraph from Ferdowsi, the tenth-century author of the Persian epic *Shahnameh*, typifies his ambition. As we saw in chapter 1, it was not unusual for Company employees to be proficient in Persian—it was the administrative language of the Mughal Empire—or to appeal to Persian poets like Hafez and Ferdowsi in the way Irwin does here. Their invocation offers an example of how a traveling author could "consecrate the ground" like those "heroes" that came before him by traveling through it.[49] The epigraph from Ferdowsi likewise consecrates the ground of Irwin's poem.

But in addition to recounting Irwin's travels through the Tigris and Euphrates River basin—"these fair Banks like Paradise"—his poem also describes how Irwin entered Palmyra, the capital of an empire that in the late third century CE incorporated parts of present-day Syria, Turkey, and Egypt and competed with the Roman Empire.[50] Palmyra was an important trading intersection in the Near East, allowing Roman and Mediterranean traders access to the Indian Ocean via the Persian Gulf, and Irwin undoubtedly followed this trade route when he was reinstated to his old position and returned to Madras from England in 1780.[51] Palmyra had been a "Guardian of arts, and Freedom's younger child!" and a home to philosophers such as Longinus, but by the time Irwin arrived, it had surrendered its importance to become merely an

> Ill-fated servant of the tuneful train!
> This scene renews their sympathetic pain.
> Mid yonder sheds, while Fancy points thy grave,
> Immortal tears the hallow'd spot shall lave.[52]

Though the poem implies the ground itself is weeping at the loss of Longinus and Palmyra, the syntax also makes it seem that Irwin weeps at this hallowed spot to attach a nearly faded classical tinge to his own travels. These tears are a tribute but also a resuscitation of Palmyra's past, accentuated by his insistence on writing about its deleted history in the present tense, so that his poem mingles him with those defunct cultures and ghostly figures that he can still hear and record. Irwin composes poetry and illustrations in assembly with the dead, using that most conventional conceit of artistic creation to conceive of Palmyra as an aesthetically vibrant locale once more.

Irwin explicitly blames the Ottoman Empire for the continued desolation of cities like Palmyra and Baghdad, the latter of which is completely absent of human life in Irwin's depiction, without even the herders and birds that had occupied the ruins around Pompey's Pillar (fig. 11). "Beneath the Othman [Ottoman] banner Glory dies; / Taste rends her vail, and Industry his ties," Irwin exclaims, while poetry "sings in chains."[53] His dislike of the Ottomans accords with his general distrust of Islam. The Kingdom of Mysore, in particular, which became the Company's most vigorous competitor during Irwin's

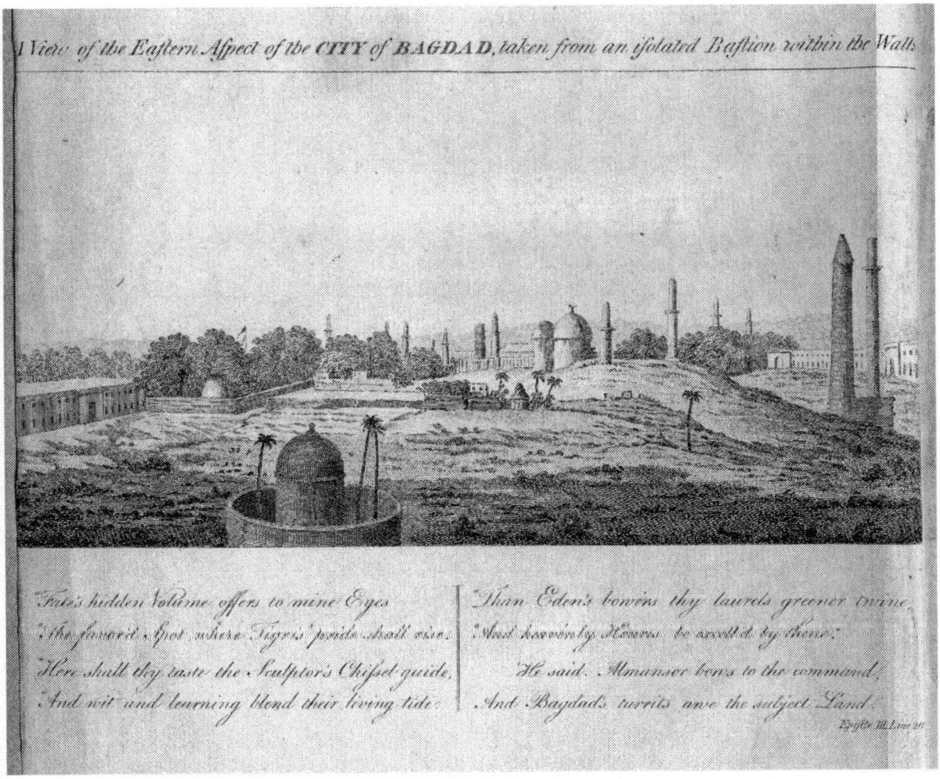

Figure 11. Eyles Irwin's sketch of Baghdad's ruins, included in his *Occasional Epistles* (1783). Courtesy of the Library Special Collections, Charles E. Young Research Library, UCLA.

residency in India, was led by sovereigns who appealed to Islam. European reactions to Islam were "conditioned" by a "dialectical engagement" with the instruments of Islamic states.[54] As Irwin roves through the Eurasian world, he associates Islam with piracy, the barbaric captivity of Christians, and religious heresy but also with radical freethinking traditions and Republicanism.

Perhaps because of this dialectical engagement, Irwin insists on Europeans' complicity in the grand historical swerves from antagonism to astonishment, which suggests that he learned a modicum of cultural relativism after his part in the Pigot affair. For example, while stranded on the Arabian Peninsula during his 1777 voyage to England, he remembers being gawked at by Muslim crowds and claims it was like the "first arrival of a Cherokee Indian in Europe."[55] He probably refers to the 1762 embassy to London from the Cherokee Nation, which, while not the first arrival, provoked so much attention from Britons that it overwhelmed the Native Americans' sensibilities and caused them anxiety.[56] The comparison places Irwin alongside the Cherokee and insinuates that Europeans may not be superior to other populations around the world. He laments that Turks barred Christians from seeing the "Saviour's shrine" in the Holy Land but admits such actions were simply the "sad end" of the religious Crusades from centuries earlier, when

> Europe's bigots bled on Asia's coast:
> Far different then th' imperious Christian came,
> Glowing with monkish zeal and promis'd fame;
> With claims unjust he fann'd the raging fire,
> While myriads in the mad crusade expire.[57]

Irwin holds Europeans partly responsible for the ruins he sees around him, naming them "bigots" with "unjust" claims. But he also implies that authors like himself might help to revive Near Eastern culture, in much the same way his sonnet to Charlotte Smith argued that his writing in Canton and Macau woke China from an aesthetic slumber. "Far different then" those Christian crusaders were when compared to the Company's enlightened artists like himself.

Irwin's poetic assemblages, therefore, might be characteristic acts of cultural appropriation for national aggrandizement, but they are also something more. His travel poetry and narratives consistently argue that past examples, like those of Palmyra and Baghdad, and present ones, like the Ottoman Empire, should temper overzealous British imperialism and correct its aspirations. The inclusion of Ferdowsi, whom he names the "the lofty

Homer of the East," signals his attempt to use his complex attitudes toward the differing histories of orientalized spaces as a means of aligning himself with a pre-Islamic past (*Shahnameh*) rather than Islam's contestatory present (the Ottomans).[58] He warns about the dilemma of competing with other empires for the future of British imperium. In this sense Irwin's worry is not that London may eventually become desolate and unartistic, like Baghdad or Palmyra, but that Britain may create those desiccated cities elsewhere by unwittingly eliminating the aesthetic possibilities of the places it occupies. It is more important to him that they create the Madras Lyceum than another version of Pompey's Pillar.

By combining the past and the present, Irwin's poetry connects different places on the globe, making them relational in the same way its artifacts are. The histories of these locations can be detached and made analytically new again by their mobility. The aim of his travel writing is to turn the dialectic of past and present, of antiquity and modernity, into a means of assessing the consequences of empire formation. Irwin is able at once to situate himself as the inheritor and regenerator of earlier cultural and artistic histories by collecting its objects and recording his assemblage of them in literary texts.[59] But rather than integrate these objects into a version of the "imperial sublime" that always sees colonies as in need of improvement, Irwin instead portrays ruins as a repeated series of interconnected cautions.[60] The objects that he gathers are valuable because of the contexts in which they were found, and they remain valuable because in being appropriated and deterritorialized, they carry that context with them rather than render it decorative or inert. He assembles these artifacts into a new framework whose primary focus is soliciting readers' encounters with the larger history that they represent. The objects form a macrostructure that has an obvious global and imperial dimension to it but is manifested as a set of discrete, intricately linked associations. The same patterns repeat from his travel writing, from his aesthetics of vagrancy, and from the cultural militancy of the Madras Lyceum, in which the conventional image of the "dying ember" blown back into flame is an explicit opposition to the story told by the ruins of the Near East's pre-Islamic empires.

Collaboration and Interimperial Assemblages

Irwin's pursuit of his decades-long project to rejuvenate English literature from Asia required robust collaborations and exchanges across oceanic networks but also within local and regional ones. While readers located in Britain remained the primary exponent of his literary hopes, Irwin also sought to develop audiences in India. He argued for the innovation of his verse (and of his authorship) by emphasizing that he wrote from Asia, demonstrating with his epigraphs, translations, and sketches how his travels rooted him in a distant past and a multi-imperial present, even as he worked in largely conventional genres. He understood the dilemma of being an anglophone author distant from a Britain-centered reading world. Curating his portable literary reputation required imaginative associations, like those found in his poem to Charlotte Smith, and more concrete collaborations that depended on the mobility of texts, especially books and correspondence. He desired literary success in Britain but comprehended that India offered an advantage for a writer in the late eighteenth-century marketplace. In an unpublished poem to his wife he laments the difficulties of sustaining such a continent-crossing reputation, promising that "no subject borrow'd from an orient Clime" or "Pagan's Spirit mounting to the Sky, / Pure, tho' misled" will "obtrude upon thy time."[61] In another letter he laughed that an epic poem, the *Ruins of Madura*, would meet "the objection which critics may start to the barbarous names of Indostan [India]."[62] But, he insists, if the poem were "devoid of oriental terms," as his critics would like, its insights might "equally be applied to the ruins and gardens of Europe," something he wanted to avoid.[63] He sought to write poetry that was unique to the place, even if that place seemed to extend beyond an immediate geographical location into the deep time of the imperial past.

To understand the portable reputation of Anglo-Indian authors like Irwin requires understanding those social relations that permitted the "international circulation of books [that] begin to foster a transnational sensibility of local differences."[64] In Irwin's case "circulation" was facilitated primarily by William Hayley, who acted as a correspondent, collaborator, and liaison to publishers in London while Irwin operated in India's market. Irwin sent Hayley works by packet ship and often apologized for the "trouble" they might cause him in overseeing their publication.[65] He empowered Hayley to make necessary "revisions and amendments" before the poems were "sent to the press," and he was thrilled when Hayley commended his poetic descriptions of Baghdad, remarking "what effect the sight of the Tigris and Euphrates with the august ruins upon their banks" may have on poetry "the Event must determine," referring to the publication of his poems.[66] Even from afar, he hoped his Indian poems would contribute immediately to public discussions in Britain. Another letter to Hayley included an "Ode on the Death of Hyder Ally," referring to the British antagonist, Haidar Ali, the Muslim king of Mysore. Irwin hoped Hayley could publish the poem while its subject, the second Anglo-Mysore War, was still "recent in the minds of the public."[67] In yet another letter Irwin notes that he has sent a copy of this same ode—for safety and redundancy—with a fellow Company merchant who was traveling through Bombay and Basra back to Britain in hopes that it could appear quickly "to have purpose."[68]

But he was careful of his literary reputation within the Indian subcontinent as well. He tried to persuade his publisher, Dodsley, about the advantages of "sending out an edition of my works to the several Presidencies" of India, referring to Calcutta, Madras, and Bombay. Irwin assured Dodsley that he was "convinced that curiosity and knowledge of me would get them off." But Dodsley, Irwin gripes, sent only "half a dozen" copies because he was "above taking advice."[69] Irwin sold the manuscript of his travel account, *A Series of Adventures*, to Dodsley in 1780 for two hundred copies of the eventual printed work, perhaps to distribute them himself in India.[70] Irwin believed (probably correctly) that he understood better than did Dodsley how the topicality and quality of his writing and his status as an EIC merchant would provide access to the lucrative marketplace of India, which, as we saw in chapter 1, accounted for nearly 20 percent of British book exports by the 1770s.[71]

The "curiosity" that made authors like Irwin attractive to British audiences seems to have reverberated through India's colonial locales as well. Irwin published an "Ode to the Nile" that drew from his travels through Egypt in a 1781 issue of the *India Gazette, or Calcutta General Advertiser*, which is noteworthy because Irwin was never stationed in Calcutta.[72] It was one of the few poems attributed to an identifiable author in that newspaper, and Irwin likely pursued it because it would expand his reputation among readers in India at a moment when there was no newspaper in Madras. Months later, the *India Gazette* published an appreciation of Irwin's poem from a lieutenant in Madras that refers to Irwin as an "ingenious Bard!" and mentions his earlier publications, suggesting that his London-printed poems were read in India as well.[73] While Irwin worried that "amid the din of Arms, and the toils of business," he had little time in "bringing of these fugitive poems to their present state," he also seems to have recognized that his employment as a colonial administrator contributed to the creation of his verse and to his mobile reputation. For Irwin, the profit of his commercial obligations was access to those "orient Clime[s]" that seemed to be so useful as the subject for poetry and the home of his closest readers.[74]

The significance of Irwin's career is not the typical story of how print aided British colonialism, although it reveals how empire assisted his reputation-making. Colonial administration provided him with monetary support and with subjects attractive to English audiences. It forced him to travel throughout the world but also offered new locations that he converted into his translocal poetics. He embodied the contradictions of an Anglo-Indian author, and he illustrates why his literary successors, like Sir William Jones and Anna Maria, the Della Cruscan poetess of Calcutta whom I document in the next chapter, intrigued London audiences with their novelty. Unusual identities and far-flung subject matter created sustainable literary reputations for Anglo-Indian authors.

Mary Favret thinks that competition between the British and other empires—both contemporaneous ones (like the Ottomans) and those long past (like Rome and Carthage)—required the British to adopt a "position beyond the contemporaneous: a universalizing and transhistorical view of their role in the world."[75] Irwin's career shows something else: imperial authors may have been transhistorical, but they were more translocal than universal, assembling together the particular places of the globe, themselves portals to lessons learned from the art and ruins of empires and states long gone. His writing and drawing accessed the global "deep time" of the classical Mediterranean, Qing China, and the Muslim Near East, which in turn allowed him to envision the world's imperial sovereignties and ethnoreligious orders as versions of his own artistic revival. Recovering these political and social contexts cannot begin without recognizing those affiliations beyond the immediacy of the local or the impositions of the global and imperial. It means turning instead toward "interimperial assemblages," with their overlapping sedimentation of time, place, and textuality, that form the bedrock of Irwin's artistic beliefs. His poetry thematizes the distances of those separations, presenting them as an excitingly alien yet intelligible account of foreign locales. The vagrant publics and spectral historical audiences that his literature conjures were not just a shared space for himself and his fellow administrators who exchanged writing and passed books and letters to one another. It was also the unstable relations of authors and audiences designed to be constantly in process, altering and being reshaped by the mobility and elasticity required for making an artistic reputation in anglophone Asia.

CHAPTER FOUR

Undoing Britain in Bengal

This chapter extends my examination of translocal poetics by focusing on two authors who were essential to late eighteenth-century Calcutta's growing literary scene: the orientalist scholar and jurist Sir William Jones, and the pseudonymous "Anna Maria," whose collection of poems provoked celebrations from Calcutta reviewers about the vibrancy of Bengal's anglophone literary culture. Jones, who was Anglo-India's most lauded eighteenth-century author, arrived in Calcutta from England in 1784 to take up a position on the Supreme Court of Bengal.[1] While in Calcutta, he composed imitations of Sanskrit hymns and wrote numerous letters about the nature of British dominion over India arguing that India's native inhabitants should be governed by their own laws.[2] At the same time, a woman named Anna Maria published a collection of poetry to acclaim in Calcutta, subsequently selling it in London. I have paired the two here because their translocal literary and cultural identities define the "new institutions of sociality" of late eighteenth-century British Bengal.[3] Although the debate about the identity of Anna Maria continues, the two poets' translocalism results from the interpenetration of seemingly antithetical spaces and extended temporalities. They serve as a representative couple for literary Calcutta because each experimented with several versions of the local as a way to transcend geographical and temporal differences.

"The term local and its derivatives, locality and localism," Mike Featherstone notes, "have generally been associated with the notion of a particular bounded space with its set of close-knit social relationships based upon strong kinship ties and length of residence."[4] In this chapter I propose an alternative to this definition of *localism*, with its implicit opposition of the global and the local, by focusing on those "close-knit social relationships" that paradoxically are experienced across the vast distances and extended temporalities that define translocalism. Jones imagines India as a way to rejuvenate British literature, which he found stodgy and stale, calling Sanskrit a "fountain head" that antedates the classical cultures of Greece and Rome and from which new inspiration could be drawn.[5] Anna Maria takes up this "fountain head" in her verse, mixing current literary trends like Della Cruscanism, a fashionable movement active in 1780s London, with representations of colonial India and Hindu Brahmins. Her translocal poetry provokes excitement about what the Calcutta newspaper proprietor William Duane called her "anglo-asiatic taste," yet it also reveals the difficulties of participating in the rapid cultural change of England from a place as removed as Bengal.[6] Jones's belief in British liberty and his advocacy for governing Indians according to their local laws, together with Anna Maria's comingling of Della Cruscanism's extended sociability with depictions of Hinduism, demonstrate that translocalism muddies the prevailing image of India as an anglicized domain imitative of English cultural fashions.

Pursuing these kinds of connections requires an "unthinking . . . of national identity" but also of "nationalist historiography and of the European exceptionalism that underpins the dichotomy between tradition and modernity," in David Porter's estimation.[7] In that they articulate alternative versions of localism, Jones and Anna Maria pull against the gravitational force of national culture to describe Anglo-India as originating out of a wide range of translocal exchanges. They illustrate that the translocal in eighteenth-century India had both expansive and contracting geographical and temporal dimensions, especially in those instances when they imagine ways to span the vast spatial disconnection between Britain and India. The translocalism of their writing cannot be thought of as purely geographical or contiguously constrained (*this* city, *that* region), nor can it be thought of as extending only to the small and space-bounded communities of Anglo-India. Scholars are comfortable describing national and transnational literary interactions as cultures meeting in middle grounds or in the "contact zones" of the globe's intercultural borderlands, but what about those geographical and social categories that do not fit within our notions of national literary production or the peripheral and provincial?[8] To understand the compositions of Jones and Anna Maria requires applying the lessons of translocalism, a category of analysis that might reveal other elements of literary and institutional artistic production ignored by those looking for the more common vocabulary of nation, borderland, and periphery. Translocalism pushes us to think about connections that creatively transcend space and time and therefore must be explored, as with Benedict Anderson's definition of the nation, according to the style by which they are imagined.[9]

A "British Brahma": Sir William Jones and the Politics of Translocalism

One striking example of this style appears in what is now probably the best-known of Jones's compositions, his 1785 poem "Hymn to Náráyena." This poem is one in a series of intricate and dense English verse adaptations of Sanskrit *vedas*, and its broad topic is the collision of ideas about poetic creation and the divine. Kate Teltscher argues that Jones wrote this poem for an audience in Britain, which meant he was more concerned with finding ways to "minimize" its "cultural dissonance" by demonstrating the "ease with which Indian myths can be absorbed into the English literary tradition," making it an "exercise in poetic appropriation."[10] Jerome McGann included Jones's "Hymn to Náráyena" as the first entry in his *New Oxford Book of Romantic Period Verse* (1993) to argue that the influences of the British Romantic period were wider than the stylistic innovations of the *Lyrical Ballads* and the political controversies of the French Revolution, extending all the way to the "renaissance" brought about by Indian orientalism.[11] Thomas Trautmann suggests Jones's translations and language learning were an "ethnological project" rather than a literary or linguistic one: an attempt to produce a synthetic origin of the differentiated populations of the world and to demonstrate its force through writing.[12] Tony Ballantyne understands Jones's translations to be part of a "comparative framework" that reconciled a "local" Indian culture with the "pattern of human history at the global level" that eventually produced the idea of Aryan culture.[13]

To their understandings I would add that Jones's writing was also a product of the surging Anglo-Indian print world. Jones composed the "Hymn to Náráyena" at the same time as he was composing other similar Sanskrit-inspired imitations with the assistance of fellow orientalists from the Asiatick Society of Bengal, particularly Charles Wilkins, who collaborated on the first Bengali printed book, *A Grammar of the Bengal Language* (1778) and was the first English-language translator of the Bhagavad Gita. His poems were published and circulated in India before they were received in Britain. He asked the East India Company printer Francis Gladwin to run copies for distribution to friends; afterward, it was included in a volume printed in Calcutta.[14] A contemporaneous poetic celebration of Jones printed in the *Calcutta*

Gazette "By a Person Unknown" compares Jones to a "British Brahma" and a "Pundit" (referring to *pandits*, Hinduism's Brahminical scholars). Jones, this anonymous author hopes, could "reclaim us—for our guilt atone; / Bid India's nations pardon all our wrongs."[15]

Jones's other poetic endeavors, typically imagined for a British audience, often started in necessarily local contexts. His translation *Sacontalá, or the Fatal Ring* (1789) reworks a fifth-century CE Sanskrit drama, *Shakuntala* by Kalidasa, about an eponymous rural maiden and her nearly tragic relationship with a king, Dushyanta, a tale derived from the ancient Indian epic the Mahabharata. It was meant to be an "authentick picture of old Hindu manners" from the "Shakspear of India."[16] *Sacontalá* was published and offered for sale by Joseph Cooper, who ran the *Calcutta Chronicle*, with its profits devoted to the "relief of insolvent debtors" in the city, confirming the generosity of Bengal's gentry elite (Jones) and merchant printers (Cooper) and their strong connection to the place.[17] Although *Sacontalá* has come to be seen as a crucial text for understanding Hindu culture and an inspiration for pan-European Romanticism, its first function was as a Calcutta publishing and charity event.[18]

Jones's local publishing confirms the "intellectual diversity of Calcutta" during the 1780s, in Michael Franklin's apt description, but also the self-conscious defensiveness of a European community that was already aware of the deleterious effects of the colonial apparatus it was creating.[19] The local response to Jones's printing abolishes notions of near and far, of familiar and alien, by drawing the British and the Brahminical into the same orbit. It imagines poetry and translation as orientalist appreciation but also an atonement for guilt and a pardon for "our wrongs," which is an astonishing admission of culpability at an early moment of Indian colonialism and an impossible enthusiasm about the power of Anglo-Indian literature.

Rediscovering Liberty

The local circumstances of Jones's imitations and translations show that his publications, and the responses to them, had political valences, not just artistic inspirations. Intervening in politics was a persistent motive in Jones's writing career. Before he arrived in India, Jones demonstrated a passion for social justice, pro-American sympathies, and a disdain for what he perceived as oppressive monarchy.[20] He turned to India, America, and Wales for new models of political liberty, even as each of them offered ambivalent prospects for its discovery.[21] (Jones, for example, described his appointment as a legal administrator of EIC colonialism in India as his scheme to become wealthy enough to avoid the need for patronage and reform the system; he hoped—naively—that Indian wealth would lead to personal and political independence.)[22]

These models complicate the assertions of Said and others that Jones's orientalism is simply an extension of the imperatives of empire. Said is accurate when he describes Jones as "codifying, tabulating, comparing" the "Orient with [the] Occident," but the effect of these actions was not always to "domesticate" the Orient, as Said claims.[23] By connecting India with Wales and America, Jones seeks clues to the divergent futures of these places within the British Empire, establishing affinities among what we now think of as fundamentally dissimilar colonial peripheries.

Jones had already begun to reinvent the ties between British and Indian traditions before he even arrived in India, sketching out a lengthy epic poem that he hoped would lock the two ancient traditions together. He composed the poem, titled *Britain Discovered*, while he sailed aboard the *Crocodile*.[24] He drew on his knowledge of Celtic druidic culture and his experience of Welsh politics to mediate the relationship between Britain and India.[25] Linking Celticism with British India was not uncommon, since the "Celtic Revival and the Oriental Renaissance have complex cultural, ethnological, political and poetical interconnections."[26] The nationalist resistance to Britain in Scotland and Wales was intensified, Franklin argues, by "Britain's exposure to Eastern mythologies."[27] Jones borrowed from these tensions to craft a connection between Britain and India as translocal and temporally transcendent, often routing it through his experience with Wales. The republican tinge of his political sympathies and his emphasis on liberty and suffrage were indebted to his Welsh origins, as Franklin has shown, particularly Jones's "love of liberty" and his longing for independence.[28] Wales served as a primary example of his principle that the struggle for independence was an "inseparable property of happiness."[29] Celticism represented a unique cultural tradition that ostensibly had resisted Roman invasion but recently had been suppressed by the centralization of power in a state dominated by England. Jones repeatedly advocated for a degree of Welsh autonomy within Britain, and he left for India disappointed about what he perceived as the increasing curtailment of rights.[30]

The status of Wales during the eighteenth century, however, was uncertain. Officially annexed by the English Crown in 1536, Wales was the earliest constituent unit of what became Great Britain and thus was a culturally distinct region within a larger nation. These ambiguities about the status of Wales and its role in British overseas colonialism begin to explain the affinities among Jones's advocacy of Wales, his orientalist studies in India, and his general principles about British liberty. He was an enthusiastic admirer of Britain's overseas colonies, which appeared to him as still undeveloped and therefore not yet corrupted by greed and luxury, as he believed Parliament was. While advocating for a position in India, he felt certain he was "capable of doing some good in Asia to the miserable natives, and I should like to see the country, and give the finishing stroke to my oriental knowledge; but be assured . . . that, if the *system* of government, which has insulted common sense and manliness for the last twenty years, be unchangeable or unchanged, *I will not grow old in England*."[31] Jones writes that he lobbied for the position on the Bengal Supreme Court because he hoped to have "some prospect of contributing to the happiness of millions or at least of alleviating their misery, and serving my country essentially, whilst I benefited my fellow-creatures."[32]

This idea of "serving" his country while benefiting his "fellow-creatures" was an extremely difficult balance to sustain. He saw similarities between the suppression of Wales and the "miserable" situation of India's populace.[33] Yet while in India he equivocates about his earlier radical positions, at times perceiving Indians as undeserving of liberty or freedom. "Hindus," he worries, "are incapable of civil liberty; few of them have any idea of it; and those, who have, do not wish it. They must (I deplore the evil, but know the necessity of it) they must be ruled by an absolute power; and I feel my pain much alleviated by knowing the natives themselves as well as from observation, that they are happier under us [the British] than they were or could have been under the Sultans of Delhi or petty Rajas."[34] Although Jones arrives in India with hopes for "alleviating" this misery, he eventually comes to believe that British administration, though not like the "happiness" of independence that he insists on for Wales, is better than the despotism of the Delhi Sultanate (c. 1200–1500 CE) that preceded the Mughal Empire in northern India or the Hindu kingdoms ("petty Rajas") that populated the south.[35]

Jones's disillusionment with the republican potential of India was accentuated by his fascination with America, which he believed offered an alternative model of governance based on notions of colonial manliness. In one letter, written during the controversy over American independence, he enthuses that in America "every man among them is a soldier, a *patriot*—Subdue such a people! The king may as easily conquer the moon or wear it in his sleeve."[36] Jones identified with the American Revolution, remarking that he'd rather be a "peasant with freedom" than a prince, exclaiming violently that he wished "every elector of Britain had as bright a bayonet as mine."[37] His enthusiasm aroused rumors that he might relocate to America to help write the new nation's Constitution.[38] With his adulation of America Jones sets the terms of liberty and independence within the logic of patriotism, political separation from Britain, and soldierly masculinity.

Jones connects this patriotic masculinity to the enhancement of the arts. In "The Muse Recalled" (1781), a poem that warns about the erosion of British liberties, Jones laments that the Muse has discovered a new home "beyond the vast Atlantick deep" in America, where "Truth, Justice, Reason, Valour, / . . . seek a purer soil, a more congenial sky."[39] Such manliness and "purer soil" distinguishes America from India; in one letter he hopes that Americans would not become like "the deluded, besotted Indians . . . who would receive Liberty as a curse instead of a blessing."[40]

Of course, there were significant differences between America and India. Britain's American colonies were settled by emigrating Europeans whose rapid economic and population expansion drove the growing dominance of an anglophone world, while India possessed a smaller population of European-descended men and women compared to the massive native and country-born population. Racial and gender differences are conspicuous in Jones's geopolitical ruminations, and they reinforce the perceived difference between Britain's settler colonies and its Asian possessions, which reverberate in the common stereotypes of Hindus as feminized and docile and white Americans as patriotic and manly.[41]

Where does Wales fit within this racialized and gendered calculus of anglophone colonialism? As a suppressed population of Britain, the Welsh may have been perceived by Jones as in danger of being "besotted," as Hindus ostensibly were, rather than being as fiercely independent as the Americans. And without ever advocating directly for Welsh revolt, his racialized and sexualized thinking about government provokes unintended and surprising affinities between seemingly divergent colonial groups. James Mill, in his *History of British India* (1817), dismissively compares Hindus and Highland Scots as backward, recalling an earlier derisive charge by Samuel Johnson that Highlanders were more like Eskimos or South Africans than they were like the English.[42] David Armitage argues that "constitutional liberty and imperial expansion seemed to be necessarily incompatible" to many Whigs, and Jones likewise saw Hindus and the Welsh as in the similar position of being constrained by English domination.[43] Therefore, despite his racist assessment of Hindu character, Jones creates shared political sympathies between the Welsh, who look for the "happiness" of independence, and Hindus, who though "besotted" still seem to provoke Jones's interest in cultivating liberty and the alleviation of their suffering. Jones actively considers different political trajectories for the subdued states and suppressed nationalisms of Wales and India that are fascinating for the contradiction and indecision they introduce into his political values.

Jones's ambivalent politics influence his translocal poetics, which exhibit a novel form of Celticism that connects Wales and India. The plan for his epic poem *Britain Discovered*, for example, elucidates supposedly ancient connections between Britain and India.[44] Although little of the poem was ever completed or published, his description of the poem's plot offers a variation on the popular rumor that Britain was settled by ancient Phoenicians.[45] As the poem's hero, Britan, seeks out a new home with a group of settlers, gods from numerous cultures, including India, conspire to deter his travel to the British coast. This is fundamentally a Celtic myth of Britain's origin that Jones substantiates by mentioning Roman historians and supposedly Phoenician monuments found in Ireland.[46]

Jones's peculiar Indo–Celtic–Near Eastern origin story of Britain knits together cultures and locales that sometimes even he dismissed in other contexts. While he defines Hindus in his letters as by nature perpetual slaves, in his poetry he gives their deities a fundamental role in the foundation of Britain. In one episode Ganga, the deity of the Ganges, addresses a council of Indian gods that has been convened in the Himalayas. She advises "the most vehement opposition" to the foundation of Britain that although it will "prove the origin of a wonderful nation," it will also "possess . . . her [the Ganges] . . . , profane her waters, mock the temples of the Indian divinities, appropriate the wealth of their adorers, [and] introduce new laws, a new religion, a new government."[47] In the final book of the poem Jones describes the "nuptials of *Britan* and *Albione*, or allegorically, of *Royalty* and *Liberty* united in the constitution of *England*."[48] The marriage is presided over by a Celtic druid, who predicts "the glories of the country, and its disasters," and "recommends the government of the *Indians* by their own laws," a peculiar addition to their nuptial vows.[49] The slippery collision of the country's namesake "Britan" with Jones's mention of the "constitution of *England*" only exacerbates the poem's political and geographical intertwining of different places, traditions, and temporalities, where an ancient wedding comments on eighteenth-century imperial politics.

Anne-Julia Zwierlein sees this poem as an example of literature preempting the future "demise of empire" by imagining it as already having been defeated in the past.[50] This accords with the general trend, beginning in the late eighteenth century, toward "imperial liberalism," which sought to resolve an expanding empire with devotion to English liberties.[51] But I think the complications of these poems arise from producing an alternative imperial history in which Indians are governed by their own laws. Jones is not like his successor Percy Bysshe Shelley, who invests the East with potential for a "revolutionary desire" that had been frustrated in Europe.[52] He is more ambivalent about the role of the British in India, though *Britain Discovered* suggests an enduring relationship between the two locations defined by connections across space and time.

That a Celtic druid has any position on the governance of India exemplifies Jones's interest in these kinds of translocal and transhistorical linkages. Jones situates the action of the poem to "around" 883 BCE, after the fall of Troy, meaning the Celtic druid speaks about political events thousands of years in the future.[53] Linking localities across the globe thus necessitates the creation of temporal proximities as well, much as it did for Irwin's Near Eastern ruins and relics that I described in the previous chapter. Retrospection and prophecy are an essential element of the poem and are integral to its geopolitical ties. It is noteworthy that in the poem Britain's relationship with India dates from before Britain was even a nation: these two regions have *always* been tethered together, meant for each other. From Jones's vantage in Calcutta, the administrative work of late eighteenth-century orientalism could be seen as simply another iteration of their bond.

Many of Jones's Indian poems reconsider empire from the vantage of someone who was an instrument of British dominion and proximate to India's inhabitants. His poetry redefines a global imperial venture as translocal and regional. The strange reverse chronology imagined in *Britain Discovered* is a version of what Srinivas Aravamudan called a "temporal postcolonial form": a form of "archaic modernity" in which, in Jones's telling, the past is rediscovered to point the way to an aspirational future.[54] But the curtailment of Welsh liberties, the revival of Celticism, and the femininity of Hindus offer warnings about their futures. Instead, it is in America that Jones sees a system and a setting for securing independence and rights. His politics of interconnection are located in diverse geographies (America, India, and Wales), differing temporalities (Britain's Celto-Phoenician past and contemporary Indian governance), and genres (poetry, political tracts, legal customs) that Jones affiliates without explicitly appealing to notions of nationalism or transnationalism. Instead of seeking to anglicize India or to form an internally coherent aboriginal British tradition dating back to antiquity, he weaves India into Celtic and British history and contrasts that history with the contemporary American colonies. Jones anticipates with his translocalism the globally interconnected twentieth-century British Empire that is, in Elleke Boehmer's vivid description, "at once decentred and multiply centred, a network, one might say, of interrelating margins."[55]

A Della Cruscan in Calcutta

Whereas Jones drew on Celtic revivalism, Hindu religious traditions, and discourses of revolution and republicanism to craft his translocal poetics, Anna Maria drew on one of the most current English literary trends—Della Cruscanism—for her inspiration. The Della Cruscan movement originated among British expatriates in Italy but became prominent in the late 1780s when Robert Merry published "The Adieu and Recall to Love" under the name "Della Crusca" in a London newspaper, *The World*. His highly sentimentalized plea to "let me, let me love again" despite the pain of previous romantic failures incited numerous responses from other authors, all of whom adopted pseudonyms as he did.[56] The ensuing publications formed an ongoing poetic dialogue about life and love.[57] The movement was fashionable, short-lived, and potentially dangerous for its emphasis on emotion and its sympathies with the French Revolution. Merry was made into a proto-Byronic hero, an object of women's affections, and a target of conservative authors and politicians.

Anna Maria participated in this literary fashion from afar, adopting a pseudonym and imitating the movement's style. Her Della Cruscanism, Mary Ellis Gibson suggests, creates a "sense of immediacy," even as her poetry charts the "inability to create poetry in the metropolitan moment," an "estrangement from the metropole" that is both "limiting and productive."[58] Rather than demonstrate the inability to exist within the metropolitan moment or an estrangement (even a productive one), Anna Maria's translocal poetics reveal an unexpected scope and flexibility with eighteenth-century conceptualizations of the translocal and the colonial. In bringing together London and Calcutta, Anna Maria illustrates the intersecting traditions that forge eighteenth-century Anglo-Indian literature. She puts Della Cruscanism in an Indian framework, turning it into an artistic movement anchored in many locations and derived from current as well as ancient cultural customs, in much the same way that Jahan Ramazani describes twentieth-century black British poets as "dislocat[ing] the local into translocation" to "see the metropolis afresh."[59]

What would it mean for scholars to detach the techniques of translocalism from the tactics of racial and cultural oppression that have been seen as governing relationships between colonizers and colonized and instead make it a feature of colonizing modernity, as I describe in my introduction? And what happens when those authors who see the metropolis afresh do so from the colonies that they inhabited as privileged rather than oppressed participants, as in the case of Anna Maria?

Of course, when *The Poems of Anna Maria* was published in 1793 in Calcutta, the city had not yet become the administrative capital known as the "City of Palaces," as it would in the nineteenth century. Nonetheless, it was already massive in population, avowed to be the center of Britain's rapidly expanding presence in Asia. From a population of about fifteen thousand in 1704, Calcutta grew to nearly two hundred thousand by 1780, with the central city along the river dominated by white Europeans and their servants. Surrounding them were native Indian as well as Armenian and Jewish neighborhoods, though some recent scholars suggest the city was more like a "gray" town of racial mixing akin to that shown in Thomas Daniell's engraving of a 1780s Calcutta street with whites and nonwhites, including in the foreground what appears to be a Western-dressed man and an Indian woman sharing a parasol (fig. 12).[60]

Calcutta was also a crucial hub in the regional multilingual literary culture of Asian anglophony, an innovator of newspaper publication, and the locus of Company-supported art and print.[61] Just in the year she published her volume of poems, printers in Calcutta also released almanacs, a dictionary of "Bengalese and English" that claimed "to assist beginners in learning the Bengal language," spelling-books, and an essay concerning "thoughts on duelling." Anna Maria's poetry competed with a "heroic epistle" of the recent war against Tipu Sultan in southern India and a first-person prose narrative of the same conflict "written chiefly in the field, amidst the scenes."[62] Her volume was purchased by many of Calcutta's primary intellectual and literary figures, such as the future governor-general John Shore, the Supreme Court justice John Hyde, and even Jones himself, but also by numerous

Figure 12. Thomas Daniell, plate 9 from *Views in Calcutta* (1788). Looking along a broad street in central Calcutta where people with parasols stroll or ride on an elephant. Hand-colored aquatint. Courtesy of SPL Rare Books.

low-level Bengal Army lieutenants, printers like William Duane (who championed her verse), and Joseph Cooper (for his Calcutta circulating library).[63] Also among the subscribers are thirty-three women, nearly all of them married.

Women were a small population of Europeans in Anglo-India, but Anna Maria was not the only female author there. Kathryn Freeman has described the interactions between women writers and the Asiatick Society of Bengal, an institution whose discourse (orientalism) is often seen as separate from women.[64] Newspaper verse was another venue in which women seem to have access to publication, though the evidence for how many is inconsistent since many of the contributors claim to act as intermediaries for women who did not want to submit material themselves or did not imagine themselves as authors. However, selections from *The Poems of Anna Maria* appeared in at least two of Calcutta's weekly newspapers, the *Asiatic Mirror* and the *Calcutta Morning Post*. Duane's newspaper, *The World*, was so excited by the appearance of her poetry that it lauded her as marking a turning point for Anglo-Indian arts, one that showed the "excellence" of literature in Bengal so much that "it might be more *correct* in addressing [her] as a tenth muse," and devoting a large portion of that issue to a discussion of her aesthetics.[65]

The two Della Cruscan poems in her collection provoked enormous interest among readers both in India and Britain and may have been inspired by the republication of Robert Merry's work in Anglo-Indian newspapers.[66] The expansive aesthetic ideology of Della Cruscanism probably appealed to an author like Anna Maria, who was positioned in India. As John Mee argues, Della Cruscanism sought "an expanded and potentially limitless public sphere" of "extended sociability."[67] William Gifford, the Della Cruscans' most savage critic, worried about the possibility of this limitless, anonymous public sphere, claiming that the movement was a disease so virile that "not a day passed without an amatory epistle . . . and a thousand other nameless names caught the infection."[68] Gifford's critique, when combined with Mee's analysis, explains why an aspiring poet in Calcutta might be so excited by the Della Cruscan movement. The "nameless names" that worry Gifford are precisely the feature that allows for an extended sociability and a poetics of pseudonymity that forms new identities through intimate collaborations across vast distances. The Della Cruscan movement was an ideal model for an author like Anna Maria because it allowed her to craft a translocal poetics that would link her existence in Calcutta back to London's literary world while also succeeding within the contours of Calcutta's regional literary culture. She follows many of the conventions of the Della Cruscans in her poems, publishing her collection under a concealed name ("Anna Maria") that consciously recalls better-known Della Cruscan authors like "Anna Matilda" (the dramatist Hannah Cowley) or "Laura Maria" (the London poet Mary Robinson).

Her poetry also displays the highly sentimentalized verse that came to characterize Della Cruscanism. In her "Ode to the Memory of Della Crusca," Anna Maria eulogizes Merry, whom she incorrectly thought had died.[69] She implores Merry's ghost to "teach Me to grace thy magic Lyre" (24) so that she may "with wild and trembling Verse, / . . . deck the Plumes of DELLA CRUSCA'S Hearse!" (26). In her subsequent "Ode to Della Crusca" she rejoices that Merry is alive, feeling again the "proud impassion'd Glow, / Thro' every trilling Fibre flow" (45). She apprentices herself to him, asking him to "induct" her "through the hallow'd Glade" and to "lead" her to "drink the chaste Olympian Dews" (46) so that she might

> Derive from *Thee* the lucid Ray,
> That dignifies the modern Lay;
> My Muse with wild Ambition fire,
> And bid the burning Thought to Fame aspire.
> (47)

While feeling these wild, trembling, thrilling emotions, Anna Maria also makes her readers conscious of her distance from the movement and its center in London. She imagines India as an alternative route by which she could feel passion and pursue poetic inspiration and claims that she either will "bid the burning Thought to Fame aspire,"

> Or, I will stray by Night's pale Orb;
> Whose Beams the lesser Lights absorb:
> Where INDIA'S GOD in secret roves,
> Through the rich consecrated Groves;
> Where BRAHMA pours his pious Pray'r,
> To the religious, list'ning Air.
> And from the Fervor of his Lays,
> I'll weave a Wreath of magic Praise;
> Shall circle round thy crescent Brows,
> *Proud Token of far distant Vows!*—
> (47, emphasis in original)

In this model, Europe may be the burning sun, but India is the moon ("Night's pale Orb"), with its own set of inspirations and prerogatives. This passage establishes the possibility of fulfilling Della Cruscan imperatives of feeling, sentimentality, and apprenticeship in a network of extended sociability by listening to the "pious Pray'r" of the Brahmin and understanding the "Fervor of his Lays." With this fervor our speaker will "weave a Wreath of magic Praise" to Della Crusca that acts as a "*Proud Token of far distant Vows*": a token, that is, from across the world and from another cultural idiom, at least in spirit if not in form. Anna Maria reconfigures the Brahmin's passionate song into her English verse-offering, thereby substituting Calcutta for European inspiration and fame. Hindu traditions become both a source of inspiration in a multinodal poetic movement and a tribute to Della Cruscanism and its literary center in London, where her volume of poetry was eventually republished.[70]

This Indian-inflected Della Cruscanism requires invention and personal emotion to be immediately available between authors and readers, even at great distances. For example, while addressing her poems to Della Crusca, she also remarks:

> And should'st *Thou* e'er my hapless Verse peruse,
> Pause on the Line, and own the simple Muse;
> Say, that in Regions far from laurel'd Fame,
> MARIA wept o'er DELLA CRUSCA's name.
> (47–48)

The scenes of writing and reception accentuate the temporal and geographical distance between Calcutta and London, yet Anna Maria's weeping and readers' appreciation of her emotion, she hopes, will repudiate these differences and permit emotional effusions to cross space and time. Her contribution to the Della Cruscan movement is not so much to make it worldly—it already had origins in Italy and attachments to the French Revolution—but to theorize how these different locations allow emotions to be expressed at a distance. Jerome McGann claims that Della Cruscan writing came to such "rapid cultural dominance" because it "explicitly encouraged further writing, whether response or elaboration." The basic structure of the verse is erotic and connective, he claims, because it "proceeds by acts of intercourse that are at once perfectly immediate and purely imaginative."[71] Of course, they are "perfectly immediate" *because* they are "purely imaginative." Paradoxically, Anna Maria's distance from Merry and the Della Cruscan movement, which had crested in popularity five years before, make possible her feelings of immediate and intense connection.

These "acts of intercourse," moreover, are textual: they are facilitated by print's ability to distribute literary fashions widely and encourage authors like Anna Maria to participate virtually in fashionable British culture while overseas. It is easy to see how Anna Maria might feel remote from the London scene of Della Cruscanism, but her response was to turn that distance into novelty—into the possibility of seeing a metropolitan fashion afresh by rewriting it in "Regions far from laurel'd Fame." In this sense, as a Della Cruscan in Calcutta, she further confirms the importance of textual intercourse and of printed communication for the movement. When examined from the edges of Britain's empire, Della Cruscanism seems even more insistently concerned with what Mee describes as an extended public sphere and what McGann calls "response and elaboration." By following Della Cruscan conventions, Anna Maria not only makes herself part of the phenomenon but adapts it to the peculiarities of her surroundings. She is able to imagine an Indian Della Cruscanism as a translocal literary phenomenon.

The significance of this translocal poetry, and the literary identity that it necessitates, were especially evident to reviewers. Anna Maria's *Poems* was reviewed in at least half a dozen journals from London and Calcutta. The responses ranged widely. In one laudatory review the editors of *The World*—the Calcutta newspaper run by William Duane—proclaim that her poems illustrate the "degree of excellence to which printing has been lately brought in this country." The reviewer argues that her poetry was "a specimen that is at once honourable to anglo-asiatic taste in charming poetry, and elegant and correct printing."[72] That Anna Maria's printers, Archibald Thomson and Paul Ferris, "acquired their knowledge of the invaluable art [of printing] in this country" is only further evidence of Anglo-India's growing pride.[73]

In a facing page of *The World*, a correspondent named "Madone" included an encomium, "To Anna Maria," that cheers her for proving that poetry could be composed in India, despite what British critics might argue. Its author, perhaps Duane himself, remarks that while India "has been long held unpropitious to the muses," Anna Maria has "proved that to be a prejudice." He then goes on to say that if his praises are "favorably received," then other writers will be "encouraged to pursue the path of fancy and feeling," presumably composing poetry much as she does.[74] *The World* accepts that she is an Indian Della Crusca—a muse in her own right—who arouses passion in her readers and instructs them in the "path of fancy and feeling." Anna Maria combined "charming poetry" with Asian subjects, creating an "anglo-asiatic taste" indicative of the "excellence" of Calcuttan poetry. Her poetry, therefore, is undoubtedly the poetry of place, but it is of a place that, at least from the vantage of Duane, is insurgently competitive with England and London, which are thought to be both its aspiration and its progenitor. She is held up as someone who simultaneously confirms the specificity of a poetic locale and an example of an indigenous Anglo-Indian tradition even as she borrows heavily from the most current of Britain's literary trends and seeks to transcend that locality.

It is precisely this transport back and forth between Britain and India, between London and Calcutta, that is a theme of her collection. In her final poem, "Adieu to India," Anna Maria makes this transit an aspect of her translocal poetic career. In bidding farewell to India, she laments that she will leave "INDIA'S fertile plains, / Where *Brahma's* holy Doctrine reigns" (66); she also notes:

> I hasten to my NATIVE Shore,
> Where *Art* and *Science* blend their Lore:
> There *Learning* keeps her chosen Seat—
> A million Vot'ries at her Feet,
> Ambitious of the LAUREL BOUGH,
> To wind about their honor'd Brow.
> (66)

The reviewers at the *British Critic* worried that if Anna Maria's poems were successful, British poets might "emigrate" to India.[75] Despite their perhaps satirical concerns, Anna Maria acknowledges in "Adieu to India" that London remains the center of English poetry. She laments leaving India because it was there that she was encouraged in her verse-making, yet her success in Asia makes her hope for "future fame" in England, where "a million Vot'ries" vie for attention. In a sense her time in Calcutta was training and apprenticeship—to the Muse; to Della Crusca—before returning in hopes of further fame in Britain.

It was likely no surprise to her that the success of her collection in Britain was established by her identity as an Anglo-Indian poet, much as it was for Eyles Irwin. Eighteenth-century reviewers were interested in her poetry for much the same reason that I am: she presents the fascinating novelty of a Della Cruscan in Calcutta. Every reviewer of her poems notes that they were first published in Calcutta, and most of the reviews focus on her two Della Cruscan poems, even though there are over a dozen more conventional ones in her collection. Some critics, such as those from the *Monthly Review* in London, were unconvinced of the "anglo-asiatic" quality of her writing, remarking that it seemed "little influenced by the local habitation of the author" and not much different from other Della Cruscans.[76] For these reviewers Anna Maria's poems are not Indian enough. Reviewers, whether they appreciated her poetry or not, whether they saw it as an example of a rising "anglo-asiatic taste" or a fraud, were intrigued by a translocal literary identity that could reconcile London and Calcutta. They were curious to know what kind of imaginative literature was being written in eighteenth-century India, as scholars still are today.

Anna Maria's poems, therefore, thematize a translocal identity conscious of place as a marker of authorial persona and the requisite fashions and styles that attend to it. This style is constructed from numerous constituent parts, some of which are borrowed from overseas, others of which are drawn from more local settings. The Della Cruscan phenomenon provides her with a template for colonial authorship at a time when the English literary culture of Calcutta was still developing. Not only did she model successful poetry that works translocally between English fashion and Anglo-Indian adaptation, but she reveals some of the vocabulary used during the late eighteenth century to understand Calcutta's collaborative literary culture. Her poetry engages in international exchanges and relays, and she is keenly aware that the Della Cruscan imperative to conversation and poetic dialogue serves to unite different locales.

Anna Maria is an example of participating virtually in contemporary literary fashions from afar. Yet even as she participates, she becomes a peculiar example of Anglo-Indian artistic culture, working within multiple traditions, mapping them onto one another while thematizing the difficulties of doing so. Her translocalism made publishing opportunities available that might not exist without being in Calcutta and certainly were not readily available to Indians in Britain. In much the same language as Eyles Irwin used, when he argued for Madras as an "Indian Parnassus," and Jones used, when he described India as a "fountain head" for verse-making, Anna Maria becomes an exemplum of a new taste for newspaper publishers like Duane. Judith Pascoe has argued that the Della Cruscan tradition allowed women writers to assert themselves in the public sphere.[77] When adapted to Calcutta, Della Cruscanism also opens up the opportunity for the anonymous Anna Maria to be an example of a new colonial literature. Away from the "million Vot'ries" of London's chaotic literary scene, whose admiration seems to be her goal, a woman writer like Anna Maria could distinguish herself and contribute to the founding of its public sphere.

Forgetting Asia

Although the importance of Sir William Jones and Anna Maria differed considerably during their lives and their literary posterities, both sought out strategies to connect with audiences across great distances. For both, translocal poetics emphasizes impossible temporalities of global authorial identities rather than the spatial language of connected places. Translocalism, in this model, becomes an alternative to the current model of the local as closely knit communities bound in space and time. It also overcomes the balkanization in studies of the global and the local, which focus primarily on the twentieth century and attempt to determine if the local enables or resists the circulation of global capital, by synthesizing alternatives within complexly overlapping timelines.[78]

In the stadial theories of Enlightenment philosophers, non-European cultures were models of early stages of civilization. Poems like *Britain Discovered* take a different route, perceiving civilized British and besotted Hindus as united at their inception and linked throughout their histories. The supple coercive power of the implausibly lengthy temporal span of *Britain Discovered* is that it imagines this connection to exist even when the parties do not acknowledge it. Jones readily admits that this interconnected history is more "allegorical" than literal but nonetheless presents Britain and India as interdependent units, whether they like it or not.[79] He reconceptualizes the translocal connections of his modern literary aesthetic to be the prophetic fulfillment of relationships that had existed from the distant human past. Much like Irwin's Near Eastern relics, Jones's translocalism is transhistorical at its foundation. Likewise, Anna Maria finds in a Brahmin past a route to literary fame in contemporary Britain and turns the time lags that seem to make her distant from English fashions, such as when she mistakes Merry for having been dead long after this knowledge was out of date, into a testimony of her passion.

It is obvious that these authorial positions include customs of other cultures, appropriated to the forms of Anglo-Indian literature. Modern scholars are understandably reluctant to lend credence to authors' claims to be authentic agents of a new indigenous aesthetic that combines the Anglo and the Asiatic by conveniently pairing them in the mists of distant time, as Jones does, or by sympathizing with Brahminical songs and prayers as inspiration for English verse, as Anna Maria does. Suvir Kaul suggests that these authors "still thought of themselves as writing for a metropolitan audience" and worries that Anna Maria, in particular, represents "formulaic exercises in contemporary English poetics" that do not "suggest any elements of her experience of India" and contain "precious little" internationalism.[80] Mary Ellis Gibson sees Anna Maria as "foundering" and "stranded" away from metropolitan domains, an atomized figure who seems to be "talking to herself alone."[81]

But there was an enthusiastic audience for Anna Maria's literary productions. She, like Jones, contributed to Anglo-India's nascent literary institutions, though his contributions were undoubtedly considered more significant at the time. Still, for both authors the combination of cultural traits—the "anglo" and the "asiatic"; the "British" with the "Brahma"—was not simply an outlet for European ideas, nor was it merely a reservoir of authentic arts to be contributed to Europe's world centers of literary dissemination. When evaluated on their own terms, their poems emphasize temporal displacement and geographical movement for the construction of an anglophone literary aesthetic in India. Despite their different circumstances, to understand the literary outputs of Jones and Anna Maria requires recognizing that the deep time of Anglo-Indian verse-making operated against, not always in harmony with, the gravity of the metropolis.

The historical significance of these spatial-temporal recombinations is revealed by David Porter, who notes that a choice was made during the Enlightenment for Europeans to see themselves as exceptionally modern, unlike the rest of the globe. This epistemological shift necessitated an "instrumental amnesia" in which Europeans ignored the modernity of other cultures.[82] Yet if we think of translocalism as a means of aggregating and connecting geographical locales and cultural values across space and time, then we find precursors to Porter's call for scholars to "historicize this act of [European] forgetting."[83] In Jones we uncover at least one eighteenth-century author who historicizes this forgetting by unthinking the nation-state, temporalizing as much as spatializing its connections and countering the international politics of imperialism at the same time as he participates in it. The historical and aesthetic interconnection that occurs with the writing of Jones and Anna Maria offers an alternative to the rigid separation of English and Indian traditions and cultures eventually exemplified by Thomas Macaulay's 1835 "Minute on Indian Education," in which he calls for the creation of a "class" of Indians in origin but English in manners who would act as "interpreters" between the British and those "millions whom [they] govern."[84] To follow Porter's call to historicize forgetting, to appreciate the peculiar connections found in the translocalism of these two authors, necessitates that we describe the multiply located literary identities and imaginations of their writing, which neither wholly resists colonialism nor always celebrates it. In this uncomfortable mixture of complicity and critique we begin to see a place and time between globalism and localism and start to identify artistic traditions that acknowledged categories of comparative thinking that went beyond the nation long before the rise of scholarly transnationalism.

CHAPTER FIVE

Tristram Shandy in Bombay

What has been lost over the past two decades as scholars have emphasized geographical connectivity and intersection, rather than local roots and adaptability, in models of public-making and identity formation among Asia's British colonizers? As we have seen, peculiar identities emerged from the imagination of Anglo-Indian writers at the nascency of their literary institutions. By the beginning of the twenty-first century the identities formed out of European colonialism, whether in the Atlantic or the Indian Ocean world, were seen primarily as the result of reciprocal forces of knowledge exchange, imperial intimacies, and cultural hybridity. These schematic models, which visualize empire as a web of cosmopolitan actors, a "set of networks," or a series of connections represented as "dots and dashes" on the globe, have successfully opened up fresh analytical categories and new archives, especially in regard to gender.[1] Postcolonial gender studies and new imperial histories have examined global anglophone theater (Kathleen Wilson), hygiene and sexual regulation (Philippa Levine, Durba Ghosh), intimacy and subject formation (Anne McClintock, Ann Laura Stoler, Antoinette Burton and Tony Ballantyne, Mrinalini Sinha), and "travelling metaphors" (Elleke Boehmer), demonstrating that cultural identities crossed the diverse geographical and social boundaries of empire.[2] The result has been more attention to the identity as "a relation and a mode of differentiation" that involves agency and coercion, with the British national identity, in particular, seen as emerging from the oceanic networks that it helped to secure.[3]

Subdued within these models were the local identities created by members of those increasingly coherent regional colonial publics that I have described throughout this book. Their existence suggests it may be time for scholars to take more seriously the translocal and regional analysis of the

British Empire. Translocal regionalism offers an answer to the problem of how to understand the links among empire's different scales, not only how these scales construct colonial identities in racial and gendered frameworks but also how they explain the physical and rhetorical infrastructure of colonial cultural creation. Translocal regionalism asks for analysis that does not see the local or the regional as natural or inevitable but rather examines them as historical concepts that are contested and changing. It opens up imperialism from the inside, avoiding the tendency toward "internal homogenization" or the reification of categories that inevitably occurs with comparative thinking.[4]

The neglected interstices of translocalized colonial identity are the focus of this chapter, which examines the gendered representations of Bombay's literary publics and cultural spheres in the writing of one of its earliest participants, the author and Bombay Army officer James Romney (1745–1807). Throughout the late eighteenth century Romney involved himself in a staggering array of literary activities, which included composing poems for Bombay newspapers, drafting plays, and adapting English novels for Indian theatrical audiences. His career reveals how Bombay residents imagined themselves to be creating and participating in a semiautonomous literary culture that exceeded its European influences. Analyzing his corpus through the logic of translocalism and regionalism offers a new vantage on the role of women's society and sociability in the creation of what Mrinalini Sinha calls an "imperial social formation."[5]

Anglo-Indian women's sociability involves the interplay between codes of conduct and manners. It also involves the meeting places where human interactions occur and the literary genres that assess and describe the contours and significance of those interactions. Eighteenth-century sociability was organized around a culture of politeness. It drove the emergent "associational world," which replaced more rigid parish fraternities and trade guilds with voluntary gatherings in clubs and societies.[6] Peter Clark believes the sense of belonging fostered by these clubs and societies was "eminently exportable." He suggests that their imitation overseas was a means of distributing English cultural values throughout the British Empire.[7] Seema Alavi calls these exported societies "imperial assemblages," referring to the social networks that were instrumental for producing and maintaining colonial identities.[8] Mrinalini Sinha specifically names British India's social club as an "intermediate zone" between the metropolitan public spheres (defined primarily by the operations of reason and rational critique within civil society) and the indigenous customs of India.[9] She claims that India's exclusive clubs were a crucial part of "fashioning a white British self" that solidified overseas and looked back to the European homeland.[10]

Romney hints at different outcomes and alternative histories of South Asian social life than those described as the imperial assemblages of exclusive Anglo associations. He depicts artistic productions and public engagements of Anglo-Indian Bombay as flexible, fluid, and locally defined, often in conscious departure from European models. The associations found in Romney's writing are less like those specific members' clubs that Sinha focuses on in her scholarship or the scholarly societies and organizations that were also important for maintaining the artistic vibrancy of British India (such as the Madras Lyceum and the Asiatick Society of Bengal). Instead, he details a mixed society of visiting and assembly that was the primary domain of women's publicity.[11] Romney writes fluently about these domains and how they can rejuvenate two essential institutions of Bombay's literary publics: the newspaper and the theater. These infrastructures were vehicles for Romney's imagination of women's roles in the cultivation of Anglo-Indian civic and artistic life.

Romney's contributions to these communal ventures often reveal a distaste for Bombay dulled by meritless social stratification. He occasionally criticizes the hierarchies of the EIC armies, offering a differential from many of the other military men who were prominent authors in eighteenth-century Anglo-India, such as John Horsford, the Bengal Army officer and contemporary of Romney who, as Suvir Kaul notes, wrote gentlemanly verse that sought to turn martial India into "poetic ground."[12]

To revitalize these systems, Romney imagines an alliance with elegant Anglo-Indian women and "agreeable" gentlemen in a model that is at times loosely based on that of the EIC, which I describe in the first section. In the second section I show how the portrayal of women and native Indians in Romney's dramas rooted oceanic fashions in Anglo-Indian customs. I extend this argument to one of Romney's most ambitious adaptations, his rewriting of Laurence Sterne's *Life and Opinions of Tristram Shandy, Gentleman* (1761–67). In the final sections I turn to one of Sterne's literary inspirations, the India-born Company wife, Elizabeth Draper, who advocates for seeing affinities and intimacies between white and nonwhite women, much like those briefly represented in Romney's play.

To see imperial social formations as the result of translocal and regional forces, rather than local manifestations of global concerns, is to suggest new ways that imperial identities and publics are formed. A "global social analytic," as Sinha observes, can misrecognize the adjustments that were made in localized settings, even as it brings metropole and colony together.[13] Defining the components of what Romney calls Bombay's "metropolitical empire"—an urban sociable public dependent on women who fashion their own scene—adds to what Gillian Russell and Clara Tuite call the "alternative history of empire," which is focused less on war and commerce and more on intimacy and socializing. Sociability was an essential reservoir for Anglo-Indian literature and a distinct "form of cultural work" that, when examined more closely, uncovers more about the local and regional networks of Bombay's colonial inhabitants.[14]

Metropolitical Empire

James Romney was born in 1745 in England but did not arrive in India until 1777, when he was a middle-aged cadet in the Bombay Army (significantly older than the civilian employees, who typically started working in India at fifteen or sixteen). He is rarely recalled now except as the younger brother of the well-known British portraitist George Romney (and a distant cousin of 2012 US presidential candidate Mitt Romney).[15] George Romney included James in some of his early paintings, such as *A Conversation* (1766), which depicts him standing with a blank look amid statuary while another brother, Peter, gestures toward a page of mathematics (fig. 13).[16] James was the eighth of eleven children, ten of them boys and many of whom seem to have been pushed by economic necessity into Britain's imperial system, where fortune was unkind to them. Romney's older brothers William and Lawrence traveled to the West Indies in 1762, and both of them died there as young men. One of Lawrence's letters to his family from Antigua agonizes that he has not received any word from his family in four years, pleading, "I do not stay here by choice, and to be neglected in such a manner makes me very unhappy."[17]

Romney may have left England out of economic necessity as well. He recalls in one letter that he was a man of "many different climates" and in another that he was not an artistic "novice," which, combined with his later interest in writing plays, suggests that he may have pursued a career in London's theater and, failing at that, received an East India Company appointment to stabilize his finances, perhaps with the help of his brother George.[18] During his twenty-five years in India (until 1803) Romney rose steadily through the ranks from cadet to lieutenant colonel in the Bombay Army, generally as an officer among native infantry battalions.[19] His duties required

Figure 13. George Romney, *A Conversation (The Artist's Brothers Peter and James Romney)* (1766). James is standing. Courtesy of the Yale Center for British Art, Paul Mellon Collection.

frequent travel among the imperial outposts of western India; he was primarily stationed in Bombay but also resided in Surat, Calicut, and "Paulghautcherry" (also known as Palghaut and now as Palakkad), a fortress town in southwestern India, where he was commander from 1795 until 1800.[20] He fought in the third Mysore War against Tipu Sultan and was attached to an 1801 British expedition to Egypt and the Red Sea intended to blunt an anticipated advance by Napoleon on India that never materialized.[21]

George Romney's son, John, remembered his uncle James as "a man of gentlemanly demeanour," who "had a taste for literature, could write complimentary verses to the ladies, and trifle agreeably on the violin." On James Romney's death, John Romney inherited his papers, which included the numerous plays on Asian subjects "in so slovenly a hand," as his nephew called them, none of which have been examined until now.[22] Romney's archive offers an aperture into Bombay urbanity and sociability and gives some sense of how he engaged with Bombay's literary public and some evidence for how it responded to him. He seems to have written often and tenaciously to the city's just-founded newspapers and cultivated a personal relationship with them, agreeing in one note attached to a poem submitted to the editors of the *Bombay Gazette* that "neither you nor I are novices" in cultural matters and warning them about his poetic competitors whose words "convey no meaning."[23] Some of his poetry devised startlingly innovative syntax from the language of Hindu religious traditions. In a poem about inspiration, for instance, the speaker implores:

> You who from Brama claim your high descent
> To whom the Bramen Gods have wisdom lent
>   By you my Muse
>   By you My Muse is big . . . [24]

It is not clear to whom this poem is addressed, but it refers to gymnosophists, a Greek tradition that was syncretized with medieval European portrayals of India's Brahmins as naked ascetics.[25] But its repetition and syntax experiment with the incantatory aspects of Hinduism, perhaps devotionals in Tamil, a language Romney may have read and spoken.[26] Like Irwin's inspirational vagrancy, Jones's imperial prophecies, or Anna Maria's Brahminical affinities that I describe in other chapters, Romney's "big" Muse collected translocal and transhistorical influences, broadening the range of his writing while also infusing it with details specific to India.

The majority of his poems were conventional songs, pastorals, love lyrics, and satires, most assigned to pseudonyms like Amintor, Hugh Proteus, Hugh Protius, Simon Highforth, or Patrick Traverse.[27] He lacquered pennames on top of one another with playful sophistication, as with his poem "From the Manuscript Amusements of Hugh Protius Esq," which is nonetheless attributed to another persona, "Eugenius."[28] His personal correspondence indicates that many of these poems were submitted to Bombay's newspapers, and there is evidence that some of them were published (though few Bombay newspapers are extant from before 1800).[29]

Anglo-India's social stratification, its increasingly aristocratic social order, and the prevalence of patronage as a mechanism of governance were frequent topics of his poetry and letters. His archive reveals the labor force that supported what Ashley Cohen has called India's "aristocratic imperialists."[30] Romney often rebels against the strictures of aristocratic privilege and reveals the frustrations of lower-level colonial functionaries like himself. In his professional communications he was always cordial, even solicitous, but his pseudonymous poems and private correspondence included enraged scribbles and darkly funny vignettes about his superiors. In a dreary note from the 1780s, for example, Romney laments his persistent physical ailments, his lack of professional advancement, and vapid hierarchies: "I have as little prospect of getting well, as I have of getting a battalion," meaning a promotion to a better-paying position of command.[31] In another letter he scoffs at the idea of being a "lieutenant without any further prospect" while in yet another he boasts that he is "not capable of submitting to the strictures of any man . . . particularly in this country [India]," insisting that he possessed an "experience in life . . . inferior to none."[32] Joining the EIC armies was a "speculative risk" by "men on the make," Raymond Callahan argues, and while Romney's poems and letters about Bombay society indicate he was keenly aware of these risks, he responded with aggrievement and mirth alike when his career was blocked or dismissed.[33]

Theatricality propels these personal invectives, as in one mischievous essay-length reply that Romney imagines receiving from a superior's wife, who is tired of hearing Romney's complaints about bad health and poor pay. In his fantasy Romney mimics her speech upbraiding him for his low station and reminding him that no one "gave you leave" to address her husband, his superior, "as if he was a poor subaltern like yourself. You write to a Councillor! You, a subaltern! You write to my husband? . . . Sir, you are an impertinent fellow." She breaks off by warning him that she will "hound you about the town" and "hunt you till not a house in Bombay shall secure you within its doors," in effect ostracizing him from polite company.[34] Here, as in the characters from Romney's plays that I describe later, women are powerful social movers who intertwine with Anglo-India's more obvious aristocratic, economic, and racial hierarchies.

With such writing Romney sought to cut through the rigidity of Bombay, arguing to the editors of the *Bombay Gazette* that if its readers could find "a nearer resemblance between one class of men and another," they would be forced to "lay aside their fear of superior talents," with the effect that newspapers would be "more generously flattered, by men of wit and understanding" than by the "whispering sycophants" and the "distinguished etcetras—best company—people who had means" that he claimed typically dominated the settlement.[35] He lampoons Bombay's self-regarding men of rank as "apes and blockheads" and mindless conformists in a poem called "The Set: A New Song."[36] In a letter to the *Bombay Courier* Romney asserts that though the city had been "disturbed" by "Folly," he knows that the "wit + urbanity will not . . . meet with discouragement" from the newspaper's editors.[37] A poem titled "The Invitation to Reason" (composed 1794), without naming Bombay explicitly, depicts Reason mercilessly correcting a vacuous society composed of "Folly" and the "Gift of Gab" by teaching them "to know thy neighbor and thyself."[38] Romney asserted the need for a local literary culture of Bombay, which he was developing with his writing, against what he perceived as the tendency toward foolishness among the city's elites.

Throughout his career Romney planned to renovate Bombay's social and artistic worlds to emphasize the role of women. Underscoring the civilizing or inspirational force of women was not unique to Romney nor to Anglo-India, but the most developed of his plans inventively merged women's sociability with the colonial governance of the EIC. In 1793 Romney penned a series of letters to "Mrs Town," who is also called the "Patroness of Public Amusements."[39] Mrs. Town is never identified in the letters, though contextual details suggest a prominent female figure. Romney's letters, signed in manuscript under the name "Unanimity," propose to regularize the "urbanical assembly" of Bombay by facilitating the "communication between one section of your metropolitical empire and another"—that is between men and women of western Indian society.[40]

His use of the phrase "metropolitical empire" to describe Bombay's social scene suggests that the "metropolitan" is made in India, not Britain, and that Bombay might act as its own social "empire."[41] While Sugata Bose worries that scholars' overvaluing of trade in histories of empire has obscured the importance of culture, Romney sees commercial governance as an example to demonstrate how Anglo-Indian social and artistic forms could follow in the wake of the EIC's imperial ambitions.[42] He proposes to modernize Mrs. Town's metropolitical empire by relocalizing the Company's hierarchy to Bombay, appealing to the model of a Grand Ball at which ladies of "high rank (Duchesses &c.)" convene a "Board of Controul," adopted from London and reminiscent of the Parliament-appointed board that oversaw the operations of the EIC after the passage of the 1784 India Act.[43] This Board of Controul is joined by an "inferior assembly," the "Court of Controul," that consisted of the "wives of men of fortune, citizens, Lawyers &c.," akin to the EIC's Court of Directors, which was the ultimate arbiter of Company decisions. No one is admitted into this group, "either as subscribers or visitors," without first being "presented to, and approved" by, the "Lady Patronesses" who are "assisted in this office by a few gentlemen who are fashionable."[44] Those "elected" to the assembly would have "absolute power to correct disorders and irregularities of every kind" in the social world; those found to have violated these rules would be "immediately impeached and called to the bar of the Court of Controul."[45] References to Boards of Control, impeachment, and courts draw explicitly from the fierce debates about governance of the EIC that dominated the late eighteenth century, during which Parliament established its control over the Company and impeached its governor-general, Warren Hastings, for corruption.

Noteworthy in Romney's reimagination of Bombay's social world is that it collapses what was a transoceanic governmentality into the more immediate domain of Bombay. By making women's sociability with men into a potent governing paradigm, he offers a colonial counterpoint to Kathleen Wilson's insight that the "feminine" was perceived to have "no place in the political imaginary" of the British nation-state between the 1760s and the 1780s.[46] Alongside the economic and political functions of the EIC, Romney establishes a parallel order for Bombay composed of prominent women and witty and fashionable men who together would regulate Bombay's communal life. His proposal organizes the city according to principles borrowed from the governing structure of the EIC and society London but introduces essential responsibilities for women. In much the same way that the republic of letters adopts elements of the state to describe the operation of a literary public sphere, Romney borrows from the function of the cultural company-state to expound new principles and structures for Bombay sociability.[47] For Romney the state supplies a model, not just a contrast, to organize the colonial public spheres of Bombay.[48]

Yet his keen attention to social stratification and his aversion to what he perceived as unmerited eminence and aristocratic lethargy indicate the difficulty of reforming Bombay's polite culture while being a relatively impoverished low-level military officer. Preferring women's outsized role in the social realm is an avenue for his advancement, while also an explicit recognition that imperial masculinity was insufficient to support his aims. He admits to Mrs. Town, for instance, that Anglo-Indian men "do not know how [to interact with women], or they are too deeply engaged in other pursuits of pleasure, which separate them from female society and weaken their relish for mixed assemblies."[49] Lurking in Romney's confessions about Anglo-Indian men are insinuations about excessive homosociality or suggestions that they direct too much attention to those nonwhite women that Durba Ghosh has documented as essential to Indian sexual life from the outset of empire.[50] Romney concludes that it is time for Anglo-Indian men to join Mrs. Town's metropolitical empire, even though he worries they are too busy forging the military and economic ones that undergird it.

There is some internal evidence that Romney's letters to Mrs. Town were addressed to a specific woman in Bombay.[51] In one contribution to the *Bombay Gazette*, for example, submitted under the name "Adolphus Adept," he claims defensively that he had no intention "to assign or implicate certain characters of society" with his critique of Mrs. Town, as if backpedaling from social pressure (while also suggesting these letters may have been intended for newspaper publication).[52] It is possible that Romney saw his Town Letters as genuine attempts to reorganize Bombay social life, but it seems more likely that his idea of forcing Bombay's urbanity to conform to the governance of the EIC was a means of satirizing the overzealous social stratifications he found so onerous for his own literary and professional success. Through this satirical allegory Romney imagines, instead, how Bombay urbanity could be driven by enthusiasm for art-making and social interaction that was figured forth with the publication of poems and essays in the city's nascent newspaper culture. Romney aspires for the infrastructure of Bombay's communal life to embrace local features and distinguish itself from that of Britain while drawing from its imperial network. He explains Bombay to his readers by appealing to the outsized importance of the EIC and the peculiar sexual and racial relations of Company men and indigenous women. That particular social life is perceived by Romney to be in turns vibrant and poisonously debilitating. Despite these oscillating fortunes, Bombay social life remained a foundational engine for distinct Anglo-Indian identities that appeared most forcefully within Romney's plays.

Oriental Traits

Much like his proposals to revise Mrs. Town's "metropolitical empire," Romney's handwritten plays include significant roles for women in ways that overturn the idea that India was simply a reproduction of British society.

Women had maintained an important role in British theater for nearly a century by the time Romney was writing in India, but his depictions of them alter our sense of the gendered "imperial social formation" that Mrinalini Sinha argues consolidated a white British self overseas.[53] His depictions of women extend beyond the "clubland" that Sinha claims functioned as an "oasis" of European culture in India and that ensured elements of "home" were "transplanted to the colonies."[54] Romney shows how local cultures reshaped the forces of empire, departing from European progenitors to remake Bombay into an origin of its own metropolitan understandings.

Theater was a significant component of Anglo-Indian identity. In Calcutta the earliest theater dates from 1753, but it was not until the 1780s and 1790s that theatergoing increased in popularity there. In Madras there was a "Committee of the Theatrical Society to Government" set up in 1786 to "erect a permanent Theatre," though it was never built.[55] The Madras Exchange, completed in the early 1790s, included space for "public meetings, lottery drawings, and occasionally for entertainments," and another public meeting place, called "The Pantheon" (built before 1789), comprised a ballroom, a theater, and verandahs, which hosted suppers, dances, and dramatic performances.[56] Most plays performed in Anglo-India were British, and, as Bridget Orr notes, dramas that were especially sensitive to questions about empire building were popular.[57] But the theater also linked empire and nation to turn identity into a problem to be addressed by performances.[58] Kathleen Wilson has shown that the colonial theater was a site of racial mixing, and she describes Calcutta as a "zone of interculture."[59] Rich Bengali natives came to watch theatrical productions in Calcutta, and the first native Bengali production onstage was in 1795 at the "Bengally Theater" and was produced by a Russian musician in India.[60] Newspaper verse explicitly addressed this intercultural mixture; for example, one poem described how during a 1784 Calcutta staging of John Home's play *Douglas* (1756), "Blacks with Britons swell the notes / And ladies strain their tuneful throats," referring, perhaps, to a chorus of the anthem "Rule Britannia," which first appeared in that play.[61] This mixing of "Blacks" and "Britons" runs alongside Daniel O'Quinn's evidence that the goal of artistic culture of Calcutta (he mentions both amateur theater and print media) was to "immerse the audience in British culture" and to consolidate "a sense of British identity through contact with metropolitan plays" and through participation in that culture.[62]

In Romney's Bombay there was one area playhouse, the Bombay Theater, which opened in 1770 or 1776, and no evidence exists that it staged his works.

His plays appear in different states of completion and are pitched to different audiences; some seem to be for coteries of friends, whereas others, which include lavish stage directions, seem intended for larger theatrical presentation. All of the players were men until the 1780s, which makes the depictions of women in his plays even more intriguing.

Romney composed two plays during the 1780s and 1790s about what he called "oriental traits." One of these plays, a two-act comedy titled "Oriental Traits," follows the flirtations and love affairs of Anglo-India's inhabitants, who are concerned with money and marriage. A five-act play, titled "The Pavilion," is centered on an extended flirtation between the young Company wife Belinda Amaranth, whose husband had left Bombay to enrich himself at the Maratha Confederacy's capital, Pune, and Colonel Amourville, who was an army officer and "poor as a rat."[63] It follows Amaranth's and Amourville's frustrated attempts to meet privately while pursued by Bombay's "town . . . inquisitive and ill-natured."[64] The other men in the "The Pavilion"—such as Tulip and Marwell, the latter of whom works in the EIC's Politics department (akin to its secret intelligence service)—discuss marriage and love and complain about overbearing mothers who protect their enticing daughters.[65]

What distinguishes these social comedies from those of the London stage are moments when Romney contrasts Anglo-Indian settings with British norms. To become Anglo-Indian is portrayed as a process of acclimation, one that is compared to learning a language. For instance, the women in "Oriental Traits"—Mrs. Purvelli, Mrs. Ample, and Mrs. Barefoot—discuss a "pilgrimage" to a Hindu temple, explaining to their newest member, Miss Clarissa Dashwould, that she will need months more among them before she would "understand the dialect" of their interactions.[66] In their example Anglo-Indians are like an unusual dialect of an otherwise familiar language that needs to be experienced at length before its nuances are understood accurately.

Explicit critiques of Britain abound in these plays. "Oriental Traits" begins with an EIC employee who exclaims, "D[am]n England! Who can live there unless they are as rich as nabobs," and exhorts the crowd that he "likes this country [India] devilishly."[67] The Oldstanders, a humorously judgmental elderly couple found in "The Pavilion" who have resided in India for twenty-five years, dismiss British life in favor of India. Mrs. Oldstander prefers the more dignified one-story Indian bungalows to "clambering up and scrambling down stairs" in multilevel houses, which is "a labour fit only for your

Europe folks, who have been accustomed to live in a garrett."[68] They declare their association with regional identities that conflict with Europe, such as when Mrs. Oldstander imagines herself as a white woman *sati*. After her husband jokes that she should "go to England" if she wants relief from India's heat, she retorts that she would rather "go to the devil," insisting that she will "turn Braminy first, and stay in India to be burnt alive with you my dear."[69] In addition to proposing the remarkable idea that a white woman might convert to Hinduism ("turn Braminy") and identify with its "good wife," Mrs. Oldstander's remarks also vehemently reject England as worse than going "to the devil."[70] Only a decade after Samuel Foote's *The Nabob* (1772) solidified the image of the Company's rich indulgent employees returning to Britain and corrupting its values, the characters in Romney's plays dispel that image of Anglo-Indians as homesick nabobs.[71] Figures like the Oldstanders might be perceived as buffoonish geriatrics (or self-satisfied colonizers), but they also embody an affirmation of long-resident Anglo-Indian life, as their surname suggests. Their exclamations demonstrate explicitly that England was no longer the "normative starting point" of their identity but rather its departure.[72]

These instances suggest that the "oriental traits" of Romney's characters emerge from the localizing of the globe's increasingly kinetic cultural features. In this version of translocalism Anglo-Indian identity coheres with the more populous native communities with whom they lived. Although Romney does not offer lengthy portrayals of native Indians or describe the sophisticated intercultural dynamics of brokers that made colonial trade possible, the presence of indigenous figures is palpable in these plays. Delia Petal, a "buxum girl at nineteen," is carried through town in a palanquin while gossiping with her servant and confidant, Feyd, who runs alongside her, offering advice.[73] The flamboyant and socially competitive Tulip complains about his fellow Anglo-Indians to a *munshi* (language teacher), who tries in vain to instruct him in Persian, and another servant, Fatima, sings a "Hindostani song," while men play on the drums and "jingle a little bell" (the musical instruments of the *nautch* dancers who provided background entertainment).[74] In an early scene of "Oriental Traits" an Anglo-Indian reclines on a couch smoking a hookah and reading a poem while one servant combs his hair, another trims his nails, and a third massages his legs.[75] Nearby a *dubash*—an interpreter and business agent—receives directions while "a peon stands by, with a pen and ink," and "some musical boys" play drums and bells in the background.[76]

Romney's plays about Anglo-Indian life are profuse with these kinds of exaggerated depictions, which would be familiar to his white audiences of India. But it is his use of Africanized literary dialect to represent the speech of Indian servants that demonstrates the energetic translocal influences of his regional settings. Some servants' voices are written in ways that suggest black African speech from the British stage. In the opening scene of "Oriental Traits," for example, a *banyan* (merchant) accosts a junior EIC employee to ask about an unpaid debt, muttering in broken English: "Massa! I got one little bill, please, can pay?" He goes on to plead: "My family, not have vitils—one month massa have owe."[77] In "The Pavilion" a servant, Abdella, when asked by her sneaky Anglo-Indian employer, Delia Petal, about whether the street is deserted so they can spy on Amaranth and Amourville, replies: "ebry ting quiet."[78] These few instances of nonstandard English syntax and vocabulary are combined with frequent uses of "massa" or "mattam" (madam) to refer to white Anglo-Indians.[79]

Romney's Indians speak much like other nonwhite characters found in contemporaneous literary works, such as Caesar, the enslaved servant who calls his owner "Massa" in Mariana Starke's play *The Sword of Peace* (1788), which was set in Madras but staged in London,[80] or the Tahitian of John O'Keefe's 1785 Covent Garden dramatic pantomime *Omai, or A Trip Round the World*, who describes his journey to England:

In de big canoe
I o'er ocean swim me . . .
Den to London comme.[81]

Although the term *massa* is recorded as early as 1766 in an issue of the *South Carolina Gazette*, the likely source for these instances of Africanized speech is the dialogue that Charles Dibdin devised for the black servant Mungo in the comic opera *The Padlock* (1768), whose "merry, muttering" sound was so successful that it was performed around the world, including 1780s India.[82]

Dorothy Couchman suggests that Mungo may have been imagined initially as a "blacked-up Irish servant" with a name that "hails from Scotland," so that instead of embodying an essential blackness, as scholars and dramatists believed well into the twentieth-century, Mungo begins in racial multiplicity. Perhaps that explains why Romney adopts Mungo's Africanized speech patterns as a model for his indigenous Indian characters. Mungo's racially multifarious origins were magnified into his slippery posterity as a "prototype" of nonstandard English.[83] Mungo comes to signify all bad talk.

In a way that precedes twentieth-century language experiments that appropriated black dialect, such as those of T. S. Eliot or Ezra Pound, Romney's plays adopt Africanized stage speech to characterize South Asians. In the process he flattens racial differences and links the racial and class structures of Bombay's urban scene to the Atlantic slave trade and black pidgins. Figures like Mungo, Caesar, and Abdella indicate rapid, near-simultaneous shifts in popular and private depictions of nonnative English speakers that coincide with the acceleration of British territorial imperialism (and military violence) during the late eighteenth century. Everyone began to sound like the English-muttering Mungo.

Shared vocal patterns and lexicons did not mean that Africans and Indians were both subjected to the same "lowly status" within Europe's empires of slavery and colonialism, however, as David Dabydeen claims.[84] That the servants of Romney's plays say "massa" does not mean that they were like enslaved black Africans nor that they are always being lampooned as inferior to whites. Instead, at this moment in South Asian history, "massa" represents an uncertain, socially fragile relationship whose significance has not yet been decided.[85] Indian traders and servants would have been performed on the stage of 1780s Bombay by white men, most likely EIC servants and military officers like Romney, though evidence suggests that Julius Soubise, a mixed-race former slave born in Jamaica, performed Mungo and Othello on the Calcutta stage.[86] A companion of the Duchess of Queensbury, Soubise had to flee Britain after being accused of rape; in Calcutta he was an equestrian and fencing instructor, as well as a thespian.[87]

There is no indication that Romney knew of Soubise's performances or that Soubise ever traveled to Bombay, and information about *how* these parts were played, in terms of costume and facial decoration, is limited. But there was an avidity in Anglo-India for exotic costuming, as evinced by accounts of lavish masquerades where white participants dressed as *subahdars* (Mughal officers), *munshis* (governmental scribes), or in "the Hindostany, French, Turkish or Egyptian style."[88] Sheikhs and scimitars were the norm at these galas. Broken speech, therefore, does not tell us that Romney's Indians were perceived to be inherently subordinate to whites. Frequently this dialect indexes differences among Indian servants themselves: though Abdella and the *banyan* are represented with broken spellings and choppy syntax, the speech of Delia Petal's counselor Feyd is represented in fluid, grammatically perfect English.

Speech has always been perceived as the access point to characters' interiority, and the varying impersonation of Indian voices in English was a means of differentiating among the sensibilities of these speaking subjects, at times offering demeaning representations of their linguistic inferiority within the anglophone world but at other times representing them as collaborators among a growing South Asian English-speaking population. The effect of this differentiation among European colonizers and the Asians that serve them, and among Asian servants themselves, is not liberation or equality, but an encrusting of differences in social status using racial terms and representations—the reverse of what David Cannadine has argued was the "ornamentalism" of the British Empire.[89] Romney's Indian servants signify the vocal equivalent of "oriental traits," distinguishing the contents and characters of his play with its settings and vocalizations. To speak broken English to Anglo-Indian audiences exposes them to what Roxann Wheeler calls the Caliban-like vitality of "bad English" for "theatrical and print culture practices."[90] But by adopting these practices, Romney also reveals the dispersed terrain for experimenting with the creation of nonwhite performance dialects that subtly undercut white cultural superiority. Romney's Indians are a unique motor for Anglo-Indian theatrical experimentation: Mungos transformed into the Abdellas and *banyans* of Bombay.[91] The themes and topics of Romney's play might be quite familiar to British literature—love, marriage, money, social status—but the setting and climate bend them into new shapes, drawing examples from across the oceanic world yet abutting them with the orientalized traits of his Anglo-Indian and South Asian characters.

Rewriting *Tristram Shandy* in Bombay

Because he wrote for an Anglo-Indian audience knowledgeable of (but with highly variable access to) British experimental traditions, surveying novels for inspiration was a common tactic of Romney's career. Domestic theatrical dramas had been the vehicle for assessing questions of empire, national identity, and exotic cultures since the English Restoration.[92] Romney's plays reverse this calculus by rewriting the domestic English novel, especially its female characters. Bridget Orr argues that foreign cultures are the "screen" on which local anxieties were projected, but in Romney's theater Britain supplies the contrast from which Anglo-Indians could assess their world and its deviations from British fashions.[93] One tactic was represented by Mrs. Oldstander in "The Pavilion," who repudiates England for Anglo-India (and the funeral pyre). In another play, Romney adapts Laurence Sterne's *Tristram Shandy* to the localized imperialism of Mrs. Oldstander's and Mrs. Town's

Bombay. His dramatic adaptation of Sterne's novel remains untitled but begins with the note "Scene First. At Mr. Shandy's" and seems to be nearly complete at more than one hundred folio pages. It does not account for the vast scope of Sterne's novel but uses many of its characters, following them through secret romances that converge into a conclusive final act. Romney combines domestic discussions between Walter Shandy and his brother Toby with action set in the streets and taverns of London, during which Tristram schemes with the Widow Wadman and courts Delia Longjaw, the daughter of a local justice of the peace and a woman who has been promised to an old friend of her aristocratic father. The play ends with the virtuous being married, the villainous being exposed, and familial integrity maintained in a straightforward way that differs considerably from Sterne's novel.

Absent from the play are many features of *Tristram Shandy* that make the novel notable, including the unwound clock, the window sash, and accounts of Tristram's birth, which, as he argues in the novel, require him to trace everything "*ab Ovo*"—from the beginning.[94] Gone, too, is the cock-and-bull story, the narrator's addresses to his female interlocutor, and the graphical richness of Sterne's visual text—its black and marbled pages, its asterisks and omissions. Romney's play reads like a prequel to Sterne's novel, with a young Tristram studying for the law in London and acting the part of a rake in its polite social world. This is not the Tristram plagued by "pitiful misadventures and cross accidents" that he can blame on his conception and the irregularity that emerged from it.[95] The "Shandean System" of Walter's philosophizing and Toby's modest nature, earned at the siege of Namur with his groin injury, is transformed into something more like a Restoration comedy, with cross-dressing, imprisonment, duped fathers, and witty, ultimately worthy young gentlemen like Tristram securing the women they love.

In the place of Sterne's formal innovations, however, are startling plot revisions that reimagine the relationship between Tristram and women, especially Wadman, as sexual attractions explained through the language of empire. He flirts with women on the street, telling one she is a "pretty goddess" who might "kill poor mortals as you pass for your mornings amusement."[96] In another scene he describes himself as "like a bee" that "would not pass a flower without a taste."[97] In still another he claims to Wadman that he is seeking the "empress of my heart."[98] Tristram's claim that he is searching for the "empress" of his heart prompts Wadman to volunteer that if she were "a princess and in the list for such an empire" she would "try with all my heart to be at least as near the throne as my sister candidates."[99] To her,

Tristram is a "gay youthful fellow" and love's emperor—perhaps its Mughal emperor—but Toby is merely a "sober sedate gentleman."[100] In one address directed to the theater audience, she admits that "if Mr. Tristram ~~Shandy~~ should make [an] offer to me—I should be puzzled and disturbed to death—for I could not marry him." She continues: "I have liked him since he was a child" and admits "should I see him often—my heart would be in danger." She resolves to "struggle against a passion so improper, and that would be so embarrassing to us all."[101] The pauses, breaths, and dashes indicate a style familiar with the mid-eighteenth-century novels of Eliza Haywood and Sterne but reimagined as a bawdy Restoration romance for Anglo-Indian audiences. By the play's end, Toby and Wadman are predictably reunited but not before she is jilted by Tristram for Delia, which leaves her cursing her "silly heart" and vowing "vengeance" on Tristram, while he grumbles about the misunderstandings that arise from treating women with "too much kindness!"[102] Delia sees her own matrimonial chances in imperial terms, too; when she is promised to a decrepit family friend rather than Tristram, she pleads to be sent into the "fishing fleet" of eligible women in India: "Let me marry any thing, send me an adventurer to Bengal."[103] Her father, seeming to direct an innuendo at knowing spectators, jokes that India "will neither mend your morals nor procure you a better husband."[104] A laughing Anglo-Indian audience might understand these lines quite differently than their English cousins would.

References to love, money, and imperial matrimony are part of a larger pattern by which Anglo-India supplies the backdrop against which to reimagine sociability as governed by women while depicting a sexual system that endorses their active desires. Felicity Nussbaum associates eighteenth-century India with the potential for "unorthodox femininity," and Michael Franklin claims India was a "transgressive space" for Anglo women.[105] Their descriptions are underpinned by the relative scarcity (and thus high value) of marriageable European women, but Romney's play suggests another possibility. Typically, adaptations of Sterne's fictions are dismissed as "Sterneana," less original than their prototype. In the place of Sterne's narrative and graphical innovations, however, Romney's "Tristram Shandy" promotes Anglo-Indian women's social power and assertive desires, as found in Mrs. Town and then reflected by Wadman's and Delia's sexual vocabulary of empire. Long before scholars emphasized Sterne's "sexual comedy," Romney had identified its potential, turning *Tristram Shandy* into a comedy of manners that scrambles and realigns the gender, sexual, and class affiliations of its characters. Rather than strengthen *Tristram Shandy*'s place in the "tradition of anti-feminist satire" or the novel's productive misogyny, Romney redefines midcentury fashionability by amalgamating it with Anglo-India's "oriental traits" and thus rewriting Wadman and Delia as versions of Bombay's "metropolitical empire."[106] Romney repurposes Sterne's literary experimentalism within a colonial theatrical world whose Mrs. Oldstanders would rather "turn Braminy" than exchange India for England.

The liberating sexual possibilities of Anglo-India's theatrical women should not be exaggerated: the scarcity of British women in India and the hazy existence of the "fishing fleet," which produced incentives for certain women to travel to India for better economic prospects through marriage, meant that women were dependent on their employed husbands, many of whom had prior relationships and families with native women. Sexual relationships between white men and indigenous women were extremely common in eighteenth-century India, introducing their own complicated dynamics, especially around the issue of mixed-race children, the conditions for whom changed rapidly from relative social acceptance to denial among Anglo-Indians during the exact period that Romney was stationed in India.[107] Such social gambles for white women could be dangerous and presented pressures unique to the place.

Despite this legal and structural inequity, women figured prominently in Romney's Bombay dramas, much as they did in his conception of Mrs. Town's metropolitical empire. He even used their example to argue for his own potential as a writer. In one poem, dated from February of 1779 and meant to serve as a prologue to Samuel Foote's play *The Mayor of Garret* (1764), Romney writes as the cross-dressed female muse of Anglo-India. His character claims to grasp "Thalia's plume" and to "don her doublet and my jerkins crop" (Thalia was the Greek Goddess of comedy) to celebrate Foote as the "Aristophanes of modern days."[108] In this female goddess's garb Romney plants "Domestic shrubs and exotics . . . / Such as old Thames or antient Ganges haunt."[109] He recasts himself as a Greek goddess and female market gardener to explain his creative license. The geographical purview of the term *domestic* in this example is exceedingly slippery, matching "old Thames" with "antient Ganges," a riverine merging that aptly describes how English ideas might recreate Indian customs. Such combinations display enormous optimism about India's literary scene and how it might equal that of London, whose theater, Romney gloats, merely feeds its vast audience pablum while Anglo-India's authors "strive to please an audience, as our friends."[110] The friendly intimacy of such theatrical culture led Romney to opine that Bombay's literary public might undergo a substantial change, making it a place where "Wit and Amusement, in their sprightliest vein" may "rouse the drooping town to something gay" and "renovate our long forsaken scene."[111] In these moments he sees his own plays as a breakthrough against "Dulness" and "revelations" that show "a revolution may take place" in literary Bombay.[112]

"Children of the Sun"

This section continues to explore India as a site of literary innovations by focusing on the relationship between Laurence Sterne and his late-life love interest, Elizabeth Draper, who was the wife of a Company employee stationed in Bombay. Sterne met Draper in 1766 while she was convalescing with her children in England. She was born in southwestern India and, after being briefly educated in England, was married to a Bombay EIC employee. It is not possible to identify any specific individual as the model for Romney's expressive Anglo-Indian women like Mrs. Town or Mrs. Oldstander, but because of her personal and epistolary relationship with Laurence Sterne, Draper had become Bombay's most-renowned female inhabitant. She was seen as a source of geographically unique South Asian inspiration the effect of which seems to be making men susceptible to emotions that span the seas.

Later in her life, and after Sterne's death, Draper classified herself as among the "Indian fair ones" who, like "all girls destined for India," were "extremely frivolous" with too much leisure and too little proper education: a "set of Ignorants," she remarked, "unknowing in every thing, but the Rites of Venus."[113] Yet Sterne consistently praised her in letters to his friends and integrated her into his writing as a means of immortalizing her, informing her at one point that he had "brought your name, *Eliza*! And Picture into my work—where they will remain," referring to his writing of *A Sentimental Journey*.[114] After she returned to Bombay in 1767, he dedicated a handwritten journal to her, hoping to maintain an emotional connection. Above introductory remarks in the journal, he scrawled a hasty title: "Continuation of the Bramines Journal."[115] The introductory page of "the Bramines Journal" claims it was written under the "fictitious Names" of "Yorick and Draper" and "Bramin and Bramine."[116] He signed letters to her "Thy Bramin" and refers to her as "La Bramine" or calls out to her in writing "O my Bramine! My

Friend! My—future wife" while wearing a miniature engraving of her around his neck, as Yorick does in *A Sentimental Journey*.[117] One effect of Draper's inspiration, as these references show, was to incite Sterne to reimagine himself as a high-caste Indian.

Scholars have explained Sterne's association with Brahmins as a result of his being a religious figure and Draper being born in India, but his identification exceeds such literal and biographical explanations.[118] Brahmins were an elevated caste associated in the eighteenth century with Hinduism and Sanskrit learning.[119] Draper has been described by scholars as Sterne's wished-for wife, his "rent-a-muse," and the "presiding deity," "mascot," and "good-luck charm" of his *A Sentimental Journey*.[120] Carol Watts concludes that Sterne's attachment to Draper was a mechanism for "making safe the anxiety of empire as a form of love."[121] Perhaps Sterne was pleased to imagine that his impending death from tuberculosis would lead Draper to "turn Braminy" and making herself a *sati*, as Mrs. Oldstander promises to do. But it also seems apparent that his connection to an Anglo-Indian woman led Sterne to conceive of himself as an Indian religious scholar in much the same way that Bombay residents might perform indigenous Indian servants for Romney's plays or that residents might dress themselves as Persians, "Turks," *subahdars*, and *munshis* at parties. In this equation white women's sentimental effusions change Anglos into Indians, at least temporarily, with the effect of opening new ranges for their sentimentality.

Sterne enjoyed the idea that the geographical range of his writing might become literal. After Eliza's departure he looked over charts of the Atlantic and envisioned her India-bound ship "but a little way off" thinking that he "could venture after it in a Boat, methinks."[122] He pictures her aboard her ship, sitting down "to yr writing Drawer . . . as you took out yr Journal; to tell . . . Yr attachment and love for me."[123] He admires the idea that, though separated by great distances, they might both return to their "solitary Cabbin" after a "tastless meal" to "fly" to their journal writing.[124] Eliza's writing (to him) was a central engine of Sterne's imaginative productions, and the sentimentality he projects onto her acts of penmanship was meant to overcome the physical distance between them. Sterne even flirted with the idea of traveling to India, wishing only two weeks after Eliza's departure that he was "put into a Ship for Bombay" and later confessing he wanted to "fly to You to Bombay."[125] Sterne's ending his life not in London but among the merchant factors of Bombay, cohabiting with an Anglo-Indian woman, would have offered a vivid turn for English literary history.

Sterne never did travel to India, of course, but Draper became a minor celebrity and "cult figure" in England after his death, in part because of the emotional hold she was thought to have had over him.[126] Rumors about her role in Sterne's fiction and the surreptitious publication of her letters show that the sociability of Anglo-Indian women was seen as both marvelous and suspicious.[127] The *Madras Courier* published a poem in 1790 commemorating her return to Asia—which had occurred almost twenty-five years earlier, in 1767—as proving "the magic of her charms."[128] Eyles Irwin, the Madras author we met in chapter 3, depicts poets having "melted" over the funeral pyre of a smiling "Eliza" in his poem about *sati*, "Bedukah" (1776); the reference to melting equates the spectacle of women's self-immolation with the intensity of the sentimental attachment that women like Draper might provoke in men like Sterne and Irwin.[129] The *Calcutta Gazette* printed a celebration of Draper by the French philosopher Abbé Raynal in 1784.[130] Elsewhere, Raynal argued that Draper's sentimental effects on men resulted from her Indian birth, and he drew a direct connection between its warm climate and her inviting society. He believed it was "the influence of [India's] happy climate that [Draper] certainly was indebted for that almost incompatible harmony of voluptuousness and decency."[131] An article to the editors of the *Bombay Courier* even satirizes such effusions by claiming to have translated a mosquito's song celebrating having bitten the "roseate cheek of STERNE'S ELIZA": even India's mosquito cannot resist the attractive powers of white Anglo-Indian women.[132] One set of interpretations might point out how Sterne's semiprivate relationship with Draper—known to their friends and reflected in his widely read novels—intensified what John Mullan calls the "sociality of the text," reconfiguring Sterne's habit of creating close relationships between his narrators (often projections of himself) and his readers.[133] Sterne's sentimentalism toward Draper appears in his novels as the enthusiastic addresses to female readers and the needy solicitations for audience participation.

Draper's desires seem to have differed greatly from Sterne's. In her mind the advantage of Asian, rather than English, sociability was the possibility of discovering affinities with nonwhite women rather than with men like Sterne. He may have seen her as the muse of his final years, but her attention was directed elsewhere. In one letter (not addressed to Sterne) Draper argues that the world of English decorum blocks sincerity. This situation, she explains, was unlike that of "Asiatic Slaves" and "honest African[s], whose wildness is term'd Savage" but which is "far far dearer to me." To English women she exclaims, "Your persons are free, but Minds fettered."[134]

Scholars should always be cautious of Anglo-Indian women who use foreign figures to examine the effects of colonialism, as Inderpal Grewal notes.[135] Draper's identifications repeat generic late eighteenth-century appeals to slavery and liberation prevalent among the Atlantic world's abolitionist women. Still, it is significant that Draper consciously removes herself from the company of white English women and aligns herself with those she calls the "Children of the Sun."[136] To be "Bramine" leads to identifications and political affinities that are more radical than anything Sterne or Romney might surmise, since, for them, the powerful effects of Anglo-Indian women's sociability nearly always registers as inspiration for white men's artistic production. While Sterne worries about the posterity of his writing and Romney about the vibrancy of Bombay's local literary culture, Draper demonstrates a wholesale reconsideration of what writing meant for a woman who was pushed into and out of Bombay during her lifetime by the forces of colonialism and the contradictory intimacies of an unhappy marriage. Bombay is a place from which Draper imagines the reorganization of relationships among the globe's women, though one that suffers from all of the dilemmas of political affinity that scholars like Chandra Mohanty would readily identify centuries later.[137]

Romney's artistic production complements this other understanding of Bombay's growing political, social, and economic importance by adding perspective about the city's cultural infrastructure of theaters, newspapers, reading publics, authors, social assemblies, military men, and Company women, like Draper. What scholarship exists on these questions has focused on nineteenth-century institutions like the Literary Society of Bombay, which Veena Naregal describes as a place for the "early discourse" of a "modern literate sphere" in Bombay, or the Courier Press (proprietors of the *Bombay Courier*).[138] In addition to these institutions, scholars should consider the importance of urban sociability—gossip, gatherings, costume balls, and theatrical ventures—that served as an anchor for Romney's ambitions throughout western India. His engagement with and criticism of polite Bombay indicates a sphere perhaps not dominated by "transoceanic elites," "aristocratic imperialists," or affluent officers, as many historians have argued.[139] Their "oriental traits," as Romney terms them, differentiate Anglo-Indians from other white Britons, whom they physically resemble but who share, in the words of the proud Anglo-Indian women of Romney's play, a different dialect within the larger language. Such shared yet discriminating dialects are more literal with Romney's depiction of the speech of indigenous South Asians and Africanized West Indians.

This might seem to classify Romney as a provincial author, but if so, his provincialism differs considerably from those models that have focused on the small-town culture of rural England, Wales, Scotland, and (to some extent) Anglo-America. Romney demonstrates the limitations of thinking about provincialism or localism as the antithesis of eighteenth-century culture's universally recognized values such as civility or politeness. Among scholars the assumption remains that Anglo-Indian society was derivative of British metropolitan norms that were exaggerated by the isolation of its inhabitants. Yet Romney portrays a much more fluid situation, in which Bombay's urban sociability was oriented toward London but often ambivalent toward its origins and keen to revise such norms to immediate circumstances rather than adopt its universal standard as a beacon. Romney was indebted to literary figures like Sterne, but the integration of British values into Anglo-Indian representations inevitably meant their transformation to the sensibilities of the readers and audiences through simultaneous acts of emulation and variation. He creates Bombay's urban sociability by transforming British politeness into Anglo-Indian imperial formations. There may have been an "Anglicization" of Britain's empire in India at the end of the eighteenth century by which "overseas subjects" maintained a "free association" with the "mother country," in the words of H. V. Bowen, but there was also an Indianization of it, in which Anglo-Indian norms were defined by recasting or explicitly departing from Europe's metropolitan culture.[140]

CHAPTER SIX

Agonies of Empire

Captivity Narratives and the Mysore Wars, 1767–1799

Between 1767 and 1799 four separate conflicts between Britain, the East India Company, their allies, and the Kingdom of Mysore dominated diplomatic and military maneuvering in southern India. In addition to the political, economic, and personal effects—shifting alliances, killed and captured soldiers, refugee populations, and destroyed livelihoods—warfare clarified the emergent literary publics of anglophone Asia, whose members inserted themselves into a debate about imperial violence in India. Military conflict generated a distinct Anglo-Indian artistic culture that was seen as responsive to the concerns of audiences geographically proximate to and educated about the Mysore Wars. Letter circulation, newspaper publication, printed commemoration, and state-assisted sculpture and painting presented opportunities for enthusiasts of Anglo-Indian arts to argue for their successful competition with British arts. This was especially evident of the captivity narratives, prison memoirs, and incarceration poems composed in response to the Mysore Wars. These documents, produced primarily during the 1780s and the 1790s (though some were published as late as 1849), exhibit sympathy for captives, revulsion about their treatment, and uncertainty about the effectiveness of imperial conflict. Captivity distinguished Anglo-Indian authors from those imperial audiences (and, occasionally, from self-satisfied Anglo-Indian readers) who were the target of their critique. Such interventions into the burgeoning Anglo-Indian public sphere were authorized by the captives' suffering, performed movingly on the printed page.

Although the exact number of white soldiers captured by Mysore is unknown, scholars estimate that at least thirteen hundred were turned over during the 1780s as part of treaty negotiations and at least four hundred more remained in the 1790s. If true, these numbers would indicate that one out of every five white soldiers fighting on the subcontinent between 1779 and 1799 was imprisoned.[1] Some captives were incarcerated for a decade or more. They faced excruciating conditions, even though many were eventually assimilated into Mysore's political and cultural life. Only a few of these captives produced first-person prose accounts that sought to reflect their extraordinary experiences, perhaps a dozen in all, though other accounts of South Asian military conflict mention these captives and their circumstances.

Scholars have noted the category problems that these captives activated about national identity, as well as the questions they provoked about responsibility and the volition of prisoners of war. These problems, which persist into the twenty-first century, were acute in South Asia because they reveal the role of Islam in the construction of Anglo-Indian identity and trouble the alignment of Anglo-Indians with British imperial ambitions. Kate Teltscher suggests that eighteenth-century Anglo-Indian captivity narratives attempt to describe and contain the ideological (not just material) threat of Mysore to British conceptions of empire by recasting Mysore's charismatic leader Tipu Sultan (1750–99) as an "oriental despot," a "timeless, generic Eastern threat."[2] Linda Colley sees in these subcontinental captives a successful effort "to humanise Britain's armed forces in the public imagination" even as the scale and aggression of British imperialism was growing.[3] For these scholars, captivity narratives successfully personalize what otherwise seemed like the faceless expansion of British dominion in India. Through a well-financed and concerted strategy of depicting suffering captives, the "sporadic failures and disasters" of the EIC and the seesaw clashes of the British state were transformed into "a form of heroic virtue, moral improvement, and patriotic service."[4]

Teltscher and Colley present compelling cases about soldiers and global actors who often found themselves involved in conflicts over which they had limited control, bringing the "underbelly" of empire into visibility.[5] Reading these captivity narratives in a translocal and regional framework, however, reveals the differing constituencies of an emerging anglophone artistic audience and how these constituencies reacted to displays of misery and emotion. Close analysis of the captivity narratives' rhetoric, rather than their historical context, indicates pervasive ambivalence about conflict and palpable distrust of an imperial system that offered few remedies or recompenses for war. Their narratives divulge painful details about the agonies of empire, countering imperial audiences' enthusiasm for national triumph with depictions of public mortification, suffering, and abjection in ways that would appear again in Romantic period theater.[6] Eventually, Britain's imperial audiences achieved some semblance of ideological unity about eighteenth-century conflicts in South Asia, but before that happened, captivity narratives and prison poems raised awkward questions about the status of warfare's prisoners that remain unresolved within the texts themselves. How much were prisoners of war required to resist the suffering that occurred while being confined by Muslims? Is the expression of suffering sufficient to demonstrate opposition to captivity? What are the differences between force and volition, between resistance and accommodation? South Asia's Anglo-Indian captives, more starkly than their better-known Anglo-American counterparts, trouble ideas about the utility of resistance to captivity.

To answer these questions, in the first section I show how the economics of subsistence described in these captivity narratives align with authors' self-representation as authentically suffering agents of empire. Because they feel the effects of warfare, they claim they are best able to portray it and most deserving of the monetary remuneration that comes from publicizing it. The adjacency of suffering and profit, public humiliation and print, concludes with the uncomfortable assertion that imprisonment was inspiring and that captivity ignited an Anglo-Indian art. In the second section I turn to antiwar poetry published in regional newspapers that presented the Anglo prisoner as an obvious consequence of colonial expansion. These representations reach their apogee in the form of child soldiers and "dancing boys"—white adolescents captured by Mysore, circumcised, and then turned into combatants against their former compatriots or, in the most unsettling examples, cross-dressed as women to dance in front of Tipu as court entertainers. These adolescents, whom I discuss in the third section, were convertible beings incorporated into Tipu's statecraft. For this reason anglophone captivity narratives struggle to demarcate who could and could not be redeemed from imprisonment among Muslims, as I show in the fourth section. Their accounts epitomize the reluctance and dread that pervaded the project of Asian imperialism and that rested uneasily alongside European nationalism's enthusiastic jingoism and white superiority.

Mercenaries of Imperial Emotion and the Spectacle of the Jailed Author

Historians and literary scholars alike have proposed that the late eighteenth century produced the idea of a "citizen-soldier" who made imperial violence palatable to domestic audiences. Sympathy for soldiers rehabilitated the

British imperial project after the defeats of the American Revolution and the military setbacks of the early Mysore Wars. This "soldier of feeling," as Christopher Loar describes him, possessed "masculine affective entanglements" that "enfold soldier and reading public into a single sentimental national community" while making the military man someone who experienced "powerful and spontaneous emotion."[7] These military men were ostensibly the champions of British national violence overseas. When killed, they were commemorated; when captured, they were tormented by "barbarians . . . so unfeeling" that readers compensated with their pity (and their pence).[8] Captivity narratives were thought to display the effects of imperial violence to a domestic audience, who received an education about feeling collectively for the disparate parts of Britain's expanding empire with which they had little direct contact.

The scenes of anguish and exposure in Mysore captivity narratives offer a different image of the citizen-solider. Rather than a confirmation of national spirit or a providential deliverance by God, these authors describe captivity as an artistic awakening or as fair reward for suffering in an alien land. Their writing was motivated by captivity and animated by accounts of torture and hardship. This fundamental paradox—that artists benefit from the adversities they experience and the sympathy they excite—structures the Mysore captivity narratives. In this sense the soldiers of the captivity narratives are more like mercenaries of imperial emotion than they are sentimental figures of a rehabilitated fiscal-military state.

These aesthetic excitements are directly connected to the quotidian commercial life of being first a prisoner and then an author (or, as in some cases, a subject) of memoir. Many of these renderings involve the everyday social and emotional accounting that arises from the captives interacting with each other, their fellow imprisoned native allies, and their Mysore jailors while trying to survive their awful conditions. Mysore's captives were rarely isolated; in fact, they socialized, composed secret diaries, wrote letters (with each other and with allies outside of prison), and even married native women and had children. They received news about southern India's shifting political and diplomatic engagements and followed the course of military actions. Information was often gleaned from new captives, circulated among prisoners in writing and gossip, and composited into an overall picture of their chances for release. For most Anglo prisoners, incarceration involved social mixing rather than crushing isolation or constant monitoring.

Perhaps the most obvious forms of social interaction concerned the marketplace economy of prisons. While conditions in these prisons varied, depending on the benevolence of individual jailors, all of the captivity narratives commented on the persistent urgency of money and the importance of the bazaar. Captives were offered monetary stipends by their jailors to purchase "what things were absolutely necessary for [their] existence," such as clothing and food.[9] They sought loans from Hindu bankers to improve their conditions. They engaged in barter and trade with their guards and used their Indian servants, who were occasionally imprisoned with them, to acquire items from the marketplace because the servants had greater mobility as noncombatants.[10] The necessity of money was so great that one narrative asserted, improbably, that prisoners slinked out of their cells to steal silver relics from a local temple, relics that could then be melted down and made into coins.[11] Cromwell Massey kept a clandestine diary throughout his capture; he reports extensively on money, especially when there were reductions in the allowances given to captives.[12] Other prisoners slipped letters to compatriots in Madras asking for funds to supplement their diet and to repair their clothing.[13] Captives complained constantly about the prices at the bazaar; there was never enough money. The elements of this dependency on money and interactions with their jailors and native servants is captured in a pencil and ink sketch of the prisoner Alexander Foulis by an unknown artist. Standing over him is a servant extending to him a plate of food while behind him is a guard with a rifle and the turban characteristic of Mysore's uniforms. The outstretched plate and the exchange of food expresses the degree to which the sustenance of white soldiers in Mysore prisons necessitated social relationships with natives.

Attention to the realities of the monetary economy was fused with an economy of emotion. Authors appealed to the logic of the marketplace and commerce to explain their mortification at being made into spectacles, which in turn fueled complaints that they were treated as slaves rather than prisoners of war. Spectacle and visuality had long been a strategy to convey the exoticism of the captives' surroundings. Being denuded of defining objects—such as money, clothing, and personal items—is a persistent feature of narratives both in Asia and the Americas, but in the Mysore Wars it also represented the peculiar status of the prisoner treated unfairly and exposed to the unnatural observation of others.[14] After being seized at Calicut (Kozhikode) in 1779 while traveling with her husband to Bengal, Eliza Fay recounts how she was displayed to the native residents at the start of her "dreadful Captivity." She reports being compelled to "walk above a mile thro' a heavy sand, surrounded by all the mob of Calicut, who seemed to take pleasure in beholding the distress of white people." Later, with her fellow travelers, she was "detained . . . nearly an hour, in an open Square" while the city governor "sat all the while smoking his Hooka, and looking down upon us" until he had "sufficiently feasted his eyes."[15] James Bristow reports that he was "stripped of every thing I possessed" when he was seized in 1781. He compares his removal of clothing to how he was "robbed" of his "liberty" by his captors, who are described as "barbarians" because they had treated him with "cruelty and scorn," sending him "almost naked" to be inspected by Haidar Ali, the founder of the Mysore dynasty and Tipu's father. Later at Seringapatam, Mysore's southern Indian capital fortress, Bristow was "shaved . . . in the customary manner" (to show that he was a slave, not a man or a person) before being circumcised and having his right ear pierced, the "mark of slavery amongst the Mahometans," in what he calls a "diabolical ceremony."[16] John Lindsay describes his inner turmoil when he is captured in 1780 during a battle and robbed of his company's wages by a cavalryman, who also "demanded [his] accouterments" and left him "stripped naked" and "stung with rage." He presents himself as a "ludicrous figure" who wore only a dirty shirt and "trowsers" to accompany his shaved head.[17] Cromwell Massey claims that "after being plundered" when he surrendered at the 1780 Battle of Pollilur, "most of us [were] stript quite naked."[18] William Thomson insists that soldiers were "stripped of all that they had" when captured and were periodically "searched most minutely in every part, without the least regard to decency" during their captivity, looking for contraband items, especially correspondence.[19] He does not detail how far or in what ways they invaded soldiers' bodies.

Being stripped and strip-searched are among the emotional apexes of these accounts. Most Anglo authors felt that nakedness and public examination was intended to make them feel like slaves rather than honorable prisoners of war, and they rebelled against such treatment in their subsequent writing.[20] Thomson repeats the claim that Mysore captives were treated "like slaves" rather than prisoners of war when they were stripped, paraded, and consistently deprived of personal possessions and basic necessities, such as quality food.[21] Alexander Dirom, who composed a retrospective of the third Mysore War, which ended in 1792, argued angrily that Tipu treated his captives "not as prisoners of war, but as slaves, and with a degree of severity that slaves never before experienced in any age, or in any quarter of the globe," a claim whose exaggeration, when compared to the vastness of Atlantic chattel slavery and the American and West Indian plantation economy, only testifies to the trauma of these captives.[22] Lindsay notes that he was "obliged to stand in a row" without clothing and shoes so that the inhabitants of Mysore could "gratify their curiosity and make their remarks" on him. He reports that one prison commander threatened to "chastise" him in public if he "did not behave better."[23]

In narratives that recount hunger, state-sanctioned mutilation, hanging, and poisoning, it seems odd to also include public ridicule as a genuine threat, but mortification was a tool of punishment and control. Massey notes how "one of ye [the] circumcised Europeans" was punished for a transgression by being "exposed naked in ye sun all this day in ye parade in stock."[24] The Royal Navy sailor Richard Runwa Bowyer had his governor take an interest in him, becoming "very inquisitive about several Matters" that "in general were very indecent." He rages at being made into a "terrible Spectacle" in Mysore when "boys hallow'd me so much as made me very uneasy 'till I got into the Prison and even then I could not for some time forget the Indignity." After it occurred a second time, Bowyer complained to his jailor about being "so frequently made a public spectacle" and insisted that he "abide in my Prison"; private detention was more palatable than public ridicule.[25]

At other times punishment was assessed for trying to avoid public scrutiny and mortification. James Scurry, a young Royal Navy sailor imprisoned at Bangalore throughout the 1780s, remembers a captive who was beaten severely because he would not "sing and dance in the English manner, for [Tipu's son] to laugh at." Scurry chuckles darkly that the punished man was Irish, so he "could not talk much English" and knew as much about English dancing and singing "as a Hottentot"; the English and Irish all looked and sounded alike to their Mysore captors.[26] Imprisoned soldiers and travelers, like Fay, believed that such spectacular suffering was fitting only for nonwhites, especially those trapped in the Atlantic slave trade.[27] It was not being a prisoner that felt humiliating to these soldiers; in fact, soldiers regularly expressed their sense of honor for military service. Rather, their perception that they were treated more like slaves or criminals—robbed of their liberty and their possessions, repeatedly made naked, inspected by and paraded before their captors and the native populace—that was so outrageous.

The complex reactions to these spectacles disclose the basic bargain for anglophone readers of the captivity narratives that scholars so far have misunderstood. Colley claims, for example, that captives were reluctant to publish because the "particular nature" of their captivity involved military defeat, physical hardship, mutilation, and "embarrassment and shame." "Castigated . . . as losers," she asserts, they could not be celebrated until British military victories brought "a measure of confidence and success" to the nation.[28] Many of the these narrators are indeed quite eloquent about their national feelings even while being subjugated, but Colley's connection between national success and personal exposure overlooks the more immediate audiences addressed by these narratives. Whereas Colley senses reluctance to publish, I see enthusiasm among authors to capitalize on their suffering through early circulation as letters, dispatches, books, and printed columns in local and regional Anglo-Indian newspapers. Soldiers recount their humiliations in exchange for money, sympathy, and recognition from local readers; this was the redemption and compensation that captives believed they deserved. The burgeoning print market of Anglo-India provided financial and artistic encouragement to publicize their mortification and humiliation.

Some narratives remained in manuscript or were never acknowledged by their authors, but more joined the already avid market for accounts of the Mysore Wars and debates about the EIC that coincided with the Hastings impeachment trial from the 1780s and early 1790s. By 1788, only four years after the end of the second Mysore War, William Thomson was already publishing his compilation of others' accounts. By 1792, when Bristow publishes his account in Calcutta at the conclusion of the third Mysore War, he worries that the marketplace of captivity narratives is already inundated, offering a lengthy apology that explains why his narrative exists. He refers specifically to "mutilated News-paper accounts of the Author" and items "picked up from conversation," as well as those of "some of the persons . . . whose escape from Tippoo has been published since this compilation [his narrative] was undertaken."[29] He believes he needs to correct these accounts with his own. And although some narratives were published anonymously, many of the best-known were attributed from the outset, demonstrating vigorous interest in publicity. William Drake, a sailor on the *Hannibal*, a ship captured by the French and turned over to Mysore, published his account using his name in the *Madras Courier* (November 17, 1791) and the *Calcutta Gazette* (December 8, 1791), before it was then republished in at least seven different London newspapers by April of 1792.[30] Bristow likewise used his name in the title of his volume and in subsequent advertising for that volume printed in the *Calcutta Gazette*.

Why would soldiers mortified about being imprisoned, stripped, impoverished, scrutinized, starved, and perhaps circumcised broadcast that account to a marketplace of both known and unknown readers? Admittedly, such exposure is textual rather than corporeal (a crucial difference), but what is the advantage of revealing such vulnerabilities in writing and print?

Most answers to these questions have pointed toward a concerted effort to boost national sentiments by creating sympathy for their suffering among British readers. But as my brief account of this print marketplace illustrates, many captives believed their experience made for good publications, and they were not averse to sharing their suffering with a growing population of Anglo-Indian readers. Publication acts as a form of compensation for their suffering. Some imagined this compensation as artistic and reputational while others admitted it was more directly financial. Thomson, for example, suggested that imprisonment in Mysore animated captives' artistic reactions. The shortages caused by imprisonment provoked the "sensibility of our captive countrymen," calling forth the "energy of their minds" to "beguile the languor of total inoccupation."[31] In his estimation, beyond playing cards, dice, or cardboard chess, prisoners devoted their time to feeling. He describes the Mysore captives as a "deep tragedy" with almost "too perfect an [*sic*] unity of time and place" in the limited range of "action" for the captives but a great deal of "suffering," making their captivity a prototypical Aristotelian drama.[32] Authors found "relief" by "pouring forth" or by "adopting strains of affecting though unpolished poetry" to these audiences. "The strength of their sympathy with one another" and the wild swings of passion that occurred from the "desire of liberty" makes the aesthetic unity of their suffering a model for sentimental readers.[33]

In this ideology captivity narratives confirmed that prison could excite the authors' innate ability and change soldiers from objects of sympathy into its most authentic artists. Bristow admits his financial motives; the dedication to the first edition of his narrative claims it was "published chiefly with the view to benefit the children" (referring to his children). The advertisements for his narrative in the *Calcutta Gazette* claim it was published for the "sole benefit of James Bristow and his family."[34] Indeed, the publication of Bristow's narrative was aided by the cultural company-state that I detailed in chapter 1, which had only recently paid the salary he was owed during his imprisonment.[35]

Others were not as sanguine about their compatriots' conduct and the national feeling of redemption.[36] One example is especially striking: Henry

Oakes, after he was freed in 1784, recalls how the commissioners who had negotiated his release demanded money from him in exchange for food and shelter. To receive "such treatment from the enemy," Oakes admits, was to be expected, but "to receive it from one of our own countrymen . . . was cruel beyond measure" and "hurt our feelings more sensibly than any thing we had hitherto experienced" during his years of captivity.[37] He concludes that he will add "an account of the ill treatment of the prisoners by the government of Madras" when he finds a "more proper place," but that place never came. In fact, Oakes's critiques were quietly excised when his memoir was adapted as part of a larger compilation about the Anglo-Mysore Wars, migrating from its local Anglo-Indian audience toward a wider metropolitan one.[38] Local readers understood what he meant, but Britain's domestic audience would not.

I offer this meticulous description of the avid market for captivity narratives to suggest that captives were strategically business-oriented in the Anglo-Indian public sphere, not reticent and embarrassed. That public sphere possessed an insatiable appetite for published information originating from genuine sufferers. In the late eighteenth century, captives were a focal point of Anglo-India's literary publics. By the Napoleonic nineteenth century, these authors may have been transformed into figures of national outrage, but before then, they embraced more venal reasons for writing. Empire remained suspicious to these captives, but the money that came from spectacular suffering was not.

Prison Poetry and Antiwar Sentiments

The prison poetry of soldiers captured during the Mysore Wars forms an adjacent archive to the better-known captivity narratives. Never as prevalent as prose narratives, and often attached to them as an addendum to their printed volumes, these poems nonetheless demonstrate a sophisticated understanding of their readership, using the figure of the captive as a channel for the abrasive political critique of colonialism's apparatus. They assert these critiques by adopting the powerful first-person perspective of captives, making them speak about their experiences. This experiential position is essential to the exposition of these poems because they address proximate civilian audiences, critiquing those readers and, by extension, the imperial expansion that they helped to sustain. These poems illustrate the anguish of the captive soldier to those who might seek to ignore it. They reveal schisms within Anglo-India's reading audiences, which shift according to the intricate politics (and tricky distances) of Britain's imperium.

Simon Bainbridge describes the Romantic period as "an age of war poetry" because verse played a "major role in the mediation of the Revolutionary and Napoleonic wars to the British public."[39] Gillian Russell argues that the politics of early nineteenth-century warfare required civilian audiences to "'see' more than even the ordinary soldier in the field, assuming instead the position of a Wellington or a Napoleon."[40] These captivity poems utilize an opposite tactic, removing readers from the perspective of the superior officer or administrator and placing them within the claustrophobic overcrowded prison as a way of mediating the experience of warfare. Rather than sentimentalize and humanize the diffuse national project of empire, these poems specify it with detailed description of captives' conduct. As a group, these poems constitute an eighteenth-century microgenre that pointedly reappraises who benefits and who suffers from empire.[41]

Some of these prison poems call themselves "songs," performed as part of a "custom to celebrate particular days" when enough money had been collected to purchase higher quality food from the prison guards. These songs included well-known "old Scotch" ballads and improvised numbers.[42] Others seem more like written and printed poems rather than improvised songs; Richard Runwa Bowyer's manuscript account and William Thomson's *Memoirs* include "prison songs" of Seringapatam and Bangalore.[43] Kate Teltscher finds that the "Prison Song in Seringapatam," included at the end of the *Memoirs*, "undermines any sense of British identity," substituting instead a "composite European identity which seems to deny the possibility of patriotism."[44] But just as often, prison songs like this one accuse their readers of insufficiently commemorating the prisoners that warfare had created. Confronted—even humorously—with the sufferings of ordinary soldiers, Anglo-Indian readers are supposed to feel uncomfortable about their own freedom and leisure.

The "Prison Song in Seringapatam," for example, begins with a specific address to "Ye folks of Madras, / Who your time gaily pass" before brightly distinguishing the readers' leisurely lives from those of Mysore's captives. The song rejects the sympathies of reading audiences. Being moved by accounts of captives might lead to attachments to a larger community, but in the Anglo-Indian iteration the captive's account is also a critique of another's *lack* of sufficient empathy.[45] Removed from the distress of imprisonment, the residents of Madras—such as the "writer so merry, / The stiff secretary, / The gorger on turkey and ham"—continue their normal lives and so "Might laugh in his sleeve / At his friends in Seringapatam."[46] The final verse of the poem turns much more sincere and philosophical, shattering the otherwise ridiculous, mocking tone of the rest of the poem. Mockery, the poem's speaker explains, seeks to "disguise / Our sadness and sighs" and "chace away chilly despair" so that although "Resign'd to our woes, / And the chains of our foes," they still hope one day they might "open the door / Of our Jail at Seringapatam."[47] By transforming the jail's well-known deprivations into a satire of those who have read about but never experienced them, the poem intensifies the criticism of the leisurely and safe civilian population of Anglo-India.

The "Prison Song in Bangalore," in contrast, relies on directness rather than parody. Also addressed to readers in Madras, it insists that "our old friends in Madras" pay attention to the "scenes of our Bangalore jail."[48] There, the speaker claims, they were treated more like "horses . . . pent in a shade, / Like felons we're loaded with chains," with abundant time to "think on past pleasure with pain."[49] Ruminating on pain is one way that prisoners can "pass the dull hours of our time," but another is making poetry, which, together with the discordant "rattle [of] our chains," is the "music of Bangalore jail."[50]

The unnamed solider who speaks in "The Star Pagoda" (1790), also set in Bangalore, excoriates the wealth and ease of his superiors while describing his hunger and lack of liberty. The poem itself is modeled on John Philips's "The Splendid Shilling," a blank verse imitation of Milton first published in 1701, that recounts the unhappy day of a hungry poet sitting in his disheveled rooms and thinking about his debts.[51] In transporting these Miltonics to Asia, the author of "The Star Pagoda" swaps the reference to a British shilling with another coin, minted by the Company at Madras, called the "star pagoda," which shows Vishnu on one side and a five-pointed star on the other.[52] Instead of adopting the persona of a starving artist, the poem proceeds from the perspective of the captured soldier, whose explicitly anticommercial assertions include the sarcastic observation that it is a "happy . . . man" who sits in Madras, "sated" with "egg hoppers," "lemonade," and a "purse" full of star pagodas yet indifferent to war. The reader of his poem "sups Imperial," but the poem's captive is so hungry that sleep does not provide refuge. Unable to be distracted from his "ghastly Poverty" and "vacant stomach," he falls into a tricky "World of bliss" in which the feast that he dreams of is stolen by the "Knights, and Aldermen" of the city. By adapting "The Splendid Shilling" to the conflicts of southern India and shifting its perspective from the artist to the soldier, "The Star Pagoda" formulates an incisive critique about the subjugation enacted by Madras's merchants and Mysore's jailors alike.

Targeting local audiences served as a strategy for criticizing imperial warmongering. The author of "A Ditty. Written at the Conclusion of the Late War with Tippoo Sultan" (1794), which was published in the Madras newspaper *The Hircarrah*, vows that "since all our fighting is over, / Our cantonments no longer shall moulder," meaning they'll be able to return to their barracks.[53] The populace, he argues, should listen to the returning "poor war-worn soldier" because "he alone can tell what he has suffer'd." Having felt "famine, fatigue, and the weather," he patiently enumerates war's costs while nonetheless remaining optimistic that the memory of war "will last" so that readers will "Now the fruit let him reap of his labours." It was not meant to be; only five years after the publication of this poem, Mysore and Anglo-India were at war again.

A similar disdain for warfare is evident in "The Captive," which appeared in a Madras newspaper in 1791.[54] This poem rewrites Thomas Gray's "The Bard," but its author transforms the thirteenth-century Welsh bard of Gray's original poem into a British soldier captured by Haidar Ali.[55] In this model the English-Welsh antagonism of Gray's original poem is turned into an Anglo-Mysore one. As with other poems in the microgenre of eighteenth-century Anglo-Indian captivity poetry, "The Captive" offers a specific idea of how poetry should change when it is written in India.[56] Composed by Candidus, a prolific pseudonymous poet, the poem is datelined from "Camp near Nundy-droug Oct. 5, 1791," referring to a military encampment near Nandidurg, a fortress that protected an important entryway into the Kingdom of Mysore.[57] Candidus extensively substitutes the locations, figures, and circumstances of Gray's thirteenth-century Wales with southern India's embattled frontiers. Rather than a Welsh bard, the singing captive is a British soldier with "haggar'd eyes," a "loose . . . beard," and "sunburnt hair" that "stream'd like a meteor to the troubl'd air." The poem names some of the "gorgeous Chiefs and Statesman old" who in "bearded majesty appear" among the "Bramin's divine / Patanes and Moghuls of illustrious line," who make the air "tremble" with "strains of vocal transport" anticipating the decline of Tipu (and his French allies).[58]

Even as the captive remains in the "Dungeons of darkness, death, despair, and shame," his song urges revenge. In its altered geographical context, however, repeating exactly lines from Gray's poem creates unsettling connotations. While addressing soldiers killed in the Mysore Wars, for instance, the captive notes:

> Ye died amid your distant countries cries!
> No more I'll weep—they do not sleep,
> On yonder cliffs a grizly band—
> I see them set [sit]—they linger yet—
> Avengers of their native land,
> With me in dreadful harmony they join,
> And weave with bloody hand the tissue of thy line.

These lines cite Gray's poem almost exactly, yet what "native land" is imagined to be avenged? One answer can be found in a small but crucial revision that transforms Gray's "The Bard" into a captivity poem. In this excerpt Candidus's speaker refers to fallen comrades as having died amid "distant countries cries" (instead of "dying country's cries," as in Gray's original poem). The revision suggests that the "native land" is Britain, whose captives can hear their national comrades from over the ocean even in their dungeons. Yet a more controversial possibility is that the native land is Anglo-India, whose territories have been consecrated by the casualties described in "The Captive." In this reading, distance operates as a complicated proxy for issues of nativity, conquest, and sacrifice. Shifting Gray's vocabulary of "native land" and "weaving brothers" establishes a new nativity, as the poem's mode of address roots the speaker as resident to the land, made authentic by the sacrifices of imprisonment, overcoming the differences of distance and birth.

The poem ends much like Gray's, with the speaker committing suicide as a political act: the soldier plunges a dagger into his heart rather than leaping to his death, as Gray's bard does. But before he stabs with the dagger, he advocates for peace, not revenge:

> My verse adorn no more
> Fierce War or faithless foes,
> May Cannon cease to roar,
> Nor Man be curst with woes;
> Come *Peace* with all thy charming pleasures,
> With mutual love, in lively measures,
> Leading the dance, joining the song,
> While discord dies thy arts among!

Candidus endorses the imaginative possibility that art might prevail in lieu of continual war. In the place of "faithless foes" and cannons' roar, the captive predicts "mutual love, in lively measures," so that when "discord dies"—like the captive—it will be replaced with dancing, songs, and art. This kind of antiwar verse depicts art as a mechanism for legitimizing a peaceful resolution that is supposed to supersede its own prophetic pronouncements. Such optimism about art's political effects differs considerably, too, from Gray's "The Bard," whose conclusion prophesies the bloodiness of Welsh occupation and oppression.

Of course, one of Candidus's most formally compelling elements is also potentially the poem's most patronizing. By adopting Gray's articulation of Welsh vulnerability as a template for heroizing Anglo-Indian captives, the speaker calls for peace on a continent in which he is still a combatant. But here again the complex interpenetration of a rapidly globalizing eighteenth-century colonial world meets the more localizing audience of Anglo-Indian literature. Poems like "The Captive," "The Star Pagoda," and the prison songs of Seringapatam and Bangalore formulated speakers whose lived experience of warfare and captivity distinguished them from their readers, who came in for criticism rather than praise. These poems classify those who benefited from imperial violence and those who did not. Poetry may not refute patriotism directly, or explicitly undermine British colonial identities, but it separates many Anglo-Indian readers from soldiers, and both of them from metropolitan readers, who are typically presumed by literary scholars and historians to be the audiences of these poems. Soldiers ask for peace in these poems, recommending alternatives to warfare. Counterposed to the "Black Hole" of Calcutta narratives, the microgenre of the captivity poem turns the experiences of soldiers into an appeal for art rather than violence.

The Dancing Boys of Mysore

If the integrity of the captive is an indicator of the integrity of the community, then what is the consequence of captives who do not survive, who are never liberated, or, most troubling, who are converted to another ideology? Captivity narratives have flashed occasionally with these types of figures that John Demos calls "unredeemed captives."[59] They exemplify what Gary Ebersole claims is the "ultimate boundary situation," in which the "captive's world is turned topsy-turvy," and they promised readers "unmediated access" to non-European cultures, which, in Joe Snader's estimation, was an important part of the genre's appeal.[60] Of course, not all unredeemed captives or exotic worlds were thought to be equivalent, especially during the Mysore Wars, and there is ample evidence that imprisonment in Muslim nations and "turning Turk" were especially distressing to European sensibilities.[61] Honorable resisters—like William Baillie, the commanding officer defeated at the 1780 Battle of Pollilur, who died while incarcerated at Seringapatam—were celebrated as trustworthy. But there were more equivocal beings, such as those captured white adolescents who functioned as entertainers for the Mysore state during the 1780s, whose treatment signaled the most disruptive consequences of European colonialism's ideological contests with South Asian polities. Mysore's white dancing boys were an example of how armed conflict affected the integrity of empire's agents by making them its most spectacular yet enigmatic victims.

The amount of detail about the dancing boys varies among captivity narratives. All seem to agree, however, that white adolescents were captured, circumcised, and converted to Islam and integrated into the functions of the Mysore state (perhaps even into Tipu's intimate household) as performers. The total number subjected to this treatment is unclear. A list of Mysore's prisoners published in the *Madras Courier* in 1791 lists only four dancing boys, including "Thomas Thompson," a "dancer in Seringapatam," and "John Ryane," a "Dancing boy pris.[oner]."[62] Other accounts suggest the number was higher, perhaps fifteen or more.[63] Mark Wilks, a Madras Army officer and the first EIC resident at Mysore, claims that there were at least fifty captives, "chiefly boys," some of whom were "instructed to perform as singers and dancers for the future amusement of the tyrant."[64]

All of the narratives offer ambiguous descriptions of the boys' lives, often insinuating that they were sexually exploited. The anonymously authored *Narrative Sketches of the Conquest of Mysore* (1800) portrays these adolescents as involved in a "disgraceful occupation . . . entertaining the Sultaun [Tipu] in his hours of leisure, by dancing before him with all the unmanly antics that youth and activity were capable of being taught."[65] James Bristow offers a similarly menacing account, admitting that among the adolescent boys, after being circumcised, the "youngest and handsomest" were "intended for dancing boys."[66] William Drake describes how the dancing boys were given Muslim names and then "were taught dancing in the Country *style*, and forced to dance in female Dresses before Tippoo."[67]

Most scholars have focused on the fraught Anglo-Indian and British reactions to the circumcision of prisoners and their forced conversion to Islam. Circumcision was not just personal disfigurement but a "national humiliation" that turned Anglo-India's military defeats into strategic "emasculation."[68] The *Madras Courier* identified dozens of prisoners with Muslim names—such as John Alexander Dempster, who is also listed as "Sulliman Khan"—suggesting public acknowledgment by Anglo-Indians of converted captives.[69] Some prisoners may have resisted these circumcisions—and even enacted "parody circumcisions" to enrage their captors—but if the inclusion of converted Islamic names on the list of Mysore prisoners is any indication, then circumcision and conversion were common.[70] In one sense the dancing boys intensify the strategy of public mortification and spectacular suffering that had been enacted on European-descended soldiers. Tipu maintains his political legitimacy through white children, incorporating them into his kingdom and asserting his power over their bodies.[71]

But it was not just the connotation of sodomitical sex with white adolescents that troubled commenters like Wilks; it was also their association with women's work and the degraded effeminacy that it implied. Tellingly, most of these anglophone narratives compare the dancing boys to native women. They frequently mention that the dancing boys were trained in *nautch*, which involved a woman dancing and singing love songs while accompanied by men on instruments.[72] The eighteenth-century global traveler Edward Ives describes *nautch* as a series of "tumbling" movements in a dress that is "thin and light," perhaps referring to the *ghangra cholis* garb of skirts and navel-baring blouses.[73] The travel writer Jemima Kindersley adds that *nautch* involves the "continual removing [of] the shawl, first over the head, then off again; extending first one hand, then the other" while the "feet are likewise moved."[74] (Kindersley mentions sitars, bells, and drums, like those depicted in fig. 14.) There was a sense that "languishing glances, wanton smiles, and attitudes" were "not quite consistent with decency," ideas that led to the notion that *nautch* was equivalent to prostitution.[75] Donald Campbell's travel narrative of eighteenth-century India describes boys dancing as a "hideous practice," calling it an "impurity" worse than *nautch*, which, he feels compelled to point out, was "not very favourable to chastity."[76] The dancing boys were engaged in highly sexualized traditions of public erotic dancing and male transgender performance and were incorporated into a system that, as Anna Morcom notes, brought "into intimate proximity . . . high status men and low status women or effeminate men," reinforcing social hierarchies dating to South Asia's feudal past.[77]

The proximity of high-status men and low-status dancing boys offers another intimation—that the dancing boys, whether coerced or not, were traitors.

Figure 14. *A Dancing-Girl with Three Musicians*, playing cymbals, drum, and flute. Gouache, artist unknown (Tanjore [Thanjavur], India, ca. 1790s). © the Victoria and Albert Museum, London.

Some accounts described the dancing boys as intimates and confidants of the Mysore government, held "high in the estimation of Hyder [Haidar Ali]," Tipu's father, and considered "his children."[78] Thomson's *Memoirs* of the second Mysore War claims that slave boys received better treatment than their fellow prisoners, being "well clothed and fed" and "supplied with every accommodation." He claims that they were educated while in Mysore, "instructed in the Persian language, in arithmetic, and algebra," being "intended for the household of the Sultan, and to be about his person." The dancers were young ("could not be above twelve or thirteen years of age") and appeared "in the Mahomedan dress, white turbans, white linen jackets and long drawers."[79] These boys—young, impressionable, handsome—were absorbed within Tipu's sovereignty in the same way that wives and daughters of principal families were seen as an extension of his court, always allied with the sustaining of his power.[80]

Anglo-Indians' indignation about the boys' existence therefore originates not so much in concern for their welfare but in the dismay that they occupied roles more properly given to women. The depravity of the dancing boys is that they engage in erotic work that should be the domain of indigenous Indian women (and that they might receive better treatment because of it). Alterations to food, clothing, and education created the perception that European adolescents were not tortured symbols of Britain's national emasculation in South Asia but potentially agents of a foreign adversary. The conflict between Asian and European systems of sovereignty played out across the dancing boys' bodies.

Captivity as Social Regeneration

Portraying the dancing boys as a population of potential traitors raises questions about who benefits from the expansion of an empire. Little can be confirmed about what ultimately happened to the dancing boys. Many of the captivity narratives equated them with the Jews of the Babylonian captivity, referring to Psalm 137, which admonishes Jews not to sing or dance for the Babylonians lest they accept the realities of imprisonment. Wilks mentions that the "fate" of the dancing boys was to remain "unhappy beings" asked to sing their songs in a strange land.[81] Thomson compares the boys to the "captive Jews of old" who wept when they "remembered Zion," although he describes them as living in the "midst of ease and plenty."[82]

For the dancing boys, unlike the Jews of Babylon, captivity did not end with return or redemption. As far as English-language records indicate, none of the dancing boys were released. Other imprisoned soldiers, when asked about the boys, replied that they were "all dead."[83] These children, it appears, were absorbed into Mysore's private spaces of rule and were never seen or heard from again.

Most Anglo-Indians responded to the existence of the dancing boys by developing an ideological autoimmunity. They recognized that imprisonment and conversion jeopardized the symbolic edifice that explained why these children had been sent to war in the first place, so they cast them out of the community and depicted them as alien and lost. The warning is clear: imprisonment might produce artistic inspiration (and book sales), but for some prisoners lengthy immersion in Mysorean society could corrupt or, worse, convert them to an alternative spirit. Daniel O'Quinn notes that British art was concerned that in the Kingdom of Mysore "difference dissolves into similitude" as Europeans identify with Asians.[84] The dancing boys raised the possibility that captives might not maintain their connection to their former lives and so could not be trusted to reintegrate into Anglo-Indian culture.[85]

Warfare defines a collectivity more indelibly than any other communal enterprise. War is a "force that gives us meaning," as Chris Hedges argues, uniting a community by violently contrasting it with others. War forms its own culture, dominating everything it surrounds.[86] South Asia's white dancing boys were an especially potent sign of this domination. It was essential for the project of imperial violence that its casualties be explained as sacrifices among eager participants. Much like those narratives of slavery and conversion within Muslim domains ("turning Turk") that troubled early modern Britain, to acknowledge the dancing boys was also to force readers to consider the status of imperialism's white victims, something less agreeable to most Western authors than castigating Muslim antagonists as despots or barbarians. If war is indeed a force that gives community a purpose, then captivity is its dangerous by-product. The dancing boys are not celebrated as victims because their captivity eradicates the ideological differences that demanded warfare in the first place.

The inclusion of the dancing boys in Anglo-Mysore narratives indicates the larger problems that arise when imperialists are taken prisoner in strange lands. Is it better to die than to cooperate? While Anglo-India's captivity narratives are not clear, another set of answers might emerge from the surprising similarity between the dancing boys of Mysore and Tipu's two biological sons, who were provided as hostages in 1792 to guarantee the treaty ending the third Mysore War. As boys of eight and ten years old, they resided in Madras for two years, acting as security for Tipu's implementation of the territorial transfers and indemnity payments demanded by the Company and its allies after their temporary victory over Mysore.[87]

The conveyance of Tipu's sons became a crucial imaginative moment for British dominion in southern India, oft depicted in print, paintings, and monuments. At least five monuments dedicated to Lord Cornwallis after his victories in 1792 depict him shielding India's children, presenting the public with a benevolent and paternalistic image of Empire.[88] Robert Home, who traveled as part of Cornwallis's army during the third Mysore War, exhibited a painting in his rooms in Madras depicting the handover (fig. 15).[89] Scholars have argued that the visual depictions of Tipu's hostage sons like Home's were an explicit counterpoint to the captivity narratives being published at the same time, but that intriguing juxtaposition misses the similarities between Mysore's dancing boys and Tipu's kidnapped sons.[90] In both instances children were used as instruments and expressions of territorial contest and state-building. They were made into public spectacles that celebrated their captors' generosity and humiliated their unassimilated comrades. And they became instruments to extend the sovereignty of an adversarial ideological regime. Tipu's sons were portrayed as receiving the compassion of Cornwallis. Captivity narratives suggest that Tipu extended munificence to Britain's young adolescents, clothing them and educating them in physical conditions more favorable than those of their adult comrades. In each instance the head of state makes some claim for the successes of his patriarchy, which are

Figure 15. Robert Home, *The Reception of the Mysorean Hostage Princes by Marquis Cornwallis*, ca. 1793. Oil on canvas. Courtesy of the National Army Museum, London.

repeated artistically through the representations of the child's person, either as a dancer in Seringapatam or as a character in a British painting. In each instance children become the inspiration for grander tales about the promises and penalties of imperial violence.

These children differ from other "subalterns with white faces," as Linda Colley calls the low-level soldiers and laborers who suffered the impact of imperial expansion.[91] They move among the different territories, private spaces, and artistic spheres of these contests. They show how the local and regional coordinates of Anglo-India's geopolitics altered the genre of captivity narrative that throughout the British imperium explained the significance of war. The threat of sexual exploitation is integral to captivity narratives, from the early modern period until the present, but its hyperlocalization in the figure of the dancing boy reveals a new accounting about who could be redeemed from captivity and who was perceived to be lost. These adolescents are not like their near artistic cousins, the colonial women captured by Native Americans who are ultimately forgiven and reintegrated into their original society by the captivity narrative's end.[92] They are more akin to the unredeemable "renegades" who abandoned their original culture or to Barbary's Christian captives, who faced similar threats of circumcision, sodomy, and submission to Islam.[93] The inability to ascertain the fate of many of these dancing boys suggests the uncomfortable possibility that Britain's imperial authors knew they could not be commemorated or made into national martyrs. The dancing boys are indigestible shards cutting against the idea that the Mysore Wars righted the unsteady project of overseas empire. Together with Mysore's sensitive captives and their antiwar poetry, these adolescents propose an important and perhaps unexpected conclusion: the critique of empire was an essential component for the emergence of Anglo-Indian culture. Those most proximate to the violence of colonial warfare used Anglo-India's nascent public sphere to advertise themselves as the most credible illustration of empire's costs.

Literary Culture of Colonial Outposts

Penang, Sumatra, and Java, 1771–1816

The 1816 meeting in Grasmere described at length in *Confessions of an English Opium-Eater* (1822) between Thomas de Quincey and a man he calls a "Malay" has become a familiar scene for postcolonial literary critics because it demonstrates succinctly how global thinking was constituted by linguistic and cultural translation between Asia and Europe.[1] Indeed, since the late eighteenth century the Malay archipelago had proved a distant fascination for English authors such as de Quincey and, before him, Adam Smith, whose *Wealth of Nations* (1776) made the area central to an emergent "global commodity regime."[2]

The Malay archipelago may have proved essential for British fantasies, but what of those European-descended authors and artists, most of them forgotten now, who actually lived in the territories of which Smith theorized and de Quincey dreamed? Literary scholars have done little to place these figures within the scope of "English literature": they exist uneasily within the broad category of colonial discourse or remain submerged within the imperial archive. In this chapter I return to these authors to describe the local and regional orientations of an anglophone Indian Ocean world. I seek to understand better the publics, audiences, and ambitions of those authors who were involved in British incursions into Southeast Asia between the 1770s and the 1820s.

My analysis of these authors is meant to extend recent thinking about how the Indian Ocean might contribute to a "method" of economic and cultural analysis.[3] Kuan-Hsing Chen has offered Asia as an "imaginary anchoring point" from which its cultures might define "alternative horizons and perspectives" that push postcolonial studies beyond what he calls its "obsessive critique of the West."[4] These geographic alignments have necessitated that scholars rethink the impositional models that followed in the decades after Edward Said's *Orientalism* and the discursive models inspired by Homi Bhabha's mimicry and Sara Suleri's "rhetoric of English India."[5] The focus on oceanic and littoral geographies has added sophistication and specificity to late twentieth-century insights about empire as a literary and cultural, not just political and economic, endeavor.

One way to expand these new horizons and material anchoring points is to focus on the cultural and literary archives of European and Anglo-Indian authors who existed on the Asian margins of Britain's India-centered eighteenth century. Three locations are paramount. The first is Penang (Pulau Pinang), in present-day Malaysia. I discuss the development of its literary infrastructure, concentrating on Southeast Asia's first English-language newspaper, the *Prince of Wales Island Gazette*, which debuted in 1806. The second location is the island of Sumatra, where the orientalist William Marsden was stationed for most of the 1770s. While there, he composed poems and plays that argue for the advantages of distance from England. The third location is the neighboring island of Java, which the British occupied between 1811 and 1816. During this brief occupation, they established a newspaper, the *Java Government Gazette* (*JGG*), which became the locus of a mixed-language literary culture that accentuated the extensive regional nature of English writing in Napoleonic-era Asia.

All three of these examples demonstrate how scholars' emphasis on reciprocal and fluid relationships between cores and peripheries, metropoles and colonies, has obscured anglophone literary publics that were self-referential and self-organized. The institutions of these literary publics attune scholars to the local and regional networks of the Indian Ocean world that existed alongside those oceanic frameworks that typically shape our analysis of imperial literary culture. They show that while authors and institutions in anglophone Asia were still affected by the gravity of London, they also celebrated local literary geographies and aesthetics against a putatively universal imperial taste or a shared colonial discourse.

The Bay of Bengal and the Geography of "Greater India"

The British had been trading from Sumatra for nearly a century by the time William Marsden arrived in 1771 as a junior clerk for the British East India Company.[6] An expedition from Madras created an outpost to compete for the pepper trade with the Dutch on the nearby island of Java, where pepper plants were plentiful. Links across the Bay of Bengal to India persisted in the ensuing century. While stationed in Fort Marlborough, Marsden wrote a "birth-day ode" commemorating a woman who was about to leave Sumatra. In many ways his poem is an unremarkable love lyric from a young EIC employee enamored with a woman at his relatively small colonial outpost remote from his upbringing in Ireland. He celebrates her by invoking "ev'ry nymph" of the woods and each "Naiad of Sumatran floods" who describe this unnamed woman as

> our pride;
> For ne'er did mortal beauty grace
> Our isle with half so sweet a face.[7]

If we think about Marsden in terms of national identity, even with its multicountry complexities that mixed Ireland and Britain in empire, then it would seem natural to assume that when Marsden laments that this celebrated beauty will "mortify our pride, / By shining forth on t'other side," he means to refer to Great Britain. But as a footnote to the poem makes clear, "the other side" to which this lady retreats was not England but India. She had abandoned Sumatra for the "other side" of the Indian Ocean.[8]

More than a decade later, in 1788, Elisha Trapaud, a young officer with the Madras Engineers, published a travel narrative that focused on Prince of Wales Island, near Penang, a strategic harbor that he believed extended India's coasts eastward beyond Bengal.[9] In a report from another mission Alexander Kyd, sent by Lord Cornwallis, then governor-general, to investigate the utility of a settlement at Penang to counter Dutch advances, conflates present-day Malaysia with subcontinental India when he advocates for Penang as a "Naval Port" that was "necessary on this side of India," referring to the eastern edge of the Bay of Bengal.[10]

Marsden's, Trapaud's, and Kyd's phrasing clarifies some of the intraregional hierarchies and divisions within British Asia, when "the other side" is not across the world but across the Bay of Bengal and when the Malay Peninsula might be understood as the "other side" of India. These intraregional orientations were as significant historically as those networked oceanic relationships between metropole and colony that have typically defined Britain's empire. The Bay of Bengal was "a region at the heart of global history," Sunil Amrith asserts. It functioned in the early nineteenth century through the ongoing process of ecological specialization (that drove the spice trade) and human migration (that propelled cultural exchange), and became more integrated by the successes of British imperialism, which eventually governed its possessions as a "patchwork of separate territories."[11] Administrative visions like those of Trapaud and Kyd pushed the orbit of British India across the Bay of Bengal and into the Strait of Malacca (Melaka) at the end of the eighteenth century, resulting in geographical and literary imaginations that inflated the scale of British India while connecting it with distant places such as Penang, Java, and Sumatra. In this environment the literary culture of Anglo-India extended into other regions of Asia that were linked to it by relationships of dependency and, at times, antagonism, as they sought to differentiate themselves from Anglo-India.

India has always had an expansive range of connotations that fit poorly with the boundaries of the modern country that carries its name. The Bay of Bengal has been the center of a "Sanskrit cosmopolis" that extended from Afghanistan to Indonesia, and the South Indian Cholas created the first "Bay of Bengal empire."[12] Migrations of Chinese and Near Eastern Muslims collided with Hinduism's flickering aspirations for a Greater India, the ambitions of aggressive Asian polities that eventually gave way to European expansions. All of these preexisting networks aided European growth in the region, and the high-volume of trade around the Bay of Bengal made the region different, not less developed, than Europe's system of modern nation-states.[13] It can be easy to forget that during the eighteenth century the India in "Anglo-India" was not an enclosed and consistent territorial site.[14] While "Indies" suggests global connections, India also indicated historically shifting regional combinations.[15]

The EIC was a vast trading regime with agents scattered throughout the world, but because of its popular name, it is easy to forget that the Company's reach extended far beyond subcontinental India to trading outposts and residencies throughout Asia and the Atlantic.[16] The British absorbed new territories in South and southeastern Asia by comparing and subordinating them to India, creating chains of connotation among these locales as forced relationships conveyed through the vagaries of exploration and naming. Paul Giles offers the example of an 1827 map of northern Australia that names this tropical zone "Australindia" while simultaneously emphasizing the "striking similarities" between Australia and India. Giles notes that this was an explicit attempt to "naturalize" a "strange new continent" in the colonial terms of the "established British empire in India."[17] Philosophers like Adam Smith may have seen Southeast Asia as an origin for a new global perspective, but it was also during this period a place for incipient regional thinking.[10] Beginning in the nineteenth century, the British Crown made distinctions between its "Colonial Office" and its "India Office," so that *India* could refer to "the British-controlled government of India" (after 1857) or the "territory under the jurisdiction of the Raj as in 'British India' or the residents of that country as in 'Indians.'"[19] It was not a "set of strings" or "lines of telegraph wire" running from European capitals to colonial outposts but a "nodal point" in itself from which ideas, institutions, and people radiated outward.[20] Tony Ballantyne describes this radiating India as a "subimperial center" that stretched its influence across space in ways that can be found in the writings of administrators, authors, engineers, and sailors like Marsden, Trapaud, and Kyd.[21]

These regional outlooks, Ash Amin points out, have historically been correlated with "a strong public sphere composed of common interests, local orientation and active deliberation over a local way of life."[22] These strong public spheres are usually assumed to be indigenous ones that authentically resist the productions of cosmopolitan Anglophones who were attached to European ideas and cultural centers even if they adapted them to their Asian homes. But the regional extension of Anglo-India's literary publics was also created by the political contests that caused Marsden, Trapaud, and Kyd to move around the Bay of Bengal and the Indian Ocean world. One of the most significant late eighteenth-century contests occurred in Penang, founded as an EIC presidency in 1786 by Francis Light in an attempt to compete with the Dutch in the Bay of Bengal. The speculator James Scott heralded it as a "second Bombay," hoping it would anchor the British presence in Southeast Asia the way Bombay was seen to do on the Indian Ocean.[23] Penang was allied to India as a penal colony for Brahmins convicted of capital offenses, who were permanently exiled there for crimes after popular outrage over their death sentences.[24]

By the early nineteenth century, Penang had a European and European-descended population of approximately one thousand to fifteen hundred people, making it equivalent to a small provincial town (though its non-European population was significantly larger).[25] Penang was such a multilingual location that the EIC insisted that advertisements for bids on monopolies of certain commodities (arrack liquor, opium, and food staples) should appear in "the Chinese, Malayan, and the Malabar Language"; the 1806 sales resulted in most of these monopolies being purchased by natives.[26] Prominent Islamic figures such as "Tuan Syed Hussen" (Tengku Syed Hussain) offered expensive dinners for Company administrators and paid for the release of debtors on the birthday of King George III.[27]

The first primarily English-language newspaper in Southeast Asia was founded in Penang in 1806, but its printer, Andrew Burchet Bone, arrived there from Calcutta, where he had apprenticed with a prominent printer and had helped run a circulating library.[28] Before that, Bone was the proprietor of the *Madras Gazette*, which was printed in the largely indigenous populated "Black Town."[29] The *Prince of Wales Island Gazette* was explicitly modeled from Bone's experience with Anglo-Indian newspapers: he sought Company patronage for his newspaper, as his earlier Anglo-Indian counterparts did, and offered his Madras newspaper experience as evidence of having been "brought up in that particular branch of business."[30] He asked the secretary of Prince of Wales Island to consider patronizing a newspaper "conducted on the same plan as the Government Papers of Calcutta, Madras, Bombay and Ceylon," arguing the newspaper would benefit the Penang community by providing business documents cheaply.[31]

Bone's economic arguments centered on utility. Since "stationery"—referring to governmental forms—was "difficult to obtain" and its cost was "immense" to transport from India, he asked to be permitted to print these forms locally, which would also ensure they were "struck off in a uniform, neat, and correct manner."[32] The EIC authorities agreed, noting in one consultation that "printing materials" had arrived from Europe to "complete the establishment" and that their arrival was a sign of "every encouragement and support from Government" for the press that was otherwise situated "far distant from any part of civilized India."[33] India becomes the orientation for the printing industry that trained Bone in the newspaper business. The EIC saw Bone's press as its extension into new terrain.

By 1808 the *Prince of Wales Island Gazette* was advertising bookbinding services and was printing on behalf of the Court of Judicature in Penang, including forms for administering oaths, probate, wills, court summons, and habeas corpus petitions.[34] Oaths and petitions, as Sudipta Sen, Robert Travers, and others have explained, were an important part of colonial legal jurisprudence, and the founding of Penang's local court also necessitated the creation of a print apparatus that sustained Bone's business.[35] But Bone also rented houses and administered raffles (using the newspaper as publicity), while also printing and selling blank bonds, bills of lading, and powers of attorney forms, much as occurred in early newspaper economics of Calcutta and Madras.[36] After the debates of the 1790s about EIC surveillance and the significance of Company patronage for sustaining newspapers' reading publics, Bone conformed assiduously to the Company's political and economic demands, offering proof sheets to the secretary of Prince of Wales Island ("for the purpose of erasing any part which may be deemed improper to appear before the public") and even pricing his variously sized advertisements in ways Company government desired.[37] There was none of the resistance that defined the earliest Calcutta and Madras newspapers.

The readership of the *Prince of Wales Island Gazette* was "likely British," Geoff Wade suggests, but also "reached other cultures as well."[38] The newspaper included Malay language advertisements (in the Arabic-derived Jawi script), indicating that the multilingualism that motivated so many of the literary publics of Anglo-India that I described in chapter 2 was present from the outset in Southeast Asia as well. Like Anglo-India's newspapers, the *Prince of Wales Island Gazette* was integrated into the wider anglophone regional network, with the Bengal Presidency, for example, purchasing a subscription for two copies (likely as a means of monitoring events across the Bay of Bengal).[39] That information network was reciprocated, and Bone sold pamphlets imported from India on notorious subjects, such as trials for rape and murder.[40]

Yet he struggled to balance Anglo-India's regional audience with his more local one. An 1811 issue of his newspaper, for example, acknowledges that Bone has had "occasion to observe" the complaints of his newspaper colleagues in Bengal ("particularly the Hurkara" referring to the *Bengal Hurkaru*, founded in 1795) about the "paucity of information" contained in the *Prince of Wales Island Gazette* about events from Penang. Bone explains in one editor's column that Penang is small enough that everyone has heard the settlement's rumor and gossip before his paper has even printed it; what audience is there for such information in the newspaper when everyone already knows?[41] This state of affairs pushed him to sacrifice the desires of more distant readers for detailed information in favor of the immediate demands of local readers, who were the majority of his customers. His devotion to narrow resident circumstances explains what B. C. Bloomfield sees as the strange apologies to his readership for absences and weaknesses: Bone was trying to report what local gossip and conversation had not already dispersed among Penang's inhabitants.[42] The need to weigh local tales against regional readership went unresolved throughout Bone's tenure. A fire in 1814 forced him to seek a loan from the EIC, and by May 1815 he was dead.[43] An announcement in a May 1815 issue explained mournfully "to its more distant readers" what Penang residents already knew—that the newspaper had been interrupted by Bone's death. It informed these regional readers that a new editor would continue the newspaper and would make it "as interesting to the Community" as the "limited extent of local circumstances" in Penang would permit.[44] Resolving the dichotomies between readers on the eastern edge of the Bay of Bengal and its subscribers from India remained a necessity even after Bone's death.

Outpost Aesthetics: William Marsden in Sumatra

Penang was only one of the outposts around the Bay of Bengal and through the Strait of Malacca that developed an intraregional relationship with the larger presidency cities of India. Another important site was Sumatra, which served as the home of the orientalist William Marsden for nearly a decade during the 1770s. Marsden is primarily known as the author of the *History of Sumatra*, which he published in 1783 but revised throughout his life. It has been rare for literary scholars to examine the poems and plays that he composed while he was stationed at Sumatra acquiring the knowledge and experiences that would lead to his later orientalist studies. Rather than trace and reevaluate Marsden's orientalism, in this section I consider his imaginative writing as conceptualizations of what I call the outpost aesthetics of anglophone Asia. From Marsden's vantage the relationship between the Asian outpost and literary ambition was complicated. He admits that he possessed an "ardent thirst for knowledge, both for its own sake and from the flattering, however distant, hope, of its enabling me to distinguish myself, in the event of my future return to England."[45] Places like Sumatra, Java, and Penang rarely register in eighteenth- and early nineteenth-century English literary studies, in part because scholars have always assumed that before the mid-nineteenth century their cultures were negligible, unimportant, or merely imitative. Marsden shows, instead, sustained reflection about how Sumatra alters what it means to be a writer of literature in English.

British interest in Sumatra began in earnest during the 1680s as a site for pepper cultivation.[46] The EIC was enthusiastic enough that in 1686 the Madras Presidency council, which had managerial jurisdiction over factories in Sumatra, believed that its primary outpost at Bencoolen (Bengkulu) could become an important trading city, but the town was susceptible to disease and natural disasters like earthquakes. After failing to entice large numbers of Britons to settle there, the EIC eventually targeted more local migration from Dutch settlements in Java and among the large Chinese diaspora in Southeast Asia. They encouraged the construction of Chinese "publick houses" and offered funds for Chinese migrants to open businesses, such as sugar refineries and cotton mills.[47] But they also exiled convicts from India to Sumatra, such as when Robert Kitson, the sheriff and self-described "coroner" of 1770s and 1780s Bombay, recorded repeatedly in notebooks that he was "whipping" residents from "Apollo Gate to the Bazaar Gate" and then transporting them to Sumatra.[48]

The majority of Bencoolen's white population was male; it was rare for a white woman to live in Sumatra, perhaps explaining the intensity of the nymphs and naiads in Marsden's celebratory ode that I described in the previous section. Bencoolen's early eighteenth-century administrator, Joseph Collet, claimed the outpost had "but 5 White things in Petticoats" and groused that one was a "Bawd," another was "non-compos"—that is, crazy—and had to be "confin'd to a Dark room and straw," while another was "as well shap'd as a Madagascar Cow."[49] The situation appears not to have changed decades later when the American sailor Dudley Leavitt Pickman complained there was "but one European Lady" and that she added "little to the morals" of the place.[50] The lack of white women, together with the always volatile economics of spice cultivation and trading, may have contributed to the deputy governor Walter Ewer's sense in 1800 that Bencoolen was "a Batavian settlement, not an English one"—that is, a place composed of multiple ethnicities and religions, none of which predominated.[51] A 1782 census seems to confirm that the small garrison at the EIC factory of Fort Marlborough in Bencoolen was extremely multinational and multiracial, composed of about two-thirds "natives of Great Britain and Ireland" but the rest made up of Dutch, French, American, Portuguese, and "Topases" (referring to mixed race Portuguese-Asians); soldiers and natives extended the population.[52] This diverse group meant that race was forefront in Bencoolen, leading one white officer to wonder in 1757: "What if the Chinese and the Malya's [Malays] here were of the same Colour with us; who then could tell by all that Appears, who was the Pagan, who the Mahometan, who this Nomenal Christian."[53]

William Marsden arrived at this variegated environment in 1771 as a "writer"—a junior accountant—for the EIC. He traveled to Sumatra because his two older brothers also worked for the Company; the oldest, Thomas, died in Madras in 1771, and another brother, John, was stationed with William in Fort Marlborough.[54] On arriving in Sumatra, Marsden gushed over the "luxuriant verdure and picturesque scenery of the coast," describing it as a "terrestrial paradise."[55] William thrived and was eventually promoted to secretary of Fort Marlborough in 1776, where, as he notes, his job was to translate into English the local Malayan speech, "studying the written character, and exercising myself in the perusal of epistolatory [*sic*] correspondence"; he also compiled a study of Sumatran customs and laws (*adat*).[56] By 1779 he had departed Sumatra, but it was this training, he later argued, that "laid the foundation of that degree of knowledge" that enabled him to publish his "Grammar and Dictionary of the language."[57]

While stationed in Sumatra for those eight years, Marsden contributed avidly to its literary culture and sought to expand its artistic world. He composed poems that he described as the "offspring of happy hours"; Marsden recounts his EIC employment as "not very urgent or laborious" and recasts his ample leisure time as enabling of his early literary pursuits.[58] "During my residence abroad," he notes, "poetry both afforded an agreeable relaxation from business, and acted as the handmaid to more substantial studies," presumably referring to those ethnographical observations that would form the *History of Sumatra*, which secured him the recognition in Europe that he craved.[59] But he also felt like poetry was a prophylactic against the disorganization of outpost life by "elevating the taste, to prevent the indulgence in idle habits into which young persons who find themselves independent of moral control are too apt to fall."[60] While in Sumatra, Marsden claims he "made translations of the Greek odes of Anacreon and Sappho."[61] Before it became the guiding topic of his orientalist writing, the local social scene was also the audience of his poetry, which was written, he claims, for the "perusal, of a few intimate friends" that formed the assemblies and coteries of Sumatra's society.[62] It must have been a somewhat sizable reading population, the archivist Graham Shaw speculates, to justify the shipment in 1776 from London to Bencoolen (and onward to Canton) of nearly three hundred books, some technical manuals and dictionaries but other works of literature by Shakespeare, Gray, Sterne, and Goldsmith, as well as printings of *The Tatler*, *The Spectator*, and *The Rambler*.[63]

The poems that Marsden shared with these intimates were conventional, such as one "song" to a lady's beauty and another epigram that he claims was merely a "saucy joke" about how women, whether "modest, pert, submissive, [or] loud," were the "cheer" and "torment" of men.[64] Sumatran society served as both inspiration and vehicle for his poetry, most clearly thematized in an untitled ode from 1773 addressed to his brother John, who had left Bencoolen for the "wild country" of the interior island to survey pepper plantations. The poem describes Fort Marlborough society and his brother John's interaction with a Sumatran society. It asks that his "dear brother":

. . . come away
from *Pâli*.
Pray think how lonely we are here,
Deprived of all we hold most dear;
To try our heavy hearts to cheer
were folly.[65]

Though John Marsden travels through "rude deserts" and "thick woods and torrents too," presumably to reach "Pâli," when he arrives, Marsden imagines his brother to be "lull'd to rest" at night "with songs . . . of rural goddesses." These "rural goddesses," a footnote explains, were the "unmarried daughters of the principal inhabitants (termed *gadês*, or virgins, in the language of the country, but by Europeans goddesses)," who "soothe, or disturb, the rest of the wearied stranger" with their "unceasing melodies"—literalized versions of the Sumatran nymphs and naiads who sing in Marsden's other poems.[66]

From this rather enticing situation Marsden seeks to call his brother back to the outpost art world that they shared. Part of the pleasure of John Marsden's company derived from their roles in Fort Marlborough's fledgling amateur theater. The majority of the roles William performed were female, he remembers, including "Belvidera, Calista, the Mourning Bride, Mrs. Beverley," referring to characters from Thomas Otway's *Venice Preserv'd* (1682), Nicolas Rowe's *The Fair Penitent* (1703), William Congreve's *The Mourning Bride* (1697), and Susanna Centlivre's *The Gamester* (1705).[67] In addition to their persistent popularity throughout the eighteenth century, staging these plays was a means of mobilizing and contesting English cultural hegemony far away from the British Isles.[68]

Restoration-era drama may have dominated the amateur theatrical productions of Fort Marlborough but not Marsden's own plays. While in Sumatra, he reports he composed at least one play, *Maon and Moriat* (ca. 1776–77), which was set in Ireland during a hazy antique period and written in "the spirit of romantic adventure" among "active and warm-blooded [Irish] countrymen."[69] It seems unlikely that the play was performed on Sumatra's stage, though it may have been read in small assemblies.[70] Marsden's play follows Maon's quest to reclaim the kingship of Ireland from his uncle, Kimbath, who had usurped and killed Maon's father. Along the way Maon falls in love with Moriat, the daughter of Maon's ally, the king of Munster. It is easy to imagine how the play's obvious issues of sovereignty and servitude, together with scenes in which families are destroyed by bribes of "all-prevailing gold," might resonate with the exercise of British power in the Asian imperium, especially owing to the importance of family alliances for securing political power in Sumatra.[71] The play combines the dramatic qualities and stilted, antiquated syntax of James Macpherson's Ossian poems with elements of Shakespearean dramas like *Hamlet* and *Macbeth*.

Kathleen Wilson has argued that Marsden remakes Sumatra into the "center of a new world history and a comparative linguistics" so that the provinces of the British Empire might see themselves as participating in the "center."[72] She has documented more specifically how the English theater, and especially plays like Rowe's *The Fair Penitent*, were instruments for inculcating "routines and ideologies of rule but also rites of possession and dominion" throughout British colonies, reconfiguring a "'national' culture in global settings."[73] But, as Marsden's artistic productions show, he achieves another goal, too. When Marsden performs Calista from Rowe's *Fair Penitent*, writes a medieval Irish version of *Macbeth* while in Sumatra, or composes poems for Fort Marlborough's nascent theater, he does not necessarily inculcate an easily identified national culture as much as sharpen and define its regional manifestation.

Consider Marsden's new "Epilogue" to Susanna Centlivre's *The Wonder* (1714), which he wrote to be spoken by his brother John for a 1773 production of the play in Fort Marlborough, perhaps one of the last productions at the theater before it burned down. During the production, John played Don Felix, one of the characters involved in this early eighteenth-century comedy of misinformation and courtship confusion.[74] Centlivre's original epilogue emphasized that women were "as fit for other Business as for Love," and Marsden turns this sentiment into an opportunity to address the local audience and contemplate what it means to make outpost art.[75] Still dressed as the Portuguese Don Felix, John exclaims that during his time at Fort Marlborough,

I, in dramatic wars a volunteer,
Have long sought fame with emulation here;
Anxious to please have borrow'd any shape,
From Pierre and Zanga down to Captain Cape:
And though my years have passed in this hard duty,
No Benefit acquir'd—no Nabob's booty,
Yet with mod'rate share of praise content,
I feel no cause to deem those years mis-spent.[76]

William's epilogue was inspired by John having to leave Fort Marlborough for the out-stations to survey pepper plantations that I referred to earlier. Drawing on the lengthy English and classical tradition of retirement and martial verse, John reflects on his time in Sumatra. He describes himself as having volunteered for Sumatra's "dramatic wars" but having done so without receiving "benefit" or "Nabob's booty" but rather for the "mod'rate share of praise" from the audience that leaves him contented that he has not misspent his years. He has, as he explains, "sought fame with emulation here," where the notion of "here" refers to geographical location and the prominence of the theatrical stage but also the listening audience of Fort Marlborough and Sumatra all at once. "Here" is where John sees that "so much taste, good-nature, [and] wit abounds" and where he remembers "long-lov'd scenes." Throwing away his Don Felix costume in the middle of his speech, he continues, speaking fully in his own person, that while "Once with delighted eyes I view'd these toys [his costume]," he claims they now serve as "sad mementos of forbidden joys," asking ultimately that his audience "still to this cherish'd house [the theater] your kindness show."[77] The references to "here" and "this cherish'd house" give abstract and specific definitions of Fort Marlborough's artistic culture that contrasts favorably with more distant locales in Europe. While "Europe may then her critic talents boast," in Sumatra, he insists, "pleas'd approving smiles adorn our coast."[78]

In this epilogue the Marsden brothers lay out a meticulous argument for the arts of the British outpost. Removed from London and from more local cultural centers like Madras and Calcutta, Marsden asserts the satisfactions of Marlborough's amateur theater arise from the participation of its audience. They play the parts, and for that reason, rather than engaging with the "critic talents" that Europe may "boast," they receive the pleasures of a laughing, crying, and sympathetic crowd. And in this sense sympathy is crucial—familiar with the actors and the playwrights alike, the audience may display the "pleasing smiles" that "adorn" the coasts of anglophone Sumatra. His audience seems to have agreed with John's sentiments; William writes in his *Memoirs* that his "Epilogue" produced a "sympathetic effect on the audience, not a little flattering to a juvenile poet" like himself.[79]

Marsden was not always enthusiastic about the potential of Fort Marlborough for inspiration. Though he felt the "perpetual verdure" of the country, with a "view of distant mountains" that made it a place that could "scarcely be surpassed in beauty," the "pernicious influence of the air" and failing health was the "real bane of our contentment."[80] His parody of Horace's

"Septimi Gades aditure mecum" that he titled "To My Brother" worries that both of them will

> ... pass the prime
> Of life in this barbarian clime,
> Surrounded by uncouth Malays.[81]

Yet he was not exactly enthusiastic about "home" either, worrying on his voyage back to England that in Fort Marlborough he had been "too much cherished by friends who loved me, and raised to too much consequence in the sphere (confined though it was)"; away from Sumatra and "set afloat in the world," he claims it will be necessary he should find his "proper level" again.[82]

In this way his time in Sumatra becomes an instrumental part of the imperial writing career. After first arriving in 1771, Marsden recognized the potential of Sumatra as the subject of an epic poem that he briefly called the *Malaiad.* Sumatra, with its "unaccustomed and striking objects," seemed the perfect repository for new epic material, as it would for so many other authors that arrived in Asia, such as Sir William Jones, who sketched out his never-completed epic, *Britain Discovered,* while aboard the *Crocodile* in 1783, or Eyles Irwin, who expresses the necessity for South Asian terms in his Indian epic, the *Ruins of Madura,* in letters to his friend William Hayley.[83] Arguably, it was its potential for epic poetry that led Marsden to his more obvious orientalist pursuits that ranked Sumatra, in his mind, as the most "bountiful indulgences of nature" to be "unaccountably neglected by writers."[84] It was only after Marsden abandoned his original epic poem and completed his tragedy *Maon and Moriat* that he began to collect materials for a "general account of the island, in a physical, moral, and political view" that would become his *History of Sumatra,* a text that would form the apogee of his career.[85] Marsden thinks first of poetry and plays, and only later of orientalist history, as genres that might convey the "striking objects" he perceived in Sumatra. The writing career that begins with the slow geographical displacement of traveling across the oceans continues as movement among literary modes: from epical to theatrical to historical.

Multilingualism in the *Java Government Gazette* (1812–1816)

Marsden departed from Sumatra two decades before the Indonesian archipelago erupted as a proxy for the conflicts of the French Revolution. Java, the largest island of the archipelago, was the primary location of the Dutch East India Company (the *Vereenigde Oost-Indische Compagnie* or VOC) and its headquarters in Batavia (now Jakarta). The Netherlands was "neither truly sovereign nor yet completely subordinate" during this period, subject, instead, to the transformations that also drove Napoleonic France, including the declaration of the Batavian Republic in 1795, the annexation of the Netherlands by France and the installation of Napoleon's brother as king in 1806, and a subsequent national revolt in 1813 that unified republic-minded resisters with royalist aristocrats who had fled to Britain during the 1790s.[86]

On the European continent the Dutch were stuck between the "irresistible force of Napoleon and the immovable object of British power," but in Asia naval strength meant that the British were ascendant.[87] In response to French influence in the Netherlands, the British sought to reduce Dutch colonial possessions in Africa and Asia throughout the 1790s and early nineteenth century, including parts of Sumatra, Malacca, the Cape Colony in South Africa, and Ceylon, culminating with the invasion and occupation of Java between 1811 and 1816. After the defeat of Napoleon, some territories, such as Java and Sumatra, were returned to the Netherlands, while others were not (Malacca, the Cape Colony), shifting Dutch attention during the nineteenth century toward the Indonesian archipelago as a "bounded place" of imperial economy with Java as its central node.[88]

The five-year British rule in Java was precarious. An 1815 conspiracy among Bengal sepoy infantry garrisoned in the central Java city of Yogyakarta sought to annihilate the island's Europeans and share sovereignty with its indigenous princes. (The planned insurrection was discovered and violently suppressed by British officers, who imprisoned or hanged the conspiracy's leaders.)[89] This period coincided with the massive 1815 volcanic eruption of Tambora, which brought the northern hemisphere a year without a summer in 1816 that some credit with inspiring works like Mary Shelley's *Frankenstein* (though in Java it seems, counterintuitively, to have improved rice harvests).[90]

The largest impediment to the British occupiers of Java was the established Dutch Indies (*Indische*) culture that had developed for centuries.[91] Before the VOC was dissolved in 1800 and its possessions integrated into the Batavian Republic, the European-descended and mixed-race inhabitants of Dutch Java lived in conditions that from Jean Gelman Taylor's perspective made it difficult to "remain European"; she argues that they developed a distinct "Indies society" that was "clearly not Dutch any longer" but an amalgamation of cultures "exceedingly polyglot in composition."[92] As with British India, the Dutch established institutions that studied those cultural amalgams, including the nearly two hundred member Batavian Academy of Arts and Sciences.[93] By the nineteenth century what had been the colonial society of the VOC that Taylor describes as "merely perched on the edge of Java and 'outward-looking'" toward Europe had "turned to look inland" toward indigenous cultures.[94]

The invasion of Java extended further the influence of British India into Southeast Asia, anchoring anglophone artistic culture in a new colonial outpost. The colonial capital of Batavia was a crowded city built on malarial swamps by a racially diverse population of ethnically Chinese, Japanese, mestizo, Balinese, and Ambonese people on which the Dutch had superimposed an administrative grid that the British took over with their own occupation.[95] According to the calculations of its lieutenant governor, Thomas Stamford Raffles, who would found Singapore in 1819 after Java was returned to the Dutch, there were just two thousand European or European-descended men and women in Batavia in 1811, mingled with approximately forty-five thousand indigenous Asian residents. The arrival of the British brought 324 officers and more than fifty-one hundred soldiers, appreciably changing the demographics of Batavia, and Indonesia more generally. Taylor argues that the British found the Dutch in Batavia to be "quaint, backward, even downright vulgar" and a target for the British "reforming zeal."[96] Some of this reforming zeal was directed toward the Dutch and mestizo populations, such as the creation of a Java Auxiliary Bible Society and the Java Benevolent Institution, the latter of which worked expressly to abolish slavery in Java.[97] Despite British attempts to alter the Dutch-mestizo culture of the Indonesian archipelago, however, Ulbe Bosma and Remco Raben agree that there were few drastic departures from the VOC past except among the most powerful families that sought influence with the new occupying forces.[98]

Other actions show the way that Java followed many of the regional models of British Asia, anchoring anglophone artistic culture in a new colonial outpost. They made Batavia into something akin to Madras or Calcutta, linking them through shorter and more rapid lines of communication, information, and cultural exchange than those to Europe. British occupiers transformed the eighteenth-century Academy of Batavia into the Batavia Literary Society (akin to the Asiatick Society of Bengal and the literary societies of Madras and Bombay, themselves based on the Royal Society) and imported "English spellers," "grammars," primers, and copies of Aesop's *Fables*, which seems to indicate the creation of a language-training infrastructure on the island.[99] They founded the "Military Bachelors' Theater" in 1814, a bamboo playhouse erected in the Weltevreden neighborhood outside Batavia's walls. The opening of the theater was a cause for celebration, with a report from "A." recognizing the "great beauty and taste" of the structure and applauding the "energetic superiority" of the amateur performers.[100] An "Address, Spoken on the Opening of the Theatre at Weltvreeden" trumpets the arrival of the playhouse as a means of distracting from the difficulties of life in Batavia because it revealed "what generous friends are here."[101] Much as in Marsden's "Epilogue," the "Address" turns the island's theater audience into a sustaining artistic community. But the theater was also maintained "under the patronage" of Raffles, and advertisements for its productions announced his support.[102] The plays were primarily in English, but short Dutch summaries were often printed in the newspaper before the performance and theatrical productions were paired with local performers (one named Piolle) who gave French "afterpieces."[103] The audiences were equally mixed, with one report indicating that invitations to the theater "circulated amongst our Dutch and English Friends at Batavia."[104]

Yet the most significant anchor of anglophone culture, and its contestation, was the *Java Government Gazette*, a multilingual weekly newspaper published between 1812 and 1816. Its printer, Amos H. Hubbard, was an American who arrived in Java via Calcutta, where he was also involved in newspaper publication.[105] In addition to official proclamations, information about exchange rates, notification of lottery winners, and announcements of important social gatherings, it also reprinted items from regional venues, particularly the many newspapers around the Bay of Bengal, such as the *Asiatic Mirror* in Calcutta, the *Madras Government Gazette*, the *Bombay Courier*, the *Ceylon Government Gazette*, and Bone's *Prince of Wales Island Gazette* in Penang. The *JGG* borrowed from but also competed with other regional and European newspapers. There were separate sections for republications from Indian and European newspapers, though at times European news was found to be lacking, as, for example, in the very first issue of the *JGG*, from February 29, 1812, when its editors note that the "European Extracts contained in these papers, exhibit nothing very interesting."

The *JGG* also featured a recurring poetry column, like nearly all of the Anglo-Indian newspapers published in the late eighteenth and early nineteenth centuries. Some of the issues reprinted poems from well-known authors like William Cowper, Walter Scott, Robert Southey, and especially Lord Byron.[106] Others possessed regional reputations, such as orientalist and linguist John Leyden, whose "Ode to an Indian Gold Coin" was written in India but published in the *JGG* in 1813, two years after he had perished during the invasion of Java.[107]

More prevalent than republications were original contributions of regionally proximate writers. The poetry of Indian newspapers during this same period demonstrated a "satirical and local imaginary," in the words of Daniel White, that contributed to a "local public sphere."[108] These local public spheres were not just engaged in reciprocal relationships to Britain that White has documented, but they were also interconnected into a regional network that extended through British Asia. The differing identities and range of topics in the poems in the *JGG* might offer some clues as to the extent and the perceived interests of these local publics. An anonymous Calcutta printer contributed an elegy for William Hunter, a member of the Asiatick Society of Bengal and a translator of the King James Bible into Hindi, blaming Hunter's death on Java; a soldier of the Nineteenth Regiment garrisoned in Batticaloa in Ceylon (Sri Lanka) celebrated the 1814 peace in Europe and defeat of Napoleon.[109] Other poems, many of which I discuss later, were datelined from "Samarang" (Semarang), then Java's second-most-populous city, located on the northern coast; Buitenzorg (Bogor), south of Batavia and a site of VOC administrators; Solo (Surakarta), in central Java; and Sourabay (Surabaya), on the eastern coast, demonstrating that the *JGG* reached far beyond Batavia, where it was printed and from which the British administered the island as the Dutch had before them. Poetry and letters appeared from across the island of Java and all around the Bay of Bengal.

These original contributions included numerous topics, such as relationships between the sexes, military matters, literary and theatrical culture, and satires of local life. Soldiers' poems in the *JGG* ranged from stern to ambivalent to angry about warfare, much like the captivity narratives and prison poems I analyzed in the previous chapter. An 1813 elegy commemorates two officers of the Seventy-Eighth Regiment, which was then stationed in eastern Java to resist an indigenous rebellion. Written from the perspective of their remaining soldiers, the poem acts as a "curse upon the tribe" of "insurgents" who killed the soldiers and grants "peace" to their graves in Probolinggo, an eastern Javanese port city surrounded by a mountainous interior.[110]

Other poems addressed issues of intercultural inspiration. The most frequent, and frequently cited, contributor to the *JGG* was the pseudonymous "Philo-villunda," whose ode on Semarang satirizes it as a "sweet" city "more lov'd than all the rest" because it is where the "Toast, the fav'rite girl went round" to "each compeer" who was "inspir'd by Bacchus." According to the poem these women were "Damsels in Cabayas white" (*kebaya*, a type of Indonesian blouse), roaming through its "gay streets" where "hospitality has fix'd her reign."[111] In this depiction Semarang is celebrated as a site of sexually available women dressed alluringly to entice dissipated men.

A contributor to the *JGG* named "Erasmus" extends such sexual satires of indigenous women by claiming he received so many requests to explain Philo-villunda's poem to "the Ladies of this place [Semarang]" that he rewrites it in Dutch so it could be more widely understood among readers. It begins "Vaarwel, vaarwel,—O gy geliefde vesten—" more literally meaning something like "Farewell, farewell, O city of my heart." It ends with a promise that "Myn hart zal altoos dankbaar voor U slaan!" (My heart will always beat for you in gratitude!)[112] Adopting a name that evokes the famous sixteenth-century Dutch humanist Erasmus to describe a parting scene between a Dutch-speaking woman and her English-speaking lover demonstrates how much intermixture of colonizing cultures was a topic of the *JGG*. Of course, the notion that Philo-villunda's account of drunken, promiscuous women trawling Semarang's streets should be read by those same women suggests at once the kind of sexual control that Ann Laura Stoler, Tony Ballantyne, and Antoinette Burton have noted were essential techniques of colonialism but also a sense of real excitement about the perceived libertinism of this Dutch colony.[113]

Whatever motivated Philo-villunda's satirical celebration of Semarang's women, that it was reworked into Dutch signals the conflicting elements of Anglo-Dutch-Malay literary publics. The newspaper was replete with poems, advertisements, and proclamations in Dutch directed toward the island's Dutch and mixed-race population. European and oceanic issues of warfare, rebellion, and slavery reappeared in regional manifestations that evaluated how it would affect such politically composite constituencies. One Dutch-language poem, "Het Vaderland en Oranje" (The fatherland in orange), celebrated Raffles by recounting a "National Feast" held in Batavia to honor Napoleon's exile to Elba ("Uitgesproken by het Vieren van het National Feest te Batavia . . . 1814").[114] Another poem, the Dutch acrostic ("naam-dicht") from 1814, commemorates Napoleon's defeat by spelling out "Oranje Boven"—literally "Orange on Top" (fig. 16).

The acrostic shouts that "oppressed compatriots"—perhaps native Hollanders or their occupied colonials overseas—might see "Netherlands Lions" finally free and their "courage crowned" by the return of the House of

Figure 16. A Dutch acrostic (*naam-dicht*), "Oranje Boven," from an issue of the *Java Government Gazette*, June 4, 1814, that commemorates Napoleon's defeat. Courtesy of The Hague, KB | National Library of the Netherlands.

Orange.[115] The use of "oranje" carries with it the multiple connotations of a royalist lineage but also of nationalist folk culture, such as the songs that sprang up during the seventeenth-century resistance to the Spanish occupation of the Low Countries during the Eighty Years War (itself begun decades earlier by William I). These songs were repurposed in "Oranje Boven" to proclaim that "old times have come again."[116] At a celebration of Dutch independence Raffles was even reported to have offered a toast of "Oranje Boven" (and, after a raucous round of applause, another to the "Ladies of Java").[117]

Poems like "Het Vaderland en Oranje" and "Oranje Boven" show how the *JGG* became an outlet for the expression of Dutch nationalism renewed from afar, approving British-occupied Java for the discussion of the future of the Netherlands through an anglophone organ.[118] News about the Dutch had been followed avidly by English readers since at least the sixteenth century, but this instance indicates how English-language vehicles advanced Dutch royalist aims (and British post-Napoleonic political aspirations) by publishing topics of European import to its regional audience.[119] It makes sense to see these poems as instances of shared alliances in Europe being expressed within colonial locales, but those shared alliances were imported into the *JGG* to create a sympathetic non-English audience for its regional and multilingual verse-making.

The shared hostility toward France and Napoleon did not suppress the low-level antagonism between Anglos and the *Indische* in Java. Unyielding issues, like slavery, which had been essential to the labor supply of the VOC, only intensified after the British captured the Dutch colony. Forced migration, especially between southern Africa and Batavia, created an "imperial network" that contributed to the VOC's "modular" and interconnected sovereignty within the Indonesian archipelago, piecing together different indigenous and Dutch interest groups in ways reminiscent of the Netherlands (with its competing patrimonial groups and bureaucratic apparatuses).[120] The slave trade was not a major revenue source for the VOC, but the company engaged in "debt-bondage" and possessed its own slaves, who made up a significant portion of Batavia's population.[121] There were approximately fifteen hundred slaves in Batavia by 1757 and probably thirteen thousand by 1816, with lives that were "closely entwined" with that of their owners.[122] They worked in every conceivable occupation.[123]

For abolitionist-inclined administrators like Raffles, attitudes toward the slave trade were an important differentiator of the British and the Dutch. He blamed the widespread existence of informal obligations, like debt-bondage, in which people sold themselves into slavery, on the region's tropical climate, but he believed chattel slavery resulted directly from greedy Chinese traders and the duplicitous Dutch colonial economy.[124] Enlightened British policies, he thought, would alleviate these forces, and he took material steps, such as shuttering Batavia's slave market (in 1813), forbidding EIC employees from owning slaves, and establishing a Benevolent Society for abolitionist charity.[125] During the same period, the formerly Dutch Cape Colony shifted from receiving slaves from across the Indian Ocean world to acting as the central hub of British naval interdictions against that trade.[126]

Nonetheless, practicality made the cessation of slavery in Java slow and uncertain. A proclamation, certified by Raffles and published in 1812, declared the seizure of enslaved children, and their transformation into indentured servants, "contrary to the spirit and intention of the British legislature, and without the sanction of any of the superior authorities."[127] This suggests that regulation of the slave trade to newly captured British territories was unclear, particularly with the widespread Javanese practice of selling oneself into bondage as a means of escaping hunger and poverty.[128] Poems in the *JGG* like the "The Horrors of Slavery" asked readers to "crush the cruel traffic while you can," yet at the same time, the paper's numerous Dutch advertisements publicized its continuation, such as the (perhaps facetious) 1813 announcement from "Orang Lama" of a Batavia "Directory" delineating where "the prettiest slave girls are for sale."[129] An 1814 item announced "good slaves" for sale (Uit de hand te koop, de volgende goede Slaven), including domestics Primo and Onverwagt, who were carriage drivers and tailors (koetzier [koetsier] and kledermaker), and Nortjaya, who was a "cook and housemaid" (kokin [kokkin] en huismeid) and was accompanied by her daughter, and "Bietja," who was a "sweet girl" (Lyfmeisje) (fig. 17).[130] Though they do not possess the metalinguistic features of many eighteenth-century American slave advertisements that described body type, speech, or skills, these announcements reveal an anglophone world adjacent to and impressed by other cultures and languages on which they depend (emphasized by the plea for help with two missing volumes of the "English Poets" that appears directly above the 1814 ad for "good slaves"). That dependence, revealed everywhere throughout the *JGG*, is most evident in the printed description of slaves who function in multilingual settings.[131]

Poems printed in Malay were more uncommon than Dutch-language poems but may be more historically significant. One untitled 1813 poetic con-

Advertisement.

THE undersigned has the honor to inform the Christian Public, that a considerable quantity of English, Dutch, and Arabic BIBLES and NEW TESTAMENTS have been received by Government, from the British and Foreign Bible Society at London, and in consequence thereof, the Honorable the Lieutenant Governor Raffles, President of the Java Auxiliary Bible Society, has been pleased to entrust the whole store to him for distribution, and in addition to it, he lately received some German Bibles and New Testaments, as also some French and Portuguese New Testaments, and likewise a considerable quantity of Dutch Hymn Books, small size.

All these Books, though most valuable in their nature, are however to be had for a very low price; and the Poor, who cannot pay for them, may have them gratis, if they apply to him at F. Thaper, Esq. Molenvliet.

J. C. SUPPER,
Secretary to the Java Auxiliary Bible Society.

Batavia, Dec. 16, 1814.

Advertisement.

MR. WILLIAM COLVILLE LEARMONTH, having withdrawn from the late Partnership of Robertson and Learmonth, on the 1st instant, and a new connexion having been formed by Messrs. Andrew Robertson, Joseph Reed, and Thomas Stones—Notice is hereby given, that the Business will in future be carried on by these Gentlemen, under the Firm of

Robertson, Reed and Stones,

Mr. Learmonth takes this opportunity of manifesting his grateful acknowledgements to the Public in general, and of recommending his friends under the present association.

Messrs. Robertson, Reed and Stones, Beg leave to inform their Friends and the Public in general, that they have entered into Partnership, as Merchants, and Agents, at Port Louis, and request a continuance of the favors of the Public, and the Friends of the late Firm of

Robertson and Learmonth,

to which they have succeeded, and assure them their interest will be most strictly attended to in all matters entrusted to their care.

Port Louis, Mauritius, May 1, 1814.

WANTED,

COLONIAL Paper Currency to the amount of 18,000 SPANISH DOLLARS, for Bills of Exchange on London. Apply to Messrs. *Timmerman Thyssen and Westermann.*

LOST

VOLUMES 25 and 68, of the Duodecimo Edition of 1790, of English Poets.—Any Gentlemen who may be in possession of either Volume, will oblige the owner of the set by sending it to the Gazette Office.

Weltevreden, 14th Dec. 1814.

UIT DE HAND TE KOOP,
de volgende goede Slaven,
ALS

PRIMO, Koetsier en Kleermaker,
Onverwagt, dito.
Nortjaya, Kokin en Huismeid, met haar Dogtertje
Bietja, Lyfmeisje.

Batavia, den 16 Dec. 1814. SLUYTER.

TE KOOP
Witte Tafel Ryst,
BY HEELE, HALVE EN KWART
KOYANGS,
te bevragen in de Nieuwe-poort Straat
By J. SUC.

By KRUITHOF,
IN DE
KOESTRAAT,
IS IN COMMISSIE TE BEKOOMEN
JAPANSE TARWE EN ROGGE,
jongst aangebragt.

Advertentie.

DIE iets te vorderen heeft van den ondergeteekende, wordt verzogt zig te addresseren voor den 31ste dezer, aan het Kantoor van de Heer *G. F. Meylan* op de Voorrey, des morgens tusschen 9 en 12 uuren.

Batavia, den 17 Dec. 1814. J. H. Tobias.

TO BE DISPOSED
OF BY
LOTTERY,

THE HOUSE, GROUNDS, and EFFECTS of Mr. Fichat, on the following plan, viz.—

To be composed of Eighty-four Tickets, (at 250 Spanish Dollars Paper per Ticket)—consisting of Twenty-one Prizes. The particulars of which may be seen at Mr. Fichat's, the Society House, the Vendue Office, and at Mr. Matak's.

Tickets to be paid for on Gentlemen setting their name against any number; and should the said Lottery not take place, the Money will be refunded.

On the whole of the Tickets being disposed of, due notice will be given in the Java Government Gazette, when and where the drawing of the same will take place.

J. FICHAT.

Batavia, Dec. 8, 1814.

UITLOOTING,
VAN DE
HUIZINGE, GRONDEN EN EFFECTEN
VAN DE
Hr. Fichat,
OP DE VOLGENDE VOORWAARDEN,
ALS

DE Uitlooting zal bestaan uit Vier en Tachentig Nummers, a 250 Papiere Spaansche Matten ieder Lot.

Er zullen zyn Een en Twintig Pryzen, verder narigt hieromtrend, is te bekomen by den Hr. Fichat, Harmony, Vendu Kantoor, en by den Hr. Matak.

By de tekening der naamen zal ook door de Heeren dadelyk het geld tegens afgave van hun nummers, afbetaald worden; en ingevallen de uitlooting geen plaats vind, zal hetzelve naderhand wederom worden gerestitueerd.

Wanneer de intekening kompleet zal zyn, zullen de Heeren verwittigd worden door middel van het Weekblad, wanneer en waar de verlooting zal geschieden

J. Fichat.

Batavia, den 8ste Dec. 1814.

Advertentie.

ALZOO den Hoogen Raad van Justitie te Batavia, aan den Griffier van Hooggemelden Raad *Germain Felix Meylan*, in zyn qualiteid als Curator in de Boedels van Insolvent overledene alhier, en als zodanig administrerende de Nalatenschap van wylen *Carel Christiaan de Fries* en *G. F. N. Goetz*, heeft verleend citatie ad valvas curiæ, op ende jegens alle bekende en onbekende, die eenig recht actie ofte pretentie ten lasten van de voorsz. nalatenschap vermeenen te hebben.

Zoo is het dat ik *Willem Antony van den Heuvel*, eerste gezwore Exploiteur van welmelde Hoogen Raad by deze dagvare alle bekende en onbekende die eenig recht actie of pretentie ten lasten van de nalatenschap van voornoemde *Carel Christiaan de Fries* en *G. F. N. Goetz* vermenen te hebben, omme op Woensdag den 18de January aanstaande des morgens ten half negen uuren ter Rolle van den Hoogen Raad van Justitie te Batavia, te compareeren dan wel gemagtigden te zenden, ten einde hunne pretention te instituëeren op poene, dat alle de taillanten die ten voorsz. dage en plaatse niet compareeren mogte dan wel gemagtigden te zenden, verstoken zullen zyn van hun regt ende actie.

Aldus gedaan en Gepubliceerd, na voorgaande Klokke geslag ten puye van den Raadhuize der stad Batavia, dezen 14de December, 1814.

By my,
W. A. van den HEUVEL,
Exploiteur.

Advertentie.

ALZO den Raad van Justitie te Sourabaya, aan den Secretaris van gemelde Raad *F. P. C. Kurtzen*, in zyne qualiteit, als Curator in de boedels van Insolvent overledene alhier en als zodanig administrerende de nalatenschap van wylen den Weledele Gestrenge Heer *A. Couperus*, heeft verleend citatie by edicte ad valvas curiæ, op ende jegens alle onbekende die enig recht actie of pretentie ten lasten van de voorsz. nalatenschap vermeenen te hebben.

Zoo is het dat ik *A. J. Hertveld* Gezwore Exploiteur van welmelde Raade, by deze voor de vierde maal ben dagvaardende, alle onbekende die enig recht actie of pretentie ten lasten van de nalatenschap van voorn. *A. Couperus* vermenen te hebben, omme op Woensdag den 22ste February 1815 aanstaande des morgens ten half negen uuren ter rolle van den Raad van Justitie te Sourabaya te Compareeren dan wel gemagtigde te zenden, ten einde het derde default te Purgeeren, en als nog hunne actie te Instituëeren, sub poene van een eeuwig silentium, voorts te zien dienen van Intendith met de verificatie daar toe specteerende.

Aldus Gepubliceerd en Geaffigeerd,
Door my
H. J. HERTVELD,
Exploiteur.

Sourabaya, den 28ste Oct. 1814.

Advertentie.

DIE iets te vorderen heeft van of schuldig is aan den boedel van wylen de Heer *Frans Michaël Kilian*, in leeven Oud President van het Eerwaarde Collegie van Boedelmeesteren alhier;—wordt by deezen verzogt, om binnen den tyd van zes weeken van heden af gerekend, daarvan opgave of betaling te doen, aan de Executeuren in gedagte boedel *Fredrik Pieter Seena* en *Huibert Librecht Seen van Basel*.—Wyders worden alle die geenen, waar voor de overledene zig als Borg geïnterponeerd heeft, verzogt, om binnen de tyd van twee maanden, volgens de expresse begeerte van de overledene by zyne uiterste wille, zig van andere borgen te voorzien, ten einde voormelde boedel niet langer moge worden aansprakelyk gehouden. Wordende tevens de Krediteuren, welke voorn. *Kilian* als zodanig hebben geaccepteerd, ook verzogt, om daar toe het hunne te willen bydragen, terwyl by gebreeke van dien tegen de schaden, die daar uit mogte voorkomen, zal worden geprotesteerd.

F. P. SEENA,
H. L. S. Van BASEL.

Batavia, den 8ste Dec. 1814.

Advertisement.

ALL Persons having Claims upon the Estate of the late A. J. v. KERST, Esq. M. D. or being indebted thereto, are requested to send in their Claims, and to pay their Debts to the undersigned Executors, before the end of the ensuing month.

B. W. Westermann,
F. S. Tim. Thyssen,

Batavia, Dec. 8, 1814.

Advertentie.

ALLE degeene die iets te vorderen hebben van ofte verschuldig zyn aan den boedel van wylen den Weledele Geboore Heer A. J. van KERST, M. D. worde verzogt hunne pretentien intezenden ofte betaling te doen voor ultimo January 1815, aan de ondergeteekenden als testamentaire Executeurs.

B. W. Westermann,
F. S. Tim. Thyssen.

Batavia, Dec. 8, 1814.

FOR SALE,
A Bengal-built BUGGY,
ENQUIRE AT THE
GAZETTE OFFICE.

To the Editor of the Java Govt. Gazette.

Sir,

The writer of an Address at the opening of the Theatre is the same who with unmerciful severity once criticized some lines written in praise of the Anacreon of Persia.—These lines were hastily and inconsiderately composed; let them be consigned to oblivion. * Shirazi as he chooses to call himself, if he have any modesty will join me in a similar wish respecting his Address.

The Shepherds in Virgil invited each other to contend in verse.—Let us for the future content ourselves with sober prose.—We are both of us, I am now fully convinced, better to contend in humble prose than in lofty rhyme—I am content to dismount—Let him alight from his crazy jade—I think I shall be able fully to convince my readers that he makes but a sorry figure on horseback.

You readily admitted the Essay in which the lines of J. T. were vituperated, though couched in terms of uncouth severity, and coarse invective.—I have endeavoured to measure the language of my disapprobation, feeling no other anger than that which bad Poetry naturally excites. I claim the same indulgence from you which Shirazi received, and that retributive justice which an English Public never refuses.

Though the language of Shirazi have not many charms for me either in Verse or Prose, yet, in one instance I will descend to quote his words, for when I ask no more than he asked and received; and do this too in the very language he made use of. Who shall deem my demand unreasonable?

This is the style in which he dictates to you, "make reparation, then, in your next Paper, by sacrificing this — to the just vengeance of the muse he has so rudely attempted to violate."—Let this be done, and let Shirazi, from this detection of his Plagiarisms, and this exposal of his incapacity, be taught that modesty and forbearance, the notorious absence of which has so frequently induced him to obtrude himself on the Public.

To insure to my strictures on the Address that publicity which you might think proper to refuse to them, I have transmitted a copy to Calcutta for insertion in one of the Bengal Prints.

Amicus.

* I enter my Caveat against any small criticism in this passage; my antagonist will say, perhaps, that as I am angry with his lines, I ought to be quite in a passion with my own. With the last, indeed, I am thus far dissatisfied, that I wish I had never written them. Lord Byron has said the same thing of his first Essays, and although I am not Lord B. and have foresworn poetry forever, I need not be ashamed of following his example in that particular.

* Shirazi, a native of the City of Shiraz or countryman of Hafiz, one no doubt who is an excellent judge of his writings, or perhaps, who thinks he writes like him.

For the Java Gazette.

EXAMINATION OF AN ADDRESS SPOKEN AT THE OPENING OF THE THEATRE AT ——, AND PRINTED.

Motto.—" Who but must laugh if such a man there be?"

Me thinks it is no difficult matter to discover that the Writer of the Address is in the real Land of the Upas Tree.—In the very commencement of the Poem the Poison has already touched the brain; the organ which is known in all cases to be chiefly affected by it.—The melancholy symptoms of the disorder increase in the progress of the Poem, and, towards the conclusion are so prodigiously aggravated, that the compassionate Reader begins to fear an utter extinction of the intellectual faculties.

The Writer of the Address sets forth as follows:—

" Can this be real? in this Land of Death,
" Where pale disease assails each gasping breath."

What is meant by pale disease attacking a gasping breath?—I thought before I read this that disease attacked the substantial frame, and that a gasping breath was but a consequence.

But the writer of the Address, I presume, has no other object in view, than to amuse us by this aerial and metaphorical combat, as he brings forward, in the course of the Poem, a number of other images equally unreal, for the sole purpose of knocking them in the head as Homer brings forward some of his petty Heroes.

See how his disordered imagination conjures them up, while almost in the same breath he tells you they have no existence—nothing but errant scandal, says he. Here is a Catalogue for you—Land of Death, pale disease, gasping breath, delusive heaven! fell land, chained by ravages, &c. &c.

But I must now make you acquainted with the history of the author's inoculation with the Upas Poison.—Reader! he caught the infection, as the knight of La Mancha did his madness, by reading bad and lying books; and let me inform you he wants one prominent virtue of that famous knight-errant; for not content with perusing these bad books, he steals from them, and appropriates without acknowledging like a practised Felon, garbling what he takes to prevent discovery.

But he has not, though he may think so, escaped detection.—A Bow-street runner in my employ has identified the Stolen Goods, and brought the most unequivocal proofs that they consist of some old tinsel furniture the property of the late Dr. Darwin, of Litchfield; fashionable about thirty years ago, but long fallen into merited contempt.

You judge of a writer, by the author he admires, as you form your opinion of a man by the Society he frequents.—You see Homer in Virgil, Dryden in Pope, the imitators improving upon the originals. You see Darwin in the Author of the Address, the latter debasing, or copying a bad original.

What are we to think of a writer who servilely copies the mawkish and gaudy tinsel of the Botanic Garden, a Book already fallen into merited neglect, and which no man will read, unless such a one, as, more in love with sound than sense, is content that his ear should be tickled at the expence of his understanding.

Let the Reader judge for himself; it is enough for me to transcribe the original and the copy.

" Where though plains smile, and glossy [illegible]
" Soft venture reign or [illegible]"
Address.

" Where seas of glass with gay reflection smile
" Round the gay coast of Java's palmy Isle."
Botanic Garden.

Figure 17. A Dutch advertisement for slaves ("Uit de hand te koop de volgende goede Slaven") in the *Java Government Gazette*, Dec. 17, 1814. Such advertisements were published at the same time as the *JGG* published poetry abhorring the slave trade. Courtesy of The Hague, KB | National Library of the Netherlands.

tribution from Salatiga, a city in central Java, refers to "Nonya Tuah," a title that indicates a distinguished woman.[132] The poem praises her qualities and entreats her to remember her male admirer. The orthography of this poem is irregular and does not conform to modern Malay's romanized spelling. Other poems mix the two languages, such as one from Semarang that interrupts its Malay to report in English "*Port, Madeira, Brandy, Beer,* / Tra-tau makan *Beef en Curry,* / Makanan busook, *English Heer,*" as if a checklist of quintessential Anglo-Asian importations to Java but also one that dismisses it as "putrid" or "rotten" (busook or busuk) food (fig. 18).[133]

As Mikihiro Moriyama points out, the language mixture of Java at the turn of the nineteenth century was confusing, with Malay acting as a lingua franca among Dutch officials and Sundanese aristocrats in colonial administrative or daily conversational exchanges but with Javanese and Sundanese used in different areas of Java.[134] In this sense the evident visual multilingualism of the *JGG* necessitates that scholars dispense with the idea that languages might easily "demarcate colonizer from colonized, civilized from primitive, core from periphery" in the words of Frederick Cooper.[135] Joseph Errington has discussed how the indigenous actors turned the Europeans' "custodial relation" toward their languages into "protonational, anti-imperial identities" that motivated Dutch attempts to regularize Malay as an instrument of imperial authority.[136] All of this evidence suggests that the *JGG* had an audience made up of multilingual publics, as was the case in late eighteenth-century India, but we have not yet assessed the degree to which literary production in these various languages aided the distribution of Anglo-Indian inspired newspapers like the *JGG*.

The "Samarang Hurly-Burly"

The inclusion of these Dutch and Malay poems confirm that the *JGG* was intended for a multilingual audience.[137] Yet debates about the proper audience of the newspaper's literary productions were pronounced throughout its existence. One correspondent from 1813 complained about the stereotypical "Java Poetiser" who, in the correspondent's description, has abandoned common sense yet believes himself to possess remarkable talent. This correspondent worries that the *JGG* editorial board "indulgently cherishes the *lisping-bard,* and adds fuel to the vanity" of these poets. He grumbles that the *JGG*'s "Poet's Corner" is "stuffed" with epigrams that "want nothing but *point,*" odes "destitute of *harmony,*" "impromptus" prepared at "half an hour's notice," and boring "*Jests, Puns, & Repartees.*"[138] The correspondent suggests

Figure 18. A poem in Malay and English from the *Java Government Gazette,* Jan. 2, 1813. Courtesy of The Hague, KB | National Library of the Netherlands.

that Java poetry should aim to "soar above the compting desks of a *Pay-Office* and a *Lottery-bank*."[139] References to jests and puns, and to the pay-office and the lottery-bank—lotteries were quite popular in Java as well as Anglo-India—direct an explicit critique at those writers who sought to merge English attitudes with Asian locales, characterizing them as lowly clerks and merchants.

Perhaps the most striking example of this debate about mixing European arts with Asia is a poem published in 1813 titled "The Triumph of Lopes, the Brown Poet, or the Samarang Hurly-Burly."[140] The poem's author is named "Dick" from "Scandal-Hall," and he describes his antagonist, Lopes, as "a brown son of Apollo" and as "brown Lopes," whose Dutch poetry is a "Samarang hurly-burly" (Samarang was Java's second most important city after Batavia). The references to "Samarang hurly-burly" compare its connotation of lowly loud commotion with the dizzying cultural and linguistic mixing that includes race ("the Brown Poet" whose "complexion is not of the most snowy hue"), pseudonymity, language (Dutch vs. English), and authorial competition. For example, Lopes's poetry is said to be worthy only of a "Billingsgate Beauty," meaning those poor primarily female London fish sellers whose cries were used as a metaphor for rudeness.[141] Ironically, and perhaps unintentionally so, Lopes is chastised by Scandal-Hall Dick for writing about white English women and London "as if you had actually been born there," and the poem is sprinkled throughout with examples of the hurly-burly that the title mentions, including Dutch phrases and even a moment that ventriloquizes Lopes's supporters yelling "baick, baick, baick"—Malay for "good, good, good"—to the sky in response to his poems while "mewling children shrilly cry."[142]

The reference to "hurly-burly" encapsulates the racialized language and aesthetic politics of the multilingual literary public produced not just by the British invasion but also by the ensuing instruments of cultural governance like the *JGG*. The "Samarang Hurly-Burly" jokes about the "Vrouws" (Dutch word for women) who glide in "gilded coaches," awaiting the "Courant's raillery" and cheering when the "'Post is on its way!'" and when the "*Courant* comes."[143] These references to the *Courant* refer to the *Bataviasche Koloniale Courant*, a Dutch newspaper inaugurated in 1809 and the immediate predecessor of the *JGG*.[144] Batavia was a "clearinghouse" of regional news throughout Dutch Southeast Asia by the early seventeenth century, and printing in Java dated from that same era, including both private and VOC-supported printing: a VOC-sponsored press was established in 1718, decades before Anglo-India.[145] But Dutch- and Malay-language newspapers did not proliferate in Java as they did in Anglo-India. The *Bataviase Nouvelles*, which lasted only one year, between 1744 and 1745, and the *Vendu-Nieuws* (Auction News), begun in 1776, were the only examples before the *Courant* was founded.[146]

In Scandal-Hall Dick's poem Lopes's insipid supporters still refer to the *JGG* as the "*Courant*," as if unaware that any change had occurred. With small details like this the "Samarang Hurly-Burly" puts the possibilities and problems of intermingled multilingual literary publics on display. The English-language author of the *JGG* chastises the Dutch Malay Lopes by parodying his techniques. The conflicted yet overlapping linguistic and colonial publics appear in the poem with its lampooning of Lopes's audience of "*merchants*" who "scan" Lopes's verses to declare they "flow fine."[147] From this vantage "The Triumphs of Lopes" refers to a political conflict between colonial publics and is played out as a debate about the aesthetics of multilingual poetry and readership. Bosma and Raben believe this poem to be the earliest evidence of "colour awareness" in Indonesia, but I would suggest it is difficult to know where the reader's allegiance is supposed to lie between Brown Lopes's hurly-burly and an author identified as Scandal-Hall Dick.[148]

"The Triumph of Lopes" was almost certainly provoked by an untitled poem published in the *JGG* one month earlier by "Michael Ferdinandus â lopes." Lopes's untitled poem contains a headnote—printed in English—that asks the editors of the *JGG* to publish his poetic "answer" to the newspaper's "frequent verses" ridiculing the "Ladies of Java," likely referring to the criticism of Semarang women that I noted earlier.[149] Little is known about "Ferdinandus â lopes," and it is not clear if this name refers to an actual nonwhite (perhaps Dutch Malay) author, or whether it was a fictitious projection of a nonindigenous European. The fact that "Ferdinandus â lopes" includes at its end the letters for *salopes*, a French term often translated as "sluts," would seem to ironize the poem's assertions that Lopes is a defender of women.[150] Or perhaps it intensifies these assertions—to defend these women is to be a *salope* like they are. This could point to an ongoing poetic satire about the cultural and linguistic diversity that results from the British occupation of Dutch colonies in Southeast Asia.

Lopes's poem is itself a complex multilingual document. Although it appears in Dutch, it is interspersed with English at its conclusion (and potentially with French obscenities buried in the author's name). The logic of Lopes's critique is wide-ranging. He insults his poetic competitors' masculinity, wondering whether their poems about Javanese women are in fact the scribbles of juvenile boys ("Is dat het werk een's mans of van een jongeling . . . ?" [Is that the work of a man or of a boy . . . ?]). He claims they do not understand women because they assume they are all identical ("Is spraak en vrouwe dragt in 't eene deel van London, / Als die terzelver tyd in 't andere werd gevonden?" [Is speech and women's clothing in the one part of London, / As it is found at the same time in another?]). He claims their writing is not the style of "true poets" (puik poëeten [poëten]) while positioning himself as the real ally of Parnassus, who would not violate women ("Parnassus-vriend rand hier de vrouwen aan?" [What friend of Parnassus violates the women here?]). He insists he knows these writers' identities despite their use of pseudonyms ("Gy die uw naam verzwygt, uw naam is ons bekend" [You conceal your name, your name is known to us]). Ultimately, he asks them to "please remember this short lesson from an Indian" (Wilt van een Indiaan deez' korte les onthouwen) not to shame men or women without reason ("Schimp nimmer zonder rêen op mannen of op vrouwen") but instead to stick with ("Houd U") their real pleasure, which is "roast-beef, . . . madeira, porter, beer" (these rendered as English words).[151]

Linguistic evidence and grammar indicate that whoever wrote under the pseudonym "Lopes" was a fluent user of Dutch. Language is an obvious demarcation between Lopes and his antagonists, particularly when his poem switches into English and when it describes prototypical English items like porter and roast beef. The movement among languages demonstrates how indigenous linguistic traditions absorbed and responded to English-language literature in their own localities during the Romantic period, resisting its aesthetic impositions even as it was integrated into its printing infrastructure. Scholars might think of these instances as the seeds of those "autonomous indigenous remakings" of British literature that Nikki Hessell has shown supported later nineteenth-century printing environments across South Asia and Australasia.[152]

Skin color and geography, however, accentuate the slippery language mixing of these poems. Lopes claims that although he is "brown" and an Indian, whereas his antagonists are from Europe, he is the only one who possesses respect for women ("Al ben ik bruin van vel, al zyt gy uit Euroop" [Although I am brown of skin and you are from Europe]). Manu Samriti Chander deftly points to the way that color becomes a figure for the marginality of "Brown Romantics" during this period: they are stigmatized and must defend their inclusion in ways that colonizers need not.[153] Then, as now, color acts as a proxy for adjacent issues of political power, public visibility, and aesthetic competition. The debate over who are men and who are boys, who defend women and who insult them, who writes true poetry and who writes doggerel are not just proxies but the direct action of an older mixed colonial culture encountering a new regional and British one. Color becomes one of the distinguishing features of these two camps.

But what makes this series of poems so consequential is not whether this unidentified Lopes was in fact the earliest exemplar of "color awareness," as Bosma and Raben claim. Rather, Lopes argues vigorously for the relevance of his brownness against that of English John Bull, forcing what Chander calls a "positional symmetry" between the two contestants.[154] Lopes appeals to English terms to offer a caricature of the Anglo-Indians as John Bull, in effect insulting them as nonnatives. Scandal-Hall Dick, however, does the same, integrating Dutch and Malay terms into his poem and suggesting that Lopes also writes about subjects he does not understand. Their poetic competition involves crosscutting claims to geographical inauthenticity merged with assertions about the effeminacy, ugliness, or unintelligibility of the other's verse—flaws depicted by representing the other author's language and customs. When Lopes wants to insult anglophone commentators on Javanese women, he calls their style boyish or describes it as akin to roast beef and beer. When those correspondents reply, they dismiss Lopes's writing as mere "hurly-burly," relying on Dutch (vrouwen) and Malay (baick) vocabulary. Racialization and nationality appear in the poem but only as ribs for broader claims about the geographical misplacement of the British or the tumultuous culture of the indigenous Dutch "Indiaan." Understanding the racial and cultural components of this type of multilingual publishing in anglophone institutions exceeds easy appeals to contact zones and the polyglot. Instead, the aesthetics of Asian anglophony depend on foreign linguistic material as a constitutive feature of writing, even when that multilingualism is dismissed.

Imitation in Early Nineteenth-Century Java

As I have noted throughout this book, scholars have historically seen English-language writing in Asia as the sign of an uninspired literary community, slavishly nostalgic for the fashions of their real European "home." As with their predecessors in Anglo-Indian newspapers, the correspondents to the *JGG* were often humorously self-aware about this attitude, puncturing it with the way they imitated other authors. Imitation is not necessarily a sign of devotion to outdated literary aesthetics or artistic fashions, and for these authors in eighteenth-century Southeast Asia, it was an opportunity to contemplate their relationship to an English canon: a way to defuse the "rich and intimidating" literary past and a form of self-reflexivity and "inter-art discourse."[155]

One poetic contributor to the *JGG*, identified only as "A. C.," captured this dynamic when he reflected on the pleasures of rewriting Thomas Gray's "Elegy Written in a Country Churchyard" in Java. This poem is titled "Meditations at Weltevreden," referring to a Dutch residential neighborhood outside of Batavia that, after the dissolution of the VOC in 1799, became an important center for colonial administration and artistic production (including the British "Military Bachelors' Theater" I referred to earlier).[156] The "Meditations" maintains Gray's rolling quatrains but stresses the more subdued social and political queries of the "Elegy." It replaces England's pastoral landscape with descriptions of Java's colonial state. The "curfew" that "tolls the knell of parting day" while the "ploughman homeward plods his weary way" in Gray's poem becomes the "evening gun" that in Java "proclaims the close of day" with "nightly picquets [pickets]" that "sternly challenge all who pass their way."[157] The "solemn stillness" and the "drowsy tinklings" that animate the darkening world of Gray's poem reappear in the "Meditations" as a scene of colonial indulgence, when "the gay song" and the noise of "lively glee" reveal those who meet together

> Upon the fatness of the land to dine,
> A jovial band their thirsty whistles wet,
> And drown each care in bowls of rosy wine.[158]

The contemplative speaker of Gray's poem meets the boisterous drunks of the colonial outpost.

But it is the poem's explicit climatological comparisons that offer insights into imitation as a technique of outpost aesthetics. After lamenting the loss of English winters, with their "cold reviving air of dawn" and the "rages loud" of a "pelting storm," A. C. concedes that "e'en in Java we possess some joys," such as devotion "to the sex and to the bowl," of being "placed above want," and of retaining the "listless idle hour for rhimes." The poem admits that Britain's difficulties might produce "contention and debate," but in Java they "spurn the anxious care / That checks the generous feelings of the soul." Rewriting Gray's "Elegy" in Java seems at first like an exercise on the impossibility of imitating Gray in Java; without a solemn speaker, grave mood, and wintry clime, there is apparently nothing about which to be philosophical or poetic.

Yet it is hard to see these conclusions as sincere. In the place of plowman and lowing herds, "Sentries walk" with "mosquitoes buzzing," but colonial poets also drink, rhyme, and court women for sex. The austere beauty of the cold pelting snowstorm is replaced with tropical warmth, which the speaker implicitly suggests is a promising exchange to undertake. Like the "Samarang Hurly-Burly," what seems to be skepticism about the arts of remote regional Java becomes an exposition of its improved possibilities for art. The ostensible inarticulacy, inauthenticity, or belatedness of anglophone Asia's artistic performances become transmuted into an expression of the fitness of the local climate as the subject of art, in much the same way that Irwin argued for the suitability of southern India as the new Parnassus that I mentioned in chapter 3. Scholars have tended to focus on these sentiments as expressions of exilic nostalgia and cultural debilitation without also seeing the (often sardonic) enthusiasm for imitation.

From Marsden's Sumatran revisions of early eighteenth-century English plays to Java's brown son of Apollo to the rewriting of Gray's "Elegy" in Java, there was an enormous range to the anglophone literary productions of Southeast Asia that grappled urgently with how to characterize its component parts. Imitation is a central tactic of outpost aesthetics, which satirize the distance between Europe and Asia that seems to inhibit anglophone artistic production but, on closer examination, actually accelerates a distinct Asian anglophony. There needs to be a new literary history that can acknowledge this cultural hurly-burly and combine it with the recognition that empire was a local and regional system, not just an oceanic and global one.

The anthropologist Engseng Ho has called for scholars to engage in the "disaggregation" of a method he calls "thick transregionalism," which perceives cultural connections that were "intermediate in scale."[159] Kuan-Hsing Chen somewhat similarly advocates for "Asia as method," by which Asia becomes an "imaginary anchoring point" for its own system of artistic and cultural reference that is not routed through European ideas.[160] Scholars must develop forms of literary analysis akin to Ho's thick transregionalism of intermediate scales and to Chen's Asian method to capture the regional variants of even white European colonial authors. As we do, we must consider what it means to include English-language writing in local and regional identities and literatures of Asia, not just its international or cosmopolitan ones.

One set of answers arises from noting how anglophone authors structured their writing according to the dictates of an English culture but in concert with the uniqueness of their non-European locales, what Marsden calls "this cherished place." Another set of answers emerges from complicating the idea of the Indian Ocean world as "method" by noting how anglophone authors drew upon European and Asian languages to fasten their writing to local geographies. The successive occupations of Java by rival European powers exemplifies the promise of these new methods. Understanding the reprinting of regional Indian newspapers in Java, or the mixing of Dutch, English, and Malay in an ostensibly anglophone newspaper's poems, or the debate between Brown Lopes and Scandal-Hall Dick about *Indische* women, or the ironic imitation of literary predecessors like Thomas Gray by Java-based authors requires a new framework that perceives such writing not as poor approximations of earlier innovations from Europe but rather as cultural products that arose from the politics and history of the Indian Ocean world. As we have seen, the Dutch-Malay allies of Lopes and the imitators of Gray indicate that there were many literary productions of Southeast Asia that grappled with how to characterize their constituent parts.

They make plain the necessity of thinking about India and Asia as both a region and an assemblage of locales. When examined from this perspective, the overriding focus among postcolonial scholars and imperial historians on East-West exchanges seems to neglect the significant population of writers and artists, some native to Asia and others immigrants from Britain, that formed among themselves an engine of cultural production and regional identification. This cultural production did not obviate the continued importance of British literary norms or the extensive cultural and economic connections between Anglo-India and Europe. Instead, it fashioned another coexistent layer, like a second skin, often unexamined because the assumption that metropolitan life was the lost origin and grand attraction of anglophone Asia had thus far prevailed.

Multilingualism is the marker of the entanglements and interactions inevitably produced by the economic and political contests of colonialism. These entanglements led (and still lead) to the success of a worldwide anglophony that in the twenty-first century is called "global English." In my reconception, English literature is a meeting place, forged through the violent contest and new affinities produced by colonial relationships. An Asia-centered account of the outpost literature of late eighteenth- and early nineteenth-century Penang, Sumatra, and Java would correspondingly expand our sense of this meeting place. Its anglophony can be best discerned and described through the principles of middle reading that I articulated in my introduction. These outlooks from the verge of Asia provide literary studies with a way to culminate the techniques of retroactive reading (Aravamudan), "processual perspective" (Gibson), and "back projection" (Giles), which see cultural concepts not as ideological formations but as the condition for knowledge production.[161]

To include European colonizers in these groups of Asians who devised locally emplaced methods is not to depoliticize the agents of colonialism but to rethink the intersection of colonial ideologies and imaginative creation. The politics of studying these figures necessitates that we reassess how cultural products were, wittingly or unwittingly, put in the service of harming some groups for the benefit of others. This is not the only way to understand these interconnections, of course, but it is an important one because it forces us to consider why we have studied English-language literature as we did before and how we might do so in the future with a new set of desires, objectives, and attitudes.

Introduction • Translocal Anglo-India

1. Add MS 39879. For Hastings's conflicts with the EIC and British politicians see Marshall, *Impeachment of Warren Hastings.*

2. See Marshall, *Impeachment of Warren Hastings*, 1–38.

3. Add MS 39879, f. 70b-71b.

4. Kaul, *Poems of Nation*, 9–10.

5. On the history of literature's institutionality see During, "Comparative Literature," 317.

6. For more on "white recovery project" and oppositionality as exclusion, see Cecire, *Experimental*, 34, 38.

7. William Duane, *The World* (Calcutta), Oct. 15, 1791; quoted in Shaw, *Printing in Calcutta*, 4. On "anglo-asiatic taste" see *The World* (Calcutta), Jan. 4, 1794.

8. Jacquemont, *Letters from India*, 85.

9. For an account of the steamship see Pearson, *The Indian Ocean*, 200. For more on early steamship travel in Asia and between Britain and India see Graham, "By Steam to India," 305. On steam travel changing regional Asian culture, see Frost, "Asia's Maritime Networks," 68. For an account of the nineteenth-century indigenous "cultural sphere" that moves beyond the notion of a Bengal Renaissance, see R. Chaudhuri, *The Literary Thing*. For a detailed history of lithography and South Asian language printing, see Shaw "Lithography vs. Letter Press," pts. 1 and 2.

10. C. A. Bayly describes this as an inability to produce the "creole nationalism" of other colonies; see Bayly, *Empire and Information*, 212. Peter Clark argues British India's limited white populations meant isolation for its "small, precarious local elites"; Clark, *British Clubs and Societies*, 425. P. J. Marshall claims "no clear British-Indian identity ever emerged"—as it did among settlers in North America, Australasia, and the Caribbean—because it was a "community dominated by official employment, recruited in Britain and set on returning to Britain"; Marshall, "Whites of British India," 27, 26. Marshall contends that "assimilation to metropolitan values seems to have been what most articulate British people in India also wanted"; Marshall, "British-Indian Connections," 51. He argues they pursued an "exclusively British community with a strictly British life style" whose "entertainments were those of an English provincial town"; Marshall, "British Society in India," 101. David

Gilmour suspects British society in India was "philistine" and declares that actors, musicians, and writers "seldom tried to make a career" there because they "could not attract a sufficient audience"; Gilmour, *The British in India*, 444. More broadly, James Belich suggests that settler colonialism—which, arguably, India was not subjected to—involved a system of "cloning" British institutions abroad; Belich, *Replenishing the Earth*, 165–69.

11. Theatergoing, Sudipto Chatterjee argues, was "integral" to British life in Calcutta that would "still reflect London"; S. Chatterjee, *The Colonial Staged*, 17. Music and drawing were ways that immigrant British "maintained their life in India as close to English models as possible" by "secluding themselves from contact with local culture"; Leppert, "Music, Domestic Life," 64. Soren Mentz asserts that the social life of late eighteenth-century Madras was dependent on multigenerational European families whose children were "trained in correct social behavior" in England so as to bring "the latest cultural developments in the English metropolis to India"; Mentz, "Cultural Interaction," 165. Máire ní Fhlathúin claims that the difference in the relative size of the British Indian marketplace to that of metropolis (presumably Britain) meant that Anglo-India was "still looking to 'home'" for "cultural leadership," and the importation of British-produced literature was "one of the greatest obstacles" to the emergence of a local literary culture; Fhlathúin, *British India*, 14, 16. Percival Spear, who originated much of this modern thinking about the imitation of British fashions, argues that the period between 1750 and 1785 was a "transition" from "secluded" factory life to "fevered cosmopolitanism" that led to a "brilliant if slightly tawdry imitation" of Europe among Anglo-Indians; Spear, *The Nabobs*, 23.

12. On "Our Indian Poets" see Manuel, *The Poetry of Our Indian Poets*; on "British-Indian Poetry" see Richardson, *Selections from the British Poets*, 1474.

13. On "tiny niche" see Sharp, "Anglo-Indian Verse," 93; on "minor tributary" see Iyengar, *Indian Writing in English*, 5; on "regional variety" see Tambe, *English Muse*, 2.

14. A new tradition of understanding eighteenth- and early nineteenth-century writing in English about India began with Teltscher's *India Inscribed* (1995). Since her account, there have been additions by Gilbert, *Writing India, 1757–1990* (1996); A. Chatterjee, *Representations of India, 1740–1840* (1998); Joseph, *Reading the East India Company* (2004); and Michael J. Franklin's work on Sir William Jones, cited throughout this book. Other accounts have sought to describe specific literary coteries; see, e.g., Franklin's "'The Hastings Circle.'"

15. D. White, *From Little London*, 14, 15.

16. Gibson, *Indian Angles*, 7, 6. Other scholars have noted the impact of these forces on literature, starting with Bart Moore-Gilbert in the 1990s, who observed divergences between metropolitan constructions of India like those advanced by Edward Said and the "'local' tradition of representation" produced by the "situatedness" of the Anglo-Indian population, but mostly as an example of returning Anglo-Indians adjusting slowly to metropolitan British life, rather than as an argument for considering British India as a regional literary culture; see Moore-Gilbert, "Introduction: Writing India," 24. Rosinka Chaudhuri similarly considers that Anglo-Indian writers "may have imagined" themselves to be writing for British audiences but contributed to a "broader literary sphere" than "they themselves,

perhaps, had dreamed of" in India; see her introduction to *History of Indian Poetry*, 9. Suvir Kaul, however, believes that when "British poets" lived elsewhere, they still imagined themselves to write for a "metropolitan audience"; Kaul, "English Poetry in India," 34.

17. On "alternative modernity" see D. White, *From Little London*, 15; on "complex . . . contact zone" see Gibson, *Indian Angles*, 20.

18. For new understandings of the reciprocal constitution of knowledge in colonialism see Raj, *Relocating Modern Science*; and Raposo et al., "Moving Localities."

19. See Shaw, *Printing in Calcutta*; and Ogborn, *Indian Ink*, esp. 198–265.

20. On the language of decentering print culture history and of "creative ferment" see Collier and Connolly, "Print Culture Histories," 6, 15.

21. R. Chaudhuri, introduction to *History of English Poetry*, 2.

22. Colley, *Captives*, 4.

23. Fuchs, *Poetics of Piracy*, 6; see also Fuchs, "Another Turn for Transnationalism" for arguments against the idea that literary history is national.

24. See Raman, *Document Raj*.

25. Kaviraj, "Outline of a Revisionist Theory," 504.

26. See Eisenstadt, "Multiple Modernities."

27. On "vast anonymous address" see Hofmeyr, Kaarsholm, and Frederiksen, "Introduction," 5; on "variations" see Orsini, "The Multilingual Local," 348.

28. Many have documented these links in detail, but I will note here only Cohn, *Colonialism*; Rocher, "Weaving Knowledge"; F. Ross, *Printed Bengali Character*; and Ogborn, *Indian Ink*. Viswanathan, *Masks of Conquest* and Ahmed, *Archaeology of Babel* have amply described how these orientalist structures in turn made Enlightenment knowledge function.

29. D. White, *From Little London*, 102.

30. Chander, *Brown Romantics*, 3–4, 37.

31. Glazener, *Literature in the Making*, 3.

32. Adapting Ann Laura Stoler's idea of history in a "minor key"; Stoler, *Along the Archival Grain*, 52.

33. On a "single analytic field" see Stoler and Cooper, "Between Metropole and Colony," 4. Catherine Hall reminds us that the "relations between colony and metropole were relations of power" and that those relations were "mutually constitutive" in which "both colonizer and colonized were made" (*Civilizing Subjects*, 8). She is careful, however, to note that empire cannot be understood in binaries (*Civilizing Subjects*, 16).

34. On "complex agglomeration" see Ballantyne, *Orientalism and Race*, 15; on local interactions see Metcalf, *Imperial Connections*, 6, 1.

35. Suleri, *Rhetoric of English India*; Teltscher, *India Inscribed*, 3.

36. Ogborn, *Indian Ink*, 4.

37. See Geertz, *Local Knowledge*, 167–234.

38. On humans in motion see Hannerz, *Transnational Connections*; on media-generated identities see Appadurai, *Modernity at Large*; on "agency-oriented" approaches in "cross-border social space" see Smith, "Power in Place," 6, 7.

39. On local and global levels see U. Freitag and Oppen, "'Translocality'"; on "local-to-local relations" see Kraidy and Murphy, "Shifting Geertz," 344, 347; on

"grounded transnationalism" see Brickell and Datta, "Introduction," 7; on assemblage of social movements see McFarlane, "Translocal Assemblages"; and on geopolitics see Mandaville, "Territory and Translocality."

40. See Banerjee, "Voices of the Governed."

41. On "relational" see Ramazani, "Local Poem," 676; on "rooted or rootless" see Ramazani, *A Transnational Poetics*, xiii. Daniel Katz suggests that Ramazani's translocalism is a necessary alternative to "regionalist and universalist narratives" that had previously described these authors; see Katz, *American Modernism's Expatriate Scene*, 161.

42. Greiner and Sakdapolrak, "Translocality," 375; see also D. Massey, *Power-Geometries*, 22.

43. On critical regionalism interceding between local and global, see Limón, "Border Literary Histories."

44. On the "architecture of resistance" see Frampton, "Towards a Critical Regionalism"; on the interstitial and incidental see Herr, *Critical Regionalism*, 11, 16. The term *critical regionalism* was coined in 1981 by Alexander Tzonis and Liane Lefaivre and was meant to conceptualize the region as open rather than static and closed; see their "Why Critical Regionalism Today?" Gayatri Spivak applies critical regionalist approaches to Asia when "making a claim to the *word* 'Asia,' however historically unjustified" (*Other Asias*, 213) and of regionalisms that "go under and over nationalism" (Butler and Spivak, *Who Sings the Nation-State?* 94). For Christopher Bush, Spivak's regionalism is a "kind of strategic essentialism on a continental scale" (Bush, "Areas"). For an account of architectural critical regionalism and an expression of colonial imposition see Eggener, "Placing Resistance," 228.

45. Allen and Cochrane, "Beyond the Territorial Fix," 1163. The notion of regions as not enclosed territorial sites borrows from Paul Giles's redefinition of the United States as a nation; see Giles, *Antipodean America*, 33.

46. See Limón, "Border Literary Histories," 168; see also Lösch and Paul, "Critical Regionalism," 4.

47. Griswold, *Regionalism and the Reading Class*, 12, 4.

48. Rezek, *London*, 14–15, 4.

49. Loughran, *The Republic in Print*, 74.

50. Eaton, "Nostalgia for the Exotic," 243, 242.

51. On "world literary space" see Casanova, "Literature as a World," 81; on "zigzagging movements" see C. Levine, "From Nation to Network," 657.

52. I contrast this with Anna Lowenhupt Tsing's idea that friction mobilizes adherents to universal ideas that nonetheless are enacted locally; see Tsing, *Friction*, 7–8.

53. Subrahmanyam, "Connected Histories"; Doyle, "Inter-imperiality and Literary Studies." Scholarship of the Indian Ocean has grown since the 1990s. For a detailed bibliography of its history see Hofmeyr, Kaarsholm, and Frederiksen, "Introduction."

54. On those preceding networks see Abu-Lughod, *Before European Hegemony*; K. Chaudhuri, *Asia before Europe*; and Frank, *ReORIENT*.

55. On "core-periphery" and "cross-colonial" models see Burton, *The Trouble with Empire*, 225n21. Burton also distinguishes between the "old-fashioned core-periphery

model of traditional imperial history" and the "reverse flow paradigm of the new imperial studies"; see Burton, *Empire in Question*, 276. On "market framework" see Kaufmann and North, introduction, 3; according to Kaufmann and North, specific cultural objects "emerged locally, and at the same time responded to global exchange" (3).

56. On "subimperial" see Ballantyne, *Orientalism and Race*, 35; and Metcalf, *Imperial Connections*, 7–8. On "fulcrum" see Pearson, *The Indian Ocean*, 50, 53, 196, 204. For network accounts of the British Empire see Lester, *Imperial Networks*.

57. Winterbottom, *Hybrid Knowledge*, 3.

58. Bose, *A Hundred Horizons*, 11. See also Lester, "Introduction," for an overview of networks in the history of British imperium.

59. Bose suggests that the "overemphasis on trade has tended to obscure much else that went along with it, especially the flow of ideas and culture"; see Bose, *A Hundred Horizons*, 11. Benton writes that the "world-systems perspective has done poorly in recognizing and representing the complexity of culture"; Benton, "From the World-Systems," 268. Benton calls for institutional histories, which have been compiled in imperial history but less so in literary study ("From the World-Systems," 279).

60. Savile, *A Rough Draught*, 5.

61. Shaw, *Printing in Calcutta*, 20–21.

62. For a robust account of this publishing see Pickett, *Bibliography*.

63. On a "pretty extensive library" as a "public utility" see *Transactions of the Literary Society of Bombay*, vol. 1, vi. On reduced rates see *Transactions*, vol. 3, ix. On free access see *Transactions*, vol. 3, x.

64. *Calcutta Gazette*, July 29, 1790.

65. *Calcutta Gazette*, May 1, 1788.

66. *Madras Courier*, Feb. 9, 1791. The *Calcutta Gazette*, Jan. 14, 1790, gives some sense of how this might work when it advertised postal rates among locales that included Bombay, "Poonah" (Pune), "Hydrabad" (Hyderabad), Madras, "Masulapatam" (Masulipatam, now Machilipatnam), and Calcutta for between 2 and 12 annas (about one-eighth to two-thirds of a rupee).

67. *Madras Courier*, Dec. 29, 1790 (italics in original).

68. *The World* (Calcutta), Oct. 15, 1791; quoted in Shaw, *Printing in Calcutta*, 4.

69. Boyd, *The Indian Observer*, 182.

70. English, "Now, Not Now," 396.

71. Lanser, *The Sexuality of History*, 21.

72. On "middle ground" evaluations of world systems see Benton, "From the World-Systems," 285. For a theory of mesolevel analysis of organizational behavior see House, Rousseau, and Thomas-Hunt, "The Meso Paradigm." Middle-range theorizing is extensive in analytical sociology. For a description of its origins see Merton, *Social Theory and Social Structure*, 39–72. For an overview of the middle range in sociology see Hedström and Udehn, "Analytical Sociology," esp. 64–66. On social and political accommodations of the "middle ground" see Richard White, *The Middle Ground*; and on "'middling' scale" see English, "Now, Not Now," 396.

73. On midrange theorizing and staying "rather close to the ground," see Ong, *Neoliberalism as Exception*, 13, 12.

74. Schmitt, "Tidal Conrad (Literally)," 16.

75. See K. Wilson, "Introduction: Histories, Empires, Modernities," 15. Tillman Nechtman argues that "Imperial Britons . . . envisioned identity not as geographically rooted but rather as global and performative"; Nechtman, *Nabobs*, 10.

76. For more on the "logic of autochthony" in authorship, in which birthplace is perceived as irrefutable evidence of belonging, see C. Levine, "From Nation to Network," 651. For more on how autochthony creates an "obsession with belonging" and an "exclusion of strangers" so that culture is used to adjudicate who "really belongs" by assessing "authenticity and falsehood," see Geschiere, "Autochthony," 207, 209.

77. My idea of recognizing "repetitions with change" is a spatial alternative to Geraldine Heng's temporally influenced idea of reading across time periods to identify continuities and variations in ideas about race and gender; see Heng, "Reinventing Race," 360. On "locally disparate, globally integrated" see Geertz, *Available Light*, 227.

78. Calhoun and Sennett, introduction, 1, 5.

79. For ideas of social transmission see Michael C. Cohen, "Peddlers, Poems, and Local Culture," 13. As scholars of late twentieth-century literary criticism have noted, debates about different modes of reading all shared the assumption that the objective was to discern meaning (Tompkins, "The Reader in History," 201) and that "interpretation was still the name of the game" (Radway, "What's the Matter with Reception Study?" 334).

80. H. Love, "Close, but Not Deep," 387.

81. For more on the historical studies of audiences see Rose, *The Intellectual Life*, 1–11. For a clear counter to this history of audiences as Rose conceives it, see Davis, *Society and Culture*, 192. The extensive archives of the EIC are "neither semiotically transparent nor unproblematically referential"; see Markley, "Alexander Hamilton," 240; and, more generally, Joseph, *Reading the East India Company*. But as Ranajit Guha notes, there is no way to eliminate such distortions. Scholars can only acknowledge them as constitutive of our findings and "stop pretending" that we can fully grasp this period and reconstitute it; see Ranajit Guha, "The Prose of Counter-Insurgency," 33.

82. An origin of new imperial history can be found in K. Wilson's introduction to *A New Imperial History*. For more on the new global history see Mazlish, "Global History," 406–8. For an overview of how global history intersects with space and ecology, see Lester, "Introduction," 1–15. For other accounts of the changing fortunes of imperial history in the twentieth and twenty-first century and the rise of "new imperial history," see Fieldhouse, "Can Humpty Dumpty?"; Peers, "Is Humpty Dumpty Back?"; and Hopkins, "Back to the Future."

83. The exemplary case of microhistory remains Ginzburg, *The Cheese and the Worms*. On big history see Christian, "The Case for 'Big History.'" On the long durée see Guldi and Armitage, *The History Manifesto*.

84. Greif, "Historical and Comparative Institutional Analysis." On "means of historical agency . . . intransitive" see Arac, "What Is the History?" 106.

85. H. Love, "Close Reading," 411.

86. I have adopted the concepts of minor literature and minor key from Deleuze and Guattari, *Kafka*, esp. its lack of abundant talent (17) and its "collective enunciation" (18).

87. Dharwadker, "English in India," 104.

88. Compare this with Ann Laura Stoler's notions in *Along the Archival Grain* of "minor history" (7) or the "history of empire 'in a minor key'" (52), which is characterized by ordinariness, paucity of archives, and "structures of feeling" that otherwise might seem "residual and sedimented" (101).

89. I am adapting John Brewer's suggestion that early modern clerks, copyists, and bookkeepers "have no history" because they have been ignored even though they wrote so much ("no group can ever have written so much and yet remained so anonymous"); see Brewer, *The Sinews of Power*, xvi.

90. See Hagerman, *Britain's Imperial Muse*.

91. Hoock, *Empires of the Imagination*, 278–79. For a synthetic account of this architecture see Vasunia, *Classics and Colonial India*, 159–60.

92. *Calcutta Gazette*, April 26, 1792.

93. Anonymous, *Calcutta*, 68.

94. Hoock, *Empires of the Imagination*, 282.

95. Star, "The Ethnography of Infrastructure," 379.

96. Star, "Anselm Strauss," par. 3.2, 6.3.

97. Michael C. Cohen, "Peddlers, Poems, and Local Culture," 28.

98. For examples of these effects see Margaret Cohen, "Narratology in the Archive of Literature," 52.

99. Margaret Cohen, *Sentimental Education*, 21.

100. Moretti, *Atlas*, 150.

101. Bellamy, *Commerce, Morality*, 6. Bellamy's example is the way that *Clarissa* is valuable for itself but also because it can be seen as a precursor to Frances Burney and Jane Austen.

102. Mitchell, *What Do Pictures Want?* 146.

103. On challenging the moral judgment of bad writing, see Janet Todd, John Goodridge, Bridget Keegan, and William Christmas. On morality and redemption see Bersani, *The Culture of Redemption*, 1–2.

104. The phrase "prosperity to poverty" is David Washbrook's; see Washbrook, "The Indian Economy," 45. As he notes, establishing changes to the Indian economy between 1757 and 1947 is notoriously difficult. For an overview of these changes, however, see Broadberry, Custodis, and Gupta, "India and the Great Divergence," which suggests a "relatively prosperous" Mughal India that gradually declines and deindustrializes across the nineteenth century as British wealth grew rapidly in comparison (58).

105. Chen, *Asia as Method*, 1; see also Spivak, *Other Asias*, 213.

106. Sir William Jones has served as an important origin for anglophone poetry in India. Theodore Douglas Dunn's 1921 *Poets of the John Company*—another term for the East India Company—begins with Jones, as does Máire ní Fhlathúin's collection *The Poetry of British India, 1780–1905* and Mary Ellis Gibson's *Anglophone Poetry in Colonial India, 1780–1913*.

107. On the "great unread," see Margaret Cohen, *Sentimental Education*, 23.

Chapter 1 • A Cultural Company-State

1. Dimock, *Through Other Continents*, 3. Dimock adapts her notion of literature's deep time from nineteenth-century geology, which Stephen Jay Gould argues is one of humanity's most significant concepts; see Gould, *Time's Arrow, Time's Cycle*, 1–8. Gould derives his use of the phrase "deep time" from John McPhee, *Basin and Range*, 20.

2. Hastings found Wilkins's translation inspiring for his own unpublished compositions (including short translations from the Mahabharata, the lengthy Indian epic of which the Gita was a part).

3. Dimock, *Through Other Continents*, 14–15. Thoreau cited this statement from Hastings in *A Week on the Concord and Merrimack Rivers*, 147. Hastings originally made these comments in "To Nathaniel Smith," his letter prefacing Wilkins's translation *The Bhăgvăt-Gēētā*, 13.

4. Dimock, *Through Other Continents*, 20.

5. This sentiment is suggested by Robert Fraser, among other scholars. Fraser argues that Wilkins's translation of the Gita was "simply perpetuating" its existence as an independent, primarily devotional, text to new generations of readers; R. Fraser, *Book History*, 63.

6. On these pivotal decades see Bayly, *Indian Society*, 7–44; Marshall, *Bengal: The British Bridgehead*, 93–172; Marshall, *Making and Unmaking*, 207–72; J. Richards, *The Mughal Empire*, 253–81. For more on steam travel to and throughout India see Pearson, *The Indian Ocean*, 202.

7. See Bayly, *Birth of the Modern World*, 88, 91, 27–42, 10.

8. Polasky, *Revolutions without Borders*, 2–12; Linebaugh and Rediker, *The Many-Headed Hydra*, 241; Walvin, *Black Ivory*, 218–39; DuBois, *Avengers of the New World*; DuBois, *A Colony of Citizens*.

9. Bayly, *Birth of the Modern World*, 107; Colley, *Captives*, 251.

10. Colley, *Captives*; O'Quinn, *Staging Governance*, 24; Favret, *War at a Distance*, 83–85.

11. This is, in essence, a cultural analytical form of what has come to be known as "infrastructural inversion," especially as found in Bowker and Star, *Sorting Things Out*, 34.

12. Said, *Orientalism*; Suleri, *Rhetoric of English India*, 1–4.

13. Farrington, *Trading Places*, 23. Wind and weather patterns, known as the monsoons, had the largest effect on oceanic trade with India. The regular pattern of the monsoons is that they blow from the Indian Ocean toward India from May to September and from the Asian continent across India from November to March, which meant that travel was limited in direction during these windows.

14. Stern, *The Company-State*, 6, 10. For example, none of the seventeenth-century settlements of the EIC permitted legal appeals to England (unlike the American colonies) (*The Company-State*, 28). The company moved convicts among its settlements, commuting thieves sentenced to death in Madras into slavery in Sumatra (*The Company-State*, 29). The EIC itself engaged in the slave trade until 1761 and did not prohibit slave exportation until 1789 (Spear, *The Nabobs*, 53). Copyright, Robert Fraser notes, was nearly nonexistent in India before 1830 because it required printing

from a manuscript in England with the Stationer's Company; R. Fraser, *Book History*, 147–48.

15. Marshall, "British-Indian Connections," 46.

16. Quoted in Marshall, 46. Marshall estimates the EIC extracted £18 million revenue in administration, manufacture, and trade for six thousand people by 1815 (45). Rajat Kanta Ray estimates that £1.3 million a year were sent from India to Britain between 1783 and 1793; see Ray, "Indian Society," 514.

17. Pearson, *The Indian Ocean*, 151; see also Eacott, *Selling Empire*, 419.

18. J. Richards, "Imperial Finance," 16–17.

19. Farrington, *Trading Places*, 69.

20. Pearson, *The Indian Ocean*, 193.

21. Pearson, 197.

22. J. Richards, "Imperial Finance," 17.

23. J. Richards, 31–33.

24. Carson, *East India Company and Religion*, 139–45. Carson argues the provision against missionaries before 1813 was pragmatic and largely unenforced but that aiding conversion by the EIC was sanctioned until 1813 (58–59).

25. Stern, *The Company-State*, esp. 212–14.

26. On the Ottoman Empire see Hoerder, *Cultures in Contact*, 174–85; on China's economic output in comparison to Europe see Maddison, *Contours of the World Economy*, 117; for a discussion of the difficulties of calculating Chinese economic output see von Glahn, "Economic Depression," 85–88.

27. Hoerder, *Cultures in Contact*, 175, 184–85.

28. Hoerder, 175.

29. Pearson, *The Indian Ocean*, 165.

30. E. Alpers, *The Indian Ocean in World History*, 84–85.

31. Sood, *India and the Islamic Heartlands*, xi, 248.

32. J. Richards, *The Mughal Empire*, 282. Richards differs from a subsequent generation of Mughal scholars in seeing the state as an "intrusive, centralizing system" rather than dispersed and distant (1).

33. Alam and Subrahmanyam, introduction, 1–71.

34. Keay, *India*, 385; see also 391–92.

35. Marshall, introduction, 3–13. Sudipta Sen also suggests that the British sought to retain the legitimacy of Mughal sovereignty until the EIC dissolution in 1858; see Sen, *Distant Sovereignty*, xiii.

36. Brittlebank, *Tipu Sultan's Search for Legitimacy*.

37. The EIC was not even the only European trading company to have territorial ambitions within India: the Dutch possessed stations in Travancore in southern India, and the French sought prominence alongside the British around Madras (keeping possession of Pondicherry until 1954, after Indian independence from the British); see Ramachandra Guha, *India after Gandhi*, 184–86.

38. J. Wilson, *The Domination of Strangers*, 29. Wilson additionally asserts this was as true of Britain in the eighteenth century as it was of Bengal.

39. There have been numerous accounts of these transformations. For overviews see Bayly, *Indian Society*; Bayly, *Empire and Information*; Marshall, introduction; J. Wilson, *Domination of Strangers*; and Alavi, *Eighteenth Century in India*. These

works generally suggest a gradual yet concerted effort to decouple the East India Company from the revenue and information reservoirs of Mughal agents, local landowners (*zamindars*), and self-interested merchants as it created an increasing informational and territorial dominance of India that fully emerged as the Raj. These assessments are opposed by those who argue that eighteenth- and early nineteenth-century British India was nothing but "piecemeal policies and uncoordinated direction" to the British in India (Keay, *India*, 395) or that the British were "absent-minded imperialists" (B. Porter, *The Absent-Minded Imperialists*). For a short overview and assessment of the accidental empire thesis see P. Levine, *The British Empire*, 92–94. The sentiment of absent-mindedness is traceable to John Seeley's remark that "we seem, as it were, to have conquered and peopled half the world in a fit of absence of mind"; Seeley, *The Expansion of England*, 8. Oft cited, Seeley's statement was actually a rejection of analysis that separated English history from its colonies overseas as absurd.

40. P. Chatterjee, *The Black Hole*, 76.

41. Husain, *Dreams of Tipu Sultan*, 84. Translation of IO Islamic 3563, f. 12r.

42. K. Chaudhuri, *Trading World of Asia*, 51.

43. The exact numbers of European-born and European-descended individuals in East India Company domains varies widely, though all presume there were somewhere between two thousand and twenty thousand people. There was little accounting of the overall population, and estimates are based on individual cities and settlements. Suresh Ghosh claims approximately seven hundred European-descended men and eighty women were in Calcutta in 1756; S. Ghosh, *Social Condition*, 61. P. J. Marshall claims there were 286 in the Bengal civil service in 1783 and more than 1,550 military officers in 1772; Marshall, "British Society in India," 98, 96. See also Marshall, *East Indian Fortunes*, 15. H. V. Bowen estimates that there were seventy thousand or seventy-five thousand Britons total in India by the early 1830s; Bowen, *The Business of Empire*, 262–63. Raymond K. Renford numbers 585 nonofficial residents in Calcutta in 1793 and an additional 281 in the countryside around Bengal, and by 1804 there were more than sixteen hundred; Renford, *The Non-official British*, 4–5. The armed forces increased these figures substantially, which makes their absence from descriptions of literary culture all the more puzzling. Linda Colley believes there were only 645 "white male civilians" who worked for the East India Company in Bengal between 1707 and 1775 but "just over 10,000 white soldiers" in India during the late 1770s alone; Colley, *Captives*, 251, 260. John F. Richards calculates that by 1781, the Company armies numbered 124,000 soldiers, of which 23,000 were European-descended; J. Richards, "Imperial Finance," 25. The East India Company maintained a large standing army and reimbursed the Crown for British regiments that were stationed and fought on its behalf.

The number of European women in India is even more elusive. In the 1730s estimates concluded that there were about thirty to forty-five women in Madras at any one time. Calcutta in 1756 included 750 Europeans of which only 80 were women, and some may have been native according to Catherine Whinyates. There were fifty women in Bombay in 1781 (of which half were Eurasian). The author Elizabeth Hamilton reports on one hundred attending a ball around the same time in Calcutta.

By 1810 estimates of women in Bengal rose to 250 to 300, though there are few attempts at precise measurement until the late nineteenth century. All of these figures for women are summarized from Raza, *In Their Own Words*, xix, 78.

44. Clark, *British Clubs and Societies*, 425–28. Clark concludes there was a more relaxed attitude toward indigenous participation in Calcutta than in the West Indies, but he still thinks it was limited (426).

45. Spear, *The Nabobs*, 34.

46. Marshall, "Whites of British India," 26.

47. Marshall, "British-Indian Connections," 51; Marshall, "British Society in India," 101, 102, 107.

48. Bayly, *Empire and Information*, 212.

49. Marshall, "British Society in India," 100.

50. See Mishra, "More Trouble," his review of William Dalrymple's *White Mughals*. See also Dalrymple's reply, "Assimilation and Transculturation." "People apart" is from Marshall, "British Society in India," 101.

51. See Shaw, "India," 457–58. For more on the Scottish participation in the East India Company appointments see Bowen, *The Business of Empire*, 272–75. Michael Fry suggests that by the late eighteenth century, half of the East India Company employees were Scotsmen; see Fry, "'Keys to Their Hearts,'" 138.

52. For Soubise as an instructor see *Calcutta Gazette*, July 8, 1784. He had fled from Britain to Calcutta in 1777, perhaps to escape charges of rape; see Fryer, *Staying Power*, 73. He had an earlier performance career in Britain; see Scobie, *Black Britannia*, 91; and Miller, *Slaves to Fashion*, 63. For an assessment of his theatrical career in Calcutta see O'Quinn, "Theatre and Empire," 234–35.

53. Evidence indicates that of 508 civil servants in Bengal between 1762 and 1784, only 37 returned to Britain, the rest either having died in India or still living in Bengal; see Misra, *The Bureaucracy in India*, 52.

54. See Nechtman, *Nabobs*.

55. On these aristocrats and their social culture see Bayly, *Imperial Meridian*; and A. Cohen, "The 'Aristocratic Imperialists.'"

56. Callahan, *The East India Company*, xi.

57. Linda Colley suggests that before 1775 nearly two-thirds of Britons died in India in the early years of their appointment and that after 1775 that rate was reduced to one quarter; Colley, *Captives*, 251. Mark Harrison supplies evidence that although climate was a consideration, it was not a universal assessment among Europeans that Asian climates were potentially deadly (an assumption aligned with a later period than the eighteenth century); see Harrison, *Climates and Constitutions*, 215–16.

58. On one hundred white women in Bengal see Raza, *In Their Own Words*, xix. Colley suggests that there were eighty-five European-descended women and children in Madras in 1771; see Colley, *Ordeal of Elizabeth Marsh*, 164. Nechtman calls white women "demographically insignificant" in eighteenth-century India; Nechtman, *Nabobs*, 188.

59. On social fluidity see Mickelson-Gaughan, *The "Incumberances"*; on "transgressive space" see Franklin, introduction, xxxi; on "unorthodox femininity" see Nussbaum, *Torrid Zones*, 176. Peter Robb disagrees, claiming that white women were

not uncommon and that there were definite class distinctions between women of status, most often attached to families by marriage, and single women, often the widows of soldiers, who were more prevalent; Robb, *Sex and Sensibility*, 10.

60. Colley, *Ordeal of Elizabeth Marsh*, 191–212.

61. Alavi, introduction, 7–8.

62. Sudipta Sen argues that the British apprehension over distant sovereignties ensured a "gradual segregation" of British and Indian components so that British India would never be a "creole society" or a settler colony; Sen, *Distant Sovereignty*, xxv. Amal Chatterjee says that the anglophone writers of this period "never really encountered the subcontinent they described because they were limited by the intellectual and political debates that raged around trade, religion, and, eventually, race," as if these subjects were somehow importations from Europe; A. Chatterjee, *Representations of India, 1740–1840*, 4. Bernard Cohn describes the British in India as producing a "fossil culture" that was recruited from among the English middle- and upper-class and was "cut off from close contact with home" (*Anthropologist among the Historians*, 545). Soren Mentz claims that "social interaction . . . was kept to an absolute minimum" between whites and nonwhites, at least in Madras from 1650 to 1740; Mentz, "Cultural Interaction," 164. Durba Ghosh describes how racial and gender hierarchies always structured interracial sexual intimacies and that while the East India Company opened opportunities for indigenous women, it was through rigid hierarchies; D. Ghosh, *Sex and the Family*, 2, 3, 10, 11, 16. Pankaj Mishra argues eighteenth-century colonists could not "break free of their larger national and imperial destiny," as he terms it, in their sympathy with the natives whom they colonize; Mishra, "More Trouble," 438.

63. Rajat Kanta Ray writes that "this was an encounter in which both sides merged into the other"; Ray, "Indian Society," 510. Peter Robb suggests that our sense of eighteenth-century British India as highly segregated is a result of nineteenth-century narratives, not actual historical sources; see Robb, *Clash of Cultures?* 5n14. Rozina Visram argues that in the early years of the seventeenth century the British were encouraged to engage with Indian women, so there "was much mixing between black and white"; see Visram, *Ayahs, Lascars, and Princes*, 3.

64. These estimates are based on parish records, which show one-third of wills included bequests to native Indian companions or their children; see Hawes, *Poor Relations*, 4. See also Robb, "Children, Emotion," esp. 175–76. For a popular account of the intermixture see Dalrymple, *White Mughals*.

65. D. White, *From Little London*; Gibson, *Indian Angles*. On "partial Anglicization" see Dharwadker, "English in India," 103–4.

66. Parthasarathi, "South Asia," 554; see also Durga, "Western Influence."

67. Seid-Gholam-Hossein-Khan, *Translation of the Sëir Mutaqharain*, 1:22, 23.

68. For more on "Old Nell" see Otis, *Hicky's Bengal Gazette*, 70–71. Her letter is in the Sept. 29, 1781, issue of *Hicky's Bengal Gazette*. Nell never explicitly claims to be what we now call mixed race, but her Irish father and references to darker skin suggest that was the case.

69. For more on Muhammad's writing and Indian travelers to Britain, see Fisher, *Travels of Dean Mahomet*; and Fisher, *Counterflows to Colonialism*.

70. See Garcia, "Stranger's Love," 233.

71. On imperial Britons see Nechtman, *Nabobs*, 10–11, 16; on "go-betweens" and cultural brokers see Schaffer et al., *The Brokered World*; on "trans-imperial subjects" see Rothman, *Brokering Empire*.

72. S. Ghosh, *Social Condition*, 57n1. The census even defined the term in 1931; see *The Census of India* 1931, par. 180, pp. 429–30. Ghosh argues that many of these terms also applied to descendants from other nationalities, like Portuguese, Dutch, and French.

73. Mary Ellis Gibson explains that nationalism primarily drove the shifts in meaning, when after independence in 1947, *Anglo-Indian*, which had referred to writing by Europeans in India, came to mean writing in English by Indians (Gibson, *Indian Angles*, 3). Mrinalini Sinha uses *Anglo-Indian* to refer to "British officials and non-officials in India," though she claims by the 1920s and 1930s it had come to mean "offsprings of mixed European and Asian or Eurasian descent" (though this may have happened much earlier) (M. Sinha, *Colonial Masculinity*, 23).

K. R. Srinivasa Iyengar offers another idea of "Anglo-Indian literature" as having no "racial significance at all" but merely indicating a literature that is "a product of Indo-English literary relations. England and India had come together, or had been accidentally thrown together; and out of their intimacy—whether legitimate or illegitimate—had come this singular offspring that is Anglo-Indian literature." To avoid racial significance, he argues that scholars settle on Indo-Anglian literature, which he claims is "Indian literature and a variation of English literature." See Iyengar, *Indian Writing in English*, 2, 6.

74. Lester, *Imperial Networks*, ix.

75. Dharwadker, "Print Culture and Literary Markets," 112.

76. K. Chaudhuri, *Trading World of Asia*, 74–75; Ogborn, *Indian Ink*.

77. Add MS 35918, f. 222; Shaw, "British Book in India," 566.

78. Dodwell, *The Nabobs of Madras*, 47.

79. On "missionary societies" see Shaw, "South Asia," 132. Giles Barber suggests that book exports to India accounted for 10 percent of all exports in 1750 but 19 percent by 1773 (Barber, "Books," 203, 218; Barber, "Book Imports and Exports," 101). James Raven has slightly different figures for the longer time frame of 1700 to 1780; see Raven, *The Business of Books*, 144.

80. Shaw, "South Asia," 132.

81. Shaw, "English Books around the World," 189. These figures are based on Barber, "Books," 213–18.

82. Zachs, *The First John Murray*, 37. He claimed explicitly in early advertisements for his bookshop that he "Executes East India or foreign Commissions," and he purchased stock in the East India Company in 1769. He himself knew and corresponded with friends in the Indian military service.

83. Fraas, "Expanding the Republic."

84. On the formation of these libraries see Ohdedar, *Growth of the Library*, 14–16.

85. Salmon, *Modern History*, 31; IOR/H/260, "A Catalogue of Books in the Library of Fort St. George with the Letter and Number of Their Places." Graham Shaw claims that this catalog numbers 1,235 works in total; Shaw, "South Asia," 131; see also Shaw, "British Book in India," 563.

86. D. Lockyer, Mss Eur Photo Eur 153, 72, 108. By 1805, Lockyer reports, there were "two Indian librarians in charge of Tipu Sultan's library, one Indian librarian in

charge of Oriental publications, and one English librarian in charge of the European section" at the Fort William College library (106).

87. D. Lockyer, 76.

88. D. Lockyer, 39, 43.

89. D. Lockyer, 183; *Calcutta Gazette*, Feb. 21, 1788.

90. *Calcutta Gazette*, Feb. 21, 1788; *Madras Courier*, Nov. 24, 1790.

91. Kesavan, *History of Printing*, 62. There is some evidence that a London printer, Henry Hill, operated briefly in Bombay in 1674 and 1675 before returning to England, though it is still inconclusive; see *Exotic Printing*, 8.

92. See Mukhopadhyay, *Hicky's Bengal Gazette*, 36–41, 60–62, for examples of how the newspaper not only followed Anglo-India's wars and heroized its armed forces but also criticized the Hastings administration for missed payments to soldiers. For more on how the perception of war meant increased readerships see IOR/H/537, 187.

93. *Calcutta Gazette*, March 2, 1786.

94. Collegins, "Literary Characteristics," 109.

95. Shaw, *Printing in Calcutta*, 3; Dharwadker, "Print Culture and Literary Markets," 108–9.

96. For more on these two typefoundries see Shaw, "From Goa to the Gutenberg Award," 13.

97. Shaw, "From Goa to the Gutenberg Award," 13.

98. A. Ghosh, *Power in Print*, 111–12.

99. For more on Hastings as a patron see Marshall, "Warren Hastings as Scholar"; and Franklin, "'The Hastings Circle.'" For more on the Calcutta madrassa see Zastoupil and Moir, *Great Indian Education Debate*, 73–76.

100. See Ballantyne, *Orientalism and Race*, 24–25.

101. "Whether in Persian": quoted in F. Ross, *The Printed Bengali Character*, 19; on "liberal" and "enlightened government" see IOR/H/207, 178. See also IOR/P/50/15, 202–3 (Jan. 8, 1779) for more on the suggestion of establishing an office. As with any bureaucracy, there was not unanimity among its participants. Even after agreeing to establish an office, EIC administrators often debated about small details, with the Court of Directors in London, for instance, insisting that while it would pay for Wilkins's travel expenses, it would not increase his salary (IOR/H/207, 472–73).

102. Ogborn, *Indian Ink*, 220–21.

103. Ogborn, 225. As Ogborn notes, Company support could be inconsistent and subject to its shifting politics.

104. On the Calcutta madrassa see Zastoupil and Moir, *Great Indian Education Debate*, 78; this is an excerpt from a letter by Jonathan Duncan, resident at Benares, to Cornwallis in 1792. For a summary of Company debates about cost and control see Franklin, *Representing India*, v–vii.

105. Halhed, *Grammar of the Bengal Language*; Rocher, *Orientalism, Poetry*, 76. On the idea of "historical grammars" as tools of cultural knowledge, not just language learning, see Ahmed, *Archaeology of Babel*, 53.

106. Ogborn, *Indian Ink*, 243; F. Ross, *The Printed Bengali Character*, 4–12. After working with Wilkins and Halhed, Karmakar produced more typefaces, such as

those that were used to print the Cornwallis Code in 1793, and eventually joined the Serampore Press; see Ogborn, *Indian Ink*, 243.

107. Ogborn, *Indian Ink*, 244.

108. IOR/P/50/8, 949.

109. A. Ghosh, "An Uncertain," 26.

110. Cohn, *Colonialism*, esp. chaps. 2 and 3.

111. Though Wilkins does not mention him, Karmakar might have literally set his name into the book, composing a line of type that refers to the "Ponchanon"—meaning five-faceted—that serves as a "version" of Karmakar's first name; see R. Fraser, *Book History*, 15.

112. Ogborn, *Indian Ink*, 220–22.

113. See Halhed's introduction to *A Code of Gentoo Laws*.

114. IOR/H/207, 172–73. See also Mss Eur F324/1. Hastings was a poet, as well, and after his lengthy trial for corruption concluded, he composed his own unpublished translations of episodes from the Mahabharata. A handwritten preface notes that his aspiration was to celebrate the Mahabharata as an "original and ancient Production" that demanded knowledgeable translators who understood its cultural contexts because pedestrian attempts to render it "more pleasing to an English Ear" would harm the text's "fidelity" (Add MS 39891, f. 1b).

115. Translation quoted from F. Ross, *The Printed Bengali Character*, 33.

116. IOR/H/207, 172–73.

117. Ogborn, *Indian Ink*, 221–22.

118. K. Hall, "Eighteenth- and Early Nineteenth-Century Evolution," 91.

119. Hoock, *Empires of the Imagination*, 17–19. Hoock's "cultural state" is an addition to John Brewer's idea of the eighteenth-century fiscal-military state; see Brewer, *The Sinews of Power*, esp. xvi–xvii.

120. Stern, *The Company-State*.

121. Quoted in Stern, 3, 4. Sudipta Sen argues that complex sovereignties were self-interested ways for the EIC to acquire territory but still avoid British critics who argued that only the Crown could possess territory, a situation he describes as "company Raj" (that is company rule) opposed to "English common law"; Sen, *Distant Sovereignty*, xx.

122. Robins, *The Corporation*, 16.

123. This project would expand Gauri Viswanathan's observations about how "English literature" appeared as a subject for examination in Indian civil service education decades before it arose as a subject in Britain for whites (which, during the early nineteenth century, still engaged in classical and belletristic modes of analysis); Viswanathan, *Masks of Conquest*, 3. Similarly, Siraj Ahmed has suggested that foundational humanistic concepts, like "historical truth" and "authentic texts," depended on "state-administered" cultural projects; see Ahmed, *Archaeology of Babel*, 18–19.

124. On the "circle" see Franklin, "'The Hastings Circle'"; on the Asiatick Society see Steadman, "Asiatick Society of Bengal"; on European artists see Archer, *India and British Portraiture*.

125. Barns, *The Indian Press*, 68.

126. H. D. Love, *Vestiges of Old Madras*, 3:359–60.

127. Quoted in H. D. Love, 3:359–60.

128. IOR/H/539, 401–2.

129. IOR/H/539, 411, 405–7.

130. Darnton, *Censors at Work*, 229–31.

131. Shuger, *Censorship and Cultural Sensibility*, 2, 4.

132. See Bayly, *Empire and Information*, 3–6.

133. Mss Eur F380/4, n.p.; Charles Forbes to Alexander Gray, Dec. 7, 1794.

134. Quoted in Little, *Transoceanic Radical*, 85.

135. Pearce, *Memoirs and Correspondence*, 279, 287.

136. These were devised for Calcutta but eventually extended to Bombay and Madras. On these regulations see Cassels, *Social Legislation*, 366.

137. Anon., *Hicky's Bengal Gazette*, Dec. 16, 1780. This was almost certainly written and printed by James Augustus Hicky.

138. Firminger, "Selections," 49, 51.

139. IOR/H/537, 8, 25.

140. IOR/H/537, 92.

141. IOR/H/537, 90.

142. See Little, *Transoceanic Radical*, 152.

143. *Madras Courier*, Sept. 15, 1791.

144. On the use of China as a critique of British politics see Ballaster, *Fabulous Orients*, 205–18. On how early modern envy of China turned to Enlightenment loathing, see D. Porter, "Sinicizing Early Modernity."

145. IOR/H/539, 3, 4.

146. IOR/H/539, 26, 32–33, 38.

147. IOR/H/539, 33.

148. The censor recorded that Humphreys suggested "an attention and tender friendship . . . rather more than fraternal"; IOR/H/539, 58.

149. IOR/H/539, 57, 58.

150. IOR/H/539, 143, 84.

151. IOR/H/539, 260–61.

152. IOR F/4/98/1992, 19, 25.

153. IOR/H/539, 130–42.

154. IOR/H/539, 130–42.

155. On these complex sovereignties and legalities see Travers, "Constitutions," 103. For more on the uncertainty over rights and jurisdiction in Calcutta see S. Sen, "Imperial Subjects on Trial," 547–48.

156. IOR/H/539, 161.

157. Munro, *Major-General Sir Thomas Munro*, 2:287, 288.

158. On "servile" see Barns, *The Indian Press*, 77. Michael Franklin calls the press a "counter-public sphere"; Franklin, "'The Hastings Circle,'" 196. Graham Shaw and Mary Lloyd argue that the relationship was "fluctuating"; Shaw and Lloyd, *Publications Proscribed*, vii. Partha Chatterjee sees decade-long struggles over liberalism; P. Chatterjee, *The Black Hole*, 114–15. See also Otis, *Hicky's Bengal Gazette* for an argument that this was a struggle for press freedom.

159. See Said, *Orientalism*; Cohn, *Colonialism*, 4, 16; and Bayly, *Empire and Information*, 52, 143.

160. For an overview of these efforts in the metropolitan context, see Black, *The English Press*, esp. 141–88.

161. Eaton, *Mimesis across Empires*, 34–36.

162. Smith, *An Inquiry*, 2:641, 1:91.

163. The East India Company was technically a joint-stock company chartered by the Crown and thus was not legally incorporated in the modern sense of the term, though it performed many of the same functions that incorporation offered in nineteenth-century Britain. See Stern's *The Company-State* for a history of the changing legal status of the company. For a succinct overview of incorporation in Britain see Stout, *Corporate Romanticism*, 23–25.

164. See Boehmer, *Empire*; and Hofmeyr, *Gandhi's Printing Press*.

165. On the intertwining of modern media and the public sphere see Kellner, "Habermas," 35.

166. See Boggs, *The End of Politics*.

167. O'Brien, *Literature Incorporated*, 1.

168. For more on this debate see Livesey, *Civil Society and Empire*, 11–12. Reconsiderations of the Habermasian public sphere, especially among scholars of America, have tried to account for the impact of colonialism. See, e.g., Brooks, "Early American Public Sphere"; Jacob, "The Mental Landscape"; and Warner, *Letters of the Republic*, esp. 36, 118–22. For Warner these developments are closely tied to the transformation of the colonial American public sphere into a national one; of course, the eighteenth-century Anglo-Indian public sphere did not respond to those same national desires.

169. Yazdani, *India*, 109.

170. Alavi, "'Fugitive Mullahs'"; M. Sinha, *Colonial Masculinity*, 2. Sinha calls the "colonial public sphere" the "quintessentially imperial institution" because it was "a privileged site for mediating the contradictory logic of Eurocentrism in the creation of a distinctive colonial public sphere that the European social club acquires its centrality as an imperial institution in colonial India"; see M. Sinha, "Britishness," 491, 493.

171. P. Chatterjee, "Civil and Political Society," 172; Kaviraj, "In Search of Civil Society," 306–12. In response to Christopher Bayly's notions of "ecumene" and "information order" Chatterjee suggests that these concepts "lack theoretical clarity and analytical power" and that the "attribution of a Habermasian public sphere to the literary world of eighteenth-century northern India" is for him "too quick"; P. Chatterjee, *The Black Hole*, 75. Veena Naregal argues that the attempt to transplant features of the bourgeois public sphere, with intimate domestic relations, vernacular reading publics, and "large-scale, imperial collaborative social structures"—all of which was "backed by print"—was merely a means of creating colonial modernity and monopolizing cultural authority rather than creating civil societies; see Naregal, *Language Politics*, 9, 60–63. Dane Kennedy claims that only the nineteenth- and twentieth-century hill stations permitted the creation of a European-style bourgeois public sphere of the type that Habermas describes; see Kennedy, *The Magic Mountains*, 6–7.

172. S. Freitag, "'The Public' and Its Meanings," 7. Also see S. Freitag, "Enactments of Ram's Story," where she argues that European notions of the public "underwent significant transmutations when imported to colonial India" (87).

173. On attenuation see Bayly, who argues that there was an "attenuated sphere of public debate" that emerged in the early nineteenth century composed of "European expatriate ideologues and a handful of Indian spokesmen" and that came at the expense of indigenous information systems; Bayly, *Empire and Information*, 143. On "imperial network" see Frost, "Wider Opportunities," 937–39; on "ocean-wide" see Pearson, "Idea of the Ocean," 12. Isabel Hofmeyr dates the emergence of an "Indian Ocean public sphere"—meaning one constructed and inhabited primarily by Asian natives—to the decades between the 1880s and WWI; Hofmeyr, "Universalizing the Indian Ocean," 725.

174. See Warner, *Publics and Counterpublics*, 8, 73, 72, 75. The Anglo-Indian public sphere was not akin to those counterpublics, especially those organized by sex and gender, described by Warner as having the potential to "transform the private lives they mediate" instead of asking them to alter such identities for belonging to a unified public (Warner, *Publics and Counterpublics*, 56–62). Nor was it a version of those "competing publics" or "subaltern counterpublics" labeled by Nancy Fraser as having "emancipatory potential" because of their ability to engage dialectically with a "dominant public"; N. Fraser, "Rethinking the Public Sphere," 124, 128. And they have a larger physical reality and sociability than those suggested by Erin Mackie and Anna Dean, who examine public spheres that were "largely figurative and rhetorical" (Mackie) or a "figure of speech" (Dean); see Mackie, "Being Too Positive," 84; and A. Dean, *Talk of the Town*, 11.

175. See, in particular, P. Bennett, *Poets in the Public Sphere*; E. Richards, *Gender and the Poetics*; Levander, *Voices of the Nation*; and Brickhouse, *Transamerican Literary Relations*.

176. H. D. Love, *Vestiges of Old Madras*, 3:362.

177. On the republic of letters borrowing from the state, see McKeon, *Secret History of Domesticity*, 48.

178. M. Sinha, *Colonial Masculinity*, 1. Sinha writes that the "categories of the coloniser and the colonised are not fixed or self-evident," meaning that there is a "constant need . . . to define and re-define" the categories and their relationship, which was "neither fixed nor given for all time" but were instead "constantly rearticulated" in concert with changing political and economic situations.

179. Mackie, *Market à la Mode*, 64.

180. Livesey, *Civil Society and Empire*, 50.

181. This is contrary to the classic philosophical definition of civil society; see Calhoun, "Civil Society," 270–71.

182. Why not simply crush all dissenting institutions with state power? Ernest Gellner asks in *Conditions of Liberty*; Livesey calls this quandary the "Gellner problem" that has been inadequately answered by historians or political scientists; Livesey, *Civil Society and Empire*, 23.

183. See Becker, *Art Worlds*; Warner, *Publics and Counterpublics*; and Latour, *Reassembling the Social*.

184. Livesey, *Civil Society and Empire*, 21.

Chapter 2 • Newspaper Poetry and Reading Publics

1. Quoted in Tambe, *English Muse*, 15. Robert Sencourt is a pseudonym of Robert George.

2. Said, *Orientalism*, 77–78. There has been an extensive debate about Jones's orientalism. For an excellent overview see Wallace, *Imperial Characters*, 212n53. For a positive view of Jones's orientalism and his ambivalence about British governance of India see Franklin, "Cultural Possession," 9.

3. On "complex linguistic contact zone" see Gibson, *Indian Angles*, 20. Two anthologies in particular advanced this new picture: Gibson's *Anglophone Poetry* and Fhlathúin's *Poetry of British India*.

4. Some of this importance undoubtedly results from archival bias: because newspapers provide some of the best evidence about *other* artistic institutions, it might be thought to have had an outsized influence on Anglo-India.

5. For an overview of the importance of the newspaper to England see Barker, *Newspapers*, 2–5.

6. Franklin, "'The Hastings Circle,'" 198.

7. For an overview of newspapers and the proliferation of print see Shaw, *Printing in Calcutta*, 1–22.

8. By 1793 London readers could select from among sixteen newspapers, and by 1811 there were fifty-two; see Raven, *The Business of Books*, 258. Jon Klancher estimates four thousand periodicals started in Britain between 1790 and 1832; see Klancher, *English Reading Audiences*, ix. For an enumeration of England's provincial newspapers see Barker, *Newspapers*, 110–12.

9. For more detail see Rhodes, *The Spread of Printing*, 33–40. For an overview of Madras newspapers see Blackburn, *Print, Folklore, and Nationalism*, 77. K. P. Viswanatha Iyer argues that what became the *Madras Courier* started as a half-sheet advertising page; see Iyer, "History of Journalism," 451–58. For more on Madras's first English printed document—a power of attorney form—see Fraas, "Beyond the Atlantic."

10. There are references to the *Ceylon Government Gazette* appearing in 1802, though the earliest traced copy is from 1813.

11. See Barker, *Newspapers*, 95, 111. On "financial prop" see Raven, *The Business of Books*, 263.

12. Black, *Europe and the World*, 98.

13. Belich, *Replenishing the Earth*, 9.

14. Shaw, "British Book in India," 568.

15. On Hastings prints see the *Calcutta Gazette*, July 29, 1784; on the "Horse and Dog Painter" see the *Calcutta Gazette*, March 26, 1789.

16. On the selling of elephants see the *Calcutta Gazette*, May 6, 1784.

17. For more on reports of military news see chap. 6. For an example of a plea for a lost animal in the newspaper see *India Gazette*, Feb. 3, 1781.

18. Shaw, "India," 457. On newspapers as national institutions see B. Anderson, *Imagined Communities*. For more on the scholarly history of newspapers and nationalism see Potter, *News and the British World*, 11–12.

19. This figure is based on the author's counting.

20. For a theory of republication see McGill, *American Literature*, esp. 3–7. For recirculation as an instrument of national unity see Garvey, *Writing with Scissors*, esp. 4–6, 30.

21. Garvey, *Writing with Scissors*, 30.

22. On the nineteenth century "imperial press system" as a "mutual interdependence" between Britain and its colonies see Potter, *News and the British World*, 16.

23. More generally, Robert Griffin suggests that what Foucault named the author function operates even when the proper name of an author is absent, as in the case of anonyms and pseudonyms; Griffin, "Anonymity and Authorship," 879–80.

24. Mark Vareschi's example is the obscure political pamphlets that likely would have been discarded by scholars but are now widely read because of their attribution to Daniel Defoe and their role in explaining his development as a novelist; Vareschi, "Reading (and Not Reading) Anonymity," 4.

25. Bode, "Thousands of Titles," 292–301.

26. *Calcutta Gazette*, May 13, 1784.

27. *Madras Courier*, Dec. 29, 1791.

28. *Madras Courier*, Dec. 29, 1791.

29. *Madras Courier*, March 8, 1792.

30. *Calcutta Gazette*, August 7, 1788.

31. Datta, "Publishing and Translating," 58–60; Cohn, *Colonialism*, 23; David Kopf, *British Orientalism*, 18.

32. Quoted in Ohdedar, *Growth of the Library*, 92.

33. *Calcutta Gazette*, Feb. 8, 1787.

34. *India Gazette*, Dec. 16, 1780.

35. Senex [pseud.], "The Monitor," *India Gazette*, Dec. 16, 1780.

36. Winterbottom, *Hybrid Knowledge*, 54–55.

37. For "practical orientalism" see Bayly, "British and Indigenous Peoples," 36. For more on Enlightenment orientalism see Aravamudan, *Enlightenment Orientalism*. Bayly claims the period 1750–1850 witnessed the "epistemological and economic creation of 'indigenous peoples' as a series of comparable categories across the globe" ("British and Indigenous People," 21). He suggests that there are two general stages to European-indigenous interaction from 1750 to 1850: first, societies see some advantages from interacting with Europeans as they integrate into an indigenous system, but then, as taxation grows and resource extraction becomes more severe, they are exploited and driven off their land (30). For a counterpoint to this argument, which sees exploitation as the fundamental relationship from the outset, see Subrahmanyam, *Europe's India*.

38. Bayly, *Empire and Information*, 182, 203.

39. K. Chatterjee, "History as Self-Representation," 921–22.

40. *Calcutta Gazette*, Feb. 24, 1785.

41. A. Ghosh, *Power in Print*, 45, 3–4.

42. Blackburn, *Print, Folklore, and Nationalism*, 31.

43. Blackburn, 58–59; Shaw, *South Asia and Burma Retrospective*, 13; Joshi, *In Another Country*, 38.

44. Blackburn, *Print, Folklore, and Nationalism*, 51, 58–59.

45. On Bunyan as an "intellectual of the world" see Hofmeyr, *The Portable Bunyan*, 2. On missionaries seeking to establish trust see Blackburn, *Print, Folklore, and Nationalism*, 29–31.

46. This author's name is spelled variously as Khusrau, Khusraw, and Kosrow. For more on Khusrau see Ahmad, *Studies in Islamic Culture*, 115–18; and Schimmel, "Amīr K̲osrow Dehlavī." Ahmad describes Khusrau as an eminent poet, musician, historian, and courtier and claims that Khusrau exhibits an "irresistible attraction" to India but an "implacable hostility" to Hinduism, which remained an "unreconciled tension" in his writing (115).

47. Khusrau is associated with numerous language traditions, including Persian and (confusingly) what is called Hindavi or Hindustani, a precursor of what is identified now both as Urdu and Hindi (or Modern Standard Hindi). On Khusrau's role in these traditions see Shapiro, "Hindi," 280. For a brief history of printing calligraphic scripts, especially the Perso-Arabic scripts represented in *Nasta'liq* that are evident here, see Stark, *Empire of Books*, 35–37.

48. For a discussion of this history see de Bruijn, "*Ḡazal* I. History."

49. S. Sharma, *Amir Khusraw*, 42–43.

50. *Madras Courier*, August 25, 1791. An origin of the name may be traced to Tiberius Claudius Candidus, the second-century CE Roman general and supporter of Emperor Septimus Severus. It is not a unique name; the American revolutionary Samuel Adams published editorials in the 1770s also signed Candidus.

51. *Calcutta Gazette*, Dec. 16, 1784.

52. Losensky, "Linguistic and Rhetorical Aspects," 244, 245.

53. de Bruijn, "*Ḡazal* I. History."

54. Losensky, "Linguistic and Rhetorical Aspects," 248.

55. Fraser, *Book History*, 62; Bauer and Neuwirth, *Ghazal as World Literature I*, 22.

56. Burney, "Locating the World," 152.

57. Dabashi, *Persophilia*, 2, 7–8, 16.

58. Ahmed, *Archaeology of Babel*, 57.

59. The Anglo-Indian translator identifies "Birj" as "spoken in the province of Agra," but, in fact, it was from a wider area of what is now identified as western Uttar Pradesh; see Shapiro, "Hindi," 252.

60. Busch, *Poetry of Kings*, 6–7. The evolution of South Asian languages and dialects in the modern period is complex and the origins of Hindi in Hindavi/Hindustani remain highly contested, especially as categories like Urdu and Hindi acquired geographical, national, and religious connotations during the twentieth century. On the complicated history of Urdu and Hindi, see King, *One Language, Two Scripts*, esp. 4–11.

61. Busch, "Hidden in Plain View," 267–68; Busch, *Poetry of Kings*, 7; on Brajbhasha versus Khari Boli see Schmidt, "Urdu," 288–89. On the place of Brajbhasha in the larger "New Indo-Aryan" group of languages, themselves descended from Sanskrit, see Snell, *Hindi Classical Tradition*, 3.

62. *Calcutta Gazette*, March 20, 1788.

63. *Calcutta Gazette*, July 17, 1788. Platts defines *paheli* as a "riddle, enigma"; see Platts, *A Dictionary of Urdu*, 294. It is also known as *mukri* or *mukuri*, which Platts

defines as "a kind of short poem (or a kind of riddle in verse), of frequent use in the Braj dialect"; see Platts, *A Dictionary of Urdu*, 1058. For additional examples of this poetic genre see Snell, *Hindi Classical Tradition*, 189. Thanks to Imre Bangha for pointing me toward this tradition.

64. For the argument that in the nineteenth century poetry like this became associated with Mughal decadence and decline, see Busch, *Poetry of Kings*, 13, 16–17.

65. Busch, 19–20.

66. Busch, "Braj beyond Braj," 7.

67. Bayly, *Empire and Information*, 7.

68. Warner, *Letters of the Republic*, 62.

69. *Punch* is typically attributed to the Sanskrit term *panca*, which refers to the mixing of ingredients; see *Oxford English Dictionary*, s.v. "punch," no. 3. As the *OED* notes, this etymology is uncertain.

70. See the *Calcutta Chronicle*, Oct. 25, 1787; and *Calcutta Chronicle*, Sept. 30, 1790.

71. *India Gazette*, April 7, 1781.

72. "The Punch House," *Madras Courier*, July 21, 1790. For more on *punch* and punch houses in India see Bond, *Strange Men, Strange Places*. For more on the alignment of punch houses, politics, and news see Thompson, *Rum Punch and Revolution*; and Newman, *The Romantic Tavern*.

73. Habermas, *Structural Transformation*, 32.

74. *Madras Courier*, July 21, 1790.

75. Czennia, "Wide-Open Hemispheres," 46.

76. Czennia, 48.

77. On tobacco cultivation and the hookah see Gokhale, "Tobacco in Seventeenth-Century India," 484–85. There is some evidence that hookahs were also used to smoke other substances, such as opium; see T. Dean, "The Hookah," 13–15. Iain Gately suggests that Africa's culture of cannabis smoking originated the idea of the water pipe that was eventually imitated as the South Asian hookah; see Gately, *Tobacco*, 60–61. Mimi Nichter suggests, however, that the water pipe was invented in South Asia during the seventeenth century as a way to moderate the smoke from tobacco introduced to the region by Europeans; see Nichter, "South Asia," 575.

78. Gokhale, "Tobacco in Seventeenth-Century India," 491–92.

79. Stanhope, *Genuine Memoirs of Asiaticus*, 46. See also Yule and Burnell, *Hobson-Jobson*, s.v. "hooka-burdar."

80. *Bombay Courier*, Feb. 4, 1804.

81. *India Gazette*, Dec. 23, 1780.

82. "The Hookah," *Calcutta Chronicle*, Sept. 24, 1789.

83. *Madras Courier*, Oct. 13, 1791.

84. *Madras Courier*, Oct. 20, 1791.

85. *Madras Courier*, Nov. 24, 1791.

86. Yule and Burnell, *Hobson-Jobson*, s.v. "firinghee." Spellings of this term varied considerably.

87. Yule and Burnell, *Hobson-Jobson*, s.v. "chowk," which originates from the Hindi *chauk*.

88. Yule and Burnell, *Hobson-Jobson*, s.v. "Qui-Hi"; *OED*, s.v. "koi-hai." It was a term also used to name an indigenous servant (as a "qui-hi").

89. *Madras Courier*, Nov. 24, 1791.

90. *OED*, s.v. "cheroot." *Cheroot* is a Tamil term (*shuruttu*) that was absorbed into the French of southern India before making its way to English.

91. Star, "The Ethnography of Infrastructure," 387–88.

92. Star and Ruhleder, "Steps toward an Ecology," 113. They also suggest that infrastructure involves a tense relation between local customizable use and the "need for standards and continuity" (112).

93. Livesey, *Civil Society and Empire*, 50, 28–29; on the coffee house as a place of babble, noise, and debate see Ellis, "Coffee-Women," 33.

94. P. Bennett, *Poets in the Public Sphere*, 4–5.

95. Michael C. Cohen, "Peddlers, Poems, and Local Culture," 10.

96. D. White, "'Zig Zag Sublimity,'" 154.

Chapter 3 • The Vagrant Muse

1. See the *Oxford Dictionary of National Biography*, s.v. "Irwin, Eyles" (both the 1892 and the 2004–10 entries). For additional accounts of Irwin's life see Anon., "Memoirs of Eyles Irwin"; Rivers, *Literary Memoirs*, 1:332–33; "Eyles Irwin," in *Biographical Dictionary*, 174; Irwin's obituary in the *Gentleman's Magazine* 87 (Oct. 1817): 376; and Clarke and Mackenzie, *Voyagers and Travellers*, 465–66. Irwin's situation as at least the second generation of his family to pursue East India Company service was common; P. J. Marshall estimates that 40 percent of service members had fathers who worked for the Company (Marshall, "British-Indian Connections," 50). There is evidence Irwin's son was employed by the Company as well.

2. Other influential accounts of the representative global life include Carretta, *Equiano, the African*; Rothschild, *The Inner Life of Empires*; and the multiple narratives brought together in Ogborn's *Global Lives* or C. Anderson's *Subaltern Lives*.

3. See *Spirit of the Public Journals*, 256.

4. On empires as imperial assemblages and imperial actors as working across them, see Alavi, *Muslim Cosmopolitanism*, esp. chap. 5.

5. Clifford, *Routes*, 19, 29–30. Yet Irwin dispenses with the "bifocal" perspective that Clifford thought to be characteristic of these travelers for a multifocal one.

6. Dimock, *Through Other Continents*, 4.

7. Teltscher, *India Inscribed*, 220–21; Schürer, "The Impartial Spectator," 34–36.

8. "Ramah: or, The Bramin" in Irwin, *Eastern Eclogues*, lines 25, 120.

9. To learn more about Irwin's impersonations of Indian speakers, see Mulholland, *Sounding Imperial*, chap. 4.

10. For an overview of this embassy see Hevia, *Cherishing Men from Afar*, 57.

11. Hevia, 82.

12. Hevia, 58. For a description of the items given in exchange, see Hsü, *Rise of Modern China*, 155.

13. *Calcutta Gazette*, March 14, 1793.

14. On Smith reviving interest in the sonnet see Knowles, *Sensibility*, 46.

15. Helgerson, *Forms of Nationhood*, 162–63.

16. DeWispelare, *Multilingual Subjects*, 207. Irwin's name is listed under the subscribers to Mickle's text, incorrectly sorted under "J" rather than "I."

17. Mickle, *The Lusiad*, viii.

18. Mickle, cii. For more on this contrast of fame and wealth see Helgerson, *Forms of Nationhood*, 156–58.

19. For more on this relationship see Coates, *Macao and the British*; and Gunn, *Encountering Macau*.

20. Rajan, *Under Western Eyes*, 33.

21. Yang, *Performing China*, 15.

22. Yang, 15.

23. Irwin, "Prologue," 245.

24. For an overview of how the colonial trade depended on the concept, not just the practicalities, of militarism, see Ahmed, *The Stillbirth of Capital*.

25. For more on the pastoral's subject as "the problem of conventionality itself" see McKeon, "Surveying the Frontier," 9. For a discussion of generic shifts in pastoral across an even longer period see P. Alpers, *What Is Pastoral?* Irwin likely also sought to emulate the Virgilian career, which began in pastoral before moving toward georgic and culminating in epic.

26. See Pope, *Windsor-Forest*: "Enough for me, that to the list'ning swains, / First in these fields I sung the sylvan strains" (lines 433–34).

27. Pope, *Rape of the Lock*, 3.

28. Anon., *The Artless Lovers*, 2:162.

29. Norbert Schürer suggests we should include an "Anglo-Indian canon" to the many other canons of British literature and suggests that Irwin is likely the first poet who should qualify as "Anglo-Indian"; Schürer, "Surveying," 604.

30. Denham, "Coopers Hill," lines 6–7. Denham's original publication of the poem does not include the possessive apostrophe in its title, though I have included it in my text proper since "Cooper's Hill" is how the poem is generally known.

31. Raposo et al., "Moving Localities," 167, 169.

32. Clifford, *Routes*, 3.

33. Hayley Manuscripts, vol. 9, Letter 47, July 23, 1783.

34. For one excellent overview of this mechanism see Kaul, *Poems of Nation*, esp. 23–33.

35. See Mulholland, *Sounding Imperial*, esp. chap. 4.

36. This list aligns with the route that Irwin took from India to England in 1777, when he passed through the Arabian Sea and Egypt before crossing the Mediterranean.

37. Pococke, *A Description of the East*; Norden, *Voyage d'Égypte et de Nubie*; Bruce, *Travels to Discover*; Constantin, *Voyage en Egypte et Syrie*. This contradiction is particularly evident when Irwin cites Pococke in the explanatory notes of later poetry collections like the *Occasional Epistles*.

38. Leask, *Curiosity*, 26–27, 46.

39. Irwin, "Epistle to the Right Honourable George Lord Pigot," 10, 5.

40. Irwin, *A Series of Adventures*, 367.

41. Irwin, "Eclogue I: Alexis: or, the Traveller," *Eastern Eclogues*, lines 81–82.

42. Mitchell, "Imperial Landscape," 10, 12. For a historical overview of the picturesque see Copley and Garside, introduction.

43. Suleri, *Rhetoric of English India*, 75–76; Leask, *Curiosity*, 168, 173.

44. Irwin, *A Series of Adventures*, 374.

45. Foote, *The Nabob*, 55.

46. See Stoler, "'The Rot Remains,'" 9.

47. Irwin, "Epistle II," 13–14 (lines 12, 34).

48. [James Boswell?], *Scot's Magazine*, vol. 45 (Jan. 1783): 600. This same review appeared in the *Gentleman's Magazine*, vol. 53 (July 1783): 688–89.

49. Irwin, "Epistle III," n.p. [23].

50. Irwin, n.p. [23].

51. Bjorkelo, Meyer, and Seland, "Definite Places," 5–6.

52. Irwin, "Epistle III," 26 (lines 79, 86–89).

53. Irwin, 35 (lines 215–16, 218).

54. On "dialectical engagement" see Garcia, *Islam and the English Enlightenment*, 3.

55. Irwin, *A Series of Adventures*, 48.

56. For a brief description of this overwhelming attention see Wright, *The Ambassadors*, 258–59. For an account of this Cherokee embassy see Oliphant, "The Cherokee Embassy."

57. Irwin, "Epistle III," 30 (lines 101, 103–7).

58. Irwin, "Epistle III," 35 (line 224). On the *Shahnameh*, and in particular the long history and present-day context of aligning Ferdowsi with Homer, see Omidsalar, *Poetics and Politics*, esp. 161–80.

59. The terminology of assemblage contains differing definitions among anthropologists, political scientists, cultural theorists, and biologists. Colin McFarlane notes that assemblage is "used in archaeology to denote a group of different artifacts found in the same context," whereas in biology the term *assemblage* "is used to connote micro- or macro-formations, such as the vertebrae skeletal muscle," and in social and political theory as a means of describing how relations among heterogeneous objects can produce new agencies and realities. See McFarlane, "Translocal Assemblages," 561–62n1. For an excellent overview of these structures see Müller, "Assemblages and Actor-Networks."

60. See Nayar, "The Imperial Sublime," 58, 69–70.

61. "Stanzas to Mrs. Irwin," lines 2–4. This poem was included in a letter to Hayley and was said to be originally written "on a blank leaf of Hayley's Poems"; see Hayley Manuscripts, vol. 9, Letter 43, Oct. 5, 1780.

62. Hayley Manuscripts, vol. 11, Letter 53, Oct. 20, 1786.

63. This poem seems never to have been published, likely at the suggestion of Hayley, who believed that it needed "a smaller compass." See Hayley Manuscripts, vol. 11, Letter 54, Feb. 15, 1787.

64. Piper, *Dreaming in Books*, 6.

65. Hayley Manuscripts, vol. 9, Letter 44, Jan. 28, 1782.

66. Hayley Manuscripts, vol. 9, Letter 44, Jan. 28, 1782. Hayley Manuscripts, vol. 9, Letter 43, Oct. 5, 1780.

67. Hayley Manuscripts, vol. 9, Letter 46, Feb. 21, 1783.

68. Hayley Manuscripts, vol. 9, Letter 47, July 23, 1783.

69. Hayley Manuscripts, vol. 9, Letter 49, April 20, 1784.

70. Tierney, *Correspondence of Robert Dodsley*, Appendix E, 562. The note is dated April 3, 1780, and reads: "JD agreed to purchase I.'s *Series of Adventures* . . . for 200 copies of the same."

71. See Barber, "Books," 203.

72. "Ode to the Nile," *India Gazette, or Calcutta General Advertiser*, June 23, 1781.

73. See "On Reading the Ode to the Nile, Written by Eyles Irwin, Esq; and Published in the *India Gazette*, June 23, 1781," Dec. 8, 1781.

74. Hayley Manuscripts, vol. 9, Letter 44, Jan. 28, 1782; and Hayley Manuscripts, vol. 9, Letter 43, Oct. 5, 1780.

75. Favret, *War at a Distance*, 95.

Chapter 4 • Undoing Britain in Bengal

1. For more on the life of Sir William Jones see Cannon, *Life and Mind of Oriental Jones*; and Franklin, *Orientalist Jones*.

2. See Franklin, "Cultural Possession," 8–12.

3. Gibson, *Indian Angles*, 22. The poems of Anna Maria have typically been attributed to Anna Maria Jones, Sir William Jones's wife, who accompanied him to India in 1784. Mary Ellis Gibson asserts that these poems are not written or published by Anna Maria Jones but instead by another anonymous woman who takes the name Anna Maria as a potential homage to the Della Cruscans. Gibson points out inconsistencies with the subject matter of the poems (too "middle-brow" for an elevated woman like Anna Maria Jones), the list of subscribers (where the Joneses appear), and the datelines that indicate some of the poems may have been written in London when the Joneses were in Asia. For her complete argument about attribution see Gibson, *Indian Angles*, 55–56. For a detailed description of Anna Maria's career and for additional debates about *The Poems of Anna Maria*, see Shaw, *Printing in Calcutta*, 163; Ashfield, *Romantic Women Poets*, 107–8; Feldman, *British Women Poets*, 358–59; and Franklin, *Orientalist Jones*, 244–45 and throughout.

4. Featherstone, "Localism," 47.

5. See Cannon, *Letters of Sir William Jones*, 2:714 (Oct. 5, 1786). (Hereafter abbreviated *LWJ*.) There is a longer genealogy to this notion that goes back to early British orientalism in India; see Ahmed, "Orientalism and the Permanent," 176–80.

6. *The World* (Calcutta), Jan. 4, 1794.

7. D. Porter, "Sinicizing Early Modernity," 299.

8. On middle grounds see R. White, *The Middle Ground*; on contact zones see Pratt, *Imperial Eyes*; on intercultural borderlands see Choudhury, *Interculturalism and Resistance*.

9. B. Anderson, *Imagined Communities*, 5–6.

10. Teltscher, *India Inscribed*, 208.

11. See McGann, *The New Oxford Book*, xxi–xxii. For another origin of the argument that orientalist knowledge inspired Romantic revolutions, see Schwab, *The Oriental Renaissance*.

12. Trautmann, *Aryans and British India*, 41.

13. Ballantyne, *Orientalism and Race*, 29. Trautmann describes this as Jones "finding India's place" (*Aryans and British India*, 52).

14. Franklin, *Orientalist Jones*, 232–33.

15. *Calcutta Gazette*, May 26, 1785.

16. Jones, *Sacontalá, or the Fatal Ring*, iii, v.

17. *Sacontalá*'s profits were advertised as for charity in the *Calcutta Gazette*, Oct. 8, 1789. On the career of Joseph Cooper see Shaw, *Printing in Calcutta*, 43–45.

18. For the claim about Jones's *Sacontalá* being seen as an early key to Hindu culture, see Ahmed, *Archaeology of Babel*, 162–63.

19. Franklin, *Orientalist Jones*, 232.

20. From 1780 to 1783 Jones wrote four political tracts, the most famous and influential of which was his inquiry into the legality of British laws to suppress riots. Another pamphlet, *The Principles of Government*, was published anonymously in 1782 and was deemed libelous by the British government. Jones reprinted it with his identity revealed as its author; the landmark legal case that resulted eventually led to the Libel Act of 1792, which advanced some basic elements of nineteenth-century press freedoms. While practicing law in Wales, he was often "aligned . . . with the under-privileged, frequently representing the colonised Welsh without a fee"; Franklin, "Sir William Jones, the Celtic Revival," 28.

21. For more on this theme see Mulholland, "Connecting Eighteenth-Century India."

22. Franklin, *Orientalist Jones*, 161.

23. Said, *Orientalism*, 77–78. There has been an extensive debate about Jones's orientalism. For an excellent overview see Wallace, *Imperial Characters*, 212n53. For a more positive view of Jones's orientalism and his ambivalence about British governance of India see Franklin, "Cultural Possession," 9.

24. Jones composed an early plan for this poem, which focused primarily on the advantages of the British constitutional tradition. He revised this plan while in India, increasing the role of Hinduism and its deities; see Cannon, *Life and Mind of Oriental Jones*, 198, 276–77.

25. See Cannon, 198.

26. Franklin, "Sir William Jones, the Celtic Revival," 20.

27. Franklin, 21.

28. See Franklin, *Sir William Jones*, 2.

29. Cannon, *LWJ*, 1:312.

30. Franklin, *Orientalist Jones*, esp. 92–95.

31. Cannon, *LWJ*, 2:516 (emphasis in original).

32. Cannon, 2:578.

33. The source of this misery is unclear in the context of this letter. In general, Jones believed that British dominion was for Hindus an improvement over Muslim Mughal rule while advocating that Hindus and Muslims would be judged according to their own laws.

34. Cannon, *LWJ*, 2:712–13.

35. The idea of Muslim tyranny was a motivating stereotype of British orientalism; see Ballaster, *Fabulous Orients*.

36. Cannon, *LWJ*, 2:517 (emphasis in original).

37. Cannon, *LWJ*, 2:517, 2:527.

38. See Cannon, 161–62; see also Baylen and Gossman, *Biographical Dictionary*, 1:273–74.

39. Jones, *The Muse Recalled*, 7.

40. Cannon, *LWJ*, 2:847.

41. For an overview of the settling and rapid growth of the anglophone world, and for an analysis of its racial explanations of the settler phenomenon, see Belich, *Replenishing the Earth*, esp. 4–9 and 21–23. On the stereotype of Hindus as feminine see Sinha, *Colonial Masculinity*.

42. See Mill, *History of British India*, 567. Mill cites Johnson as his example, showing Johnson's narrative of his Highlands journey was the origin for this comparison. Mill notoriously and controversially describes Hindus as "the offspring of a wild and ungoverned imagination . . . [which] mark[s] the state of a rude and credulous people" (33). See also S. Johnson, *Journey to the Western Islands*, 51. Many Scots perceived similarities between the Highland Clearances, which moved poor tenants off their land for wealthy landowners, and the rapacity of the British in India. See Pittock, "Dissolving the Dream," 131–32. For more on Scottish orientalists and their comparison of Scotland and India's Hindus, see Rendall, "Scottish Orientalism."

43. Armitage, *Ideological Origins*, 11.

44. Jones, *Collected Works*, 2:429–54.

45. Jones composed only four stanzas and prose "Arguments" for all twelve of the books in the epic; see Cannon, *Life and Mind of Oriental Jones*, 276. He must have published at least a limited amount, as a printed version of the prose arguments can be seen in the papers of his friend and correspondent Viscount Althorp; see Add MS 75979, Althorp Papers. There was extensive discussion among antiquarians of the possibility of a Phoenician lineage for Britain; see Weinbrot, *Britannia's Issue*, 488–91.

46. Jones, *Collected Works*, 2:452.

47. Jones, 2:445–46.

48. Jones, 2:451.

49. Jones, 2:451–52.

50. Zwierlein, "Travelling through (Post-)Imperial Panoramas," 254.

51. For an overview of this trend see Pitts, *A Turn to Empire*, 4–5.

52. For more on this potential see Leask, *British Romantic Writers*, 108–9.

53. Jones, *Collected Works*, 2:452.

54. Aravamudan suggests, instead, that archaic modernity makes the present seem "whole": Aravamudan, *Enlightenment Orientalism*, 14. "Archaic modernity" derives from Prakash, *Another Reason*, esp. chap. 4.

55. See Boehmer, *Empire*, 6.

56. See Merry, "Adieu and Recall to Love," 36–37, line 44.

57. For more on the Della Cruscan movement see Hargreaves-Mawdsley, *The English Della Cruscans*. For more on women authors and Della Cruscanism see Pascoe, *Romantic Theatricality*, 68–94.

58. Gibson, *Indian Angles*, 54, 55, 57.

59. Ramazani, *A Transnational Poetics*, 165.

60. For these figures, and the scholarship from which they arise, see Stern, *The Company-State*, 183 and 275n157. For more on the idea of a "grey town" Calcutta see P. Sinha, *Calcutta in Urban History*, esp. 7–8. Disagreement persists about how much physical and cultural mixing there was. R. Mukherjee calls Calcutta the "forever England" ("'Forever England'"), but Swati Chattopadhay claims there is little

evidence for a divided Calcutta and argues instead for a "hybrid colonial culture" (Chattopadhay, "Blurring Boundaries," 176–77).

61. For more on the publication history of this volume consult Shaw, *Printing in Calcutta*, 63.

62. Shaw, 157–62. For an excellent overview of late eighteenth-century Calcutta's literary scene see Gibson, *Indian Angles*, 22–26.

63. A list of subscribers is included at the beginning of *The Poems of Anna Maria.*

64. See K. Freeman, *British Women Writers.*

65. *The World* (Calcutta), Jan. 4, 1794.

66. Merry's "Serenade" was published in the *Calcutta Gazette*, May 27, 1790, likely republished from the *European Magazine* (London: Sept. 1789), 217.

67. Mee, "'Reciprocal Expressions of Kindness,'" 104.

68. Quoted in McGann, *The Poetics of Sensibility*, 74.

69. See Maria, *Poems of Anna Maria*. She acknowledges this misinformation in her subsequent poetry but takes no steps to revise or edit her initially incorrect premise, revealing how difficult it can be to participate in literary fashions from thousands of miles away.

70. It is not clear whether Anna Maria's poetry was reprinted and sold in London or whether it was shipped from Calcutta. Because of cost, however, it was unusual for books to be printed and shipped from Calcutta to Britain in the eighteenth century.

71. McGann, *The Poetics of Sensibility*, 81–82.

72. *The World* (Calcutta), Jan. 4, 1794.

73. *The World* (Calcutta), Jan. 4, 1794.

74. *The World* (Calcutta), Jan. 4, 1794.

75. See *British Critic and Quarterly Theological Review* 5 (1794): 297–98. The reviewer remarks on the enormously high price of her collection and claims, perhaps jokingly, "surely our poets will emigrate" to India.

76. *Monthly Review* (London: Nov. 1794), 352.

77. Pascoe claims that Della Cruscanism is "particularly advantageous for women writers" who "strategically appropriated Merry's verse" as a means of composing their own poetry and ushering themselves into print; see Pascoe, *Romantic Theatricality*, 71–72, 81–82.

78. For an overview and history of these debates about the global and the local see Wilson and Dissanayake, *Global/Local.*

79. Jones uses this term to describe the action of *Britain Discovered*; see Jones, *Collected Works*, 2:431.

80. Kaul, "English Poetry in India," 32.

81. Gibson, "Transforming Late Romanticism," 64. Nigel Leask claims about Anglo-Indian poetry more generally that one has to "look hard" for the "direct influence of Asian poetical styles" not already "encoded" within the "metropolitan discourse of the primitive or the exotic" ("Towards an Anglo-Indian Poetry?" 55).

82. D. Porter, "Sinicizing Early Modernity," 304.

83. D. Porter, 305.

84. Macaulay, *Macaulay*, 729.

Chapter 5 • Tristram Shandy *in Bombay*

1. On web of cosmopolitan actors see Games, *The Web of Empire*; on "set of networks" see Glaisyer, "Networking," 474. On "dots and dashes" Harm Stevens writes of seventeenth-century Dutch empire: "if this was an empire it was one of dots and dashes. The dashes represented the trading routes controlled by the VOC; the dots the Company's overseas bases"; H. Stevens, *Dutch Enterprise*, 87. For an early overview of the use of network metaphors for empire see Lester, "Imperial Circuits and Networks." The art historian and archaeologist Finbarr Flood claims that the first use of networks to explain South Asia was Cohn and Marriott, "Networks and Centres."

2. K. Wilson, *Strolling Players of Empire*; P. Levine, *Prostitution, Race, and Politics*; McClintock, *Imperial Leather*; Stoler, *Carnal Knowledge*; Ballantyne and Burton, *Moving Subjects*; M. Sinha, *Colonial Masculinity*; Boehmer, *Colonial and Postcolonial Literature*, 49.

3. K. Wilson, *The Island Race*, 2, 4–5.

4. M. Sinha, "Is 'Region' Still Good to Think?" 266.

5. M. Sinha, *Colonial Masculinity*, 2. See also M. Sinha, "Mapping the Imperial Social Formation."

6. On the "culture of politeness" see Klein, *Shaftesbury*, 3–8. For "associational world" see Clark, *British Clubs and Societies*; and Clark, *Sociability and Urbanity*, 6–7.

7. Clark, *Sociability and Urbanity*, 12.

8. Alavi, "'Fugitive Mullahs,'" esp. 1337–38.

9. M. Sinha, "Britishness," 492.

10. M. Sinha, "Britishness," 504.

11. Michèle Cohen, *Fashioning Masculinity*, 65–67.

12. Kaul, "English Poetry in India," 35.

13. M. Sinha, "Mapping the Imperial Social Formation," 1077. Sinha borrows this notion from Hennessy, *Materialist Feminism*.

14. For more on sociability as "cultural work" see Russell and Tuite, "Introducing Romantic Sociability," 4.

15. James Romney was the first cousin, once removed of Miles Romney, who converted to Mormonism, traveled to America, and was the great-great-grandfather of Mitt Romney; see Hebblethwaite, "Mitt Romney's Mormon Roots." See also A. Bennett, *Guide for Genealogical Research*, 154, 156.

16. It was exhibited at the Free Society of Artists in 1766; see Chamberlain, *George Romney*, 229. This description of which brother is which appears in John Romney's *Memoirs* (1830), 53.

17. Chamberlain, *George Romney*, 381.

18. On "many different climates" see Mss Eur F198/3/1 f. 11v; on "novice" see Mss Eur F198/3/2 f. 15r; on receiving his brother's help securing a commission, see J. Romney, *Memoirs*, 178.

19. The total provenance of Romney's archive is not known. His nephew John Romney (the painter George Romney's son) mentions possessing manuscripts of his plays. This may indicate that James Romney traveled to England from India in 1803 with his records, and then, on his death, without any immediate family, they were

turned over to his nephew. From that point in the mid-nineteenth century there was no mention of Romney's archive until it went for sale at Sotheby's in 1992, at which point it seems the archive was split into two pieces and purchased by the British Library and the Australian Defence Force Academy Library in Canberra.

20. Romney was a cadet on his arrival, but in 1794 he was listed as a captain of the "second Battalion of European Infantry" and temporarily in Surat in 1794 (*Bombay Courier*, Feb. 15, 1794) before being transferred to the Second Native Infantry battalion stationed in Calicut (*Bombay Courier*, Oct. 24, 1795) and then stationed in Palghaut in 1795, a fortress near the present city of Palakkad and Coimbatore, that same year as a major (see *East India Military Calendar*, 114–15). After his expedition to the Red Sea Romney left India as a lieutenant colonel, having served for twenty-five years, approximately half his life.

21. For more on Romney's account of his expedition and its diplomacy see a description dated April 15, 1801, in IOR/H/476, 195–200.

22. J. Romney, *Memoirs*, 6.

23. On "novices" see Mss Eur F198/3/2, f. 15r. On "convey no meaning" see Mss Eur F198/3/2, f. 11v. He forgives the *Bombay Gazette* editors for their "inattention," which, when combined with the volume of his manuscript drafts to them, suggest he wrote so often that they sometimes ignored him; Mss Eur F198/3/2, f. 6r.

24. Mss Eur F198/5/3, f. 76r.

25. For two accounts of this lengthy tradition see Juncu, *India in the Italian Renaissance*, 87; and Hilton, "Speaking Truth to Power," 206–7.

26. Among his archive is a collection of letters he received in Tamil, which implies his knowledge of that language; see Mss Eur F198/6/19.

27. For examples of Amintor see Mss Eur F198/3/2/ f. 14v. For examples of Hugh Proteus see F198/6/5. For examples of Hugh Protius see Mss Eur F/198/6/5 f. 5r. For examples of Simon Highforth see Mss Eur F198/3/2 f. 3r. For examples of Patrick Traverse see Mss Eur F198/6/14.

28. Mss Eur F198/6/5 f. 5r-6v.

29. In an appreciative reply to the *Bombay Gazette*, Romney expresses happiness at seeing a poem in the previous week's issue (Mss Eur F198/3/2, f. 16v).

30. For an account of the importance of aristocratic patronage see A. Cohen, "The 'Aristocratic Imperialists.'"

31. Mss Eur F198/3/1 f. 11r. Romney eventually received his promotion but not until the mid-1790s. For more on how his concerns with promotion reflect East India Company army structure, see Callahan, *The East India Company*, esp. 21–24.

32. On "without further prospect" see Mss Eur F198/3/1 f. 6r; on "submitting" and "inferior to none" see Mss Eur F198/3/1 f. 9r.

33. Callahan, *The East India Company*, xi, 4.

34. Mss Eur F198/3/1 f. 8r-8v. This vignette appears in Romney's hand and is titled "Mrs. —— Letter, taking her husband's part," which leads me to conclude it was an imagined soliloquy rather than a genuine reply from the wife of a member of Bombay's government. There is, however, the possibility that he was copying a reply that he actually received, which might indicate the fragility of his social life in Bombay that appears in his poems and letters, or that he was trying out a scene for one of his plays (though this appears among his personal papers).

35. On "nearer resemblance" and "whispering sycophants" see Mss Eur F198/3/2 f. 1v; on "distinguished etcetras" see Mss Eur F198/6/5 f. 11r.

36. Mss Eur F198/5/1 f. 5v.

37. Mss Eur F198/6/5 f. 9r.

38. Mss Eur F198/6/5 f. 1r–1v.

39. Mss Eur F198/3/3 f. 1r.

40. On "unanimity" see Mss Eur F198/3/3 f. 4r; on "metropolitical empire" and the creation of an "urbanical assembly" see Mss Eur F198/3/3 f. 2r.

41. Mss Eur F198/3/3 f. 2r. *Metropolitical* is synonymous with *metropolitan* (though it also has a religious definition of the exact extent of a diocese); see *OED*, s.v. "metropolitical."

42. Bose, *A Hundred Horizons*, 11.

43. Mss Eur F198/3/3 f. 3r.

44. Mss Eur F198/3/3 f. 3r.

45. Mss Eur F198/3/3 f. 3v.

46. K. Wilson, *The Sense of the People*, 185–205, esp. 203.

47. On the republic of letters borrowing from the state see McKeon, *Secret History of Domesticity*, 48.

48. This position contrasts with Michael Warner's assertion from *Publics and Counterpublics* that a public "must be organized by something other than the state" (68).

49. Mss Eur F198/3/3 f. 2v.

50. D. Ghosh, *Sex and the Family*, 1–2, 12–15.

51. Romney notes that he has written to her twice since he has left the "delightful neighbourhood" of her charms (and this might be somewhat literal, since Romney seems to have been restationed by 1793) (Mss Eur F198/3/3 f. 5r). In another letter Romney responds to her request of his opinion of the production of *She Stoops to Conquer* performed by the "gentlemen volunteers of the theatrical society" (Mss Eur F198/3/3 f. 9r).

52. Mss Eur F198/3/2 f. 4r.

53. M. Sinha, "Britishness," 504. For women in early modern British theater see M. Anderson, *Female Playwrights*; L. Freeman, *Character's Theater*; Lowenthal, *Performing Identities*; and Rosenthal, *Playwrights and Plagiarists*.

54. M. Sinha, "Britishness," 489–90.

55. Love, *Vestiges of Old Madras*, 369.

56. On the Madras Exchange see H. D. Love, *Vestiges of Old Madras*, 367; on the Pantheon see H. D. Love, 419. For more on theater in pre-1800 Madras see Thurston, *Coinage of the Territories*, 259; and Lawson, *Memories of Madras*, 266.

57. Orr, *Empire on the English Stage*, 11.

58. See K. Wilson, *The Island Race*, 2–4, 16; and K. Wilson, *Strolling Players of Empire*.

59. See K. Wilson, "Lure of the Other," 523–24, 529. Wilson draws from the language of Choudhury, *Interculturalism and Resistance*.

60. For more on Bengali attendance at Calcutta theaters, and their own native Bengali theater, see S. Chatterjee, *The Colonial Staged*, 24–26.

61. *Calcutta Gazette*, August 12, 1784.

62. O'Quinn, "Theatre and Empire," 239.

63. "Oriental Traits" was another title written on the manuscript of "The Pavilion," suggesting that "The Pavilion" may have been an expansion of the two-act play Romney titled "Oriental Traits"; see F198/4/31 f. 1r. On Belinda Amaranth see Mss Eur F198/4/31 f. 2r. On Pune see Mss Eur F198/4/31 f. 18v. On Amourville's description as "poor as a rat" see Mss Eur F198/4/31 f. 1v.

64. Mss Eur F198/4/31 f. 25r.

65. On Marwell's service in politics see Mss Eur F198/4/31 f. 20r; on their discussions of marriage see Mss Eur F198/4/31 f. 1r–v.

66. Mss Eur F198/4/15 f. 4r.

67. Mss Eur F198/4/15 f. 1r.

68. Mss Eur F198/4/31 f. 13r.

69. Mss Eur F198/4/31 f. 3v.

70. For a genealogy of *sati* as "good wife," see A. Sharma et al., *Sati*, 77.

71. The historical record shows that the image of the nabob was something of a social fiction: few became wealthy and left India.

72. Nechtman, *Nabobs*, 24.

73. On Delia as a "buxum girl at nineteen" see Mss Eur F198/4/31 f. 27r. For the palanquin scene between Delia and Feyd see Mss Eur F198/4/31 f. 23r.

74. Mss Eur F198/4/31 f. 11r. *Nautch* is a term derived from Hindi, and before that Sanskrit, for dancing; see Yule and Burnell, *Hobson-Jobson*, s.v. "nautch."

75. The actual phrase is that a servant is "shampooing his legs," with "shampooing" referring to muscle massage rather than its modern connotation of hair-washing.

76. Mss Eur F198/4/15 f. 10r.

77. Mss Eur F198/4/15 f. 1v.

78. Mss Eur F198/4/31 f. 34r.

79. Mss Eur F198/4/31 f. 18r.

80. See Starke, *The Sword of Peace*.

81. O'Keefe and Shields, *A Short Account*, 16.

82. *OED*, s.v. "massa." *The Padlock* was performed at the Calcutta Theater in 1787 (*Calcutta Chronicle*, Jan. 4, 1787) and in Madras in 1782 (reported in the *India Gazette*, Dec. 28, 1782) and in 1794 (where *The Hircarrah* called the performance of "merry, muttering Mungo" all "dance and sing"); *The Hircarrah*, Feb. 18, 1794. There is no definitive evidence it was performed in Bombay.

83. Couchman, "'Mungo Everywhere,'" 705, 707; on "prototype" see Cooley, "An Early Representation," 53

84. Dabydeen, *Hogarth's Blacks*, 34–36.

85. Andrew Elfenbein suggests, for example, that nineteenth-century black characters appeared together with other dialect speakers and were differentiated from them primarily by lexical markers such as "massa"; Elfenbein, *Romanticism*, 78.

86. For the evidence of Soubise on the Calcutta stage see O'Quinn, "Theatre and Empire," 234. This evidence, drawn from newspaper accounts, is even more extensive than O'Quinn can cite. For more on Soubise as a performer in Britain see Scobie, *Black Britannia*, 91.

87. For more on Soubise in India and his importance as a figure for blackness in British and Indian imaginations, see Fryer, *Staying Power,* 73; and Miller, *Slaves to Fashion,* 62–63.

88. Romney refers to these costumes in a letter to a friend in which he asks for information about the "last Gala of the Hon. Governor," likely referring to Bombay's governor ("Hon. Governor" is scratched out in the letter but clearly legible from the fading of the ink) (Mss Eur F198/3/6 f. 13r). Accounts and reviews of these types of costumes were published in newspapers; see, e.g., the March 24, 1785, *Calcutta Gazette* account of a masquerade.

89. Cannadine, *Ornamentalism,* 1–4.

90. Wheeler, "Sounding Black-*ish,*" 64.

91. For a modern example of this experimentation see North, *The Dialect of Modernism,* 14–15.

92. Orr, *Empire on the English Stage,* 11.

93. Orr, 11.

94. Sterne, *Tristram Shandy,* 8.

95. Sterne, 10.

96. Mss Eur F198/4/29, f. 11r.

97. Mss Eur F198/4/29, f. 21v.

98. Mss Eur F198/4/29, f. 23r.

99. Mss Eur F198/4/29, f. 23r.

100. Mss Eur F198/4/29, f. 14r.

101. Mss Eur F198/4/29, f. 20r.

102. "Silly heart": Mss Eur F198/4/29 f. 85r; "Vengeance": Mss Eur F198/4/29, f. 85v; "Too much kindness!": Mss Eur F198/4/29, f. 84r.

103. Mss Eur F198/4/29 f. 80r. For some references to the "fishing fleet" see MacMillan, *Women of the Raj,* 4–5.

104. Mss Eur F198/4/29 f. 80r.

105. Nussbaum, *Torrid Zones,* 176; Franklin, introduction to *Hartly House, Calcutta,* xxxi.

106. On "anti-feminist satire" see Benedict, "'Dear Madam,'" 495–96; on productive misogyny see Harries, "Words, Sex, and Gender," 121. For more on Sterne as the apogee of midcentury European modernity see Keymer, *Sterne, the Moderns,* 2–3.

107. On the importance of relationships between white men and indigenous women see D. Ghosh, *Sex and the Family.* On the changing status of mixed-race children see Hawes, *Poor Relations.*

108. Papers of James Romney, MSS 313, box 1, "An Occasional Prologue," n.p. [2, 1].

109. Papers of James Romney, MSS 313, n.p. [2].

110. Papers of James Romney, MSS 313, n.p. [7].

111. Papers of James Romney, MSS 313, n.p. [12–13].

112. Papers of James Romney, MSS 313, n.p. [13–14].

113. Wright and Sclater, *Sterne's Eliza,* 12, 121.

114. For the reference to bringing in her picture in *A Sentimental Journey* and the *Bramine's Journal,* see Sterne, *The Florida Edition,* 6:3, 202.

115. For more on the composition and publishing history of the *Bramine's Journal* see New, introduction to *The Florida Edition,* 6:xvii–xxiv. It is called a "continuation"

because, scholars suspect, it is the only remaining journal of three that Sterne kept during his acquaintance with Draper (xxiv). (There are also ten letters addressed to Draper from Sterne; see Sterne, *The Florida Edition*, vol. 8, *The Letters, Part II: 1765–68*.

116. Sterne, *The Florida Edition*, 6:169.

117. I. Ross, *Laurence Sterne*, 401; Sterne, *The Florida Edition*, 8:531; I. Ross, *Laurence Sterne*, 366.

118. On the numerous origins and motives of Sterne's association with Brahmins see Watts, *Cultural Work of Empire*, 273, 276.

119. For more on the notion of class and colonial India see Dirks, *Castes of Mind*.

120. On Eliza as Sterne's wished-for wife, presiding deity, mascot, and good luck charm see Guest, "Sterne, Elizabeth Draper," 27, 12; on "rent-a-muse" see Festa, *Sentimental Figures of Empire*, 107.

121. Watts, *Cultural Work of Empire*, 277.

122. *The Florida Edition*, 6:173.

123. *The Florida Edition*, 6:194.

124. *The Florida Edition*, 6:179.

125. *The Florida Edition*, 6:184, 196.

126. Cash, *Laurence Sterne*, 346.

127. There were two prominent collections of letters: *Letters from Yorick to Eliza*; and *Sterne's Letters to His Friends on Various Occasions*.

128. Anon., "To Eliza on Her Return to India," *Madras Courier*, Oct. 20, 1790.

129. Irwin, *Bedukah, or the Self-Devoted*, lines 9, 16.

130. *Calcutta Gazette*, Dec. 23, 1784.

131. Raynal, *Philosophical and Political History*, 87–88.

132. *Bombay Courier*, June 2, 1804.

133. Mullan, *Sentiment and Sociability*, 159.

134. Wright and Sclater, *Sterne's Eliza*, 92–93.

135. Grewal, *Home and Harem*, esp. 9–11.

136. Wright and Sclater, *Sterne's Eliza*, 92–93.

137. See Mohanty, "Under Western Eyes."

138. Naregal, *Language Politics*, 149; *Bombay Courier*, Jan. 5, 1793.

139. On *transoceanic elites* see Bowen, *Elites*, 104–5. On "aristocratic imperialists" see A. Cohen, "The 'Aristocratic Imperialists,'" following Bayly, *Imperial Meridian*.

140. See Bowen, *Elites*, 103.

Chapter 6 • Agonies of Empire

1. Colley, *Captives*, 276.

2. Teltscher, *India Inscribed*, 233. Teltscher submits that the British were interested in stereotyping Tipu because he "vindicates British military action against Mysore" but also because doing so "contains and limits the menace posed by the sultan" to the superiority of the British colonial system (238).

3. Colley, *Captives*, 300, 303; and Colley, "Going Native, Telling Tales," 176. She indicates that these captivity narratives are "often ambivalent, even subversive documents" because they are about Britons who have been defeated (*Captives*, 303).

4. Colley, *Captives*, 305.

5. Colley, 4.

6. David Worrall argues the Romantic period stage produced "nuanced receptions" of figures like Tipu among its audiences; see Worrall, "Islam on the Romantic Period Stage," 167.

7. Loar, "Soldiers of Feeling," par. 1, 9. Loar claims that sympathetic soldierly manhood is not limited to British soldiers but is also extended at times to their Mysore antagonists and these affective attachments (par. 18, 1).

8. Thomson, *Memoirs*, 2:8.

9. Lindsay, "Journal of an Imprisonment," 3:269.

10. For more historical details about these loans and monetary exchanges see Colley, "Going Native, Telling Tales," 179.

11. Bristow, *Sufferings of James Bristow*, 45. It seems unlikely that captive soldiers looted religious items to manage a secret mint, but the claim itself implies how important money was for those imprisoned at Mysore.

12. C. Massey, *Diary of Col. Cromwell Massey*, 42 and throughout. This is a printed version of a manuscript book, hand-sewn and measuring four inches by two inches, that Massey kept while imprisoned.

13. Consider, for example, Alexander Maitland's letter written from Bangalore in 1783, while he was being held captive by Hyder Ali, in which he asks for "a small supply of mony [*sic*]" so that he can do more than simply "buy wood to dress [cook] our rice" allowance from Tipu; see Maitland and Rorison, Manuscript letter.

14. See Castro, "Stripped."

15. Fay, *Original Letters from India*, 110, 120.

16. Bristow, *Sufferings of James Bristow*, 6–7, 15–16.

17. Lindsay, "Journal of an Imprisonment," 3:264.

18. C. Massey, *Diary of Col. Cromwell Massey*, 8.

19. Thomson, *Memoirs*, 2:2, 247.

20. Colley suggests that British prisoners were keenly interested in making and mending clothing, which she sees as an extension of their attempts to maintain a national and cultural identity as Britons; Colley, "Going Native, Telling Tales," 178–79.

21. Thomson, *Memoirs*, 2:105.

22. Dirom, *Narrative of the Campaign*, 100.

23. Lindsay, "Journal of an Imprisonment," 3:277, 280.

24. C. Massey, *Diary of Col. Cromwell Massey*, 24.

25. Mss Eur A94, Memoirs of Richard Runwa Bowyer, 98, 102, 107.

26. Scurry, *Captivity, Sufferings, and Escape*, 214.

27. For more on the alignment of spectacle and suffering see Mallipeddi, *Spectacular Suffering*.

28. Colley, *Captives*, 293–94.

29. Bristow, *Sufferings of James Bristow*, xi.

30. Colley discusses anonymity in *Captives*, 293. The Calcutta and Madras newspapers seemed to reprint similar items a few months apart. The London newspapers were *The Times*, April 10, 1792; *London Gazette*, May 18, 1792; *The Star*, April 7, 1792; *Public Advertiser*, April 9, 1792; *General Evening Post*, April 10–12, 1792; *London Chronicle*, April 10–12, 1792; and *Diary or Woodfall's Register*, April 9, 1792.

Many of these papers received this information from Cornwallis himself; for an account of his transmission to the *London Gazette* see Marshall, "'Cornwallis Triumphant,'" 95. See also Ronald, *Youth, Heroism, and War Propaganda.*

31. Thomson, *Memoirs*, 1:v.

32. Thomson, 1:iv. Aristotle discusses the unities of time, place, and action in the *Poetics.*

33. Thomson, 1:v–vi.

34. Bristow, *Sufferings of James Bristow*, ii; on the "sole benefit" see *Calcutta Gazette*, March 22, 1792. These claims also were meant to suppress the idea that he was motivated by others to publish his account.

35. Bristow, *Sufferings of James Bristow*, 107. Nonetheless, in his public pronouncements he wanted to make clear that his writing was his own and its benefits accrued to himself.

36. As both Teltscher and Colley have noted, there were vigorous debates throughout the 1780s in print about the conduct of British warfare with Tipu, especially claims about atrocities committed by soldiers that some commentators suggested led to reprisals by Tipu.

37. Oakes, *An Authentic Narrative*, 51–52.

38. Oakes, 66–67. Thomson's *Memoirs*, which compiles many different accounts, including Oakes's, quietly removed these critiques, as well as another portion of Oakes's narrative that asserted captives in Bangalore were "better treated" because they "received frequent supplies of cash from Madras," unlike captives at Seringapatam or Mysore (56).

39. Bainbridge, *British Poetry*, vii, 2.

40. Russell, *The Theatres of War*, 78.

41. For a definition of the microgenre see A. Stevens, "The Season Novel, 1806–1824," 81–82.

42. Wilks, *Historical Sketches*, 2:524.

43. Thomson claims these poems were composed by an imprisoned soldier named Lieutenant Thewlis, without more explanation. Thewlis's name does not appear on the (admittedly incomplete) list of captives published in 1791 in the *Madras Courier.* But the poems' appearance in the manuscript of Richard Runwa Bowyer and the recurring use of "ye," a writing style also utilized by Bowyer, indicate that he may be the author.

44. Teltscher, *India Inscribed*, 242, 243.

45. On feeling for captives as attachment to a larger community see Burnham, *Captivity and Sentiment*, 1.

46. Thomson, *Memoirs*, 2:289

47. Thomson, 2:296.

48. Thomson, 2:297.

49. Thomson, 2:298.

50. Thomson, 2:299.

51. For a thorough discussion of the poem see Philips, "An Imitation of Milton."

52. Anon., "The Star Pagoda," *Madras Courier*, Oct. 27, 1790. For more on the history of this coin see Thurston, *Coinage of the Territories*, 14–15.

53. *The Hircarrah* (Madras), July 8, 1794. The poem includes a Latin address, suggesting its author was an educated officer.

54. *Madras Courier,* Nov. 3, 1791.

55. A headnote makes explicit its rewriting of Gray's "The Bard," indicating that the poem was *"Taken from Gray's Ode entitled the BARD, in the Character of a Prisoner with the late HYDER ALLY.* Prophetic of the fall of his Family."

56. See Mulholland, *Sounding Imperial,* chap. 4.

57. Two weeks after this poem was supposed to have been composed, on Oct. 19, the combined British and allied forces overcame Nandidurg and captured it from Tipu. But the poem itself is set in the 1780s—Haidar Ali died in 1782—making it a reminiscence of an earlier military campaign projected into the contemporary fiscal-military politics of the third Mysore War. In other issues of the *Madras Courier* Candidus is identified as a military officer; for more see chap. 2.

58. *Madras Courier,* Nov. 3, 1791.

59. See Demos, *The Unredeemed Captive.* He writes specifically about seventeenth-century America.

60. See Ebersole, *Captured by Texts,* 7; and Snader, *Caught between Worlds,* 3.

61. See Vitkus, *Turning Turk*; and Styer, "Barbary Pirates," esp. 211–50.

62. *Madras Courier,* Nov. 17, 1791.

63. Mss Eur A94, Memoirs of Richard Runwa Bowyer, 179.

64. Wilks, *Historical Sketches,* 2:519–20.

65. Anon., *Narrative Sketches,* 82. Here the *Narrative Sketches* refers to the account from Bristow as corroboration.

66. Bristow, *Sufferings of James Bristow,* 22–23.

67. See "Narrative of Mr. William Drake," in the *Madras Courier,* Nov. 17, 1791.

68. Colley argues, for example, that circumcision was intended as "a mark of new ownership" rather than as a sincere attempt at conversion to Islam, with mutilation functioning as an "indelible symbol of these men's incorporation into the Mysore state"; Colley, *Captives,* 289.

69. These names were printed in the *Calcutta Gazette* (December 15, 1791) and in the *London Gazette* (May 18, 1792), though they likely originated from the *Madras Courier.*

70. For an extensive discussion of this phenomenon see Teltscher, *India Inscribed,* 240–44. William Dalrymple estimates that three hundred soldiers were circumcised and converted, but he does not explain the origin of this statistic; see Dalrymple, "Tipu Sultan."

71. Brittlebank, *Tipu's Search for Legitimacy,* 9, 91–92. For more on incorporative theories of South Asian sovereignty see Dirks, *The Hollow Crown,* 47–48; and Pearson, *Legitimacy and Symbols,* 25–26.

72. These performing boys might be examples of what are called variously *ramzani* or *ramjani,* a subclass of *hurukiya,* who were performing women akin to European courtesans. For references to *ramzani* see Colley, *Captives,* 289; and Marshall, "'Cornwallis Triumphant,'" 95. According to Madhu Trivedi, *ramjani* became "eminent" during the seventeenth century, when they were perceived to be "learned and subtle orators, eloquent in speech," and were associated with "finesse in their conversations," not just sexual fulfillment; M. Trivedi, "Tradition and Transition," 97–98, 109. For more on *hurukiya* see B. Wade, "Visual Sources," 305.

During the nineteenth century *ramjani* were viewed as sexually transactional rather than companionate relationships, with the massive glossary of Anglo-Indian life, *Hobson-Jobson*, insisting that at least "among soldiers and sailors" the *ramjani* (or as that dictionary describes it "rum-johnny") were prostitutes; see Yule and Burnell, *Hobson-Jobson*, s.v. "Rum-Johnny." Anna McNeil, however, describes *ramjani* as a branch of the *kalawant* subcaste, a community whose members pursued the "profession of singing, dancing and prostitution"; McNeil, "Mirasis," 52. See also Sherring, *Tribes and Castes of Rajasthan*, 200. François Balthasar Solvyns suggests that *ramjani* was the name for those individuals who engaged in *nautch* rather than a separate class or style of dancing; see Hardgrave, *Portrait of the Hindus*, 261. Another possibility is that these white adolescents were modeled on the *balak* tradition of male dancers who were often included in *nautch* performances as young children. Solvyns compared *balak* dances to those of *ramjanis* but noted that "few *Baulaks* are to be met except among the true Hindoos" (Hardgrave, 267). *Balaks* no longer danced but became musicians when they reached adulthood. In sum, it seems that, culturally, the dancing boys existed at the intersection of a number of entertainment castes and positions that included *nautch*, *ramjani*, and *balak*.

73. Ives, *A Voyage from England*, 75–76. For more on this suggestion that the dancers wore *ghangra cholis* see Dalrymple, "Tipu Sultan."

74. J. Kindersley, *Letters from the Island*, 231, 229.

75. Bhattacharya, "Behind the Veil," 283. For more on this shift see I. Sen, "Devoted Wife/Sensuous Bibi"; and Bearce, "Intellectual and Cultural Characteristics," 4.

76. Campbell, *A Narrative*, 253–54.

77. These highly sexualized dance traditions include *kothi*, *zanana*, and *jankha*; see Morcom, *Illicit Worlds*, 10.

78. Scurry, *Captivity, Sufferings, and Escape*, 59.

79. Thomson, *Memoirs*, 2:145, 108.

80. Brittlebank, *Tipu's Search for Legitimacy*, 97.

81. Wilks, *Historical Sketches*, 2:520.

82. Thomson, *Memoirs*, 2:148.

83. Thomson, 2:276.

84. O'Quinn, *Staging Governance*, 324–26. Colley conveys similar perspectives when she claims that the danger of captivity was "being dragged across a line of sorts" between different cultures, a drift whose consequences were the reexamination of established ideas about nation and power; Colley, *Captives*, 16.

85. This differs from North American captivity narratives, which scholars argue are defined by the resourcefulness of white captives, especially women, with maintaining connections to their home culture. For more see Armstrong and Tennenhouse, *The Imaginary Puritan*, chap. 8; and Burnham, *Captivity and Sentiment*, 10–40. Another possibility is to see these dancing boys as part of what Mary Louise Pratt has capaciously described as the genres of "survival literature," those "first-person stories of shipwrecks, castaways, mutinies, abandonments, and . . . captivities" that have been popular from the fifteenth century to the present; Pratt, *Imperial Eyes*, 86–87.

86. Hedges, *War Is a Force,* esp. chap. 3. I disagree, however, with Hedges's assertion that "in wartime the state seeks to destroy its own culture" before it begins "to exterminate the culture of its opponents" (62).

87. Bayly, *The Raj,* 154.

88. Burnage, "Commemorating Cornwallis," 173.

89. C. A. Bayly argues that Home was present at the occasion of the handover; Bayly, *The Raj,* 154. For an account of Home displaying his painting *The Reception of the Mysorean Princes by Marquis Cornwallis* in his rooms in Madras in 1795 before it eventually appeared at the Royal Academy exhibition in 1797, see Harrington, *British Artists and War,* 57–58. On hostage pictures in general see Marshall, *"Free though Conquering People"*; and Moon, *British Conquest,* 257–60.

90. Teltscher argues that these depictions inverted the captivity narratives of Europeans in Mysore by enacting visually and verbally the "British appropriation of the East," in which Tipu's sons "embody the concept of a subdued Mysore"; Teltscher, *India Inscribed,* 248–49. Holger Hoock suggests the hostage princes shift the imagination of empire, whereby "British martyrdom balanced the plight of the young princes"; Hoock, *Empires of the Imagination,* 190. Barbara Groseclose notes that in all of the hostage pictures "adult Indians are either obsequious or unable to care properly for their children"; Groseclose, *British Sculpture,* 65.

91. Colley, *Captives,* 316.

92. Burnham, *Captivity and Sentiment,* 26.

93. On the unredeemed see Demos, *The Unredeemed Captive*; on the "renegade" see Sayre, "Renegades from Barbary," 354–56. For Barbary pirates and the threat of sodomy and submission see LaFleur, *Natural History of Sexuality,* 67–69, 100–101.

Chapter 7 • Literary Culture of Colonial Outposts

1. For more on that meeting between de Quincey and the Malay see Lindop, *The Opium-Eater,* 217–18.

2. Krishnan, *Reading the Global,* 76. Krishnan suggests the Malay is a phantasm, an idea supported by Lindop's speculation that de Quincey hallucinated his meeting with the Malay after seeing the frontispiece of William Marsden's recently revised 1811 edition of the *History of Sumatra* (Lindop, *The Opium-Eater,* 218).

3. For more on the Indian Ocean world as method see Burton et al., "Sea Tracks and Trails."

4. Chen, *Asia as Method,* 212, 1; see also Burton et al., "Sea Tracks and Trails."

5. See Bhabha, "Of Mimicry and Man"; and Suleri, *Rhetoric of English India.*

6. Bastin, *British in West Sumatra,* xi.

7. Marsden, *A Brief Memoir,* 18.

8. Marsden, 18.

9. See Trapaud, *A Short Account.*

10. Quoted in Langdon, *Penang,* 5.

11. Amrith, *Crossing the Bay,* 1, 3.

12. On "Sanskrit cosmopolis" see Pollock, "Cosmopolitan and Vernacular," esp. 23–27; see also Pollock, *Language of the Gods,* 15–16; and Pollock, "The Sanskrit Cosmopolis, 300–1330." For "Bay of Bengal empire" see Amrith, *Crossing the Bay,* 14.

13. Abu-Lughod, *Before European Hegemony*; Pomeranz, *The Great Divergence*; K. Chaudhuri, *Trading World of Asia*; Ho, *The Graves of Tarim*.

14. I borrow from Paul Giles's sense that to study "US cultural geography transnationally" necessitates that scholars "move away from the identification of the United States . . . as an enclosed territorial site"; Giles, *Antipodean America*, 33.

15. For more on the Indies as a term for global connection see A. Cohen, *The Global Indies*.

16. I say its popular name because its official one was different, and the company was often known as the Honorable Company. These other non-Asian locales included factories in the Near East, possessions in southern Africa, and the Atlantic island of St. Helena.

17. Giles, *Antipodean America*, 14.

18. On Smith's placing Southeast Asia at the center of global industrialization, see Krishnan, *Reading the Global*, 27, 28, 31.

19. Metcalf, *Imperial Connections*, xii.

20. Metcalf, 6, 1.

21. See Ballantyne, *Orientalism and Race*, 35.

22. Amin, "Regions Unbound," 37.

23. Quoted in Amrith, *Crossing the Bay*, 64.

24. S. Sen, "Imperial Subjects on Trial," 547.

25. Geoff Wade concludes that Europeans were between 2 percent and 4 percent of the total population; see Wade, "New Ways of Knowing." Wade draws these population numbers from Ken, "Revenue Farms." My thanks to Geoff Wade for sharing this material before it had been published.

26. For the language admonition see IOR/G/34/18, 1037. For an overview of sales see Wade, "New Ways of Knowing," 141–42.

27. Wade, "New Ways of Knowing," 151, 164n88.

28. See Bloomfield, "A. B. Bone," 9–11. Bloomfield's is the most comprehensive history of Bone, but see also Shaw, *Printing in Calcutta*, 43–44. While the *Prince of Wales Island Gazette* is the first English-language newspaper, a newspaper in Dutch Batavia first appeared in 1745–46 and is likely the first printed newspaper in Southeast Asia. For more on this Batavian newspaper see Graaf, *The Spread of Printing*, 26.

29. Bloomfield, "A. B. Bone," 9.

30. Quoted in Bloomfield, 12.

31. Quoted in Bloomfield, 12. See also IOR/G/34/13, 48–49, for Bone's petition. The Company's response can be found at IOR/G/34/13, 61–62.

32. IOR/G/21/67, 19.

33. IOR/G/34/18, 971–72.

34. Bloomfield, "A. B. Bone," 24, 26. Versions of these documents can be found at IOR/G/34/8 f. 64v, f. 108; IOR/G/34/8 f. 52r, f. 83; and IOR/G/34/8 f. 50r, f. 79.

35. See S. Sen, "Imperial Subjects on Trial," 550–52; Travers, "Indian Petitioning."

36. Bloomfield, "A. B. Bone," 15.

37. Quoted in Bloomfield, 13.

38. Wade, "New Ways of Knowing," 134.

39. Bloomfield, "A. B. Bone," 21.

40. Bloomfield, 15.

41. *Prince of Wales Island Gazette*, July 27, 1811.

42. Bloomfield claims that he cannot figure out the reason for Bone's including these apologies, but his negotiation of his local readership with a smaller more distant one explains this situation (29).

43. Bloomfield, "A. B. Bone," 30–31.

44. *Prince of Wales Island Gazette*, May 20, 1815.

45. Marsden, *A Brief Memoir*, 11.

46. For a detailed account of the financial and trade aspects of western Sumatra see Kathirithamby-Wells, *British Western Sumatran Presidency*.

47. Stern, *The Company-State*, 74–75.

48. IOR/H/732, 2.

49. Quoted in Bastin, *British in West Sumatra*, xxi. See also Collet, *The Private Letter Books*, 33. For more on Collet's attempts to regulate the sexual economies of Fort Marlborough, see K. Wilson, "Rethinking the Colonial State," 1302–6.

50. Quoted in Bastin, *British in West Sumatra*, xxi; from *Journals of Dudley Leavitt Pickman*.

51. Quoted in Bastin, 103–4.

52. Harfield, *Bencoolen*, 289. The exact census was ninety-one "Natives of Great Britain and Ireland," forty "Dutchmen," six "Frenchmen," two "Americans," one "Native of Portugal" and eleven "Topases," with soldiers and natives extending the population.

53. Quoted in Harfield, 593.

54. Marsden, *A Brief Memoir*, 7.

55. Marsden, 7.

56. Marsden, 12, 15; Kathirithamby-Wells, *British Western Sumatran Presidency*, 210.

57. Marsden, *A Brief Memoir*, 15. Marsden is referring to *A Dictionary and Grammar of the Malayan Language* (1812).

58. Marsden, *A Brief Memoir*, 12–13.

59. Marsden, 11.

60. Marsden, 11.

61. Marsden, 11.

62. Marsden, 16.

63. Shaw, "English Books around the World," 190–91. For a more detailed description of this book shipment see Musty, "Going to China."

64. Marsden, *A Brief Memoir*, 17.

65. Marsden, 13.

66. Marsden, 14.

67. Marsden, 16.

68. K. Wilson, "Introduction: Three Theses," 377. For more on these issues of gender, identity, family, and the state on the early modern stage see Lowenthal, *Performing Identities*; Chernaik, "Unhappy Families"; and Rosenthal, *Playwrights and Plagiarists*.

69. Marsden, *A Brief Memoir*, 20. The full title is *Maon and Moriat, a Tragedy*, and it is included within Marsden's *A Brief Memoir* as a separate section with its own

pagination. For clarity I will cite the play as *Moan and Moriat* to distinguish it from the separately paginated *A Brief Memoir.*

70. The theater in Fort Marlborough was destroyed in 1774 (Marsden, *A Brief Memoir,* 16) and seems not to have been rebuilt, so it is unlikely that the play was performed in Sumatra, as Diana J. Carroll suggests it was; see Carroll, "William Marsden and Patterns," 277n32.

71. *Maon and Moriat,* in Marsden, *A Brief Memoir,* 17.

72. K. Wilson, "Performing *The Wonder* in Sumatra."

73. K. Wilson, "Rowe's *Fair Penitent,*" 232.

74. See Marsden, *A Brief Memoir,* 8.

75. See Centlivre, *The Wonder,* n.p. [80].

76. Marsden, *A Brief Memoir,* 8–9.

77. Marsden, 9.

78. Marsden, 9.

79. Marsden, 10.

80. Marsden, 22.

81. Marsden, 22, lines 1–3.

82. Marsden, 31.

83. Marsden, 21.

84. Marsden, *The History of Sumatra* (1783), b [iii]. Of course, this neglect is only apparent among writers of English.

85. Marsden, *A Brief Memoir,* 21.

86. Schama, *Patriots and Liberators,* 2, 640–41.

87. Israel, *The Dutch Republic,* 1127.

88. Taylor, *Indonesia,* 219, 210. This geopolitical situation was confirmed with the 1824 Anglo-Dutch Treaty of London.

89. For more on this plot see Carey, *Destiny,* 162–63.

90. For these local effects see Carey, *The Power of Prophecy,* 393–94. For their worldwide implications see Wood, *Tambora,* 9–11.

91. *Indische* means both "colonial," as in the name of the VOC, and mixed-race and mestizo; on these meanings and their limitations see Bosma and Raben, *Being "Dutch" in the Indies,* xiv–xv.

92. Taylor, *Social World of Batavia,* 85, 78. For a political and commercial account of the decline of the VOC see Nierstrasz, *In the Shadow,* esp. 1–6 and 209–17. For an overview of "Indies society" see Gaastra, *Dutch East India Company,* 21, 66–68.

93. Taylor, *Social World of Batavia,* 86.

94. Taylor, 53.

95. See Blussé, *Strange Company,* 4–5.

96. Taylor, *Social World of Batavia,* 97.

97. Taylor, 101.

98. Bosma and Raben, *Being "Dutch" in the Indies,* 91–94.

99. Taylor, *Social World of Batavia,* 104, 102. Many of these books were advertised in the *JGG* and were sold from its printing office.

100. *JGG,* Oct. 22, 1814.

101. *JGG,* Oct. 22, 1814.

102. *JGG*, March, 23, 1816. The advertisement does not make clear the form of Raffles's patronage.

103. Bosma and Raben, *Being "Dutch" in the Indies*, 92. Bosma and Raben also argue that the Military Bachelor's Theater was intended for the "lower classes" (but not Muslims) because tickets could be purchased through barter (92). On French "afterpieces" and the Military Bachelor's Theater see Winet, *Indonesian Postcolonial Theater*, 21–24, 76–77, 113.

104. *JGG*, Oct. 22, 1814.

105. Bastin, *Sir Stamford Raffles*, 139n198. Hubbard later returned to Connecticut, where he and his family became papermaking industrialists and publishers of a Norwich, Connecticut, newspaper; see Nord, *Faith in Reading*, 70. For more on the Hubbards in Connecticut see Staley, *Norwich in the Gilded Age*.

106. Byron's poetry was especially prominent in the *JGG*; see, e.g., "Address on the Opening of Drury Lane Theater," *JGG*, Sept. 25, 1813 (the Byron poem is actually titled "Address, Spoken at the Opening of Drury-lane Theater"); "Ode to Napoleon Buonaparte," *JGG*, Sept. 24, 1814; selections from *The Corsair*, *JGG*, Oct. 8, 1814; "Unpublished Lines (inscribed on the Monument of a Favorite Dog) by Lord Byron," *JGG*, Oct. 22, 1814; "Ode on the Death of Sir Peter Parker," *JGG*, July 15, 1815; and "Description of Sleep," from *Lara*, *JGG*, August 19, 1815.

107. *JGG*, Feb. 20, 1813.

108. D. White, "'Zig Zag Sublimity,'" 154, 151.

109. *JGG*, July 17, 1813; *JGG*, Jan. 28, 1815.

110. *JGG*, July 31, 1813. For a report on the soldier's graves see the *Celtic Monthly* 5, no. 7 (April 1897): 140.

111. *JGG*, June 20, 1812.

112. *JGG*, Dec. 5, 1812.

113. Stoler, *Along the Archival Grain*; Ballantyne and Burton, *Moving Subjects*.

114. *JGG*, August 27, 1814.

115. *JGG*, June 4, 1814. A rough literal translation of the Dutch version might read:

> Oppressed compatriots
> Rescue (and) freedom are near
> Do not hesitate—freshly joined
> Dutch Lion is free again!!
> Rejoice, you noble sons of Freedom
> Before long you will see your courage crowned
> Batoos children shall show Gallien
> Whether they can be taunted unpunished!
> Flee, quarrel and anger, from our side
> "One head, one heart" is our choice
> Nassau bravely leads us to war.

The reference to Batoos likely refers to the *Bato*, a Dutch ship that was destroyed at the Battle of Blaauwberg off the coast of South Africa in 1806 that marked the end of Dutch aspirations to African colonies. The translation from the Dutch here, and throughout this chapter, was assisted by Annette Dowd.

116. "Old times" occurs in a folksong quoted in Schama, *Patriots and Liberators*, 641. For more on Dutch resistance to the Spanish, initiated by William II of Orange, see Darby, *Origins and Development*. See also Tracy, *Founding of the Dutch Republic*.

117. *JGG*, August 27, 1814.

118. England and then Britain had been in turns an antagonist and ally of the Netherlands for centuries. For an argument about the United Provinces as a model for nationalist England, see Jardine, *Going Dutch*.

119. See Dunthorne, *Britain and the Dutch Revolt*, xiii–xvi, 1–29.

120. Ward, *Networks of Empire*, 6–7, 12, 14–15.

121. For "debt-bondage" see Anthony Reid, introduction, 8–12; and Ward, *Networks of Empire*, 18–19, 21–22.

122. Taylor, *Social World of Batavia*, 70–71. On thirteen thousand slaves see Abeyasekere, "Slaves in Batavia," 288.

123. Reid, introduction, 22–23.

124. See Wood, "The Volcano Lover," 38–39.

125. Wood, 46.

126. Ward, *Networks of Empire*, 304.

127. *JGG*, Sept. 19, 1812.

128. For more on this practice of selling oneself into bondage, see Reid, "'Closed' and 'Open' Slave Systems," 168.

129. On "The Horrors of Slavery" see *JGG*, May 11, 1816; on "prettiest slave girls" see *JGG*, March 6, 1813.

130. *JGG*, Dec. 17, 1814.

131. DeWispelare, *Multilingual Subjects*, 4, 6, 28–29.

132. *JGG*, Jan. 30, 1813. Kratz argues that "nyonya" was used to refer to married women of distinction and usually of "European extraction" ("Like a Fish Gasping for Water," 256).

133. *JGG*, Jan. 2, 1813. See Echols and Shadily, *An Indonesian-English Dictionary*, s.v. "busuk."

134. Moriyama, *Sundanese Print Culture*, 12. Raffles, while stationed in Java, suggested incorrectly that Javanese and Sundanese were dialects of a larger generic language (Moriyama, 12–13).

135. Cooper, *Colonialism in Question*, 4.

136. Errington, *Linguistics in a Colonial World*, 125. For the modern consequences of administrative Malay see Errington, *Shifting Languages*, 3–6.

137. Taylor, *Social World of Batavia*, 98.

138. *JGG*, April 3, 1813.

139. *JGG*, April 3, 1813.

140. *JGG*, April 3, 1813.

141. *JGG*, April 3, 1813. On "Billingsgate eloquence" see McDowell, *Invention of the Oral*, 193.

142. For contemporary usages of "baick" see Bowrey, *Dictionary*, s.v. "baick," which he translates as "good, well." See also Echols and Shadily, *An Indonesian-English Dictionary*, s.v. "baik."

143. "Vrouws" should probably be rendered "Vrouwen" in more proper Dutch.

144. There is uncertainty about whether the *Courant* was continued as the *Java Government Gazette* or a separate instrument discontinued when the British invaded; see Adam, *The Vernacular Press*, 4; Termorshuizen, "In Search of the Noble Savage," 112–13; and Kahin, *Historical Dictionary of Indonesia*, 324.

145. Faber, *Short History of Journalism*, 14; Graaf, *The Spread of Printing*, 19.

146. Faber, *Short History of Journalism*, 20. The *Vendu-Nieuws* was successful enough that the Malayan words for newspaper remained *surat lelang* (auction news) into the nineteenth century.

147. *JGG*, April 3, 1813.

148. Bosma and Raben, *Being "Dutch" in the Indies*, 86.

149. *JGG*, March 6, 1813.

150. Thanks to Annette Dowd for noticing this buried word in the name.

151. *JGG*, March 6, 1813.

152. Hessell, *Romantic Literature*, 4.

153. Chander, *Brown Romantics*, 3.

154. Chander, 4.

155. Bate, *Burden of the Past*, 4; Hutcheon, *A Theory of Parody*, 2.

156. Zandvliet, *Dutch Encounter with Asia*, 32.

157. *JGG*, Jan. 16, 1813.

158. *JGG*, Jan. 16, 1813. Gray's "Elegy" in Lonsdale, *Poems of Gray*, lines 1–8.

159. Ho, "Afterword," 885, 886, 888.

160. Chen, *Asia as Method*, 212.

161. Aravamudan, *Tropicopolitans*, 11; Gibson, *Indian Angles*, 7; Giles, *Antipodean America*, 34.

BIBLIOGRAPHY

Manuscripts Cited

British Library (BL)

Add MS 35918, Hardwicke Papers
Add MS 39879, Warren Hastings Papers
Add MS 39891, Warren Hastings Papers
Add MS 75979, Althorp Papers
IO Islamic 3563
IOR/F/4/98/1992
IOR/G/21/67
IOR/G/34/8
IOR/G/34/13
IOR/G/34/18
IOR/H/207
IOR/H/260
IOR/H/476
IOR/H/537
IOR/H/539
IOR/H/732
IOR/P/50/8
IOR/P/50/15
Mss Eur A94, Memoirs of Richard Runwa Bowyer
Mss Eur F324/1
Mss Eur F380/4

PAPERS OF JAMES ROMNEY

Mss Eur F198/3/1
Mss Eur F198/3/2
Mss Eur F198/3/3
Mss Eur F198/3/6
Mss Eur F198/4/15
Mss Eur F198/4/29
Mss Eur F198/4/31
Mss Eur F198/5/1
Mss Eur F198/5/3
Mss Eur F198/6/5
Mss Eur F198/6/19

Other Manuscripts

Hayley Manuscripts. Fitzwilliam Museum. University of Cambridge.

Journals of Dudley Leavitt Pickman 1799–1804. Peabody Essex Museum. Cat. no. 656/1799B.

Maitland, A., and William Rorison. Manuscript letter to a Dr. Spalding in Madras, India. July 1783. National Museum of Scotland, M.1996.52.

Papers of James Romney. Australian Defence Force Academy Library. MSS 313.

Newspapers Cited

Asiatic Mirror, and Commercial Advertiser (Calcutta)
Bombay Courier
Bombay Gazette
British Critic and Quarterly Theological Review (London)
Calcutta Chronicle; and General Advertiser
Calcutta Gazette; or, Oriental Advertiser
Calcutta Morning Post and General Advertiser
Diary, or, Woodfall's Register (London)
General Evening Post (London)
Gentleman's Magazine
Hicky's Bengal Gazette (Calcutta)
The Hircarrah (Madras)
India Gazette (Calcutta)
Java Government Gazette (*JGG*)
London Chronicle
London Gazette
Madras Courier
Monthly Review (London)
Prince of Wales Island Gazette (Penang, Malaysia)
Public Advertiser (London)
The Star (London)
The Times (London)
The World (Calcutta; also known as the *Indian World*)

Published Articles and Books

Abeyasekere, Susan. "Slaves in Batavia: Insights from a Slave Register." In *Slavery, Bondage, and Dependency in Southeast Asia*, edited by Anthony Reid, with the assistance of Jennifer Brewster, 286–314. New York: St. Martin's, 1983.

Abu-Lughod, Janet L. *Before European Hegemony: The World System A.D. 1250–1350*. New York: Oxford University Press, 1989.

Adam, Ahmat B. *The Vernacular Press and the Emergence of Modern Indonesian Consciousness (1855–1913)*. Ithaca, NY: Cornell University Press, 1995.

Ahmad, Aziz. *Studies in Islamic Culture in the Indian Environment*. Oxford: Clarendon Press, 1964.

Ahmed, Siraj. *Archaeology of Babel: The Colonial Foundation of the Humanities*. Stanford, CA: Stanford University Press, 2018.

——. "Orientalism and the Permanent Fix of War." In *The Postcolonial Enlightenment: Eighteenth-Century Colonialism and Postcolonial Theory*, edited by Daniel Carey and Lynn Festa, 167–206. Oxford: Oxford University Press, 2009.

——. *The Stillbirth of Capital: Enlightenment Writing and Colonial India*. Stanford, CA: Stanford University Press, 2012.

Alam, Muzaffar, and Sanjay Subrahmanyam. Introduction to *The Mughal State, 1526–1750*, edited by Muzaffar Alam and Sanjay Subrahmanyam, 1–71. Oxford: Oxford University Press, 1998.

——. "The Making of a Munshi." *Comparative Studies of South Asia, Africa, and the Middle East* 24, no. 2 (2004): 61–72.

——. "Witnesses and Agents of Empire: Eighteenth-Century Historiography and the World of the Mughal Munshi." *Journal of the Economic and Social History of the Orient* 53, no. 1/2 (2010): 393–423.

Alavi, Seema, ed. *The Eighteenth Century in India*. New Delhi: Oxford, 2002.

——. "'Fugitive Mullahs and Outlawed Fanatics': Indian Muslims in Nineteenth-Century Trans-Atlantic Imperial Rivalries." *Modern Asian Studies* 45 (Nov. 2011): 1337–82.

——. Introduction to *The Eighteenth Century in India*, edited by Seema Alavi, 1–56. Oxford, 2002.

——. *Muslim Cosmopolitanism in the Age of Empire*. Cambridge, MA: Harvard University Press, 2015.

Allen, John, and Allan Cochrane. "Beyond the Territorial Fix: Regional Assemblages, Politics, and Power." *Regional Studies* 41, no. 9 (Dec. 2007): 1161–75.

Alpers, Edward A. *The Indian Ocean in World History*. New York: Oxford University Press, 2014.

Alpers, Paul. *What Is Pastoral?* Chicago: University of Chicago Press, 1996.

Amin, Ash. "Regions Unbound: Towards a New Politics of Place." *Geografiska Annaler* 86, ser. B, no. 1 (2004): 33–44.

Amrith, Sunil S. *Crossing the Bay of Bengal: The Furies of Nature and the Fortunes of Migrants*. Cambridge, MA: Harvard University Press, 2013.

Anderson, Benedict. *Imagined Communities: Reflections on the Origin and Spread of Nationalism*. London: Verso, 1983.

Anderson, Clare. *Subaltern Lives: Biographies of Colonialism in the Indian Ocean World, 1790–1920*. Cambridge: Cambridge University Press, 2012.

Anderson, Misty G. *Female Playwrights and Eighteenth-Century Comedy: Negotiating Marriage on the London Stage*. New York: Palgrave, 2002.

Anon. *The Artless Lovers: A Novel*. 2 vols. London: J. Wilkie, 1768.

——. *Calcutta: A Poem*. London: J. J. Stockdale, 1811.

——. "Memoirs of Eyles Irwin, Esq." *European Magazine and London Review* 15 (London: 1789): 179–81.

——. *Narrative Sketches of the Conquest of Mysore, Effected by the British Troops and Their Allies, in the Capture of Seringapatam, and the Death of Tipoo Sultaun, May 4, 1799*. 2nd ed. London: W. Justins, 1800.

Appadurai, Arjun. *Modernity at Large: Cultural Dimensions of Globalization*. Minneapolis: University of Minnesota Press, 1996.

Arac, Jonathan. "What Is the History of Literature?" *MLQ* 54, no. 1 (March 1993): 105–10.

Aravamudan, Srinivas. *Enlightenment Orientalism: Resisting the Rise of the Novel*. Chicago: University of Chicago Press, 2012.

——. *Tropicopolitans: Colonialism and Agency, 1688–1804*. Durham, NC: Duke University Press, 1999.

Archer, Mildred. *India and British Portraiture, 1770–1825*. Totowa, NJ: Sotheby Parke Bernet, 1979.

Armitage, David. *Ideological Origins of the British Empire*. Cambridge: Cambridge University Press, 2000.

Armstrong, Nancy. "Captivity and Cultural Capital in the English Novel." In *Revolutionary Histories: Transatlantic Cultural Nationalism, 1775–1815*, edited by W. M. Verhoeven, 104–21. Houndmills, Basingstoke: Palgrave, 2002.

Armstrong, Nancy, and Leonard Tennenhouse. *The Imaginary Puritan: Literature, Intellectual Labor, and the Origins of Personal Life*. Berkeley: University of California Press, 1992.

Ashfield, Andrew, ed. *Romantic Women Poets, 1770–1838*. Manchester: Manchester University Press, 1995.

Bainbridge, Simon. *British Poetry and the Revolutionary and Napoleonic Wars: Visions of Conflict*. Oxford: Oxford University Press, 2003.

Bakhle, Janaki. *Two Men and Music: Nationalism in the Making of an Indian Classical Tradition*. Oxford: Oxford University Press, 2005.

Ballantyne, Tony. *Orientalism and Race: Aryanism in the British Empire*. Houndmills, Basingstoke: Palgrave, 2002.

——. "Rereading the Archive and Opening Up the Nation-State." In *After the Imperial Turn: Thinking with and through the Nation*, edited by Antoinette Burton, 102–21. Durham, NC: Duke University Press, 2003.

Ballantyne, Tony, and Antoinette Burton. *Moving Subjects: Gender, Mobility, and Intimacy in an Age of Global Empire*. Urbana: University of Illinois Press, 2009.

Ballaster, Ros. *Fabulous Orients: Fictions of the East in England, 1662–1785*. Oxford: Oxford University Press, 2005.

Banerjee, Subhabrata Bobby. "Voices of the Governed: Towards a Theory of the Translocal." *Organization* 18, no. 3 (May 2011): 323–44.

Barber, Giles. "Book Imports and Exports in the Eighteenth Century." In *Sale and Distribution of Books from 1700*, edited by Robin Myers and Michael Harris, 77–105. Oxford Polytechnic, 1982.

——. "Books from the Old World and for the New: The British International Trade in Books in the Eighteenth Century." *Studies on Voltaire and the Eighteenth Century* 151 (1976): 185–224.

Barker, Hannah. *Newspapers, Politics, and Public Opinion in Late Eighteenth-Century England*. Oxford: Clarendon Press, 1998.

Barns, Margarita. *The Indian Press: A History of the Growth of Public Opinion in India*. London: George Allen and Unwin, 1940.

Bastin, John. *The British in West Sumatra (1685–1825)*. Kuala Lumpur: University of Malaya Press, 1965.

——. *Sir Stamford Raffles and Some of His Friends and Contemporaries: A Memoir of the Founder of Singapore*. Singapore: World Scientific, 2019.

Bate, Walter Jackson. *The Burden of the Past and the English Poet*. Cambridge, MA: Belknap Press, 1970.

Bauer, Thomas, and Angelika Neuwirth. Introduction to *Ghazal as World Literature I: Transformations of a Literary Genre*, edited by Thomas Bauer and Angelika Neuwirth, 9–31. Würburg: Ergon, 2005.

Baylen, Joseph O., and Norbert Gossman, eds. *Biographical Dictionary of Modern British Radicals: 1770–1830*. 2 vols. Hassocks: Harvester Press, 1979–84.

Bayly, C. A. *The Birth of the Modern World, 1780–1914*. Malden, MA: Blackwell, 2004.

——. "The British and Indigenous Peoples, 1760–1860: Power, Perception, and Identity." In *Empire and Others: British Encounters with Indigenous Peoples, 1600–1850*, edited by Martin Daunton and Rick Halpern, 19–41. Philadelphia: University of Pennsylvania Press, 1999.

——. *Empire and Information: Intelligence Gathering and Social Communication in India, 1780–1870*. Cambridge: Cambridge University Press, 1996.

——. *Imperial Meridian: The British Empire and the World*. London: Longman, 1989.

——. *Indian Society and the Making of the British Empire*. Cambridge: Cambridge University Press, 1988.

——, ed. *The Raj: India and the British, 1600–1947*. London: National Portrait Gallery, 1990.

Bearce, George D. "Intellectual and Cultural Characteristics of India in a Changing Era, 1740–1800." *Journal of Asian Studies* 25, no. 1 (Nov. 1965): 3–17.

Becker, Howard S. *Art Worlds*. Berkeley: University of California Press, 1982.

Beecroft, Alexander. "The Sanskrit Ecumene." *New Left Review* 72 (Nov./Dec. 2011): 153–60.

Belich, James. *Replenishing the Earth: The Settler Revolution and the Rise of the Anglo-World, 1783–1939*. Oxford: Oxford University Press, 2009.

Bellamy, Liz. *Commerce, Morality, and the Eighteenth-Century Novel*. Cambridge: Cambridge University Press, 1998.

Benedict, Barbara. "'Dear Madam': Rhetoric, Cultural Politics, and the Female Reader in Sterne's *Tristram Shandy*." *Studies in Philology* 89, no. 4 (Autumn 1992): 485–98.

Bennett, Archibald F. *A Guide for Genealogical Research*. Salt Lake City: Desert News Press, 1951.

Bennett, Paula Bernat. *Poets in the Public Sphere: The Emancipatory Project of American Women's Poetry, 1800–1900*. Princeton, NJ: Princeton University Press, 2003.

Benton, Lauren. "From the World-Systems Perspective to Institutional World History: Culture and Economy in Global Theory." *Journal of World History* 7, no. 2 (Fall 1996): 261–95.

Bersani, Leo. *The Culture of Redemption*. Cambridge, MA: Harvard University Press, 1990.

Bhabha, Homi K. "Of Mimicry and Man: The Ambivalence of Colonial Discourse." 1994. In *The Location of Culture*, 121–44. London: Routledge, 2004.

Bhattacharya, Nandini. "Behind the Veil: The Many Masks of Subaltern Sexuality." *Women Studies International Forum* 19, no. 3 (1996): 277–92.

Bickerstaffe, Isaac. *The Padlock*. London: W. Griffin, 1768.

A Biographical Dictionary of the Living Authors of Great Britain and Ireland. London: Henry Colburn, 1816.

Bjorkelo, Anders, Jorgen Christian Meyer, and Eivind Heldaas Seland. "Definite Places: Translocal Exchange." In *The Indian Ocean in the Ancient Period: Definite Places, Translocal Exchange*, edited by Eivind Heldaas Seland, 3–8. Oxford: Archaeopress, 2007.

Black, Jeremy. *The English Press in the Eighteenth Century*. Philadelphia: University of Pennsylvania Press, 1987.

——. *Europe and the World, 1650–1830*. London: Routledge, 2002.

Blackburn, Stuart. *Print, Folklore, and Nationalism in Colonial South India*. Delhi: Permanent Black, 2003.

Bloomfield, B. C. "A. B. Bone and the Beginning of Printing in Malaysia." In *India Office Library and Records: Report for the Year 1979*. Foreign and Commonwealth Office, 1980.

Blussé, Leonard. *Strange Company: Chinese Settlers, Mestizo Women, and the Dutch in VOC Batavia*. Dordrecht, Netherlands: Foris Publications, 1986.

Bode, Katherine. "Thousands of Titles without Authors: Digitized Newspapers, Serial Fiction, and the Challenges of Anonymity." *Book History* 19 (2016): 284–316.

Boehmer, Elleke. *Colonial and Postcolonial Literature: Migrant Metaphors*. 2nd ed. Oxford: Oxford University Press, 2005.

——. *Empire, the National, and the Postcolonial, 1890–1920: Resistance in Interaction*. Oxford: Oxford University Press, 2002.

Boggs, Carl. *The End of Politics: Corporate Power and the Decline of the Public Sphere*. New York: Guildford Press, 2000.

Bond, Rusking. *Strange Men, Strange Places*. New Delhi: Rupa, 1992.

Borsay, Peter. *English Urban Renaissance: Culture and Society in the Provincial Town, 1660–1770*. Oxford: Clarendon Press, 1989.

Bose, Sugata. *A Hundred Horizons: The Indian Ocean in the Age of Global Empire*. Cambridge, MA: Harvard University Press, 2006.

Bosma, Ulbe, and Remco Raben. *Being "Dutch" in the Indies: A History of Creolisation and Empire, 1500–1920*. Translated by Wendie Shaffer. Athens: Ohio University Press, 2008.

[Boswell, James?]. *Gentleman's Magazine* 53 (July 1783): 689.

——. *Scot's Magazine* 45 (Jan. 1783): 600.

Bowen, H. V. *The Business of Empire: The East India Company and Imperial Britain, 1756–1833*. Cambridge: Cambridge University Press, 2006.

——. *Elites, Enterprise, and the Making of the British Overseas Empire, 1688–1775*. Palgrave Macmillan, 1996.

Bowker, Geoffrey C., and Susan Leigh Star. *Sorting Things Out: Classification and Its Consequences*. Cambridge, MA: MIT Press, 1999.

Bowrey, Thomas. *A Dictionary, [of] English and Malayo, Malayo and English*. London: Sam Bridge, 1701.

Boyd, Hugh. *The Indian Observer by the Late Hugh Boyd, Esq. [. . .] by Lawrence Dundas Campbell*. London: T. Cadell, Jun. and W. Davis, 1798.

Brewer, John. *The Sinews of Power: War, Money, and the English State, 1688–1783*. Cambridge, MA: Harvard University Press, 1990.

Brickell, Katherine, and Ayona Datta. "Introduction: Translocal Geographies." In *Translocal Geographies: Spaces, Places, Connections*, edited by Katherine Brickell and Ayona Datta, 3–22. Burlington, VT: Ashgate, 2011.

Brickhouse, Anna. *Transamerican Literary Relations and the Nineteenth-Century Public Sphere*. Cambridge: Cambridge University Press, 2004.

Bristow, James. *A Narrative of the Sufferings of James Bristow, Belonging to the Bengal Artillery, during Ten Years Captivity with Hyder Ally and Tippoo Saheb*. Calcutta: Honorable Company Press, 1792.

Brittlebank, Kate. *Tipu Sultan's Search for Legitimacy: Islam and Kingship in a Hindu Domain*. Delhi: Oxford University Press, 1997.

Broadberry, Stephen, Johann Custodis, and Bishnupriya Gupta. "India and the Great Divergence: An Anglo-Indian Comparison of GDP Per Capita, 1600–1871." *Explorations in Economic History* 55 (Jan. 2015): 58–75.

Brooks, Joanna. "The Early American Public Sphere and the Emergence of a Black Print Counterpublic." *William and Mary Quarterly* 62, no. 1 (Jan. 2005): 67–92.

Brown, Vincent. "Social Death and Political Life in the Study of Slavery." *American Historical Review* 114, no. 5 (Dec. 2009): 1231–49.

Bruce, James. *Travels to Discover the Source of the Nile in the Years 1768, 1769, 1770, 1771, 1772, and 1773*. 5 vols. London: G. G. J. and J. Robinson, 1790.

Buddle, Anne, Iain Gordon Brown, Pauline Rohatgi. *The Tiger and the Thistle: Tipu Sultan and the Scots in India*. July 29–Oct. 3, 1999. Edinburgh: National Gallery of Scotland, 2000. www.tigerandthistle.net/tipu314.htm.

Burke, Edmund. *India: Madras and Bengal 1774–1785*. Vol. 5 of *Writings and Speeches of Edmund Burke*. Edited by Paul Langford and William B. Todd. Oxford: Clarendon Press, 1981.

Burnage, Sarah. "Commemorating Cornwallis: Sculpture in India, 1792–1813." *Visual Culture in Britain* 11, no. 2 (July 2010): 173–94.

Burney, Fatima. "Locating the World in Metaphysical Poetry: The Bardification of Hafiz." *Journal of World Literature* 4 (2019): 149–68.

Burnham, Michelle. *Captivity and Sentiment: Cultural Exchange in American Literature, 1682–1861*. Hanover, NH: University Press of New England, 1997.

Burton, Antoinette. *Empire in Question: Reading, Writing, and Teaching British Imperialism*. Durham, NC: Duke University Press, 2011.

———. *The Trouble with Empire: Challenges to Modern British Imperialism*. Oxford: Oxford University Press, 2015.

Burton, Antoinette, Madhvi Kale, Isabel Hofmeyr, Clare Anderson, Christopher J. Lee, and Nile Green. "Sea Tracks and Trails: Indian Ocean Worlds as Method." *History Compass* 11, no. 7 (July 2013): 497–502.

Busch, Allison. "Braj beyond Braj: Classical Hindi in the Mughal World." *IIC Occasional Publications* 12 (2009): 1–33.

———. "Hidden in Plain View: Brajbhasa Poets at the Mughal Court." *Modern Asian Studies* 44, no. 2 (March 2010): 267–309.

———. *Poetry of Kings: The Classical Hindi Literature of Mughal India*. New York: Oxford University Press, 2011.

Bush, Christopher. "Areas: Bigger Than the Nation, Smaller Than the World." *State of the Discipline Report*. American Comparative Literature Association, 2014–15. https://stateofthediscipline.acla.org/entry/areas-bigger-nation-smaller-world.

Butler, Judith, and Gayatri Chakravorty Spivak. *Who Sings the Nation-State? Language, Politics, Belonging*. Kolkata: Seagull, 2007.

Calhoun, Craig. "Civil Society and the Public Sphere." *Public Culture* 5, no. 2 (Winter 1993): 267–80.

Calhoun, Craig, and Richard Sennett. Introduction to *Practicing Cultures*, edited by Craig Calhoun and Richard Sennett, 1–12. London: Routledge, 2007.

Callahan, Raymond. *The East India Company and Army Reform, 1783–1798*. Cambridge, MA: Harvard University Press, 1972.

Campbell, Donald. *A Narrative of the Extraordinary Adventures, and the Sufferings by Shipwreck & Imprisonment, of Donald Campbell [. . .]*. 3rd ed. London: Vernor and Hood, 1798.

Candidus [pseud.]. "The Captive." *Madras Courier*, Nov. 10, 1791.

——. "An Ode. Translated from Anacreon." *Calcutta Gazette*, Nov. 18, 1784.

——. "An Ode on the Introduction of the Cold Weather." *Calcutta Gazette*, Nov. 4, 1784.

——. "A SONG of Amir Khoseru, *translated*." *Calcutta Gazette*, Dec. 16, 1784.

——. "To the Editors of the *Madras Courier*." *Madras Courier*, July 28, 1790.

——. "Verses Addressed to a Lady in England on the Anniversary of Her Birth-day by an Officer with the Grand Army in India." *Madras Courier*, August 25, 1791.

Cannadine, David. *Ornamentalism: How the British Saw their Empire*. Oxford: Oxford University Press, 2001.

Cannon, Garland, ed. *The Letters of Sir William Jones*. 2 vols. Oxford: Clarendon Press, 1970.

——. *The Life and Mind of Oriental Jones: Sir William Jones, the Father of Modern Linguistics*. Cambridge: Cambridge University Press, 1990.

Carey, Peter. *Destiny: The Life of Prince Diponegoro, 1785–1855*. Bern: Peter Lang, 2014.

——. *The Power of Prophecy: Prince Dipanagara and the End of an Old Order in Java, 1785–1855*. Leiden: KITLV Press, 2007.

Carretta, Vincent. *Equiano, the African: Biography of a Self-Made Man*. Athens: University of Georgia Press, 2005.

Carroll, Diana J. "William Marsden and Patterns of British Scholarship in the Malay Peninsula." *Indonesia and the Malay World* 39, no. 114 (2011): 269–74.

Carson, Penelope. *The East India Company and Religion, 1698–1858*. Suffolk: Boydell Press, 2012.

Casanova, Pascale. "Literature as a World." *New Left Review* 31 (Jan./Feb. 2005): 71–90.

Cash, Arthur H. *Laurence Sterne: The Later Years*. London: Methuen, 1986.

Cassels, Nancy Gardner. *Social Legislation of the East India Company: Public Justice versus Public Instruction*. New Delhi: Sage, 2010.

Castro, Wendy Lucas. "Stripped: Clothing and Identity in Colonial Captivity Narratives." *Early American Studies* 6, no. 1 (Spring 2008): 104–36.

Cecire, Natalia. *Experimental: American Literature and the Aesthetics of Knowledge*. Baltimore: Johns Hopkins University Press, 2019.

The Census of India. 1931. Vol. 1, pt. 1.

[Centlivre, Susanna]. *The Wonder: A Woman Keeps a Secret. A Comedy*. London: E. Curll, 1714.

Chamberlain, Arthur Bensley. *George Romney*. New York: Charles Scribner, 1910.

Chander, Manu Samriti. *Brown Romantics: Poetry and Nationalism in the Global Nineteenth Century*. Lewisburg, PA: Bucknell University Press, 2017.

Chandler, David. "'The Athens of England': Norwich as a Literary Center in the Late Eighteenth Century." *Eighteenth-Century Studies* 43, no. 2 (Winter 2010):171–92.

Chatterjee, Amal. *Representations of India, 1740–1840: The Creation of India in the Colonial Imagination*. New York: St. Martin's, 1998.

Chatterjee, Kumkum. "History as Self-Representation: The Recasting of a Political Tradition in Late Eighteenth-Century Eastern India." *Modern Asian Studies* 32, no. 4 (1998): 913–48.

Chatterjee, Partha. *The Black Hole of Empire: History of a Global Practice of Power*. Princeton, NJ: Princeton University Press, 2012.

——. "On Civil and Political Society in Postcolonial Democracies." In *Civil Society: History and Possibilities*, edited by Sudipta Kaviraj and Sunil Khilnani, 165–78. Cambridge: Cambridge University Press, 2001.

Chatterjee, Sudipto. *The Colonial Staged: Theater in Colonial Calcutta*. Calcutta: Seagull, 2007.

Chattopadhay, Swati. "Blurring Boundaries: The Limits of 'White Town' in Colonial Calcutta." *Journal of the Society of Architectural Historians* 59, no. 2 (June 2000): 154–79.

Chaudhuri, K. N. *Asia before Europe: Economy and Civilization of the Indian Ocean from the Rise of Islam to 1750*. Cambridge: Cambridge University Press, 1990.

——. *The Trading World of Asia and the English East India Company, 1660–1760*. Cambridge: Cambridge University Press, 1978.

Chaudhuri, Rosinka. Introduction to *A History of Indian Poetry in English*, edited by Rosinka Chaudhuri, 1–18. Cambridge: Cambridge University Press, 2016.

——. *The Literary Thing: History, Poetry, and the Making of a Modern Literary Culture*. Oxford: Oxford University Press, 2013.

Chen, Kuan-Hsing. *Asia as Method: Toward Deimperialization*. Durham, NC: Duke University Press, 2010.

Chernaik, Warren. "Unhappy Families: The Family and the State in Otway, Lee, Filmer, and Dryden." *Restoration and 18th Century Theatre Research* 22, no. 1/2 (Summer-Winter 2007): 72–90.

Choudhury, Mita. *Interculturalism and Resistance in the London Theater, 1660–1800: Identity Performance, Empire*. Lewisburg, PA: Bucknell University Press, 2000.

Christian, David. "The Case for 'Big History.'" *Journal of World History* 2, no. 2 (Fall 1991): 223–38.

Christmas, William. *The Lab'ring Muses: Work, Writing, and the Social Order in English Plebeian Poetry, 1730–1830*. Newark: University of Delaware Press, 2001.

Clark, Peter. *British Clubs and Societies, 1580–1800: The Origins of an Associational World*. Oxford: Clarendon Press, 2000.

——. *Sociability and Urbanity: Clubs and Societies in the Eighteenth-Century City*. Leicester: Victorian Studies Center, 1986.

Clarke, William, and Robert Shelton Mackenzie. *Voyagers and Travellers; Philosophers and Men of Science; Authors*. Volume 3 of *The Georgian Era: Memoirs of the Most Eminent Persons, Who Have Flourished in Great Britain [. . .]*. London: Vizetelly, Branston, 1832–34.

Clifford, James. *Routes: Travel and Translation in the Late Twentieth Century*. Cambridge, MA: Harvard University Press, 1997.

Coates, Austin. *Macao and the British, 1637–1842: Prelude to Hong Kong*. Hong Kong: Hong Kong University Press, 2009.

Cohen, Ashley. "The 'Aristocratic Imperialists' of Late Georgian and Regency Britain." *Eighteenth-Century Studies* 50, no. 1 (Fall 2016): 5–26.

——. *The Global Indies: British Imperial Culture and the Reshaping of the World, 1756–1815*. New Haven: Yale University Press, 2021.

Cohen, Margaret. "Narratology in the Archive of Literature." *Representations* 108, no. 1 (Fall 2009): 51–75.

——. *The Sentimental Education of the Novel*. Princeton, NJ: Princeton University Press, 1999.

Cohen, Michael C. "Peddlers, Poems, and Local Culture: The Case of Jonathan Plummer, a 'Ballad-Monger' in Nineteenth-Century England." *ESQ: A Journal of the American Renaissance* 54, nos. 1–4 (2008): 9–32.

——. *The Social Lives of Poems in Nineteenth-Century America*. Philadelphia: University of Pennsylvania Press, 2015.

Cohen, Michèle. *Fashioning Masculinity: National Identity and Language in the Eighteenth Century*. New York: Routledge, 1996.

Cohn, Bernard S. *An Anthropologist among the Historians and Other Essays*. Delhi: Oxford University Press, 1987.

——. *Colonialism and Its Forms of Knowledge: The British in India*. Princeton, NJ: Princeton University Press, 1996.

Cohn, Bernard, and McKim Marriott. "Networks and Centres in the Integration of Indian Civilisations." *Journal of Social Research* 1, no. 1 (1958): 1–9.

Collegins, John. "Literary Characteristics of the Most Distinguished Members of the Asiatic Society." *Asiatic Annual Register*. London: J. Debrett and T. Cadell Jun. and W. Davies, 1802.

Collet, Joseph. *The Private Letter Books of Joseph Collet*. Edited by H. H. Dodwell. London: Longmans, Green, 1933.

Colley, Linda. *Captives: Britain, Empire, and the World, 1600–1850*. New York: Anchor, 2002.

——. "Going Native, Telling Tales: Captivity, Collaboration, and Empire." *Past and Present*, no. 168 (August 2000): 170–93.

——. *The Ordeal of Elizabeth Marsh: A Woman in World History*. London: Harper, 2007.

Collier, Patrick, and James J. Connolly. "Print Culture Histories beyond the Metropolis: An Introduction." In *Print Culture Histories beyond the Metropolis*, edited by Frank Felsenstein, Kenneth R. Hall, James J. Connolly, Patrick Collier, and Robert G. Hall, 1–25. Toronto: University of Toronto Press, 2016.

Constantin, Comte de Volney. *Voyage en Égypte et Syrie, pendant les années 1783, 1784, & 1785*. Paris: Volland, 1787.

Cooley, Marianne. "An Early Representation of African American English." In *Language Variety in the South Revisited*, edited by Cynthia Bernstein, Thomas E. Nunnally, and Robin Sabino, 51–58. Tuscaloosa: University of Alabama Press, 1997.

Cooper, Frederick. *Colonialism in Question: Theory, Knowledge, History*. Berkeley: University of California Press, 2005.

Copley, Stephen, and Peter Garside. Introduction to *The Politics of the Picturesque: Literature, Landscape and Aesthetics since 1770*, edited by Stephen Copley and Peter Garside, 1–12. Cambridge: Cambridge University Press, 2002.

Couchman, Dorothy. "'Mungo Everywhere': How Anglophones Heard Chattel Slavery." *Slavery & Abolition* 36, no. 4 (2015): 704–20.

Cowper, William. *Selected Poems*. Edited by Nick Rhodes. New York: Routledge, 2003.

Czennia, Bärbel. "Wide-Open Hemispheres: Punch Bowls, Punch, and World Citizenship in Eighteenth-Century British Culture." In *Citizens of the World: Adapting in the Eighteenth Century*, edited by Kevin L. Cope and Samar Anne Cahill, 43–68. Lewisburg, PA: Bucknell University Press, 2015.

Dabashi, Hamid. *Persophilia: Persian Culture on the Global Scene*. Cambridge, MA: Harvard University Press, 2015.

Dabydeen, David. *Hogarth's Blacks: Images of Blacks in Eighteenth-Century English Art*. Athens: University of Georgia Press, 1987.

Dalrymple, William. "Assimilation and Transculturation in Eighteenth-Century India: A Response to Pankaj Mishra." *Common Knowledge* 11, no. 3 (Fall 2005): 453–85.

——. "Tipu Sultan: Noble or Savage?" *Open* (Nov. 26, 2015): www.openthemagazine.com/article/voices/tipu-sultan-noble-or-savage.

——. *White Mughals: Love and Betrayal in Eighteenth-Century India*. New York: HarperCollins, 2002.

Darby, Graham, ed. *The Origins and Development of the Dutch Revolt*. New York: Routledge, 2001.

Datta, Kitty Scoular. "Publishing and Translating Hafez under Empire." In *Books without Borders*. Vol. 2, *Perspectives from South Asia*, edited by Robert Fraser and Mary Hammond, 58–70. Basingstoke, Hampshire: Palgrave Macmillan, 2008.

Darnton, Robert. *Censors at Work: How States Shaped Literature*. New York: Norton, 2014.

Davis, Natalie Zemon. *Society and Culture in Early Modern France: Eight Essays*. Stanford, CA: Stanford University Press, 1975.

Dean, Ann. *Talk of the Town: Figurative Publics in Eighteenth-Century Britain*. Lewisburg, PA: Bucknell University Press, 2007.

Dean, Tessa. "The Hookah, Orientalism, and Colonialism in Eighteenth-Century India: An Analysis of *Colonel Polier Watching a Nautch*." Master's thesis, University of North Carolina, 2004.

de Bruijn, J. T. P. "ḠAZAL i. HISTORY." *Encyclopædia Iranica*, X/4, 354–58. www.iranicaonline.org/articles/gazal-1-history.

Deleuze, Gilles, and Félix Guattari. *Kafka: Toward a Minor Literature*. Translated by Dana Polan. Minneapolis: University of Minnesota Press, 1986.

Demos, John. *The Unredeemed Captive: A Family Story from Early America*. New York: Vintage, 1995.

Denham, John. "Coopers Hill." In *Poems and Translations, with "The Sophy."* London: H. Herringman, 1668.

De Quincey, Thomas. *Confessions of an English Opium-Eater and Other Writings*. Edited by Grevel Lindop. Oxford: Oxford University Press, 1985.

DeWispelare, Daniel. *Multilingual Subjects: On Standard English, Its Speakers, and Others in the Long Eighteenth-Century*. Philadelphia: University of Pennsylvania Press, 2017.

Dharwadker, Vinay. "English in India and Indian Literature in English: The Early History: 1579–1834." *Comparative Literature Studies* 39, no. 2 (2002): 93–119.

——. "Print Culture and Literary Markets in Colonial India." In *Language Machines: Technologies of Literary and Cultural Production*, edited by Jeffrey Masten, Peter Stallybrass, and Nancy J. Vickers, 108–33. New York: Routledge, 1997.

Dimock, Wai Chee. *Through Other Continents: American Literature across Deep Time*. Princeton, NJ: Princeton University Press, 2006.

Dirom, Alexander. *A Narrative of the Campaign in India, Which Terminated the War with Tippoo Sultan, in 1792*. London: W. Bulmer, 1793.

Dirks, Nicholas B. *Castes of Mind: Colonialism and the Making of Modern India*. Princeton, NJ: Princeton University Press, 2001.

——. *The Hollow Crown: Ethnohistory of an Indian Kingdom*. 1987. 2nd ed. Ann Arbor: University of Michigan Press, 1993.

Dodwell, Henry. *The Nabobs of Madras*. London: Williams and Norgate, 1926.

Doyle, Laura. "Inter-imperiality and Literary Studies in the Long Durée." *PMLA* 130, no. 2 (2015): 336–47.

DuBois, Laurent. *Avengers of the New World: The Story of the Haitian Revolution*. Cambridge, MA: Belknap Press, 2004.

——. *A Colony of Citizens: Revolution and Slave Emancipation in the French Caribbean, 1787–1804*. Chapel Hill: University of North Carolina Press, 2004.

Dunn, Theodore Douglas. *Poets of the John Company*. Calcutta: Thacker, Spink, 1921.

Dunthorne, Hugh. *Britain and the Dutch Revolt, 1560–1700*. Cambridge: Cambridge University Press, 2013.

Durga, S. A. K. "Western Influence on Indian Music: 'Nottusware Sahithya' or Muthuswami Dikshitar: An Intercultural Musical Form." *Journal of the Indian Musicological Society* 41 (2011/12): 31–35.

During, Simon. "Comparative Literature." *ELH* 72, no. 2 (2004): 313–22.

Dwyer, Rachel, and Divia Patel. *Cinema India: The Visual Culture of Hindi Film*. New Brunswick, NJ: Rutgers University Press, 2002.

Eacott, Jonathan. *Selling Empire: India in the Making of Britain and America, 1600–1830*. Chapel Hill: University of North Carolina Press, 2016.

The East India Military Calendar: Containing the Services of General and Field Officers in the Indian Army. Vol. 3. London: Kingsbury, Parbury, and Allen, 1826.

Eaton, Natasha. *Mimesis across Empires: Artworks and Networks in India, 1765–1860*. Durham, NC: Duke University Press, 2013.

——. "Nostalgia for the Exotic: Creating an Imperial Art in London, 1750–1793." *Eighteenth-Century Studies* 39, no. 2 (Winter 2006): 227–50.

Ebersole, Gary. *Captured by Texts: Puritan to Postmodern Images of Indian Captivity*. Charlottesville: University Press of Virginia, 1995.

Echols, John M., and Hassan Shadily. *An Indonesian-English Dictionary*. Ithaca, NY: Cornell University Press, 1961.

Eggener, Keith. "Placing Resistance: A Critique of Critical Regionalism." *Journal of Architectural Education* 55, no. 4 (May 2002): 228–37.

Eisenstadt, S. N. "Multiple Modernities." In *Multiple Modernities*, edited by S. N. Eisenstadt, 1–29. Piscataway, NJ: Transaction, 2002.

Elfenbein, Andrew. *Romanticism and the Rise of English*. Stanford, CA: Stanford University Press, 2009.

Ellis, Markman. "Coffee-Women, *The Spectator*, and the Public Sphere in the Early Eighteenth Century." In *Women, Writing, and the Public Sphere, 1700–1830*, edited by Elizabeth Eger, Charlotte Grant, Clíona Ó Gallchoir, and Penny Warburton, 27–52. Cambridge: Cambridge University Press, 2001.

English, James. "Now, Not Now: Counting Time in Contemporary Fiction Studies." *Modern Language Quarterly* 77, no. 3 (Sept. 2016): 395–418.

Errington, J. Joseph. *Linguistics in a Colonial World: A Story of Language, Meaning, and Power.* Malden, MA: Blackwell, 2008.

——. *Shifting Languages: Interaction and Identity in Javanese Indonesia.* Cambridge: Cambridge University Press, 1998.

Exotic Printing and the Expansion of Europe, 1492–1840: An Exhibit. Bloomington: Lilly Library, Indiana University, 1972.

Faber, G. H. von. *A Short History of Journalism in the Dutch East Indies.* Sourabaya: G. Kolff, 1930.

Farrington, Anthony. *Trading Places: The East India Company and Asia, 1600–1834.* London: British Library, 2002.

Favret, Mary. *War at a Distance: Romanticism and the Making of Modern Wartime.* Princeton, NJ: Princeton University Press, 2010.

Fay, Eliza. *Original Letters from India.* New York: New York Review Books, 2010.

Featherstone, Mike. "Localism, Globalism, and Cultural Identity." In Wilson and Dissanayake, *Global/Local*, 46–77.

Feldman, Paula, ed. *British Women Poets of the Romantic Era: An Anthology.* Baltimore: Johns Hopkins University Press, 1997.

Festa, Lynn. *Sentimental Figures of Empire in Eighteenth-Century England and France.* Baltimore: Johns Hopkins University Press, 2006.

Fhlathúin, Máire ní. *British India and Victorian Literary Culture.* Edinburgh: Edinburgh University Press, 2015.

——. *The Poetry of British India, 1780–1905.* Vol. 1. London: Pickering and Chatto, 2011.

Fieldhouse, Douglas. "Can Humpty Dumpty Be Put Back Together Again? Imperial History in the 1980s." *Journal of Imperial and Commonwealth History* 12, no. 2 (1984): 9–23.

Firminger, W. K. "Selections from the Notebooks of Justice John Hyde." *Bengal: Past and Present* 3 (1909): 27–64.

Fisher, Michael H. *Counterflows to Colonialism: Indian Travellers and Settlers in Britain, 1600–1857.* Delhi: Permanent Black, 2004.

——, ed. *The Travels of Dean Mahomet: An Eighteenth-Century Journey through India.* Berkeley: University of California Press, 1997.

Flood, Finbarr B. *Objects of Translation: Material Culture and Medieval "Hindu-Muslim" Encounter.* Princeton, NJ: Princeton University Press, 2009.

Foote, Samuel. *The Mayor of Garret.* London: P Vaillant, 1764.

——. *The Nabob; a Comedy, in Three Acts.* Dublin: W. Kidd, 1778.

Forman, Ross G. *China and the British Imagination: Empires Entwined.* Cambridge: Cambridge University Press, 2013.

Fraas, Mitch. "Beyond the Atlantic: British India, Book Circulation, and the Transmission of Knowledge in the Eighteenth Century." Lecture given at the Rare

Books School, Kislak Center, University of Pennsylvania Library, July 7, 2015. www.youtube.com/watch?v=NvtwE6znMoA.

——. "Expanding the Republic of Letters: India and the Circulation of Ideas in the Late Eighteenth Century." *Mapping Books* (blog). Presentation for the Society for the History of Authorship, Reading, and Publishing Conference, University of Pennsylvania, July 20, 2013. http://mappingbooks.blogspot.com/2013/07/expanding-republic-of-letters-india-and.html.

Frampton, Kenneth. "Towards a Critical Regionalism: Six Points for an Architecture of Resistance." In *The Anti-Aesthetic: Essay on Postmodern Culture*, edited by Hal Foster, 16–30. Port Townsend, WA: Bay Press, 1983.

Frank, Andre Gunder. *ReORIENT: Global Economy in the Asian Age*. Berkeley: University of California Press, 1998.

Franklin, Michael J. "Cultural Possession, Imperial Control, and Comparative Religion: The Calcutta Perspectives of Sir William Jones and Nathaniel Brassey Halhed." *Yearbook of English Studies* 32 (2002): 1–18.

——. "'The Hastings Circle': Writers and Writing in Calcutta in the Last Quarter of the Eighteenth Century." In *Authorship, Commerce, and the Public: Scenes of Writing, 1750–1850*, edited by E. J. Clery, Caroline Franklin, and Peter Garside, 186–202. London: Palgrave Macmillan, 2002.

——. Introduction to *Hartly House, Calcutta*, by Phebe Gibbes. Edited with an intro. by Michael J. Franklin, xi–lvii. Oxford: Oxford University Press, 2007.

——. *Orientalist Jones: Sir William Jones, Poet, Lawyer, and Linguist, 1746–1794*. Oxford: Oxford University Press, 2011.

——, ed. *Representing India: Indian Culture and Imperial Control in Eighteenth-Century Orientalist Discourse*. Vol. 7, *The Asiatick Researches*. London: Routledge, 2000.

——. *Sir William Jones*. Cardiff: University of Wales Press, 1995.

——. "Sir William Jones, the Celtic Revival, and the Oriental Renaissance." In *English Romanticism and the Celtic World*, edited by Gerard Carruthers and Alan Rawes, 20–37. Cambridge: Cambridge University Press, 2003.

Fraser, Nancy. "Rethinking the Public Sphere: A Contribution to the Critique of an Actually Existing Democracy." In *Habermas and the Public Sphere*, edited by Craig J. Calhoun, 109–42. Cambridge, MA: MIT Press, 1992.

Fraser, Robert. *Book History through Postcolonial Eyes: Rewriting the Script*. New York: Routledge, 2008.

Freeman, Kathryn. *British Women Writers and the Asiatic Society of Bengal, 1785–1835: Re-Orienting Anglo-India*. Farnham, Surrey: Ashgate, 2014.

Freeman, Lisa A. *Character's Theater: Genre and Identity on the Eighteenth-Century English Stage*. Philadelphia: University of Pennsylvania Press, 2002.

Freitag, Sandria. "Enactments of Ram's Story and the Changing Nature of 'the Public' in British India." *South Asia* 14, no. 1 (1991): 65–90.

——. "Introduction: 'The Public' and Its Meanings in Colonial South Asia." *South Asia* 14, no. 1 (1991): 1–13.

Freitag, Ulrike, and Achim von Oppen. "'Translocality': An Approach to Connection and Transfer in Area Studies." In *Translocality: The Study of Globalising Processes from a Southern Perspective*, edited by Ulrike Freitag and Achim von Oppen, 1–24. Leiden: Brill, 2010.

Frost, Mark Ravinder. "Asia's Maritime Networks and the Colonial Public Sphere, 1840–1920." *New Zealand Journal of Asian Studies* 6, no. 2 (Dec. 2004): 63–94.

——. "Wider Opportunities: Religious Revival, Nationalist Awakening, and the Global Dimension in Colombo, 1870–1920." *Modern Asian Studies* 36, no. 4 (Oct. 2002): 937–67.

Fry, Michael. "'The Keys to Their Hearts': Scottish Orientalism." In *Scotland and the 19th-Century World*, edited by Gerard Carruthers, David Goldie, and Alastair Renfrew, 137–57. Amsterdam: Rodopi, 2012.

Fryer, Peter. *Staying Power: The History of Black People in Britain*. London: Pluto, 1984.

Fuchs, Barbara. "Another Turn for Transnationalism: Empire, Nation, and Imperium in Early Modern Studies." *PMLA* 130, no. 2 (2015): 412–18.

——. *Poetics of Piracy: Emulating Spain in English Literature*. Philadelphia: University of Pennsylvania Press, 2013.

Gaastra, Femme. *The Dutch East India Company: Expansion and Decline*. Zutphen, Netherlands: Walburg, 2003.

Games, Alison. *The Web of Empire: English Cosmopolitans in an Age of Expansion, 1560–1660*. Oxford: Oxford University Press, 2008.

Garcia, Humberto. *Islam and the English Enlightenment, 1670–1840*. Baltimore: Johns Hopkins University Press, 2012.

——. "A Stranger's Love for Ireland: Indo-Irish Xenophilia in *The Travels of Mirza Abu Taleb Khan* (1810, 814)." *Common Knowledge* 23, no. 2 (May 2017): 232–53.

Garvey, Ellen Gruber. *Writing with Scissors: American Scrapbooks from the Civil War to the Harlem Renaissance*. Oxford: Oxford University Press, 2013.

Gascoigne, John. *Joseph Banks and the English Enlightenment: Useful Knowledge and Polite Culture*. Cambridge: Cambridge University Press, 1994.

Gately, Iain. *Tobacco: A Cultural History of How an Exotic Plant Seduced Civilization*. New York: Grove, 2001.

Geertz, Clifford. *Available Light: Anthropological Reflections on Philosophical Topics*. Princeton, NJ: Princeton University Press, 2000.

——. *Local Knowledge: Further Essays in Interpretive Anthropology*. 3rd ed. New York: Basic Books, 1983.

Gellner, Ernest. *Conditions of Liberty: Civil Society and Its Rivals*. London: Allen Lane, 1994.

Geschiere, Peter. "Autochthony: Local or Global?" In *Translocality: The Study of Globalising Processes from a Southern Perspective*, edited by Ulrike Freitag and Achim von Oppen, 207–28. Leiden: Brill, 2010.

Ghosh, Anindita. "Literary Traditions in Pre-Print Bengal and Their Legacy in the Age of Print." In *On Modern Indian Sensibilities: Culture, Politics, History*, edited by Ishita Banerjee-Dube and Sarvani Gooptu, 234–58. New York: Routledge, 2018.

——. *Power in Print: Popular Publishing and the Politics of Language and Culture in a Colonial Society, 1778–1905*. New Delhi: Oxford University Press, 2006.

——. "An Uncertain 'Coming of the Book': Early Print Cultures in Colonial India." *Book History* 6 (2003): 23–55.

Ghosh, Durba. *Sex and the Family in Colonial India: The Making of Empire*. Cambridge: Cambridge University Press, 2006.

Ghosh, Suresh Chandra. *The Social Condition of the British Community in Bengal, 1757–1800*. Leiden: Brill, 1970.
Gibson, Mary Ellis. *Anglophone Poetry in Colonial India, 1780–1913*. Athens: Ohio University Press, 2011.
——. *Indian Angles: English Verse in Colonial India from Jones to Tagore*. Athens: Ohio University Press, 2011.
——. "Transforming Late Romanticism, Transforming Home: Women Poets in Colonial India." In *A History of Indian Poetry in English*, edited by Rosinka Chaudhuri, 64–81. Cambridge: Cambridge University Press, 2016.
Giles, Paul. *Antipodean America: Australasia and the Constitution of U.S. Literature*. Oxford: Oxford University Press, 2014.
Gilmour, David. *The British in India: Three Centuries of Ambition and Experience*. Allen Lane, 2018.
Ginzburg, Carlo. *The Cheese and the Worms: The Cosmos of a Sixteenth-Century Miller*. Translated by John Tedeschi and Anne Tedeschi. Baltimore: Johns Hopkins University Press, 1980.
Gladwin, Francis. *Ayeen Akbery: or, The Institutes of the Emperor Akber*. 3 vols. Calcutta: 1783.
Glaisyer, Natasha. "Networking: Trade and Exchange in the Eighteenth-Century British Empire." *Historical Journal* 47, no. 2 (June 2004): 451–76.
Glazener, Nancy. *Literature in the Making: A History of U.S. Literary Culture in the Long Nineteenth Century*. Oxford: Oxford University Press, 2016.
Gokhale, B. G. "Tobacco in Seventeenth-Century India." *Agricultural History* 48, no. 4 (Oct. 1974): 484–92.
Goldberg, Jonathan. *Sodometries: Renaissance Texts, Modern Sexualities*. Stanford, CA: Stanford University Press, 1992.
Goodridge, John. *Rural Life in Eighteenth-Century English Poetry*. Cambridge: Cambridge University Press, 1996.
Gould, Stephen Jay. *Time's Arrow, Time's Cycle: Myth and Metaphor in the Discovery of Geological Time*. Cambridge, MA: Harvard University Press, 1987.
Graaf, H. J. de. *The Spread of Printing: Eastern Hemisphere*. Vol. 6, *Indonesia*. Amsterdam: Vangendt, 1969.
Graham, Gerald S. "By Steam to India." *History Today* 14, no. 5 (May 1964): 301–12.
Greif, Avner. "Historical and Comparative Institutional Analysis." *American Economic Review* 88, no. 2 (May 1998): 80–84.
Greiner, Clemens, and Peter Sakdapolrak. "Translocality: Concepts, Applications, and Emerging Research Perspectives." *Geography Compass* 7, no. 5 (May 2013): 373–84.
Grewal, Inderpal. *Home and Harem: Nation, Gender, Empire, and the Cultures of Travel*. Durham, NC: Duke University Press, 1996.
Griffin, Robert J. "Anonymity and Authorship." *New Literary History* 30, no. 4 (Autumn 1999): 877–95.
Griswold, Wendy. *Regionalism and the Reading Class*. Chicago: University of Chicago Press, 2008.
Groseclose, Barbara S. *British Sculpture and the Company Raj: Church Monuments and Public Statuary in Madras, Calcutta, and Bombay to 1858*. Newark: University of Delaware Press, 1995.

Guest, Harriet. "Sterne, Elizabeth Draper, and Drapery." *The Shandean* 9 (1997): 9–33.

Guha, Ramachandra. *India after Gandhi: The History of the World's Largest Democracy.* New York: Ecco, 2007.

Guha, Ranajit. "The Prose of Counter-Insurgency." *Subaltern Studies II: Writings on South Asian History and Society,* edited by Ranajit Guha, 1–42. Delhi: Oxford University Press, 1983.

Guldi, Jo, and David Armitage. *The History Manifesto.* Cambridge: Cambridge University Press, 2014.

Gunn, Geoffrey C. *Encountering Macau: A Portuguese City-State on the Periphery of China, 1557–1999.* Boulder, CO: Westview, 1996.

Habermas, Jürgen. *The Structural Transformation of the Public Sphere: An Inquiry into a Category of Bourgeois Society.* Translated by Thomas Burger, with the assistance of Frederick Lawrence. Cambridge, MA: MIT Press, 1989.

Hagerman, C. A. *Britain's Imperial Muse: The Classics, Imperialism, and the Indian Empire, 1784–1914.* Houndmills, Basingstoke: Palgrave Macmillan, 2013.

[Halhed, Nathaniel Brassey]. *A Code of Gentoo Laws [. . .].* London, 1776.

——. *A Grammar of the Bengal Language.* Bengal, 1778.

Hall, Catherine. *Civilizing Subjects: Colony and Metropole in the English Imagination, 1830–1867.* Chicago: University of Chicago Press, 2002.

Hall, Kenneth R. "The Eighteenth- and Early Nineteenth-Century Evolution of Indian Print Culture and Knowledge Networks in Calcutta and Madras." In *Print Culture Histories beyond the Metropolis,* edited by James J. Connolly, Patrick Collier, and Robert G. Hall, 88–122. Toronto: University of Toronto Press, 2016.

Hannerz, Ulf. *Transnational Connections: Culture, People, Places.* New York: Routledge, 1996.

Hardgrave, Robert L., Jr. *A Portrait of the Hindus: Balthazar Solvyns and the European Image of India, 1760–1824.* Oxford: Oxford University Press, 2004.

Harfield, Alan. *Bencoolen: A History of the Honourable East India Company's Garrison on the West Coast of Sumatra (1685–1825).* Barton on Sea, Hampshire: A and J Partnership, 1995.

Hargreaves-Mawdsley, W. N. *The English Della Cruscans and Their Time, 1783–1828.* The Hague, Netherlands: Martinus Nijhoff, 1967.

Harper, T. N. "Empire, Diaspora and the Languages of Globalism, 1850–1914." In *Globalization in World History,* edited by A. G. Hopkins, 141–66. London: Pimlico, 2002.

Harries, Elizabeth W. "Words, Sex, and Gender in Sterne's Novels." In *The Cambridge Companion to Laurence Sterne,* edited by Thomas Keymer, 111–24. Cambridge: Cambridge University Press, 2009.

Harrington, Peter. *British Artists and War: The Face of Battle in Paintings and Prints, 1700–1914.* London: Greenhill, 1993.

Harrison, Mark. *Climates and Constitutions: Health, Race, Environment, and British Imperialism in India, 1600–1850.* New Delhi: Oxford University Press, 1999.

Hastings, Warren. "To Nathaniel Smith." In Wilkins, *The Bhăgvăt-Gēētā,* 5–16.

Hawes, Christopher. *Poor Relations: The Making of a Eurasian Community in British India, 1773–1833.* Richmond, Surrey: Curzon, 1996.

Hebblethwaite, Cordelia. "Mitt Romney's Mormon Roots in Northern England." BBC News. June 13, 2012. www.bbc.com/news/magazine-18422949.

Hedges, Chris. *War Is a Force That Gives Us Meaning*. New York: Public Affairs, 2002.

Hedström, Peter, and Lars Udehn. "Analytical Sociology and Theories of the Middle Range." In *The Oxford Handbook of Analytical Sociology*, edited by Peter Hedström and Peter Bearman, 25–48. Oxford: Oxford University Press, 2009.

Helgerson, Richard. *Forms of Nationhood: The Elizabethan Writing of England*. Chicago: University of Chicago Press, 1992.

Heng, Geraldine. "Reinventing Race, Colonization, and Globalisms across Deep Time: Lessons from the *Longue Durée*." *PMLA* 130, no. 2 (2015): 358–66.

Hennessy, Rosemary. *Materialist Feminism and the Politics of Discourse*. London: Routledge, 1993.

Herr, Cheryl Temple. *Critical Regionalism and Cultural Studies: From Ireland to the American Midwest*. Gainesville: University Press of Florida, 1996.

Hessell, Nikki. *Romantic Literature and the Colonised World: Lessons from Indigenous Traditions*. New York: Palgrave Macmillan, 2018.

Hevia, James L. *Cherishing Men from Afar: Qing Guest Ritual and the McCartney Embassy of 1793*. Durham, NC: Duke University Press, 1995.

Hilton, John. "Speaking Truth to Power: Julian, the Cynics, and the Ethiopian Gymnosophists of Heliodorus." In *Intellectual and Empire in Greco-Roman Antiquity*, edited by Philip R. Bosman, 205–16. Abingdon, Oxon: Routledge, 2019.

Ho, Engseng. "Afterword: Mobile Law and Thick Transregionalism." *Law and History Review* 32, no. 4 (Nov. 2014): 883–89.

——. *The Graves of Tarim: Genealogy and Mobility across the Indian Ocean*. Berkeley: University of California Press, 2006.

Hoerder, Dirk. *Cultures in Contact: World Migrations in the Second Millennium*. Durham: NC: Duke University Press, 2002.

Hofmeyr, Isabel. *Gandhi's Printing Press: Experiments in Slow Reading*. Cambridge, MA: Harvard University Press, 2013.

——. "The Globe in the Text: Towards a Transnational History of the Book." *African Studies* 64, no. 1 (July 2005): 87–103.

——. *The Portable Bunyan: A Transnational History of "The Pilgrim's Progress."* Princeton, NJ: Princeton University Press, 2004.

——. "Universalizing the Indian Ocean." *PMLA* 125, no. 3 (May 2010): 721–29.

Hofmeyr, Isabel, Preben Kaarsholm, and Bodil Folke Frederiksen. "Introduction: Print Cultures, Nationalisms, and Publics of the Indian Ocean." *Africa* 81, no. 1 (2011): 1–22.

Hoock, Holger. *Empires of the Imagination: Politics, War, and the Arts in the British World, 1750–1850*. London: Profile, 2010.

Hopkins, A. G. "Back to the Future: From National History to Imperial History." *Past & Present* 164 (August 1999): 198–243.

House, Robert, Denise M. Rousseau, and Melissa Thomas-Hunt. "The Meso Paradigm: A Framework for Integration of Micro and Macros Organizational Behavior." *Research in Organizational Behavior* 17 (1995). 71–114.

Hsü, Immanuel C. Y. *The Rise of Modern China*. 6th ed. New York: Oxford University Press, 2000.

Husain, Mahmud. *The Dreams of Tipu Sultan*. Karachi: Pakistan Historical Society, 1957.

Hutcheon, Linda. *A Theory of Parody: The Teachings of Twentieth-Century Art Forms*. Urbana: University of Illinois Press, 2000.

Irwin, Eyles. *Bedukah, or the Self-Devoted. An Indian Pastoral. By the Author of St. Thomas's Mount*. London: J. Dodsley, 1776.

——. *Eastern Eclogues: Written during a Tour through Arabia, Egypt, and Other Parts of Asia and Africa in the Year MDCCLXXVII*. London: J. Dodsley, 1780.

——. "Epistle II. From Laodicea." In Irwin, *Occasional Epistles*, 10–21.

——. "Epistle III. From Coorna, on the Conflux of the Tigris and Euphrates." In Irwin, *Occasional Epistles*, 23–37.

——. "Epistle to the Right Honourable George Lord Pigot, On the Anniversary of the Raising of the Siege of Madras." London: J. Dodsley, 1778.

——. *Napoleon: or, the Vanity of Human Wishes. Part II*. London: J. Hatchard, 1814.

——. *Nilus; An Elegy Occasioned by the Victory of Admiral Nelson over the French Fleet, on August 1, 1798*. London: W. Bulmer, 1798

——. *Occasional Epistles: Written during a Journey from London to Busrah, in the Gulf of Persia, in the Years 1780 and 1781*. London: J. Dodsley, 1783.

——. *Ode to Iberia*. London: J. Asperne, 1808.

——. *Ode to Robert Brooke, Esquire: Occasioned by the Death of Hyder Ally*. London: J. Dodsley, 1798.

——. "Ode to the Nile." *India Gazette; or Calcutta General Advertiser*, no. 32 (June 23, 1781).

——. "Prologue Written for the Opening of the Lyceum at Madras 1782, Spoken by Major Maule." Senate House Library, University of London, MS 704.

——. *A Series of Adventures in the Course of a Voyage Up the Red-Sea, on the Coasts of Arabia and Egypt*. London: J. Dodsley, 1780.

——. *St. Thomas's Mount. A Poem. Written by a Gentleman in India*. London: J. Dodsley, 1774.

——. *The Bedouins: or, Arabs of the Desert: a Comic Opera in Three Acts*. Dublin: J. Archer, 1802.

——. "To Mrs. Charlotte Smith, on her Various Works." *Gentleman's Magazine* 64 (Nov. 1794).

Israel, Jonathan. *The Dutch Republic: Its Rise, Greatness and Fall, 1477–1806*. Oxford: Clarendon Press, 1995.

Ives, Edward. *A Voyage from England to India*. London: Edward and Charles Dilly, 1773.

Iyengar, K. R. Srinivasa. *Indian Writing in English*. 3rd ed. New Delhi: Sterling, 1983.

Iyer, K. P. Viswanatha. "A History of Journalism in Madras." In *The Madras Tercentenary Commemoration Volume*, 451–58. Madras: Oxford University Press, 1939.

Jacob, Margaret C. "The Mental Landscape of the Public Sphere: A European Perspective." *Eighteenth-Century Studies* 28, no. 1 (Autumn 1994): 95–113.

Jacquemont, Victor. *Letters from India; Describing a Journey in the British Dominions of India, Tibet, Lahore, and Cashmeer [. . .]*. London: E. Churton, 1834.

Jardine, Lisa. *Going Dutch: How England Plundered Holland's Glory*. London: Harper, 2008.

Jones, Sir William. *The Collected Works of Sir William Jones*. 13 vols. Edited with an intro. by Garland Cannon. New York: New York University Press, 1993.

——. *A Grammar of the Persian Language*. London: W. & J. Richardson, 1771.

——. *The Muse Recalled; An Ode Occasioned by the Nuptials of Lord Viscount Althorp and Miss Lavinia Bingham [. . .]*. Strawberry-Hill: Thomas Kirgate, 1781.

——. *The Principles of Government: In a Dialogue Between a Scholar and a Peasant*. London: Society for Constitutional Information, 1783.

——. *Sacontalá, or the Fatal Ring; An Indian Drama by Cálidás: Translated from the Original Sanscrit and Prácrit*. Calcutta: Joseph Cooper, 1789.

Johnson, Kurt A. "'Lisping Tongues' and 'Sanscrit Songs': William Jones' Hymns to Hindu Deities." *Translation and Literature* 20, no. 1 (Spring 2011): 48–60.

Johnson, Samuel. *A Journey to the Western Islands of Scotland and the Journal of the Tour to the Hebrides by James Boswell*. Edited by Peter Levi. London: Penguin, 1984.

Joseph, Betty. *Reading the East India Company, 1720–1840: Colonial Currencies of Gender*. Chicago: University of Chicago Press, 2004.

Joshi, Priya. *In Another Country: Colonialism, Culture, and the English Novel in India*. New York: Columbia University Press, 2001.

Juncu, Meera. *India in the Italian Renaissance: Visions of a Contemporary Pagan World, 1300–1600*. Abingdon, Oxon: Routledge, 2016.

Kahin, Audrey, ed. *Historical Dictionary of Indonesia*, 3rd ed. Lanham, MD: Rowman and Littlefield, 2015.

Kanda, K. C. *Urdu Ghazals: An Anthology from 16th to 20th Century*. New Delhi: Sterling, 1995.

Kaplan, Robert. *The Indian Ocean and the Future of American Power*. New York: Random House, 2010.

Kathirithamby-Wells, Jeyamala. *The British Western Sumatran Presidency, 1760–1785: Problems of an Early Colonial Enterprise*. Kuala Lumpur: Penerbit Universiti Malaya, 1977.

Katz, Daniel. *American Modernism's Expatriate Scene: The Labour of Translation*. Edinburgh: Edinburgh University Press, 2007.

Kaufmann, Thomas DaCosta, and Michael North. "Introduction—Artistic and Cultural Exchanges between Europe and Asia, 1400–1900: Rethinking Markets, Workshops and Collections." In *Artistic and Cultural Exchanges between Europe and Asia, 1400–1900*, edited by Michael North, 1–8. Farnham, Surrey: Ashgate, 2010.

Kaul, Suvir. "English Poetry in India: The Early Years." In *A History of Indian Poetry in English*, edited by Rosinka Chaudhuri, 32–47. Cambridge: Cambridge University Press, 2016.

——. *Poems of Nation, Anthems of Empire: English Verse in the Long Eighteenth Century*. Charlottesville: University Press of Virginia, 2000.

Kaviraj, Sudipta. "In Search of Civil Society." In *Civil Society: History and Possibilities*, edited by Sudipta Kaviraj and Sunil Khilnani, 287–323. Cambridge: Cambridge University Press, 2001.

——. "An Outline of a Revisionist Theory of Modernity." *European Journal of Sociology* 46, no. 3 (2005): 497–526.

Keay, John. *India: A History*. New York: Atlantic Monthly, 2000.

Keegan, Bridget. *British Labouring-Class Nature Poetry, 1730–1837*. Houndmills, Basingstoke: Palgrave, 2008.

Kellner, Douglas. "Habermas, the Public Sphere, and Democracy." In *Re-imagining Public Space: The Frankfurt School in the 21st Century*, edited by Diana Boros and James M. Glass, 19–44. New York: Palgrave Macmillan, 2014.

Ken, Won Lin. "The Revenue Farms of Prince of Wales Island, 1805–30." *Journal of the South Seas Society* 19, no. 1 (1964): 79–82.

Kennedy, Dane. *The Magic Mountains: Hill Stations and the British Raj*. Berkeley: University of California Press, 1996.

Kesavan, B. S. *History of Printing and Publishing in India: A Story of Cultural Re-Awakening*. Vol. 1, *South Indian Origins of Printing*. New Delhi: National Book Trust, 1984.

Keymer, Thomas. *Sterne, the Moderns, and the Novel*. Oxford: Oxford University Press, 2002.

Khan, M. Siddiq. "The Early Bengali Printed Books." In *Gutenberg-Jahrbuch* (1966): 200–208.

Khan, Mirza Abu Taleb, ed. *The Works of Dewan Hafez*. Calcutta: A. Upjohn, 1791.

Kindersley, Jemima. *Letters from the Island of Teneriffe, Brazil, the Cape of Good Hope, and the East Indies*. London: J. Nourse, 1777.

Kindersley, Nathaniel. *Specimens of Hindoo Literature [. . .]*. London: W. Bulmer, 1794.

King, Christopher. *One Language, Two Scripts: The Hindi Movement in Nineteenth Century North India*. New Delhi: Oxford University Press, 1994.

Klancher, Jon. *The Making of English Reading Audiences, 1790–1832*. Madison: University of Wisconsin Press, 1987.

Klein, Lawrence E. *Shaftesbury and the Culture of Politeness: Moral Discourses and Cultural Politics in Early Eighteenth-Century England*. Cambridge: Cambridge University Press, 1994.

Knowles, Claire. *Sensibility and the Female Poetic Tradition, 1780–1860: The Legacy of Charlotte Smith*. Farnham, Surrey: Ashgate, 2009.

Kopf, David. *British Orientalism and the Bengal Renaissance: The Dynamics of Indian Modernization, 1773–1835*. Berkeley: University of California Press, 1969.

Kraidy, Marwan M., and Patrick D. Murphy. "Shifting Geertz: Toward a Theory of Translocalism in Global Communication Studies." *Communication Theory* 18 (2008): 335–55.

Kratz, E. Ulrich. "Like a Fish Gasping for Water: The Letters of a Temporary Spouse from Bengkulu." *Indonesia and the Malay World* 34, no. 100 (Nov. 2006): 247–80.

Krishnan, Sanjay. *Reading the Global: Troubling Perspectives on Britain's Empire in Asia*. New York: Columbia University Press, 2007.

LaFleur, Greta. *The Natural History of Sexuality in Early America*. Baltimore: Johns Hopkins University Press, 2018.

Langdon, Marcus. *Penang: The Fourth Presidency of India, 1805–1830*. Vol. 1, *Ships, Men, and Mansions*. Penang: Arcea, 2013.

Lanser, Susan S. *The Sexuality of History: Modernity and the Sapphic, 1565–1830*. Chicago: University of Chicago Press, 2014.

Latour, Bruno. *Reassembling the Social: An Introduction to Actor-Network-Theory*. Oxford: Oxford University Press, 2005.

Lawson, Charles, *Memories of Madras*. London: S. Sonnenschein, 1905.

Leask, Nigel. *British Romantic Writers and the East: Anxieties of Empire*. Cambridge: Cambridge University Press, 1992.

———. *Curiosity and the Aesthetics of Travel Writing, 1770–1840: "From an Antique Land."* Oxford: Oxford University Press: 2002.

———. "Towards an Anglo-Indian Poetry? The Colonial Muse in the Writings of John Leyden, Thomas Medwin and Charles D'Oyly." In Moore-Gilbert, *Writing India*, 52–85.

Leppert, Richard. "Music, Domestic Life, and Cultural Chauvinism: Images of British Subjects at Home in India." In *Music and Society: The Politics of Composition, Performance, and Reception*, edited by Richard Leppert and Susan McClary, 63–104. Cambridge: Cambridge University Press, 1987.

Lester, Alan. "Imperial Circuits and Networks: Geographies of the British Empire." *History Compass* 4, no. 1 (2006): 124–41.

———. *Imperial Networks: Creating Identities in Nineteenth-Century South Africa and Britain*. London: Routledge, 2001.

———. "Introduction: New Imperial and Environmental Histories of the Indian Ocean." In *The East India Company and the Natural World*, edited by V. Damodaran, A. Winterbottom, and A. Lester, 1–15. London: Palgrave Macmillan, 2014.

Letters from Yorick to Eliza. London: Printed for the Editor, 1773.

Levander, Caroline Field. *Voices of the Nation: Women and Public Speech in Nineteenth-Century American Literature and Culture*. Cambridge: Cambridge University Press, 1998.

Levine, Caroline. "From Nation to Network." *Victorian Studies* 55, no. 4 (Summer 2013): 647–66.

———. "Infrastructuralism, or the Tempo of Institutions." In *On Periodization: Selected Essays from the English Institute*, edited by Virginia Jackson. Cambridge, MA: English Institute and American Council of Learned Societies, 2010. https://www.fulcrum.org/epubs/ws859g78b?locale=en#/6/20[div1_c02]!/4/2[div1_c02]/2/2/1:0.

Levine, Philippa. *The British Empire: Sunrise to Sunset*. 2nd ed. London: Routledge, 2013.

———. *Prostitution, Race, and Politics: Policing Venereal Disease in the British Empire*. New York: Routledge, 2003.

Limón, José E. "Border Literary Histories, Globalization, and Critical Regionalism." *American Literary History* 20, no. 1–2 (2008): 160–82.

Lindop, Grevel. *The Opium-Eater: The Life of Thomas De Quincey*. New York: Taplinger, 1981.

Lindsay, John. "Journal of an Imprisonment in Seringapatam, during the Years 1781, 1782, 1783, and part of 1780 and 1784." In Alexander Crawford Lindsay, *Lives of the Lindsays; or a Memoir of the Houses of Crawford and Balcarres*. 3 vols. London: John Murray, 1849.

Linebaugh, Peter, and Marcus Rediker. *The Many-Headed Hydra: Sailors, Slaves, Commoners, and the Hidden History of the Revolutionary Atlantic*. Boston: Beacon, 2000.

Little, Nigel. *Transoceanic Radical, William Duane: National Identity and Empire, 1760–1835*. Abingdon, Oxon: Routledge, 2008.

Livesey, James. *Civil Society and Empire: Ireland and Scotland in the Eighteenth-Century Atlantic World.* Yale, 2009.

Loar, Christopher F. "Soldiers of Feeling: Masculinity and Patriotism in Innes Munro's Military Memoirs." *Genders* 56 (Fall 2012): https://cdn.atria.nl/ezines/IAV_606661/IAV_606661_2013_57/g56_loar.html.

Lockyer, Charles. *An Account of the Trade in India [. . .].* London: Samuel Crouch, 1711.

Lockyer, Dora. BL Mss Eur Photo Eur 153. "The Provision of Books and Libraries by the East India Company in India, 1611–1858." Thesis submitted for Fellowship of the Library Association, British Library, 1977.

Lonsdale, Roger, ed. *The Poems of Thomas Gray, William Collins, Oliver Goldsmith.* London: Longman, Green, 1969.

Lösch, Klaus, and Heike Paul. "Critical Regionalism: An Introduction." In *Critical Regionalism,* edited by Klaus Lösch, Heike Paul, and Meike Zwingenberger, 1–9. Heidelberg: Universitätsverlag Winter, 2016.

Losensky, Paul E. "Linguistic and Rhetorical Aspects of the Signature Verse (*Takhallus*) in the Persian *Ghazal.*" *Edebiyât: Journal of Middle Eastern Literature* 8 (1998): 239–71.

Loughran, Trish. *The Republic in Print: Print Culture in the Age of U.S. Nation Building, 1770–1870.* New York: Columbia University Press, 2007.

Love, H. D. *Vestiges of Old Madras, 1600–1800.* Vol. 3. London: John Murray, 1913.

Love, Heather. "Close, but Not Deep: Literary Ethics and the Descriptive Turn." *New Literary History* 41, no. 2 (Spring 2010): 371–91.

——. "Close Reading and Thin Description." *Public Culture* 25, no. 3 (2013): 401–34.

Lowenthal, Cynthia. *Performing Identities on the Restoration Stage.* Carbondale: Southern Illinois University Press, 2003.

Macaulay, Thomas Babington. *Macaulay: Prose and Poetry.* Selected by G. M. Young. Cambridge, MA: Harvard University Press, 1952.

Mackie, Erin. "Being Too Positive about the Public Sphere." In *The Spectator: Emerging Discourses,* edited by Donald J. Newman, 81–104. Newark: University of Delaware Press, 2005.

——. *Market à la Mode: Fashion, Commodity, and Gender in "The Tatler" and "The Spectator."* Baltimore: Johns Hopkins University Press, 1997.

MacMillan, Margaret. *Women of the Raj: The Mothers, Wives, and Daughters of the British Empire in India.* New York: Random House, 2007.

Maddison, Angus. *Contours of the World Economy, 1-2030 AD: Essays in Macro-Economic History.* Oxford: Oxford University Press, 2007.

Mallipeddi, Ramesh. *Spectacular Suffering: Witnessing Slavery in the Eighteenth-Century British Atlantic.* Charlottesville: University of Virginia Press, 2016.

Mandaville, Peter G. "Territory and Translocality: Discrepant Idioms of Political Identity." *Millennium* 28, no. 3 (1999): 653–73.

Manuel, Thomas Philip. *The Poetry of Our Indian Poets.* Calcutta: D'Rozario, 1861.

Maria, Anna [pseud.]. *The Poems of Anna Maria.* Calcutta: Thomson and Ferris, 1793.

Markley, Robert. "Alexander Hamilton, the Mughal War, and the Critique of the East India Company." *Genre* 48, no. 2 (July 2015): 237–59.

Marsden, William. *A Brief Memoir of the Life and Writings of the Late William Marsden, Written by Himself.* London: J. L. Cox and Sons, 1838.

——. *The History of Sumatra*. London: Thomas Payne and Son, 1783.

——. *The History of Sumatra*. London: J. McCreery, 1811.

Marshall, P. J. *Bengal: The British Bridgehead, Eastern India 1740–1828*. Vol. 2, pt. 2 of *The New Cambridge History of India*. Cambridge: Cambridge University Press, 1987.

——. "British-Indian Connections c. 1780 to c. 1830: The Empire of the Officials." In *Romantic Representations of British India*, edited by Michael J. Franklin, 45–64. London: Routledge, 2006.

——. "British Society in India under the East India Company." *Modern Asian Studies* 31 (Feb. 1997): 89–108.

——. "'Cornwallis Triumphant': War in India and the British Public." In *The East India Company: 1600–1858*. Vol. 5, *War, Expansion, and Resistance*, edited with an intro. by Patrick Tuck, 82–100. London: Routledge, 1998.

——. *East Indian Fortunes: The British in Bengal in the Eighteenth Century*. Oxford: Clarendon Press, 1976.

——. *"A Free though Conquering People": Eighteenth-Century Britain and Its Empire*. Burlington, VT: Ashgate, 2003.

——. *The Impeachment of Warren Hastings*. London: Oxford University Press, 1965.

——. Introduction to *The Eighteenth Century in Indian History: Evolution of Revolution?* edited by P. J. Marshall, 1–49. Oxford: Oxford University Press, 2003.

——. *The Making and Unmaking of Empires: Britain, India, and America, c. 1750–1783*. Oxford: Oxford University Press, 2005.

——. "Warren Hastings as Scholar and Patron." In *Statesmen, Scholars, and Merchants: Essays in Eighteenth-Century History Presented to Dame Lucy Sutherland*, edited by Anne Whiteman, J. S. Bromley, and P. G. M. Dickson, 242–62. Oxford: Clarendon Press, 1973.

——. "The Whites of British India, 1780–1830: A Failed Colonial Society?" *International History Review* 12, no. 1 (Feb. 1990): 26–44.

Massey, Cromwell. *Diary of Col. Cromwell Massey, Late of the Hon'ble East India Company's Service. Kept While a Prisoner at Seringapatam*. Bangalore: Higginbotham, 1912.

Massey, Doreen. *Power-Geometries and the Politics of Space-Time: Hettner Lecture 1998*. University of Heidelberg, 1999.

Mazlish, Bruce. "Global History." *Theory, Culture, & Society* 23 (2006): 406–8.

McClintock, Anne. *Imperial Leather: Race, Gender, and Sexuality in the Colonial Conquest*. New York: Routledge, 1994.

McDowell, Paula. *The Invention of the Oral: Print Commerce and Fugitive Voices in Eighteenth-Century Britain*. Chicago: University of Chicago Press, 2017.

McFarlane, Colin. "Translocal Assemblages: Space, Power, and Social Movements." *Geoforum* 40 (2009): 561–67.

McGann, Jerome J., ed. *The New Oxford Book of Romantic Period Verse*. Oxford: Oxford University Press, 1993.

——. *The Poetics of Sensibility: A Revolution in Literary Style*. Oxford: Oxford University Press, 1996.

McGill, Meredith. *American Literature and the Culture of Reprinting, 1834–1853*. Philadelphia: University of Pennsylvania Press, 2003.

McKeon, Michael. *The Secret History of Domesticity: Public, Private, and the Division of Knowledge*. Baltimore: Johns Hopkins University Press, 2005.

——. "Surveying the Frontier of Culture: Pastoralism in Eighteenth-Century England." *Studies in Eighteenth-Century Culture*, edited by Syndy M. Conger and Julie C. Hayes, 7–28. Baltimore: Johns Hopkins University Press, 1997.

McNeil, Anna. "Mirasis: Some Thoughts on Hereditary Musicians in Hindustani Music." *Context* (2007): 45–58.

McPhee, John. *Basin and Range*. New York: Farrar, Strauss and Giroux, 1981.

Mee, Jon. "'Reciprocal Expressions of Kindness': Robert Merry, Della Cruscanism and the Limits of Sociability." In *Romantic Sociability: Social Networks and Literary Culture in Britain, 1770–1840*, edited by Gillian Russell and Claire Tuite, 104–22. Cambridge: Cambridge University Press, 2002.

Mentz, Soren. "Cultural Interaction between the British Diaspora in Madras and the Host Community, 1650–1790." In *Asian Port Cities, 1600–1800: Local and Foreign Cultural Interactions*, edited by Haneda Masashi, 162–74. Singapore: National University of Singapore Press, 2009.

Merry, Robert. "The Adieu and Recall to Love." In *The New Oxford Book of Romantic Period Verse*, edited by Jerome McGann, 36–37. Oxford: Oxford University Press, 1993.

Merton, Robert K. *Social Theory and Social Structure*. Enl. ed. New York: Free Press, 1968.

Metcalf, Thomas R. *Imperial Connections: India in the Indian Ocean Arena, 1860–1920*. Berkeley: University of California Press, 2007.

Mickelson-Gaughan, Joan. *The 'Incumberances': British Women in India, 1615–1856*. Oxford: Oxford University Press, 2013.

Mickle, Julius. *The Lusiad; or, The Discovery of India, an Epic Poem*. Oxford: Jackson and Lister, 1776.

Mill, James. *The History of British India*. Abridged, with intro. by William Thomas. Chicago: University of Chicago Press, 1975.

Miller, Monica. *Slaves to Fashion: Black Dandyism and the Styling of Black Diasporic Identity*. Durham, NC: Duke University Press, 2009.

Mishra, Pankaj. "More Trouble Than It Is Worth." *Common Knowledge* 11, no. 3 (Fall 2005): 432–44.

Misra, B. B. *The Bureaucracy in India: An Historical Analysis of Development to 1947*. Delhi: Oxford University Press, 1977.

Mitchell, W. J. T. "Imperial Landscape." In *Landscape and Power*, 5–34. 2nd ed. Chicago: University. of Chicago Press, 2002.

——. *What Do Pictures Want? The Lives and Loves of Images*. Chicago: University of Chicago Press, 2005.

Mohanty, Chandra Talpade. "Under Western Eyes: Feminist Scholarship and Colonial Discourses." *boundary 2* 12, no. 3 / 13, no. 1 (Spring-Autumn 1984): 333–58.

Moon, Penderel. *The British Conquest and Dominion of India*. London: Duckworth, 1989.

Moore-Gilbert, Bart. "Introduction: Writing India, Reorienting Colonial Discourse Analysis." In Moore-Gilbert, *Writing India*, 1–29.

——. *Writing India, 1757–1990: The Literature of British India*. Manchester: Manchester University Press, 1996.

Morcom, Anna. *Illicit Worlds of Indian Dance: Cultures of Exclusion*. Oxford: Oxford University Press, 2013.

Moretti, Franco. *Atlas of the European Novel, 1800–1900*. London: Verso, 1998.

——. *Signs Taken for Wonders: Essays in the Sociology of Literary Forms*. 1984. London: Verso, 2005.

Moriyama, Mikihiro. *Sundanese Print Culture and Modernity in Nineteenth-Century West Java*. Singapore: National University of Singapore Press, 2005.

Mukherjee, Rudrangshu. "'Forever England': British Life in Old Calcutta." In *Calcutta: The Living City*. Vol 1, *The Past*, edited by Sukanta Chaudhuri, 45–51. New Delhi: Oxford University Press, 1990.

Mukhopadhyay, Tarun Kumar. *Hicky's Bengal Gazette: Contemporary Life and Events*. Calcutta: Subarnarekha, 1988.

Mulholland, James. "Connecting Eighteenth-Century India: The Translocal Poetics of William and Anna Maria Jones." In *Representing Place in British Literature and Culture of the Long Eighteenth Century: From Local to Global*, edited by Evan Gottlieb and Juliet Shields, 117–36. Farnham, Surrey: Ashgate, 2013.

——. *Sounding Imperial: Poetic Voice and the Politics of Empire, 1730–1820*. Baltimore: Johns Hopkins University Press, 2013.

Mullan, John. *Sentiment and Sociability: The Language of Feeling in the Eighteenth Century*. Oxford: Clarendon Press, 1988.

Müller, Martin. "Assemblages and Actor-Networks: Rethinking Socio-material Power, Politics, and Space." *Geography Compass* 9, no. 1 (2015): 27–41.

Munro, Thomas. *Major-General Sir Thomas Munro: Selections from His Minutes and Other Official Writings*, edited by Sir Alexander Arbuthnot. 2 vols. London: C. Kegan Paul, 1881.

Musty, John. "Going to China: A Literary Cargo." *Antiquarian Book Monthly Review* 11, no. 4.120 (April 1984): 132–37.

Naregal, Veena. *Language Politics, Elites, and the Public Sphere: Western India under Colonialism*. London: Anthem, 2002.

Nayar, Pramod K. "The Imperial Sublime: English Travel Writing and India, 1750–1820." *Journal of Early Modern Cultural Studies* 2, no. 2 (Fall/Winter, 2002): 57–99.

Nechtman, Tillman W. *Nabobs: Empire and Identity in Eighteenth-Century Britain*. Cambridge: Cambridge University Press, 2010.

New, Melvyn. Introduction to Sterne, *The Florida Edition*, 6:xi–lxxii.

Newman, Ian. *The Romantic Tavern: Literature and Conviviality in the Age of Revolution*. Cambridge: Cambridge University Press, 2019.

Nichter, Mimi. "South Asia." In *Tobacco in History and Culture: An Encyclopedia*. Vol. 2, edited by Jordan Goodman, 575–79. New York: Scribner's Sons, 2005.

Nierstrasz, Chris. *In the Shadow of the Company: The Dutch East India Company and Its Servants in the Period of Its Decline (1740–1796)*. Leiden: Brill, 2012.

Nord, David Paul. *Faith in Reading: Religious Publishing and the Birth of Mass Media in America*. Oxford: Oxford University Press, 2004.

Norden, Frederick. *Voyage d'Égypte et de Nubie*. Copenhagen: La Maison Royale des Orphelins, 1755.

North, Michael. *The Dialect of Modernism: Race, Language, and Twentieth-Century Literature*. New York: Oxford University Press, 1994.

Nussbaum, Felicity. *Torrid Zones: Maternity, Sexuality, and Empire in Eighteenth-Century English Narratives*. Baltimore: Johns Hopkins University Press, 1995.

Oakes, Henry. *An Authentic Narrative of the Treatment of the English, Who Were Taken Prisoners [. . .]*. London: G. Kearsley, 1785.

Oaten, E. F. *A Sketch of Anglo-Indian Literature*. London: Kegan Paul Trench Trübner, 1908.

O'Brien, John. *Literature Incorporated: The Cultural Consciousness of the Business Corporation, 1650–1850*. Chicago: University of Chicago Press, 2016.

Ogborn, Miles. *Global Lives: Britain and the World, 1550–1800*. Cambridge: Cambridge University Press, 2008.

——. *Indian Ink: Script and Print in the Making of the English East India Company*. Chicago: University of Chicago Press, 2007.

Ohdedar, A. K. *The Growth of the Library in Modern India: 1498–1836*. Calcutta: World Press, 1966.

O'Keefe, John, and William Shields, *A Short Account of the New Pantomime Called Omai, or, A Trip Round the World*. London: T. Cadell, 1785.

Oliphant, John. "The Cherokee Embassy to London, 1762." *Journal of Imperial and Commonwealth History* 27, no. 1 (1999): 1–26.

Omidsalar, Mahmoud. *Poetics and Politics of Iran's National Epic, the Shāhnāmeh*. New York: Palgrave Macmillan, 2011.

Ong, Aihwa. *Neoliberalism as Exception: Mutations in Citizenship and Sovereignty*. Durham, NC: Duke University Press, 2006.

O'Quinn, Daniel. *Staging Governance: Theatrical Imperialism in London, 1770–1800*. Baltimore: Johns Hopkins University Press, 2005.

——. "Theatre and Empire." In *The Cambridge Companion to British Theatre, 1730–1830*, edited by Jane Moody and Daniel O'Quinn, 233–46. Cambridge: Cambridge University Press, 2007.

Orr, Bridget. *Empire on the English Stage, 1660–1714*. Cambridge: Cambridge University Press, 2001.

Orsini, Francesca. "The Multilingual Local in World Literature." *Comparative Literature* 67, no. 4 (2015): 345–74.

Otis, Andrew. *Hicky's Bengal Gazette: The Untold Story of India's First Newspaper*. Chennai: Tranquebar, 2018.

Oxford Dictionary of National Biography. Oxford: Oxford University Press, 2004.

Oxford English Dictionary. oed.com.

Parthasarathi, Prasannan. "South Asia: From Political Economy to Intellectual and Cultural Life." *Journal for Eighteenth-Century Studies* 34, no. 4 (Dec. 2011): 551–56.

Pascoe, Judith. *Romantic Theatricality: Gender, Poetry, and Spectatorship*. Ithaca, NY: Cornell University Press, 1997.

Pearce, Robert Rouiere. *Memoirs and Correspondence of the Most Noble Richard Marquess Wellesley*. Vol. 1. London: R. Bentley, 1846.

Pearson, Michael. "The Idea of the Ocean." In *Eyes across the Water: Navigating the Indian Ocean*, edited by Pamila Gupta, Isabel Hofmeyr, and Michael Pearson, 7–14. Pretoria: Unisa, 2010.

——. *The Indian Ocean*. London: Routledge, 2003.

——, ed. *Legitimacy and Symbols: The South Asian Writings of F. W. Buckler*. Ann Arbor: University of Michigan Press, 1985.

Peers, Douglas M. "Is Humpty Dumpty Back Together Again? The Revival of Imperial History and the Oxford History of the British Empire." *Journal of World History* 13, no. 2 (Fall 2002): 451–67.

Philips, John. "An Imitation of Milton [The Splendid Shilling]." 1701. In *Spenser and the Tradition: English Poetry, 1579–1830*, compiled by David Hill Radcliffe. http://spenserians.cath.vt.edu/TextRecord.php?textsid=37978.

Pickett, Catherine. *Bibliography of the East India Company: Books, Pamphlets, and Other Materials Printed between 1600 and 1785*. London: British Library, 2011.

Piper, Andrew. *Dreaming in Books: The Making of the Bibliographic Imagination in the Romantic Age*. Chicago: University of Chicago Press, 2009.

Pittock, Murray. "Dissolving the Dream of Empire: Fratriotism, Boswell, Byron, and Moore." *Journal of Irish and Scottish Studies* 1, no. 1 (Sept. 2007): 127–44.

Pitts, Jennifer. *A Turn to Empire: The Rise of Imperial Liberalism in Britain and France*. Princeton, NJ: Princeton University Press, 2005.

Platts, John T. *A Dictionary of Urdu, Classical Hindi, and English*. London: W. H. Allen, 1884.

Pococke, Richard. *A Description of the East, and Some Other Countries*. 2 vols. London: W. Bowyer, 1743.

Polasky, Janet. *Revolutions without Borders: The Call to Liberty in the Atlantic World*. New Have, CT: Yale University Press, 2015.

Pollock, Sheldon. "Cosmopolitan and Vernacular in History." In *Cosmopolitanism*, edited by Carol A. Breckenridge, 15–53. Durham, NC: Duke University Press, 2002.

——. *The Language of the Gods in the World of Men: Sanskrit, Culture, and Power in Premodern India*. Berkeley: University of California Press, 2006.

——. "Literary Culture and Manuscript Culture in Precolonial India." In *Literary Cultures and the Material Book*, edited by Simon Eliot, Andrew Nash, and Ian Wilson, 77–94. London: British Library, 2007.

——. "The Sanskrit Cosmopolis, 300–1330." In *Ideology and Status of Sanskrit: Contributions to the History of the Sanskrit Language*, edited by Jan E. M. Houben, 197–247. Leiden: Brill, 1996.

Pomeranz, Kenneth. *The Great Divergence: Europe, China, and the Making of the Modern World Economy*. Princeton, NJ: Princeton University Press, 2000.

Pope, Alexander. *Pastorals*. London: Jacob Tonson, 1709.

——. *The Rape of the Lock: An Heroi-comical Poem*. London: Bernard Lintott, 1714.

——. *Windsor-Forest*. London: Bernard Lintott, 1713.

Porter, Bernard. *The Absent-Minded Imperialists: Empire, Society, and Culture in Britain*. Oxford: Oxford University Press, 2004.

——. "Further Thoughts on Imperial Absent-Mindedness." *Journal of Imperial and Commonwealth History* 36, no. 1 (March 2008): 101–17.

Porter, David. "Sinicizing Early Modernity: The Imperatives of Historical Cosmopolitanism." *Eighteenth-Century Studies* 43, no. 3 (Spring 2010): 299–306.

Potter, S. J. *News and the British World: The Emergence of an Imperial Press System, 1876–1922*. Oxford: Clarendon Press, 2003.

Prakash, Gyan. *Another Reason: Science and the Imagination in Modern India*. Princeton, NJ: Princeton University Press, 1999.

Pratt, Mary Louise. *Imperial Eyes: Travel Writing and Transculturation*. London: Routledge, 1992.

Preminger, Alex, and T. V. F. Brogan, eds. *The New Princeton Encyclopedia of Poetry and Poetics*. Princeton, NJ: Princeton University Press, 1993.

Protschky, Susie. *Images of the Tropics: Environment and Visual Culture in Colonial Indonesia*. KITLV Press, 2011.

Radway, Janice. "What's the Matter with Reception Study? Some Thoughts on the Disciplinary Origins, Conceptual Constraints, and Persistent Viability of a Paradigm." In *New Directions in American Reception Study*, edited by Philip Goldstein and James L. Machor, 327–51. Oxford: Oxford University Press, 2008.

Raj, Kapil. "Refashioning Civilities, Engineering Trust: William Jones, Indian Intermediaries, and the Production of Reliable Legal Knowledge in Late-Eighteenth-Century Bengal." *Studies in History* 17, no. 2 (2001): 175–209.

——. *Relocating Modern Science: Circulation and the Construction of Knowledge in South Asia and Europe, 1650–1900*. Houndmills, Basingstoke: Palgrave Macmillan, 2007.

Rajan, Balachandra. *Under Western Eyes: India from Milton to Macaulay*. Durham, NC: Duke University Press, 1999.

Raman, Bhavani. *Document Raj: Writing and Scribes in Early Colonial South India*. Chicago: University of Chicago Press, 2012.

Ramazani, Jahan. "The Local Poem in a Global Age." *Critical Inquiry* 43, no. 3 (Spring 2017): 670–96.

——. *A Transnational Poetics*. Chicago: University of Chicago Press, 2009.

Rangarajan, Padma. *Imperial Babel: Translation, Exoticism, and the Long Nineteenth Century*. New York: Fordham University Press, 2014.

Raposo, Pedro M. P., Ana Simões, Manolis Patiniotis, and José R. Bertomeu-Sánchez. "Moving Localities and Creative Circulation: Travels as Knowledge Production in 18th-Century Europe." *Centaurus* 56, no. 3 (2014): 167–88.

Raven, James. *The Business of Books: Booksellers and the English Book Trade, 1450–1850*. New Haven, CT: Yale University Press, 2007.

Ray, Rajat Kanta. "Indian Society and the Establishment of British Supremacy, 1765–1818." In *The Oxford History of the British Empire: The Eighteenth Century*, edited by P. J. Marshall, 508–29. Oxford: Oxford University Press, 1998.

Raynal, Abbé. *A Philosophical and Political History of the Settlements and Trade of the Europeans in the East and West Indies*. Vol. 2, bk. 3. Translated by J. O. Justamond. London: W. Strahan, 1788.

Raza, Rosemary. *In Their Own Words: British Women Writers and India, 1740–1857*. Oxford: Oxford University Press, 2006.

Reid, Anthony. "'Closed' and 'Open' Slave Systems in Pre-Colonial Southeast Asia." In *Slavery, Bondage, and Dependency in Southeast Asia*, edited by Anthony Reid, with the assistance of Jennifer Brewster, 157–181. New York: St. Martin's, 1983.

——. Introduction to *Slavery, Bondage, and Dependency in Southeast Asia*, edited by Anthony Reid, with the assistance of Jennifer Brewster, 1–43. New York: St. Martin's, 1983.

Rendall, Jane. "Scottish Orientalism: From Robertson to James Mill." *Historical Journal* 25, no. 1 (March 1982): 43–69.

Renford, Raymond K. *The Non-official British in India to 1920*. Oxford: Oxford University Press, 1987.

Rezek, Joseph. *London and the Making of Provincial Literature: Aesthetics and the Transatlantic Book Trade, 1800–1850*. Philadelphia: University of Pennsylvania Press, 2015.

Rhodes, Dennis E. *The Spread of Printing, Eastern Hemisphere: India, Pakistan, Ceylon, Burma, and Thailand*. Amsterdam: Vangendt, 1969.

Richards, Eliza. *Gender and the Poetics of Reception in Poe's Circle*. Cambridge: Cambridge University Press, 2004.

Richards, John F. "Imperial Finance under the East India Company, 1762–1859." In *Decentring Empire: Britain, India, and the Transcolonial World*, edited by Durba Ghosh and Dane Kennedy, 16–50. Hyderabad: Orient Longman, 2006.

——. *The Mughal Empire*. Vol. 5, pt. 1 of *The New Cambridge History of India, Part 1*. Cambridge: Cambridge University Press, 1993.

Richardson, David Lester. *Selections from the British Poets from the Time of Chaucer to the Present Day with Biographical and Critical Notices*. Calcutta: Baptist Mission Press, 1840.

Rivers, David. *Literary Memoirs of Living Authors*. Vol. 1. London: R Faulder, 1798.

Robb, Peter. "Children, Emotion, Identity, and Empire: Views from the Blechyndens' Calcutta Diaries (1790–1822)." *Modern Asian Studies* 40, no. 1 (2006): 175–201.

——. *Clash of Cultures? An Englishman in Calcutta in the 1790s*. London: School of Oriental and African Studies, 1998.

——. *Sentiment and Self: Richard Blechynden's Calcutta Diaries, 1791–1822*. New Delhi: Oxford University Press, 2011.

——. *Sex and Sensibility: Richard Blechynden's Calcutta Diaries, 1791–1822*. Oxford: Oxford University Press, 2011.

Robins, Nick. *The Corporation That Changed the World: How the East India Company Shaped the Modern Multinational*. London: Pluto, 2006.

Rocher, Rosane. *Orientalism, Poetry, and the Millennium: The Checkered Life of Nathaniel Brassey Halhed, 1751–1830*. Delhi: Motilal Banarsidass, 1983.

——. "Weaving Knowledge: Sir William Jones and the Indian Pandits." In *Objects of Inquiry: The Life, Contribution, and Influences of Sir William Jones (1746–1794)*, edited by Garland Cannon and Kevin R. Brine, 51–91. New York: New York University Press, 1994.

Romney, John. *Memoirs of the Life and Works of George Romney*. London: Baldwin and Cradock, 1830.

Ronald, D. A. B. *Youth, Heroism, and War Propaganda: Britain and the Young Maritime Hero, 1745–1820*. London: Bloomsbury, 2015

Rose, Jonathan. *The Intellectual Life of the British Working Classes*. New Haven, CT: Yale University Press, 2001.

Rosenthal, Laura J. *Playwrights and Plagiarists in Early Modern England: Gender, Authorship, Literary Property*. Ithaca, NY: Cornell University Press, 1996.

Ross, Fiona G. E. *The Printed Bengali Character and Its Evolution*. Richmond, Surrey: Curzon, 1999.

Ross, Ian Campbell. *Laurence Sterne: A Life*. Oxford: Oxford University Press, 2001.

Rothman, E. Natalie. *Brokering Empire: Trans-imperial Subjects between Venice and Istanbul*. Ithaca, NY: Cornell University Press, 2011.

Rothschild, Emma. *The Inner Life of Empires: An Eighteenth-Century History*. Princeton, NJ: Princeton University Press, 2011.

Russell, Gillian. *The Theatres of War: Performance, Politics, and Society, 1793–1815*. Oxford: Clarendon Press, 1995.

Russell, Gillian, and Clara Tuite. "Introducing Romantic Sociability." In *Romantic Sociability: Social Networks and Literary Culture in Britain, 1770–1840*, edited by Gillian Russell and Clara Tuite, 1–23. Cambridge, 2002.

Said, Edward. *Orientalism*. New York: Vintage, 1979.

Salmon, Thomas. *Modern History: Or the State of All Nations*. London: Bettesworth and Hitch et al., 1724.

Savile, George, Marquis of Halifax. *A Rough Draught of a New Model at Sea*. London: A. Banks, 1694.

Sayre, George. "Renegades from Barbary: The Transnational Turn in Captivity Studies." *American Literary History* 22, no. 2 (Summer 2010): 347–59.

Schaffer, Simon, Lisa Roberts, Kapil Raj, and James Delbourgo, eds. *The Brokered World: Go-Betweens and Global Intelligence, 1770–1820*. Sagamore Beach, MA: Science History, 2009.

Schama, Simon. *Patriots and Liberators: Revolution in the Netherlands, 1780–1813*. New York: Alfred A. Knopf, 1977.

Schimmel, Annemarie. "AMĪR K̲OSROW DEHLAVĪ." *Encyclopædia Iranica*, I/9, 963–65. www.iranicaonline.org/articles/amir-kosrow-poet.

Schmidt, Ruth Laila. "Urdu." In *The Indo-Aryan Languages*, edited by George Cardona and Danesh Jain, 286–350. London: Routledge, 2003.

Schmitt, Cannon. "Tidal Conrad (Literally)." *Victorian Studies* 55, no. 1 (Autumn 2012): 7–29.

Schürer, Norbert. "The Impartial Spectator of Sati, 1757–1784." *Eighteenth-Century Studies* 42, no. 1 (2008): 19–44.

——. "Surveying the Eighteenth-Century Anglo-Indian Canon." *Literature Compass* 7, no. 7 (2010): 597–609.

Schwab, Raymond. *The Oriental Renaissance: Europe's Rediscovery of India and the East, 1680–1880*. Translated by Gene Patterson-Black and Victor Reinking. New York: Columbia University Press, 1984.

Scobie, Edward. *Black Britannia: A History of Blacks in Britain*. Chicago: Johnson Publishing, 1972.

Scurry, James. *The Captivity, Sufferings, and Escape of James Scurry, Who Was Detained a Prisoner during Ten Years, in the Domains of Hyder Ali and Tipoo Saib*. London: Henry Fisher, 1824.

Seeley, John. *The Expansion of England: Two Courses of Lectures*. London: Macmillan, 1883.

Seid-Gholam-Hossein-Khan [Ghulam Husain Khan Tabatabai]. *A Translation of the Sëir Mutaqharain; or, View of Modern Times, Being an History of India*. 3 vols. Calcutta: James White, 1789.

Sen, Indrani. "Devoted Wife/Sensuous Bibi: Colonial Constructions of the Indian Woman, 1860–1900." In *India Journal of Gender Studies* 8, no. 1 (2001): 1–22.

Sen, Sudipta. *Distant Sovereignty: National Imperialism and the Origins of British India*. New York: Routledge, 2002.

——. "Imperial Subjects on Trial: On the Legal Identity of Britons in Late Eighteenth-Century India." *Journal of British Studies* 45, no. 3 (July 2006): 532–55.

Sencourt, Robert [Robert George]. *India in English Literature*. London: Simpkin, Marshall, Hamilton, Kent, 1923.

Seton-Karr, Walter Scott. *Selections from Calcutta Gazettes*. Vol. 2, *1789–1792*, 257–59. Calcutta: Military Orphan Press, 1865; Calcutta: Bibhash Gupta, 1987.

Shapiro, Michael. "Hindi." In *The Indo-Aryan Languages*, edited by George Cardona and Danesh Jain, 250–85. Abingdon, Oxon: Routledge, 2003.

Sharp, Henry. "Anglo-Indian Verse." In *Essays by Divers Hands, Being the Transactions of the Royal Society of Literature of the United Kingdom*. Vol. 16, edited by G. P. Gooch. Oxford: Oxford University Press, 1937.

Shaw, Graham. "The British Book in India." In *The Cambridge History of the Book in Britain*. Vol. 5, *1695–1830*, edited by Michael F. Suarez and Michael L. Turner, 560–75. Cambridge: Cambridge University Press, 1998.

——. "English Books around the World: The East India Company and the Globalization of the English Book and Book-Trade." *Gutenberg-Jahrbuch* 88 (2013): 180–203.

——. "From Goa to the Gutenberg Award: The Story of Indian Typography." *Typo: Typografie, Grafický Design, Vizuální Komunikace: Typography, Graphic Design, Visual Communication* 49 (Autumn 2012): 8–15.

——. "India." In *The Edinburgh History of the Book in Scotland*. Vol. 3, *Ambition and Industry 1800–1880*, edited by Bill Bell, 456–64. Edinburgh: Edinburgh University Press, 2007.

——. "Lithography v. Letter Press in India." *South Asia Library Notes and Queries* 29 (1993): 1–11.

——. "Lithography v. Letter Press in India, Part II: Lithography and the Vernacular Book." *South Asia Library Notes and Queries* 30 (1994/95): 1–10.

——. *Printing in Calcutta to 1800: A Description and Checklist of Printing in Late 18th-Century Calcutta*. London: Bibliographical Society, 1981.

——. "South Asia." In *A Companion to the History of the Book*, edited by Simon Eliot and Jonathan Rose, 126–38. Malden, MA: Blackwell, 2007.

——. *The South Asia and Burma Retrospective Bibliography (SABREB) Stage 1: 1556–1800*. London: British Library, 1987.

Shaw, Graham, and Mary Lloyd. *Publications Proscribed by the Government of India: A Catalogue of the Collections in the India Office Library and Records and the Department of Oriental Manuscripts and Printed Books, British Library Reference Division*. London: British Library, 1985.

Sharma, Arvind, with Ajit Ray, Alaka Hejib, and Katherine K. Young. *Sati: Historical and Phenomenological Essays*. Delhi: Motilal Banarsidass, 1988.

Sharma, Sunil. *Amir Khusraw: The Poet of Sultans and Sufis*. Oxford: Oneworld, 2005.

Sherring, M. A. *The Tribes and Castes of Rajasthan, together with Descriptions of Sacred and Celebrated Places of Historical Value in Rajasthan*. Delhi: Cosmo, 1975.

Shore, John. *Memoir of the Life and Correspondence of John, Lord Teignmouth in Two Volumes*. Vol. 1. London: Hatchard and Son, 1843.

Shuger, Debora. *Censorship and Cultural Sensibility: The Regulation of Language in Tudor-Stuart England*. Philadelphia: University of Pennsylvania Press, 2006.

Sinha, Mrinalini. "Britishness, Clubbability, and the Colonial Public Sphere: The Genealogy of an Imperial Institution in Colonial India." *Journal of British Studies* 40, no. 4 (Oct. 2001): 489–521.

——. *Colonial Masculinity: The 'Manly Englishman' and the 'Effeminate Bengali' in the Late Nineteenth Century*. Manchester: Manchester University Press, 1995.

——. "Is 'Region' Still Good to Think?" *Comparative Studies of South Asia, Africa, and the Middle East* 33, no. 3 (2013): 264–67.

——. "Mapping the Imperial Social Formation: A Modest Proposal for Feminist History." *Signs* 25, no. 4 (Summer 2000): 1077–82.

Sinha, Pradip. *Calcutta in Urban History*. Calcutta: Firma KLM, 1978.

Smith, Adam. *An Inquiry into the Nature and Causes of the Wealth of Nations*. Edited by W. B. Todd. 2 vols. Oxford: Clarendon Press, 1976.

Smith, Michael Peter. "Power in Place/Places of Power: Contextualizing Transnational Research." *City & Society* 17, no. 1 (2005): 5–34.

Snader, Joe. *Caught between Worlds: British Captivity Narratives in Fact and Fiction*. Lexington: University Press of Kentucky, 2001.

Snell, Rupert. *The Hindi Classical Tradition: A Braj Bhasa Reader*. London: School of Oriental and African Studies, 1991.

Solvyns, François Balthasar, and William Jones. "An Hooka-Burdar." In *A Collection of Two Hundred and Fifty Coloured Etchings: Descriptive of the Manners, Customs and Dresses of the Hindoos*. Calcutta: [Mirror Press,] 1796, 1799.

Sood, Gagan D. S. *India and the Islamic Heartlands: An Eighteenth-Century World of Circulation and Exchange*. Cambridge: Cambridge University Press, 2016.

Spear, Percival. *The Nabobs: A Study of the Social Life of the English in Eighteenth-Century India*. Oxford: Oxford University Press, 1963.

The Spirit of the Public Journals for 1799. London: James Ridgway, 1805.

Spivak, Gayatri Chakravorty. *Other Asias*. Malden, MA: Blackwell, 2008.

Staley, Patricia F. *Norwich in the Gilded Age: The Rose City's Millionaires' Triangle*. Charleston, SC: History Press, 2014.

Stanhope, Philip Dormer. *Genuine Memoirs of Asiaticus*. London: G. Kearsley, 1784.

Star, S. L. [Susan Leigh]. "Anselm Strauss: An Appreciation." *Sociological Research Online* 2, no. 1 (1997): www.socresonline.org.uk/2/1/1.html.

Star, Susan Leigh. "The Ethnography of Infrastructure." *American Behavioral Scientist* 43, no. 3 (Nov./Dec. 1999): 377–91.

Star, Susan Leigh, and Karen Ruhleder. "Steps Toward an Ecology of Infrastructure: Design and Access for Large Information Spaces." *Information Systems Research* 7, no. 1 (March 1996): 111–34.

Stark, Ulrike. *An Empire of Books: The Naval Kishore Press and the Diffusion of the Printed Word in Colonial India*. Ranikhet: Permanent Black, 2007.

Starke, Mariana. *The Sword of Peace; or, A Voyage of Love*. London: J. Debrett, 1789.

Steadman, J. M. "The Asiatick Society of Bengal." *Eighteenth-Century Studies* 10, no. 4 (Summer 1977): 464–83.

Stern, Philip J. "British Asia and British Atlantic: Comparisons and Connections." *William and Mary Quarterly* 63, no. 4 (Oct. 2006): 693–712.

———. *The Company-State: Corporate Sovereignty and the Early Modern Foundations of the British Empire in India*. Oxford: Oxford University Press, 2011.

Sterne, Laurence. *The Florida Edition of the Works of Laurence Sterne*. Vol. 6, *"A Sentimental Journey through France and Italy" and "The Continuation of the Bramine's Journal."* Edited by Melvyn New and W. G. Day. Gainesville: University Press of Florida, 2002.

———. *The Florida Edition of the Works of Laurence Sterne*. Vol. 8, *The Letters, Part 2: 1765–68*. Edited by Melvyn New. Gainesville: University Press of Florida, 2009.

———. *The Life and Opinions of Tristram Shandy, Gentleman*. Edited by Ian Campbell Ross. Oxford: Oxford University Press, 1983.

Sterne's Letters to His Friends on Various Occasions. London: G. Kearsley, J. Johnson, and T. Evans, 1775.

Stevens, Anne H. "The Season Novel, 1806–1824: A Nineteenth-Century Microgenre." In *Victoriographies* 7, no. 2 (2017): 81–90.

Stevens, Harm. *Dutch Enterprise and the VOC 1602–1799*. Zutphen: Walburg, 1998.

Stoler, Ann Laura. *Along the Archival Grain: Epistemic Anxieties and Colonial Common Sense*. Princeton, NJ: Princeton University Press, 2009.

———. *Carnal Knowledge and Imperial Power: Race and the Intimate in Colonial Rule*. Berkeley: University of California Press, 2002.

———. "'The Rot Remains': From Ruins to Ruination." In *Imperial Debris: On Ruins to Ruination*, edited by Ann Laura Stoler, 1–35. Durham, NC: Duke University Press, 2013.

Stoler, Ann Laura, and Frederick Cooper. "Between Metropole and Colony: Rethinking a Research Agenda." In *Tensions of Empire: Colonial Cultures in a Bourgeois World*, edited by Frederick Cooper and Ann Laura Stoler, 1–58. Berkeley: University of California Press, 1997.

Stout, Daniel. *Corporate Romanticism: Liberalism, Justice, and the Novel*. New York: Fordham University Press, 2016.

Styer, Catherine. "Barbary Pirates, British Slaves, and the Early Modern Atlantic World, 1570–1800." PhD diss., University of Pennsylvania, 2011.

Subrahmanyam, Sanjay. "Connected Histories: Notes Toward a Reconfiguration of Early Modern Eurasia." *Modern Asian Studies* 31, no. 3 (July 1997): 735–62.

———. *Europe's India: Words, Peoples, Empire, 1500–1800*. Cambridge, MA: Harvard University Press, 2017.

Suleri, Sara. *The Rhetoric of English India*. Chicago: University of Chicago Press, 1992.

Tambe, Shrikant R. *English Muse on Indian Soil: A Study of Anglo-Indian Poetry up to 1914*. Bangalore: Ultra, 1999.

Taylor, Jean Gelman. *Indonesia: Peoples and Histories*. New Haven, CT: Yale University Press, 2003.

———. *The Social World of Batavia: European and Eurasian in Dutch Asia*. Madison: University of Wisconsin Press, 1983.

Teltscher, Kate. *India Inscribed: European and British Writing on India, 1600–1800.* Oxford: Oxford University Press, 1995.

Termorshuizen, Gerard. "In Search of the Noble Savage: Travellers' Accounts in Old Indies Government Journals (1816–1830)." In *Oriental Prospect: Western Literature and the Lure of the East,* edited by C. C. Barfoot and Theo D'haen, 111–30. Amsterdam: Rodopi, 1998.

Thompson, Peter. *Rum Punch and Revolution: Taverngoing and Public Life in Eighteenth-Century Philadelphia*. Philadelphia: University of Pennsylvania Press, 1999.

Thomson, William. *Memoirs of the Late War in Asia, with a Narrative of the Imprisonment and Sufferings of Our Officers and Soldiers: By an Officer of Colonel Baillie's Detachment*. 2 vols. London: J. Murray, 1788.

Thoreau, Henry D. *A Week on the Concord and Merrimack Rivers*. Boston: James R. Osgood, 1873.

Thurston, Edgar. *History of the Coinage of the Territories of the East India Company in the Indian Peninsula [. . .]*. Madras: Government Press, 1890.

Tierney, James, ed. *The Correspondence of Robert Dodsley, 1733–1764*. Cambridge: Cambridge University Press, 2004.

Todd, Janet. *The Secret Life of Aphra Behn*. London: Andre Deutsch, 1996.

Tompkins, Jane P. "The Reader in History: The Changing Shape of Literary Response." In *Reader-Response Criticism: From Formalism to Post-Structuralism,* edited by Jane P. Tompkins, 201–32. Baltimore: Johns Hopkins University Press, 1980.

Tracy, James D. *The Founding of the Dutch Republic: War, Finance, and Politics in Holland, 1572–1588*. Oxford: Oxford University Press, 2008.

Transactions of the Literary Society of Bombay. Vols. 1 and 3. London: Longman, Hurst, Rees, Orme, and Brown, 1819–23. Reprinted 1876.

Trapaud, Elisha. *A Short Account of the Prince of Wales's Island, or Pulo Peenang, in the East Indies [. . .]*. London: John Stockdale, 1788.

Trautmann, Thomas R. *Aryans and British India*. Berkeley: University of California Press, 1997.

Travers, Robert. "Constitutions, Contact Zones, and Imperial Ricochets: Sovereignty and Law in British Asia." In *Britain's Oceanic Empire: Atlantic and Indian Ocean Worlds, 1550–1850,* edited by H. V. Bowen, Elizabeth Mancke, and John G. Reid, 98–129. Cambridge: Cambridge University Press, 2012.

——. "Indian Petitioning and Colonial State-Formation in Eighteenth-Century Bengal." *Modern Asian Studies* 53, no. 1 (2019): 89–122.

Trivedi, Harish. "The 'Book' in India. Orality, Manu-Script, Print (Post)colonialism." In *Books without Borders*. Vol. 2, *Perspectives from South Asia,* edited by Robert Fraser and Mary Hammond, 12–33. Houndmills, Basingstoke: Palgrave Macmillan, 2008.

Trivedi, Madhu. "Tradition and Transition: The Performing Arts in Medieval North India." In *Medieval History Journal* 2, no. 1 (1999): 73–110.

Truschke, Audrey. *Culture of Encounters: Sanskrit at the Mughal Court*. New York: Columbia University Press, 2016.

Tsing, Anna Lowenhupt. *Friction: An Ethnography of Global Connection*. Princeton, NJ: Princeton University Press, 2005.

Tzonis, Alexander, and Liane Lefaivre. "Why Critical Regionalism Today?" In *Theorizing a New Agenda for Architecture: An Anthology of Architectural Theory 1965–1995*, edited by Kate Nesbitt, 484–92. New York: Princeton Architectural Press, 1996.

Vareschi, Mark. "Reading (and Not Reading) Anonymity: Daniel Defoe, 'An Essay on the Regulation of the Press' and 'A Vindication of the Press.'" *Authorship* 4, no. 1 (2015): 1–11.

Vasunia, Phiroze. *The Classics and Colonial India*. Oxford: Oxford University Press, 2013.

Visram, Rozina. *Ayahs, Lascars, and Princes: Indians in Britain, 1700–1947*. London: Pluto, 1986.

Viswanathan, Gauri. *Masks of Conquest: Literary Study and British Rule in India*. New York: Columbia University Press, 1989.

Vitkus, Daniel. *Turning Turk: English Theater and the Multicultural Mediterranean*. New York: Palgrave Macmillan, 2003.

Von Glahn, Richard. "Economic Depression and the Silver Question in Nineteenth-Century China." In *Global History and New Polycentric Approaches: Europe, Asia, and the Americas in a World Network System*, edited by Manuel Perez Garcia and Lucio De Sousa, 81–118. Singapore: Palgrave Macmillan, 2018.

Wade, Bonnie C. "Visual Sources." In *The Garland Encyclopedia of World Music*. Vol. 5, *South Asia: The Indian Subcontinent*, edited by Alison Arnold, 298–311. New York: Garland, 2000.

Wade, Geoff. "New Ways of Knowing: The *Prince of Wales Island Gazette*—Penang's First Newspaper." Paper presented at the Penang Story International Conference, Penang, Malaysia, April 19, 2002.

Wallace, Tara Ghoshal. *Imperial Characters: Home and Periphery in Eighteenth-Century Literature*. Lewisburg, PA: Bucknell University Press, 2010.

Walvin, James. *Black Ivory: Slavery in the British Empire*. 2nd ed. Oxford: Blackwell, 2001.

Ward, Kerry. *Networks of Empire: Forced Migration in the Dutch East India Company*. Cambridge: Cambridge University Press, 2009.

Warner, Michael. *Letters of the Republic: Publication and the Public Sphere in Eighteenth-Century America*. Cambridge, MA: Harvard University Press, 1990.

——. *Publics and Counterpublics*. New York: Zone, 2002.

Washbrook, David. "The Indian Economy and the British Empire." In *India and the British Empire*, edited by Douglas Peers and Nandini Gooptu, 44–74. Oxford: Oxford University Press, 2012.

Watts, Carol. *The Cultural Work of Empire: The Seven Years' War and the Imagining of the Shandean State*. Edinburgh: Edinburgh University Press, 2007.

Weinbrot, Howard D. *Britannia's Issue: The Rise of British Literature from Dryden to Ossian*. Cambridge: Cambridge University Press, 1993.

Wheeler, Roxann. "Sounding Black-*ish*: West Indian Pidgin in London Performance and Print." *Eighteenth-Century Studies* 51, no. 1 (Fall 2017): 63–87.

White, Daniel E. *From Little London to Little Bengal: Religion, Print, and Modernity in Early British India, 1793–1835*. Baltimore: Johns Hopkins University Press, 2013.

——. "'Zig Zag Sublimity': John Grant, the Tank School of Poetry, and the *India Gazette* (1822–1829)." In *A History of Indian Poetry in English*, edited by Rosinka Chaudhuri, 147–61. Cambridge: Cambridge University Press, 2016.

White, Richard. *The Middle Ground: Indians, Empires, and the Republics in the Great Lakes Region, 1650–1815*. Cambridge: Cambridge University Press, 1991.

Wilkins, Charles. *The Bhăgvăt-Gēētā, or Dialogues of Krĕĕshnă and Ărjŏŏn*. London: C. Nourse, 1785.

Wilks, Mark. *Historical Sketches of the South of India, in an Attempt to Trace the History of Mysoor [. . .]*. 3 vols. London: Longman, Hurst, Rees, Orme, and Brown, 1817.

Wilson, Jon E. *The Domination of Strangers: Modern Governance in Eastern India, 1780–1835*. New York: Palgrave Macmillan, 2008.

Wilson, Kathleen. "Introduction: Histories, Empires, Modernities." In *A New Imperial History: Culture, Identity, and Modernity in Britain and the Empire, 1660–1840*, edited by Kathleen Wilson, 1–26. Cambridge: Cambridge University Press, 2004.

——. "Introduction: Three Theses on Performance and History." *Eighteenth-Century Studies* 48, no. 4 (2015): 375–90.

——. *The Island Race: Englishness, Empire, and Gender in the Eighteenth Century*. Abingdon, Oxon: Routledge, 2003.

——. "The Lure of the Other: Sheridan, Identity, and Performance in Kingston and Calcutta." *Eighteenth-Century Fiction* 27, no. 3–4 (Spring-Summer 2015): 509–34.

——. "Performing *The Wonder* in Sumatra: East India Company Peripheries and the History of Modernity." Triangle Global British History Studies Seminar, National Humanities Center, Raleigh, NC, 2016.

——. "Rethinking the Colonial State: Family, Gender, and Governmentality in Eighteenth-Century British Frontiers." *American Historical Review* 116, no. 5 (Dec. 2011): 1294–1322.

——. "Rowe's *Fair Penitent* as Global History: Or, a Diversionary Voyage to New South Wales." *Eighteenth-Century Studies* 41, no. 2 (2008): 231–51.

——. *The Sense of the People: Politics, Culture, and Imperialism in England, 1715–1785*. Cambridge, 1995.

——. *Strolling Players of Empire: Theatre, Culture, and Modernity in the British Provinces*. Cambridge: Cambridge University Press, forthcoming.

Wilson, Rob, and Wimal Dissanayake, eds. *Global/Local: Cultural Production and the Transnational Imaginary*. Durham, NC: Duke University Press, 1996.

Winet, Evan Darwin. *Indonesian Postcolonial Theater: Spectral Genealogies and Absent Forces*. Houndmills, Basingstoke: Palgrave Macmillan, 2010.

Winterbottom, Anna. *Hybrid Knowledge in the Early East India Company World*. Houndmills, Basingstoke: Palgrave Macmillan, 2016.

Wood, Gillen D'Arcy. *Tambora: The Eruption That Changed the World*. Princeton, NJ: Princeton University Press, 2014.

——. "The Volcano Lover: Climate, Colonialism, and the Slave Trade in Raffles's *History of Java* (1817)." *Journal for Early Modern Cultural Studies* 8, no. 2 (Fall/Winter 2008): 33–55.

Worrall, David. "Islam on the Romantic Period Stage: Hyder Ali, Tippoo Saib and Beyond the Captivity Narrative." In *Unrespectable Radicals? Popular Politics in the Age of Reform*, edited by Michael T. Davis and Paul A. Pickering, 167–85. Farnham, Surrey: Ashgate, 2008.

Wright, Arnold, and William Lutley Sclater. *Sterne's Eliza: Some Account of Her Life in India: With Her Letters Written between 1757 and 1774*. London: W. Heinemann, 1922.

Wright, Jonathan. *The Ambassadors: From Ancient Greece to Renaissance Europe, the Men Who Introduced the World to Itself.* Orlando, FL: Harcourt, 2006.

Yang, Chi-ming. *Performing China: Virtue, Commerce, and Orientalism in Eighteenth-Century England, 1660–1760*. Baltimore: Johns Hopkins University Press, 2011.

Yazdani, Kaveh. *India, Modernity, and the "Great Divergence": Mysore and Gujarat (17th to 19th C.)*. Leiden: Brill, 2017.

Yule, Henry, and A. C. Burnell. *Hobson-Jobson: The Definitive Glossary of British India*. Selected by Kate Teltscher. Oxford: Oxford University Press, 2013.

Zachs, William. *The First John Murray and the Late Eighteenth-Century London Book Trade, with a Checklist of Publications*. Oxford: British Academy, 1998.

Zandvliet, Kees, ed. *The Dutch Encounter with Asia, 1600–1950*. Amsterdam: Rijksmuseum, 2002.

Zastoupil, Lynn, and Martin Moir, eds. *The Great Indian Education Debate: Documents Relating to the Orientalist-Anglicist Controversy, 1781–1843*. Richmond, Surrey: Curzon, 1999.

Zwierlein, Anne-Julia. "Travelling through (Post-)Imperial Panoramas: British Epic Writing and Popular Shows, 1740s to 1840s." In *Post-Empire Imaginaries? Anglophone Literature, History, and the Demise of Empires*, edited by Barbara Buchenau and Virginia Richter, with Marijke Denger, 243–67. Leiden: Brill Rodopi, 2015.

INDEX

Page numbers in *italics* refer to illustrations.